Communications
in Computer and Information Science   **1585**

More information about this series at https://link.springer.com/bookseries/7899

Frank Phillipson · Gerald Eichler ·
Christian Erfurth · Günter Fahrnberger (Eds.)

Innovations for Community Services

22nd International Conference, I4CS 2022
Delft, The Netherlands, June 13–15, 2022
Proceedings

 Springer

Editors
Frank Phillipson ⓘD
Netherlands Organisation for Applied
Scientific Research
The Hague, The Netherlands

Christian Erfurth ⓘD
University of Applied Sciences Jena
Jena, Germany

Gerald Eichler ⓘD
Deutsche Telekom Technology & Innovation
Darmstadt, Germany

Günter Fahrnberger ⓘD
University of Hagen
Hagen, Germany

ISSN 1865-0929   ISSN 1865-0937 (electronic)
Communications in Computer and Information Science
ISBN 978-3-031-06667-2   ISBN 978-3-031-06668-9 (eBook)
https://doi.org/10.1007/978-3-031-06668-9

This Springer imprint is published by the registered company Springer Nature Switzerland AG
The registered company address is: Gewerbestrasse 11, 6330 Cham, Switzerland

Foreword

This year, our three-day annual event, the International Conference on Innovations for Community Services (I4CS 2022), went ahead as planned despite the ongoing COVID-19 pandemic. But something else was new. Celebrating its 22nd edition, for the first time it took place in The Netherlands. We met the fellows, who had to stay at home last year, at Delft University in person, though the Organizing Committee still prepared a hybrid event.

Twenty-one years ago, at the Technical University of Ilmenau, Germany, Herwig Unger and Thomas Böhme called for the Workshop on Innovative Internet Community Systems (IICS). It has continued its success story under its revised names of I^2CS and, since 2014, I4CS. The workshop published its proceedings in Springer's Lecture Notes in Computer Science series (LNCS) until 2005, followed by Gesellschaft für Informatik (GI) and Verein Deutscher Ingenieure (VDI). I4CS had commenced with proceedings published by the Institute of Electrical and Electronics Engineers (IEEE) before it switched back to Springer's Communications in Computer and Information Science (CCIS) series in 2016 and created a permanent partnership in 2018. The unique combination of printed proceedings and the SpringerLink online edition has generated much interest from external readers, with more than 3200 downloads since June 2021.

The selection of conference locations reflects the conference concept, and members of the Program Committee (PC) offer suitable locations for us to live our passion. For 2022, the I4CS Steering Committee had the honor to hand over the organization responsibility to Frank Phillipson. Given his affiliation with TNO, The Hague, and professorships in Delft and Maastricht, there was a choice of three beautiful Dutch cities, with Delft coming out on top. Located close to The Hague, we were near to the heart of quantum computing research which perfectly reflected this year's motto "Exploring Future Computing".

We were proud to offer a good selection of scientific presentations, combined with a keynote, two invited talks – among them the conference founder – and a great social conference program to strengthen the cultural community spirit. The proceedings of I4CS 2022 comprise 15 full and five short papers that were selected from 43 submissions, received from authors in 13 countries. Interdisciplinary thinking is a key success factor for any community. Hence, I4CS 2022 covered the renewed plurality of scientific, academic, social, and industrial topics, bundled into the three key areas: Technology, Applications, and Socialization.

Technology: Distributed Architectures and Frameworks

- Data architectures and enablers for community services,
- Block chain and secure multi-party computation,
- 5G/6G technologies and ad-hoc mobile networks,
- Data models, artificial intelligence, and big data analytics,
- Distributed and hybrid quantum computing.

Applications: Communities on the Move

- Social networks, news, and mobile work,
- Open collaboration and eLearning didactics,
- Recommender solutions and context awareness,
- Augmented reality, robotics, and location-based gaming,
- Intelligent transportation, logistics, and connected cars.

Socialization: Ambient Work and Living

- Pandemic-related challenges and eHealth-assisted living,
- Smart energy and home control,
- Smart cities and municipal infrastructure,
- Internet of Things and cyber-physical systems,
- Security, identity, and data protection.

Many thanks to the 28 members of the Program Committee, representing 14 countries worldwide, for their 152 worthwhile reviews, especially to the Program Chair Christian Erfurth and furthermore to our Publication Chair Günter Fahrnberger, who continued a very successful cooperation with the Springer publishing board to keep the high reputation of I4CS, rated C-level at CORE.

Following the alternation rule, the 23rd I4CS will take place in Germany around June 2023. Due to the requirement to hold last year's I4CS completely online, as an exception, the Steering Committee decided to vote again for the University of Bamberg as host. Please check the permanent conference URL at http://www.i4cs-conference.org/ for more details.

Proposals on emerging topics as well as applications for prospective Program Committee members along with potential conference hosts and locations are kindly welcome at request@i4cs-conference.org.

Kind regards on behalf of the entire Steering Committee and the Editors' Board.

June 2022

Gerald Eichler
I4CS Steering Chair

Preface

As Conference and Program Chairs, it is our pleasure to present this CCIS volume with its unique contributions on distributed architectures and software frameworks, both classical and quantum, and advanced applications in machine learning and cryptography as well as services supporting digital communities and smart mobility. The related papers were presented at the 22nd International Conference on Innovations for Community Services (I4CS 2022), held during June 13–15, 2022, in Delft, the Netherlands.

The conference was hosted by TNO, the Netherlands organization for applied scientific research, at the venue of Delft University of Technology. TNO connects people and knowledge to create innovations that boost the competitive strength of industry and the well-being of society in a sustainable way. Information and Communication Technology (ICT) offers excellent opportunities to solve all kinds of societal challenges, ensure innovation, and continue economic growth. It is a key area for many sectors and other technologies. The rapid digital transformation of our society requires a framework for action. TNO's ambition is to help to achieve complex digital transformations by using its knowledge of technology, policy, and business models. The connection of TNO and Delft University of Technology here is a representation of the purpose of the conference, which stands not only for scientific breakthroughs but also for the connection of science to industry, giving room to present experiences and applications.

We were happy to be in Delft and have a physical event again. Delft is a popular tourist destination in the Netherlands, famous for its historical connections with the reigning House of Orange-Nassau, for its blue pottery, for being home to the painter Johannes Vermeer, and for hosting Delft University of Technology. Historically, Delft played a highly influential role in the Dutch Golden Age. In terms of science and technology, thanks to the pioneering contributions of Antonie van Leeuwenhoek and Martinus Beijerinck, Delft represents the birthplace of microbiology.

Currently, Delft is one of the main centers of quantum computing in the world. Again, TNO and Delft University of Technology have joined efforts and created QuTech, whose mission is to develop scalable prototypes of a quantum computer and an inherently safe quantum Internet, based on the fundamental laws of quantum mechanics. Quantum computing is only one example of the (fundamental) new computation techniques that will change our lives. Areas such as photonic computing will grow rapidly in the coming years. New cryptographic techniques will arise, partly assisted and forced by the rise of the quantum computer and cryptographic applications, such as secure multi-party computation. Artificial intelligence (AI) will continue to develop, enhanced by new computing techniques and driving further demands for explainability. The consideration of these trends and the effect on society was the main theme of this year's conference, having the title "Exploring Future Computing".

The keynote and invited talks gave attention to these topics, and you will find a summary of them in this volume. Thijs Veugen explained secure multi-party computation and showed some of its applications. Herwig Unger, one of the founders of the conference, gave his view on developments in Artificial Intelligence (AI), especially on brain-inspired approaches to natural language processing and explainable AI. Darian Meacham looked at the future of work and asked how all this new technology will influence the way we are working. A visit to the quantum laboratories of QuTech was an interesting excursion during the conference.

As Conference and Program Chairs, we express our gratitude to all members of the Program Committee and all external reviewers for their dedicated service, for maintaining the quality objectives of the conference, and for the timely provision of their valuable reviews. We again managed to realize at least three reviews for each submitted paper. We thank all the authors for their submitted contributions, all the speakers for their vivid presentations, and all the participants for their contributions and interesting discussions. We thank EasyChair and Springer for their excellent services.

We thank TNO and Delft University of Technology for hosting the conference, giving us the opportunity to meet again after two years of restrictions due to COVID-19 in the nice city of Delft.

It was a pleasure to work together with Gerald Eichler and Günter Fahrnberger. Together, we have realized another version of the conference and hope the tradition lives on.

June 2022

Frank Phillipson
Christian Erfurth

Organization

Conference Chair

Frank Phillipson   TNO, The Netherlands

Steering Chair

Gerald Eichler   Deutsche Telekom Technology and Innovation
Darmstadt, Germany

Program Chair

Christian Erfurth   University of Applied Sciences Jena, Germany

Publication Chair

Günter Fahrnberger   University of Hagen, Germany

Program Committee

Sebastian Apel	Technical University of Applied Sciences Ingolstadt, Germany
Gilbert Babin	University of Montréal, Canada
Gerald Eichler	Deutsche Telekom Darmstadt and Innovation Darmstadt, Germany
Christian Erfurth	University of Applied Sciences Jena, Germany
Günter Fahrnberger	University of Hagen, Germany
Hacène Fouchal	University of Reims Champagne-Ardenne, France
Sapna Ponaraseri Gopinathan	Coimbatore Institute of Technology, India
Michal Hodoň	University of Žilina, Slovakia
Mikael Johansson	CSC - IT Center for Science, Finland
Kathrin Kirchner	Technical University of Denmark, Denmark
Udo Krieger	University of Bamberg, Germany
Peter Kropf	University of Neuchâtel, Switzerland
Ulrike Lechner	Bundeswehr University Munich, Germany
Andreas Lommatzsch	Technical University of Berlin, Germany
Karl-Heinz Lüke	Ostfalia University of Applied Sciences, Germany
Raja Natarajan	Tata Institute of Fundamental Research, India
Deveeshree Nayak	University of Washington Tacoma, USA

Contents

Quantum Computing

Invited Papers

Secure Multi-party Computation and Its Applications

Thijs Veugen[1,2(✉)]

[1] TNO, Anna van Buerenplein 1, The Hague, The Netherlands
thijs.veugen@tno.nl
[2] CWI, Amsterdam Science Park, Amsterdam, The Netherlands

Abstract. There is an urgent need for secure data sharing solutions, such that different organisations can jointly compute with their data, without revealing sensitive data to each other. Secure multi-party computation is an innovative cryptographic technology that has recently become more mature, such that it can be used to obtain very secure data sharing solutions for real life applications. Its broad usability is illustrated by different use cases from various domains.

Keywords: Secure data sharing · Secure multi-party computation

1 Secure Data Sharing

In the current era of big data, artificial intelligence, and privacy, there is a growing need for secure data sharing solutions [1]. This can be explained by two conflicting developments observed within our society. The first one is the increased availability of data from different sources, and the need to add value to data by artificial intelligence, machine learning, and similar technologies [2]. By sharing various data sources we can improve services, mitigate risks, and create new business opportunities.

The second development is the improved regulation for protecting the privacy of personal data, avoiding large data lakes by commercial companies [3], and the increased awareness of people and organisations to carefully handle privacy-sensitive data. Data can be sensitive because of privacy reasons, but organisations are also reluctant to share commercially sensitive data. These two developments illustrate the apparent paradox that we have created. On one hand we want to share data and jointly compute with it to create value, but on the other hand we do not, because this will leak sensitive data to other parties, who might use it for malicious purposes.

This paradox shows the need for technical solutions that people and organisations can use to securely compute with distributed data to jointly create value, without revealing sensitive data to others. A suitable and very secure technology to tackle this problem is the innovative cryptographic field of secure multi-party computation.

© The Author(s), under exclusive license to Springer Nature Switzerland AG 2022
F. Phillipson et al. (Eds.): I4CS 2022, CCIS 1585, pp. 3–5, 2022.
https://doi.org/10.1007/978-3-031-06668-9_1

2   Secure Multi-party Computation

First introduced in 1982 [5], secure multi-party computation is a relatively new field within cryptography. It consists of a large collection of techniques to tackle a specific problem. Consider multiple parties, each having their own data. Together they want to perform a certain computation with their data, technically described as a function that given all inputs, each party having an input, will compute an output. The most important requirement is that the parties are not allowed to learn each others input during the computation of the function.

Although the developed solutions are very secure, this initially required large computational efforts by the parties, and lots of (secure) communication between them. In recent decades, new academic discoveries [6, 7] led to improvements that reduced the computational and communication effort, which has made the technology suitable for tackling real life problems. Secure multi-party computation has proven to be a serious candidate for multiple data sharing problems in various domains.

3   Applications

We mention a couple of applications of secure multi-party computation from different domains. The first example is the combat of financial fraud. Anti money laundering is a worldwide huge problem, and financial institutions are investing a lot of effort in their attempt to tackle it. A reason that this has not led to serious fraud reductions, is that banks are not allowed to share their data. This is especially a problem for anti money laundering, as these activities typically consist of large transaction chains over various banks and countries in an attempt to legalise the fraudulent money. We developed a solution to enable banks to search for fraudulent accounts within virtually joint transaction networks, without leaking their own transaction data [4].

Another problem arises from the fact that data are often fragmentary stored over different organisations. A frequently arising situation is that there are two databases containing similar items or persons, and they would like to know how many, or even which ones, they have in common, without learning the remainder of the other database. This problem is technically known as private, or secure set intersection [8]. This could e.g. be used to find people that are wanted in different countries for fraudulent actions, without revealing sensitive national black lists.

Within the health domain, sensitive medical data is stored at various organisations, like hospitals, general practitioners, pharmacies, medical research, etc. Interesting insights could be gained by running machine learning on the distributed data, such as measuring the impact of health innovations, developing personalised medicines, and finding the cause of diseases. As a concrete use-case, hospital Erasmus MC and health insurance company Achmea have data on individuals in the city of Rotterdam, which would in theory enable them to train a regression model in order to identify high-impact lifestyle factors for heart failure [9].

4 Conclusion

We explained the urgency of finding solutions for secure data sharing, where different organisations can jointly compute with their data, without revealing sensitive data to each other. Secure multi-party computation is an innovative cryptographic technology that can be used to obtain very secure data sharing solutions. Its broad usability is illustrated by different applications from various domains.

References

1. Attema, T., Worm, D.: Finally, a privacy-friendly way to harness data. Whitepaper TNO (2021). https://publications.tno.nl/publication/34637925/StFCdC/TNO-2021-technological.pdf
2. OECD: Enhancing Access to and Sharing of Data: Reconciling Risks and Benefits for Data Re-use across Societies. OECD Publishing, Paris (2019)
3. European Union: European Comission: Proposal for a REGULATION OF THE EUROPEAN PARLIAMENT AND OF THE COUNCIL on European data governance (Data Governance Act), 25 November 2020, COM (2020). 767 final
4. Sangers, A., et al.: Secure multiparty PageRank algorithm for collaborative fraud detection. In: Goldberg, I., Moore, T. (eds.) FC 2019. LNCS, vol. 11598, pp. 605–623. Springer, Cham (2019). https://doi.org/10.1007/978-3-030-32101-7_35
5. Yao, A.C.-C.: Protocols for secure computations (extended abstract). In: 23rd Annual Symposium on Foundations of Computer Science, Chicago, Illinois, USA, 3–5 November 1982, pp. 160–164. IEEE Computer Society (1982)
6. Damgård, I., Pastro, V., Smart, N., Zakarias, S.: Multiparty computation from somewhat homomorphic encryption. In: Safavi-Naini, R., Canetti, R. (eds.) CRYPTO 2012. LNCS, vol. 7417, pp. 643–662. Springer, Heidelberg (2012). https://doi.org/10.1007/978-3-642-32009-5_38
7. Keller, M., Orsini, E., Scholl, P.: MASCOT: faster malicious arithmetic secure computation with oblivious transfer. In: Weippl, E.R., Katzenbeisser, S., Kruegel, C., Myers, A.C., Halevi, S. (eds.) Proceedings of the 2016 ACM SIGSAC Conference on Computer and Communications Security, Vienna, Austria, 24–28 October 2016, pp. 830–842. ACM (2016)
8. Freedman, M.J., Nissim, K., Pinkas, B.: Efficient private matching and set intersection. In: Cachin, C., Camenisch, J.L. (eds.) EUROCRYPT 2004. LNCS, vol. 3027, pp. 1–19. Springer, Heidelberg (2004). https://doi.org/10.1007/978-3-540-24676-3_1
9. van Egmond, M.B., Spini, G., van der Galien, O., et al.: Privacy-preserving dataset combination and Lasso regression for healthcare predictions. BMC Med. Inform. Decis. Mak. **21**, 266 (2021)

Brain-Inspired Approaches to Natural Language Processing and Explainable Artificial Intelligence

Erik Deussen[1], Herwig Unger[1] , and Mario M. Kubek[2]($\boxtimes$)

[1] University of Hagen, Hagen, Germany
{erik.deussen,herwig.unger}@fernuni-hagen.de
[2] Georgia State University, Atlanta, USA
mkubek@gsu.edu

Abstract. Like no other medium, the World Wide Web became the major information source for many people within the last years, some even call it the brain of mankind. For any arising questions, any facts needed, or any multimedia content wanted, a web page providing the respective information seems to exist. Likewise, it seems that sometimes there is nothing that has not been thought, written, painted, or expressed in any other form before: most users simply feel overwhelmed by the flood of available information. Consequently, there is a need for new technologies for autonomous self-management, more timely information handling, processing, and the user's interaction with such huge amounts of data. Indeed, Einstein's saying *Look deep into nature, then you will understand everything better* is a big inspiration and challenge to find the required, new solutions. At this point, a short overview is given of existing organizational and functional principles, which have been derived from nature and in particular the human brain and which could be adapted to realize the desired, new methods for natural language processing. The methods mostly follow the strict natural design principle of locality, i.e. work without overseeing the whole system or full set of data, and exhibit a high degree of parallelism. Also, specific application fields for them will be discussed.

Keywords: Brain-inspired natural language processing · Explainable artificial intelligence · Attention

1 Introduction

Like no other medium, the World Wide Web (WWW) became the major information source for many people within the last years, some even call it the brain of mankind. For any arising questions, any facts needed, or any multimedia content wanted, a web page providing the respective information seems to exist. Likewise, it seems that sometimes there is nothing that has not been thought, written, painted, or expressed in any other form before: most users simply feel overwhelmed by the flood of available information. Consequently, there is a need for

F. Phillipson et al. (Eds.): I4CS 2022, CCIS 1585, pp. 6–10, 2022.
https://doi.org/10.1007/978-3-031-06668-9_2

new technologies and methods supporting autonomous self-management, more timely information handling, processing, and the user's interaction with such huge amounts of data. Indeed, Einstein's saying *Look deep into nature, then you will understand everything better* is a big inspiration and challenge to find the required, new solutions. Therefore, in the following sections, a short overview is given of existing organizational and functional principles, which have been derived from nature and in particular the human brain and which are currently being adapted to realize the desired, new methods for natural language processing (NLP). These methods mostly follow the natural design principle of locality, i.e. work without overseeing the whole system or full set of data, and exhibit a high degree of parallelism. Also, specific application fields for them will be discussed. However, today's existing approaches to Artificial Intelligence (AI) are not able to emulate human intelligence in the required flexibility, e.g. to transfer problem solutions and strategies of one domain to another domain, i.e. to perform a generalization. On the other hand, because they are often used as a "black box", they are not able to justify and explain certain decisions and classifications made in a way that is comprehensible to human users. Moreover, they are characterized by a usually long training phase for the creation of models, which is always strictly separated from the phase of their application.

2   Information Processing in the Human Brain

However, this approach does not correspond to the way the human brain works, where processes of learning and applying take place simultaneously and continuously in the neocortex across multiple cortical levels. In the context of the theory of memory-prediction framework presented in [1], these processes and their interconnectedness are discussed. An essential core aspect here is that sensory input sequences are stored and recognized by the cortical processing hierarchy. To this end, recurrent sequences are encoded in an invariant form (are assigned identifiers) and stored in the different levels of the hierarchy, which allows to represent facts according to their degree of abstraction. Furthermore, a prediction of expected sequence components (based on already stored inputs) and their continuous comparison with new inputs takes place. Deviations trigger a learning process in which alternative representations are captured, which in turn trigger new predictions. Implicitly, this provides for fault tolerance and allows for the correction of errors. The process of prediction is also an important basis for content generation, e.g. in speech production. Furthermore, sensory stimuli of different origins are linked in parallel on the levels of the hierarchy. In this way, a complete – from the point of view of the individual brain – but dynamically adaptable and holistic model of the (perceptible) world is created. Despite continuous improvement and extensions of techniques based on artificial neural networks for sequence modeling [2], for matching data of different domains [3] by linking the models representing them and transfer learning [4], the aforementioned mechanisms and processes are not represented by adequate technical analogues. Despite their importance for natural language understanding (NLU), the neurophysiological processes and effects occurring in the human brain such as remembering (e.g. fan effect [5]) and forgetting [6] are largely ignored in these technical solutions. Furthermore, neuroscientists have found out that during its development the human brain may not only learn many new words but is also connecting them by relations, depending on how often they have been used together. In such a manner, even spatial clusters of frequently and jointly used words appear; this process is called modular segregation [7] in neuroscience and finds a corresponding model with co-occurrence graphs [8] in natural language processing.

3   Language Acquisition and Use

The sequence learning processes addressed can be illustrated particularly well in the context of natural language processing (analysis and generation). It is shown in [9] that the classical generative model of linguistic knowledge [10], which is based on the use of static and limited resources (lexicons, grammatical rules), is unsuitable for this purpose. Instead, humans learn to use language through repeated (frequency dependence should be emphasized) and situational exposure to idiomatic turns of phrase and collocations, which allows words to be ascribed their individual meaning by the brain along with their contextual profile and frame of use, thus also allowing for the resolution of ambiguities. Linguistic experiences are therefore stored by both semantic and episodic memory. In the context of stimulus-response experiments [8], it was also shown that term associations by humans correlate well with significant co-occurrences in statistical corpus analysis. The mentioned learning processes must therefore incorporate these approaches of human language acquisition and use. As a side effect, a unique representation of the world is formed depending on the presented stimuli.

4   Brain-Inspired and Continuous Information Processing

In order to make this representation as comprehensive as possible, it is necessary to acquire as many sensory stimuli as possible and process them simultaneously in order to strengthen the mental representation through a manifold input (not exclusively linguistic). The core aspect here is that this modeling must always be oriented towards use. Furthermore, this learning process must be executed continuously, not only once or as needed, e.g. during the training phase of artificial neural networks. In this way, it is possible for the agent/computer program executing the learning process to dynamically adjust to changing situations and contexts. However, a filtering mechanism is necessary to support the aforementioned abstraction of the cortical processing hierarchy. The aim is to capture the essential information from an input sequence on the different levels of the hierarchy and to store it there in an encoded form. Current language models such as Google BERT [4] use so-called attention mechanisms to determine the importance of different input fragments. In this respect, an alternative, graph-based method was developed in [11], which determines the semantically influential terms and phrases – called source topics – of a given text or corpus. Through these, it is possible (among other things), to create topical chains of terms (even across text boundaries) and whole texts that reveal the fundamentals of topics of interest. In a natural way, this creates a kind of topic-oriented signpost system, which is able to reveal thematic dependencies and to further use them to find relevant foundational documents through (possibly repeated) interactive and automated topic tracking alike. Another advantage of this approach is its inherent explainability: topical foundations can be found by repeated backtracking, starting from source topics connected to an initial set of topics of interest. This way, these connections serve as an explanation of the topical chain. Furthermore, using those and similar procedures, an implicit extraction of relevant features from input streams of different sensory origins is possible.

5   Applications

The previous discussions stress the importance of the technical realization and modeling of the brain's neurophysiological processes in modern information systems. Especially, the extraction of semantic features along with their weights to be used in numerous tasks such as sentiment analysis as well as document classification and clustering can be greatly improved when applying them as continuously executed steps in a preprocessing pipeline. This way, the quality of the results returned by downstream text mining algorithms will be significantly improved as well. Library services are a particular important application field that can specifically benefit from these approaches. As those services are essential for learning and teaching, they are increasingly being integrated into learning management systems (LMS) [12]. For instance, the services of liaison librarians, who act as active intermediaries or contact persons and know how scientists of a certain domain use to communicate, can be offered in these systems in order to sustainably and actively support scientific works and research processes. To a certain extent, the brain-inspired approaches and methods mentioned in the previous sections can on one hand support these services on a technical level and on the other hand can take a lot of work off the librarians' hands, especially when it comes to analyzing, filtering, and screening large amounts of scientific contents. Furthermore, these services can be personalized and adapted to users' needs. As an example, they can actively support LMS-users in their specific research tasks by continuously providing pointers to relevant literature from the WWW, enriching search processes with complementary topical directions or search terms and suggesting useful scientific communities. For this purpose, large amounts of textual resources must be automatically analyzed and classified, not only with respect to content-related aspects, but to time-related ones, too. In doing so, a "Librarian of the Web" [13] is created which will act autonomously and on behalf of the LMS-users, while at the same time taking a huge leap forward towards real information literacy or competence.

6   Conclusion

This extended abstract pointed out that current approaches for artificial intelligence lack the inclusion of an adequate technical realization of neurophysiological processes in the human brain. However, the adoption and integration of brain-inspired methods in modern information systems will yield significantly better processing results, e.g. when classifying textual documents and search queries. Furthermore, they enable the creation of information literate library-services that can proactively and individually support scientists in their research tasks.

References

1. Hawkins J., Blakeslee, S.: On Intelligence. Henry Holt and Company (2004)
2. Paaß, G., Hecker, D.: Erfassung der Bedeutung von geschriebenem text. In: Paaß, G., Hecker, D. (eds.) Künstliche Intelligenz, pp. 167–248. Springer, Wiesbaden (2020). https://doi.org/10.1007/978-3-658-30211-5_6
3. Antol, S., et al.: VQA: visual question answering. In: IEEE International Conference on Computer Vision (ICCV), pp. 2425–2433. IEEE Computer Society (2015)
4. Devlin, J., et al.: BERT: pre-training of deep bidirectional transformers for language understanding. In: Proceedings of the 2019 Conference of the North American Chapter of the Association for Computational Linguistics: Human Language Technologies, vol. 1, pp. 4171–4186. ACL (2019)
5. Radvansky, G.A.: The fan effect: a tale of two theories. J. Exp. Psychol.: Gener. **128**(2), 198–206 (1999)
6. Deussen, E., Immelnkämper, M., Unger, H.: Oblivion in time-dependent information management. In: Unger, H., Kubek, M. (eds.) The Autonomous Web. Studies in Big Data, vol. 101, pp. 149–158. Springer, Cham (2022). https://doi.org/10.1007/978-3-030-90936-9_11
7. Baum, G.L., et al.: Modular segregation of structural brain networks supports the development of executive function in youth. Curr. Biol. **17**(11), 1561–1572.e8 (2017)
8. Heyer, G., Quasthoff, U., Wittig, T.: Text Mining: Wissensrohstoff Text: Konzepte, Algorithmen, Ergebnisse. W3L-Verlag (2006)
9. Taylor, J.R.: The Mental Corpus. How Language is Represented in the Mind. Oxford University Press, Oxford (2012)
10. Chomsky, N.: Knowledge of Language: Its Nature, Origin, and Use. Greenwood Publishing Group (1986)
11. Kubek, M., Unger, H.: Detecting source topics by analysing directed co-occurrence graphs. In: 12th International Conference on Innovative Internet Community Services (I2CS 2012), pp. 202–211. Gesellschaft für Informatik e.V., Bonn (2012)
12. Roos, M.: Mögliche Anforderungen an ein LMS aus Bibliothekssicht. eleed **14** (2021)
13. Kubek, M.: Concepts and Methods for a Librarian of the Web. Springer, Cham (2020). https://doi.org/10.1007/978-3-030-23136-1

Back to the Future of Work: Old Questions for New Technologies

Darian Meacham(✉)

Maastricht University, Maastricht, Netherlands
d.meacham@maastrichtuniversity.nl

Abstract. In the past decade or so the *Future of Work* question has emerged as a major policy concern at national and international level. This is in large part due to opportunities and challenges created by the development of data and AI driven automation technologies, and in the past two years by the Covid pandemic, which has led many employees and employers to rethink the ways in which they work, as individuals and organisations. In the USA, there is now talk of a *great resignation*, as many employees reconsider the value and quality of their working lives. If there is one lesson that we have already learned it is that the *future of work* question resists easy formulations and answers, nor is it primarily a matter of jobs being replaced by automation. As work touches nearly every aspect of our lives the future of work is bound to be a complex question in need to careful investigation. In this talk I won't offer predictions, but try to unpack the problem, asking not so much what is the future of work, but rather how should we ask good question(s) about it in the first place.

Keyword: Future of work

The question of the "future-of-work" has in the past decade or so re-emerged as a major field of academic and policy inquiry. Interest in this topic has spanned disciplines with significant contributions being made in economics [1, 2], sociology [3], anthropology [4] and philosophy [5]. On the policy side, reports from the European Commission [6] have been published alongside studies from major consultancies [7], European agencies such as Eurofound [8] as well as organised labour [9].

The recent storm of activity has in large part been motivated by reflection, anticipation and consternation surrounding opportunities and challenges created by the development of data and AI driven automation technologies. Over the past two years, the Covid-19 pandemic, has also led many employees and employers to rethink the ways in which they work, as individuals and organisations. In the USA, there is now talk of a "great resignation", as many employees reconsider the value and quality of their working lives. The question of the future-of-work has taken a partner: what is "good work"?

Taking a step back, a first question to ask is why this refocus on "work", and why has it sustained itself. An immediate if rather coarse answer is a concern about unknowns when it comes to both the quality and quantity of future employment. Modern forms of employment, what we normally call work or jobs, play a formative role in pretty much all aspects of how our individual and collective lives are structured in. There is really

F. Phillipson et al. (Eds.): I4CS 2022, CCIS 1585, pp. 11–13, 2022.
https://doi.org/10.1007/978-3-031-06668-9_3

nothing that we do that is not somehow touched by the work that we do or do not do and the rewards and recognition derived from that work. Employment roles have also played a decisive part in the formation of social and political identities that have constitutive roles in the ways that the legacy institutions of liberal democracy have functioned for generations. In other words, there is a sense that the structures of work could be entering a period of accelerated change. And when work changes, everything changes.

These are not new concerns. In the 1980s, the French philosopher André Gorz pointed out that the "crisis of work" [10], in terms of both its quality and quantity, is coeval with the emergence of the modern concept and practices of employment. The "future of work" question and consternation have been around since work's inception. In his seminal paper, "Economic Possibilities for Our Grandchildren" [11] from the early 1930s, John Maynard Keynes introduced the term "technological unemployment", postulating that by today productivity gains would leave citizens of technologically developed nations with such a surplus of time that it could constitute an existential crisis, provided the question of distribution was adequately addressed. Keynes got the problem backwards; it is the problem of distribution within societies of relative affluence that plagues policy makers and not a surplus of leisure time, but the conceptual framework that he introduced persists in the current debate. Functionalist anthropologists [12] have also argued for decades that the paradigmatic political structures of the modern age arose from the exigencies of transformations in the material and technological structures of employment, namely the emergence of commercial and eventually industrial economies.

It is important to revisit these old questions and debates in light of new technological environments, and specifically the development of AI. Decades of debate in these disciplines have prepared us to have different kinds of conversations about not only what structures are subject to change, but what we value more or less in those structures.

There are nonetheless several novel aspects of the current debate. First is the question of whether *this time* is somehow different from previous waves of automation. Again, an old question, but there is the possibility that the answer will be different this time around. Jobs are not monolithic entities, but rather complex practices composed of many different tasks involving diverse human capacities, and human-machine assemblages. When evaluating the potential effect(s) of automation on jobs, it makes more sense to look at what human roles, capacities and tasks are being transformed, and how jobs and roles could change qualitatively as well as quantitatively, rather than anticipating whether this or that job will exist *tout court* at some point in the future.

Something else may be different this time as well. There exist an ever-growing number of proposals for hard and soft governance mechanisms which aim to humanise, if not AI, but the socio-technical environments that AI is transforming or may transform [13]. These approaches, grouped under the umbrella of "human-centred AI", which now inform EU guidelines [14], national research funding programmes and iterations of corporate social responsibility, have something very similar to the questions and concerns that have informed the future of work debate for decades. They aim to facilitate the development and application of AI that enhances human capacities rather than replacing them, that upskills rather than deskills and that overall contributes to human flourishing rather than redundancy. The primary aim of this talk then is to better understand what the work programme that we might call "human-centred AI" can learn from the future-of-work question.

References

1. Susskind, R.E., Susskind, D.: The Future of the Professions: How Technology will Transform The Work of Human Experts. Oxford University Press, USA (2021)
2. Avent, R.: The Wealth of Humans: Work, Power, and Status In The Twenty-First Century. St Martins Press, New York (2016)
3. Dejours, C.: The Return of Work in Critical Theory : Self, Society. Columbia University Press, Politics (2018)
4. Graeber, D.: Bullshit Jobs: A Theory. Penguin, London (2019)
5. Geuss, R.: A philosopher looks at work. Cambridge University Press, Cambridge (2021)
6. Arregui, P.: The changing nature of work and skills in the digital age. In: Gonzalez Vazquez, I., et al. (eds) EUR 29823 EN, Publications Office of the European Union, Luxembourg, ISBN 978–92–76–09207–0, JRC117505 (2019). https://doi.org/10.2760/373892
7. https://www2.deloitte.com/global/en/pages/human-capital/articles/future-of-work.html
8. Eurofound Employee Monitoring and Surveillance: The Challenges of Digitalisation. Publications Office of the European Union, Luxembourg (2020)
9. Freeman, R.: Who owns the robots rules the world. IZA World Labor. **5** (2015). https://doi.org/10.15185/izawol.5
10. Gorz, A.: Critique of Economic Reason. Verso, London (2010)
11. Keynes, J.M.: Economic possibilities for our grandchildren. In: Essays in Persuasion. Palgrave Macmillan.London (2010). https://doi.org/10.1007/978-1-349-59072-8_25
12. Gellner, E., Breuilly, J.: Nations and Nationalism. Blackwell Publishing, Malden (2013)
13. International KES Conference on Human Centered Intelligent Systems. In: Zimmermann, A., Howlett, R.J., Jain, L.C., Schmidt, R. (eds.) Human centred intelligent systems. In: Proceedings of KES-HCIS 2021 Conference https://doi.org/10.1007/978-981-15-5784-2
14. European Commission. High-level expert group on artificial intelligence. Ethics Guidelines for Trustworthy AI. Publications office of the European Union (2019)

Energy Harvesting and Environment Protection

Solar Energy Harvesting for the Mobile Robotic Platform

Michal Hodoň$^{(\boxtimes)}$, Peter Ševčík, Juraj Miček, Veronika Olešnániková, Peter Šarafín, Ján Kapitulík, and Lukáš Čechovič

Faculty of Management Science and Informatics, Department of Technical Cybernetics, University of Žilina, Univerzitná 8215/1, 01026 Žilina, Slovakia
michal.hodon@fri.uniza.sk

Abstract. This paper describes the educational mobile robotic platform Solarcar. The platform is used for teaching purposes, especially for description of theoretical as well as practical aspects of using alternative energy sources in embedded system design. The robot was designed and built as the supportive material for the students of study field Computer engineering, for the subject Embedded systems. Through its usage, the principles of so called Green computing in the background of complex physics are taught in a playful, and for students interesting way.

Keywords: Solar energy · Robot · Educational platform · Green computing

1 Introduction

Electrical energy is often stored in batteries (electrochemical cell). These can be divided into primary cells that are non-rechargeable and secondary cells that can be recharged. Note that secondary electrochemical cells have a limited number of charge/discharge cycles. Capacitors are another possibility of electrical storage. Not long ago, high-capacity capacitors with the commercial name supercapacitors, or supercapacitors, or ultracapacitors, have appeared. Their capacitance is several orders of magnitude higher than that of conventional electrolytic capacitors. With their application together with solar cell as an energy harvesting technology, a kind of energy-efficient embedded system for various application fields can be revealed. The scope of this paper is not to list and discuss pros and cons of supercapacitor and batteries or other energy harvesting technologies in detail. An aim of the authors is to introduce and describe small robotic platform powered via solar panel as a simple educational tool, which can used for better explanation of various physical laws.

However, because the supercapacitor is a relatively new component, which comes hand in hand with the developments in nanotechnology, let's mention its basic properties in general. It is obvious that the supercapacitor serves to store electricity. Thanks to the very thin dielectric and large active areas of the electrodes, it achieves significantly larger capacities than conventional electrolytic capacitors. This feature predestines the supercapacitor for the energy storing. It performs the same function as rechargeable batteries. Although, at present time, it is not yet able to fully replace the batteries [1–3],

F. Phillipson et al. (Eds.): I4CS 2022, CCIS 1585, pp. 17–27, 2022.
https://doi.org/10.1007/978-3-031-06668-9_4

in many applications, especially in low-power applications, supercapacitors successfully compete with them. Gross comparison of Li-Ion batteries and supercapacitors is given in the following Table 1.

Table 1. Gross comparison of Li-Ion batteries and supercapacitor

Parameter	Battery	Supercapacitor
Energy density	100 Wh/kg*	10 Wh/kg
Power density	1000 W/kg	10 000W/kg*
Efficiency	ca. 80%	ca. 92%*
Number of battery cycle counts	400 – 2500	1 000 000*
Lifetime	4 – 6 years	15 years*
Working temperature range	-20°C to +60°C	-40°C to 100°C*
End of working	Sudden end	Predictable end
Price	0.07 – 0.2 € / kg-cycle	0.006 € / kg-cycle*

* better parameter according to the opponent

From the table is evident (light-grey filling), in which parameters supercapacitors exceeds the second type of batteries.

2 Solar Mobile Robotic Platform

The block schematic of the solar mobile robotic platform, further named as Solar car, can be seen in the Fig. 1 below.

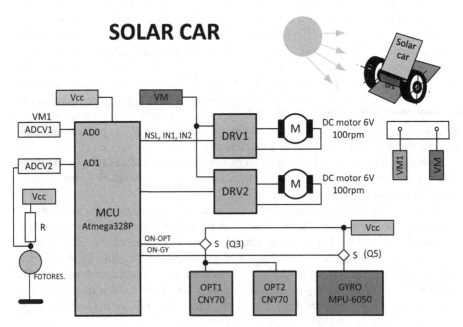

Fig. 1. A block schematic of the solar car

As can be seen from the figure above, the solar car, as the educational robotic platform, is built on the popular 8-bit AVR microcontroller Atmega328p as the main control unit. Further, there are integrated two 6V DC motors 100rpm for the robot driving, which are operated through DRV8837 1.8A low-voltage DC motor driver. Two optical sensors OPTx CNY70 together with the MPU-6050 module, which includes triple axis accelerometer and gyro sensory, allow to navigate the robot through the defined environment. Photoresistor is used for the purposes of power optimization through the light source sensing. The solar car outline can be seen in the Fig. 2.

Fig. 2. Prototype of Solarcar

We will briefly describe the energy management solution of a solar car (Fig. 3). Not everything mentioned is necessary for students when programming their applications. Knowledge of the operation of circuits that provide power to the microcontroller and motors is not necessary during programming.

Basic knowledge is that the supercapacitor C1 is continually charged from the solar panel. This is the place, where an energy is stored. If the voltage at its electrodes reaches 1.4 V, the DC/DC boost converter will start its operation to increase the input voltage to 3.4 V. All circuits including the microcontroller (MCU) are then supplied with this voltage.

From the moment the DC/DC boost converter starts working, the student (or program) can control solar car's next activity so that it can complete the task with minimum power consumption. The car is designed so the students do not have to wait for nice weather (sun) when programming and tuning programs. For this reason, it is possible to power the car's control circuits via the USBASP programmer from the computer's USB port.

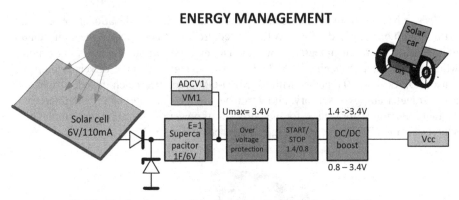

Fig. 3. Block schematic of the power-management circuit of Solarcar

3   Detailed Description of a Solar Car Power Circuitry

From the block diagram of the power-management circuitry is evident, that the protection of supercapacitor together with the protection as well as starting of the DC/DC conversion, is handled through the circuit design. It should be noted that more elegant solution would be such that these protections against higher voltage could be solved by the software. However, in this case the cars may not survive while students developing and debugging the program. For this reason, these functions are assigned to electronics, even this is not optimal solution in terms of power consumption optimization. Nevertheless, basic goal of the proposed solution is the minimization of its power consumption.

As it was already mentioned, the main source, which powers the solar car is solar panel together with the supercapacitor. The energy stored in a capacitor is given by:

$$E = \frac{1}{2}C \cdot U^2 \,[J, F, V] \tag{1}$$

The supercapacitor 1 V/6 V is used as a mean of storing energy in the solar vehicle. It has a capacity of 1 F and the maximum permissible voltage at its electrodes is 5.5 to 6 V (depending on the supercapacitor type used). It follows an amount of the energy, which can be stored in it:

$$E = 0.5 \cdot 1F \cdot (5.5\,\text{V})^2 = 15.125\,\text{J} \tag{2}$$

Power to the supercapacitor is supplied by a solar cell with a maximum power of 0.66 W. The maximum voltage is 6 V. The supercapacitor is protected against overvoltage by a Zener diode with a breakdown voltage of 5.6 V (Fig. 4).

Then, at the supercapacitor electrodes there is a voltage U which is used:

- for supplying H bridges of DRV8837 DC motors.
- for powering solar car control circuits via DC/DC boost converter (MCP16251) with 3.4 V output.

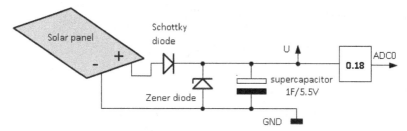

Fig. 4. Supercapacitor protection

Since the input voltage of the DC/DC converter must not exceed the output voltage (3.4 V), while the voltage on the supercapacitor can reach up to 5.8 V, the input voltage limiting circuits are essential. These circuits provide overvoltage protection at the side of DC/DC converter input (Fig. 5).

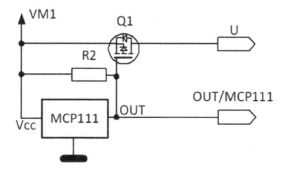

Fig. 5. Overvoltage protection of DC/DC boost module

The MCP111 monitoring circuit has at the input voltage lower than 3 V a voltage of 0 V at the OUT/MCP111 output, which causes the transistor Q1 to be open and the voltage U to be applied to the DC/DC converter input. The same voltage is applied to resistor divider R5, R6 and therefore transistor Q8 will be closed, the base of transistor Q7 will not flow. For this reason, base Q6 will be close to zero and transistor Q6 will be closed. When the voltage U reaches 3 V, the circuit U2 closes, and at its output the voltage level U (via resistor R2).

This will cause:

– closure of transistor Q1,
– opening of transistor Q6, which acts as a voltage limiter due to diode D5.

Voltage U on the emitter of Q6 transistor is equal to:

– if 3 V < U < Uz (where Uz = 3,6 V), Uv = U – Ube (where Ube = 0,6 V).
– if U > Uz, Uv = Uz – Ube = 3 V.

The described circuit part is shown in the Fig. 6.

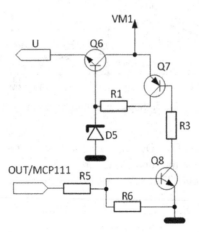

Fig. 6. Overvoltage protection circuit

To improve efficient operation, the DC/DC converter is preceded by a START/STOP circuit that starts/stops the converter - MCP16251 via the EN pin when the defined voltage levels are reached (Fig. 7).

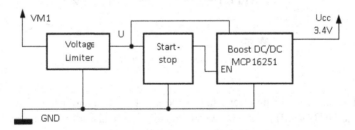

Fig. 7. Block schematic of power circuitry

Start-stop circuits are shown in the following Fig. 8.

If the voltage U1 reaches 0.4 V (Ube Q2), transistor Q2 opens, causing an increase in current to the base of transistor Q4, which opens "shortens resistance R3" causing an increase in base current Q2. The voltage at the EN input reaches a value close to U. It is apparent from the above relations that by suitable selection of resistors R1 to R3 a suitable combination of *Ustart* and *Ustop* voltages can be set over a wide range.

If we choose the values of resistors R1, R2 and R3, R1 = 1.8 MΩ, R2 = 1.8 MΩ, R3 = 2.7 MΩ, then *Ustart* = 1.4 V and *Ustop* = 0.8 V.

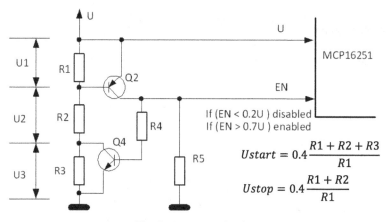

Fig. 8. Start-stop circuits

Note that the efficiency of the MCP16251 converter decreases with the decreasing input voltage. At the output voltage Vout = 3.4 V and the input voltage 3 V the efficiency at the consumption of 2 to 70 mA is above 95%, however at the voltage 1.5 V the efficiency is only at the level of 87%. The dependence of the inverter efficiency from *Iout* and *Vin* at Vout = 3.4 V is shown in the Fig. 9 below.

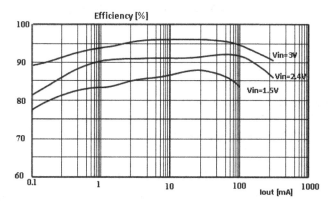

Fig. 9. Dependance of MCP16251 converter efficiency on the input voltage and current consumption [4]

4 Power Consumption of Solar Car Peripherals

The main power consumption of a solar car is the consumption of a microcontroller. Although the consumption of all other subsystems is significant, it can be controlled via the software. All subsystems are powered through MCP 16251, with following supplies:

– MCU ATMEL328P @ RCOSC 1MHz, @ 3.4V, active mode - **0.6 mA**

- control of H-bridge DRV8837 without PWM / PWM50kHz - **0.3/0.7 mA**
  (SLEEP MODE – **5 nA**)
- MPU6050 - **3.6 mA**
- optical sensors CNY 70 - **20 mA**
- LED - **2 mA**

In the figure below, all peripherals are shown in block schematic (Fig. 10).

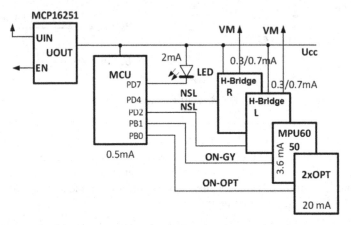

Fig. 10. Power supply of basic functional parts of a solar car

4.1 Optical Subsystem

As it follows from the above, the optical subsystem has the highest power consumption in active mode. For this reason, it is necessary to turn it only when required, for the shortest possible time. Circuitry of optical sensors is shown in the figure below (Fig. 11).

When the switch S1 is turned on, it is necessary to wait until the filter capacitors C1 and C2 are charged. The time constant of the filters, τ is:

$$\tau = R1 \cdot C1 = 0.484 \text{ ms} \tag{3}$$

If we assume that after a time of $4\tau \approx 2$ ms, the value of output OPT1 can be measured with sufficient accuracy. In the use scenario, the sensors are used for the navigation of the robot across the black path at white underlay. So 2 ms is the minimal time to decide on the reflectivity (color) of the path. The measurement then last 2.1 ms because the setting of AD converter takes 50 us and AD conversion takes 50 us at clkIO = 1 MHz.

Power used to charge capacitors C1 and C2 is equal to:

$$E = \frac{1}{2}CU^2 = 12.7 \cdot 10^{-6} \text{ J} \tag{4}$$

The total energy to charge both capacitors is 0.0254 mJ. The current flowing through the optocoupler diode can be calculated:

$$I = \frac{Ucc - U_D}{R2} = \frac{3.4 - 1.4}{220} = 9 \text{ mA} \tag{5}$$

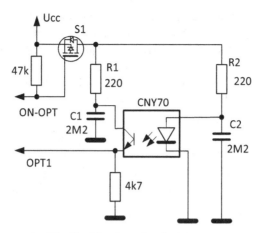

Fig. 11. Circuitry of optical sensors

The current flowing through the optocoupler transistor depends on the specific conditions (reflection of the emitting infrared radiation). In the worst case, the current through the transistor is equal to:

$$I_T = \frac{Ucc}{R3} = \frac{3.4}{4700} = 0.7 \,\text{mA} \tag{6}$$

To make it simpler, assume that a current $I = 9.7$ mA flows through the optocoupler 2.1 ms. Then the energy consumed in one measurement will be equal to:

$$E = U \cdot I \cdot t = 3.4 \cdot 9.7 \cdot 10^{-3} \cdot 2.1 \cdot 10^{-3} = 69 \cdot 10^{-6} \,\text{J} \tag{7}$$

The total energy per measurement using both optocouplers will be:

$$E = (0.0254 + 0.069) \cdot 2 = 0.19 \text{ mJ} \tag{8}$$

Recall that the energy accumulated in the supercapacitor at a voltage of 5.5 V was E = 15.125 J. A simple comparison shows that it is enough energy to perform about 80,000 measurements. Note that these considerations are too basic just to show the students how the energy intensity of the measurement process is handled. If the measurement is done every 200 ms then the mean current value is:

$$I = \frac{E}{U \cdot t} = \frac{0.19}{0.68} = 0.28 \,\text{mA} \tag{9}$$

In continual measurement, the power consumption would be around 20 mA as it was stated earlier.

4.2 Motor Drives

The DC motors of the solar car are controlled by two DRV3387 H-bridges. Their consumption in sleep mode can be neglected. It is approximately 100 times lower than the

ATmega328P @ 1 MHz MCU power consumption. In the active mode, their consumption depends on the excitation. If the inputs do not have a PWM signal, then the typical current is 0.3 mA. In the case of a 50 kHz PWM signal, the typical current is 0.7 mA. Note that the consumption of the bridge control circuits is higher than that of the MCU. For this reason, it is advisable to keep the bridges as long as possible in a sleep state. Motor drives circuitry is shown in the Fig. 12 below.

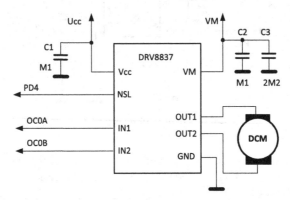

Fig. 12. Motor drives circuitry

4.3 Main Controller

The consumption of the ATmega328P microcontroller depends mainly on the frequency of the clock signal generator, the magnitude of the supply voltage and the active subsystems of the microcontroller. From the datasheet and from measurements is obvious, that current consumption at 1 MHz is about 0.5 mA. If 12 MHz external crystal oscillator would be used, the consumption of the MCU in active mode and the 3.4 V supply would rise to about 5 mA, i.e. about 10 times. In this case it is obvious, that computing power is paid by consumption rise.

5 Conclusion

In this paper, the circuit solution of the special solar car robotic platform was described in detail. Energetical requirements, necessary for its driving were discussed too. Though the solution was successfully practically implemented, there are some improvements to be applied. This solution is not ideal, because if the supercapacitor voltage rises above 3 V, the energy efficiency of the whole device decreases significantly. In the extreme case up to 55% at 5.5 V. However, we assume that much of the time the car will operate at voltages around 3 V. This is already in the hands of the SW developer. On the other hand, in the case of direct sunlight, the solar panel can supply an amount of energy that cannot be meaningfully use or conserve. Therefore, in this case, we will not be interested in the efficiency of the device. From the point of view of the optimal use of the capacity of the solar panel, it would be necessary to choose a more suitable energy processing strategy. In the simplest case, it would be necessary to ensure that the voltage on the supercapacitor is approximately equal to $Uc = 0.7Uo$ at each exposure, where Uo is the voltage on the solar cell without load. This can be solved by a two-way energy pump with secondary storage [5, 6].

Acknowledgement. "This publication was realized with support of Operational Program Integrated Infrastructure 2014 - 2020 of the project: Innovative Solutions for Propulsion, Power and Safety Components of Transport Vehicles, code ITMS 313011V334, co-financed by the European Regional Development Fund".

EUROPEAN UNION

European Regional Development Fund
OP Integrated Infrastructure 2014 – 2020

MINISTRY
OF TRANSPORT
AND CONSTRUCTION
OF THE SLOVAK REPUBLIC

References

1. Musolino, V., Tironi, E., di Milano, P.: A comparison of supercapacitor and high-power lithium batteries. In: Electrical Systems for Aircraft, Railway and Ship Propulsion, pp. 1–6 (2010). https://doi.org/10.1109/ESARS.2010.5665263
2. Andreev, M.K.: An overview of supercapacitors as new power sources in hybrid energy storage systems for electric vehicles. In: 2020 XI National Conference with International Participation (ELECTRONICA), pp. 1–4 (2020). https://doi.org/10.1109/ELECTRONICA50406.2020.9305104
3. Soni, S.R., Upadhyay, C.D., Chandwani, H.: Analysis of battery-super capacitor based storage for electrical vehicle. In: 2015 International Conference on Energy Economics and Environment (ICEEE), pp. 1–7 (2015). https://doi.org/10.1109/EnergyEconomics.2015.7235110
4. MCP16251 datasheet. http://ww1.microchip.com/downloads/en/devicedoc/20005173b.pdf
5. Kochláň, M., Ševčík, P.: Supercapacitor power unit for an event-driven wireless sensor node. In: 2012 Federated Conference on Computer Science and Information Systems (FedCSIS), pp. 791–796 (2012)
6. Kochláň, M., Žák, S., Miček, J., Milanová, J.: Control unit for power subsystem of a wireless sensor node, pp. 1239–1246 (2015). https://doi.org/10.15439/2015F355

Demonstrating Feasibility of Blockchain-Driven Carbon Accounting – A Design Study and Demonstrator

Karl Seidenfad[(⊠)], Tobias Wagner, Razvan Hrestic, and Ulrike Lechner

Computer Science Department, Universität der Bundeswehr München, Munich, Germany
{karl.seidenfad,tobias.wagner,razvan.hrestic,
ulrike.lechner}@unibw.de

Abstract. Carbon accounting calls for innovative digital infrastructures. The Paris Agreement and the 26th UN Climate Change Conference provide the frame for designing information systems for carbon accounting. This paper explores blockchain as a technology for carbon accounting and, in particular, for the Product Carbon Footprint. This article analyses core architectural designs of carbon footprints, consortia, and smart contract infrastructure. Experiences from the implementation of a carbon footprint blockchain demonstrator are reported. A coffee supply chain exemplifies the approach. Hyperledger Fabric and Minifabric from Hyperledger Labs are the technical frameworks used.

Keywords: Blockchain · Carbon accounting · Supply chain

1 Introduction

Digitalization and decarbonization are strategic topics that require considerable efforts and innovations. The Paris Agreement sets climate goals for nation-states. A recent milestone for developing the Paris Agreement [1] is marked by the 26th UN Climate Change Conference (COP26), held in November 2021 in Glasgow. In the momentum of the COP26, Article 6.2 of the Paris Agreement refers to decentralized, cooperative approaches in carbon accounting – a departure from centralized architecture and comprehensive rules of present emission trading market mechanisms [2, 3]. Blockchain as a technology comes with the value promise of decentralized architecture and secure inter-organizational information flows. This article explores blockchain technology as technical basis for carbon accounting.

Analysis and design are exemplified with the coffee supply chain. In the coffee supply chain, farmer, production, logistics, retail provide consumers with roasted coffee beans. Public authorities monitor the whole process. The use of blockchain to digitalize the coffee supply chain may address three societal problems. First, a traceable product history facilitates tracking and tracing to increase food safety [4]. Second, transparency across the supply chain helps to address concerns of quality, fairness, and sustainability as all this information can be provided to the end customer. We are interested in a third

F. Phillipson et al. (Eds.): I4CS 2022, CCIS 1585, pp. 28–46, 2022.
https://doi.org/10.1007/978-3-031-06668-9_5

application: the transactions stored in the blockchain can be enriched to enable carbon accounting use cases. This work presented in this article builds on previous work on blockchain for enabling transparency, tracking, and tracing across the supply chain [5] and the coffee supply chain is one of the use cases.

The main research interest is how to design blockchain technology for carbon accounting and what functionalities are necessary. We are also interested in how to integrate carbon accounting with other transactions in the supply chain for an efficient solution. A demonstrator validates our design. We study design options and implement a demonstrator for carbon accounting in the coffee supply chain. The article presents the design of a demonstrator for blockchain as infrastructure for a coffee supply chain and for capturing the associated carbon emissions. The article also reports on the learnings for implementing blockchain-based infrastructures.

This article is organized as follows. Section 2 summarizes related work in blockchain technology and carbon accounting. Section 3 describes the research design. Section 4 characterizes the scenario illustrated by the demonstrator. Section 5 documents the implementation results for the demonstrator. Section 6 concludes our experiences and outlines future work.

2   State of the Art

This work contributes to understanding the design of blockchain-based infrastructures for carbon accounting systems. The state-of-the-art section reviews Blockchain technology first and then moves on to carbon accounting.

2.1   Blockchain Technology and Design of Blockchain

The Distributed Ledger Technology (DLT) shapes a family of concepts with different designs, properties, and characteristics. Popular concepts such as Blockchain, block directed acyclic graphs (blockDAG), and transaction-based directed acyclic graphs (TDAG) differ in how data is concatenated. All these concepts have decentralized management of immutable data and transactions in common. Reports by the NIST [6] and its German counterpart BSI [7] provide definitions and guidelines for blockchain technology. They outline the four key DLT characteristics: decentralization, transparency, immutability, and cryptography. Classification approaches for blockchain technologies distinguish network exposure (e.g., private or public) or the right to be part of the consensus (e.g., permissioned or permissionless).

For the design process of blockchain-based information systems, Xu et al. [8] guide the multitude of configuration possibilities and variants of blockchain-based systems and summarize design decisions in a flowchart. Marchesi, Marchesi, and Tonelli [9] follow an agile approach based on user stories and iterative development for designing blockchain applications. They provide a UML activity diagram as orientation for the design process. Hoiss, Seidenfad, and Lechner [10] develop an architecture for blockchain-based systems: blockchain and the integration with business information systems and integration with services for operation are critical elements of this approach. The approach fosters a clearer annotation of tasks and responsibilities inside a blockchain-based consortium.

30   K. Seidenfad et al.

Weking et al. [11] provide a taxonomy of blockchain-based business models. The adoption of private permissioned blockchains in practice is recognized by projects such as IBM's TradeLens [12], BMW's PartChain [13], and the Catena-X Automotive Network [14]. A systematic review of applications in supply chain management contributed by Dietrich et al. [15] lists more than 40 blockchain projects. Beyond famous use cases for supply chain management, Schmiedel [16] connects an additive manufacturing machine with a permissioned blockchain to enable business models like pay-per-use or predictive maintenance.

The discussion about implementing carbon accounting and carbon markets with blockchain technology is vital, and the bandwidth of approaches ranges from public permissionless to private permissioned blockchain solutions [17–20]. Braden [21] evaluates Bitcoin, Ethereum, Hyperledger Fabric, and EOS regarding the applicability for climate policy applications, with the result that Hyperledger Fabric and Ethereum are the most promising technology stacks to date. Schletz, Franke, and Salomo [22, 23] introduce architecture to embed Article 6.2 requirements into a blockchain-based market model. In this regard, the vibrant open source community around Hyperledger Fabric [24] coined the term 'operating System for Climate Action' [25].

2.2 Carbon Accounting

Carbon accounting is how organizations track and report their greenhouse gas (GHG) emissions. In combination with pricing, these are the well-known instruments to realize cost-effective GHG mitigation [3, 26]. For interoperability, international standards such as ISO14040/14044, PAS2050, and the Greenhouse Gas Protocol [25] have been introduced. Carbon accounting aims to calculate carbon footprints, as the product carbon footprint (PCF) and the corporate carbon footprint (CCF). While the CCF collects carbon emissions associated with all the activities of a person or other entity (e.g., building, corporation, country, etc.) [27], the PCF collects all carbon emissions in producing and distributing a product along the supply chain and serves as meaningful information for consumers.

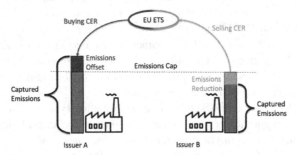

Fig. 1. The (simplified) principle of exchanging certified emissions reductions (CER) by the cap-and-trade scheme according to the German Emissions Trading Authority (DEHSt) [28]

According to the Kyoto protocol, NDC's are stored in dedicated national registries. To facilitate the exchange between national registries, the United Nations Framework

Convention on Climate Change (UNFCCC) operates the International Transaction Log (ITL) [29]. The European Union Transaction Log (EUTL) is linked with the ITL and acts as a database for the European Emissions Trading System (EU ETS) [2]. The EU ETS is the world's most extensive emission trading system [30, 31] and utilizes the cap-and-trade scheme [32] (cf. Fig. 1). In the EU ETS, an individual emissions cap is assigned for each issuer. This emissions cap acts as an annual threshold. The issuers need to decide whether to reduce emissions or buy emissions allowances for compensation. To reduce carbon emissions, the individual emissions cap is lowered by a percentage amount each year according to regulation.

According to Zhao and Chan [33], the practical problems of current cap-and-trade implementations include issues in operation and security. The current cap-and-trade systems, including transaction settlement, credit registration, compliance checking, and emissions verification, require a large amount of administrative effort. Besides the industries which already contribute to carbon markets (e.g., energy and aviation), these concerns are also mentioned in the context of onboarding new sectors to carbon markets, such as, agricultural industry [34, 35]. Also, many of the existing implementations lack effective punishment mechanisms or their non-strict execution [36]. The centralized architecture of current cap-and-trade systems makes them vulnerable to hacking and corruption [37]. Security concerns regard fraud claims for emissions and double accounting [38]. However, there is also a considerable agreement about the importance of voluntary carbon accounting (e.g., by small measures) and the challenges of incentivization and auditing [39, 40].

In 2020, the Kyoto Protocol reached its end of life, and the Paris Agreement became effective. Schneider et al. [41] compare the Kyoto Protocol and Paris Agreement. For the operationalization of the Paris Agreement, Müller and Michaelowa [42] discuss two Internationally Transferred Mitigation Outcomes (ITMO's) approaches for achieving NDC's.

3   Research Design

According to Hevner et al. [42], guided by the design science paradigm, we work in an iterative design process. Our research builds on a codebase, scenarios, a demonstrator, and an understanding of designing blockchain to increase security and resilience for the food supply chain. We have identified design principles to guide our conceptualization, design, and implementation in our work. One design principle aims for fully decentralized structures, i.e., a blockchain that runs on distributed peers operated by different organizations (in contrast to the many approaches hosted in a single cloud). This article is about a use case carbon accounting and extends the current use case, namely tracking, tracing, and resilience in the food supply chain.

The demonstrator we present in this article marks the first design iteration of blockchain for carbon accounting as part of project LIONS. Note that the scenario development for our blockchain-based carbon accounting demonstrator is strongly inspired by the theoretical work of Richardson and Xu [17].

This work extends our Blockchain design knowledge base in the fields of operation [10], design principles [43], design patterns [5], and IoT integration [44, 45].

4 The Carbon Accounting Scenario

This section is about the scenario of carbon accounting and core business and architectural design decisions. We consider three different topics with implications for the blockchain design: (1) the carbon footprint, (2) the consortium architecture, and (3) the tokens and smart contracts to run carbon accounting (and potentially compensation). The coffee supply chain scenario concludes the section.

In our analysis, we assume the existence of a blockchain-based infrastructure for food safety, similar to our approach in NutriSafe [4]. This infrastructure connects actors in the supply chain, and each actor adds information to the blockchain. The consumer then may access this information.

4.1 Carbon Footprint

There are two prominent types of carbon footprint: Product Carbon Footprint and Corporate Carbon Footprint, and both require different kinds of architectures of digital infrastructure.

Product Carbon Footprints (PCF). The first option to implement carbon accounting is with a Product Carbon Footprint. This carbon footprint is the sum of all the greenhouse gas emissions in production and distribution. To build on the blockchain-based infrastructure for food safety (similar to our approach in NutriSafe [4]).

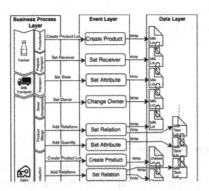
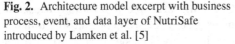
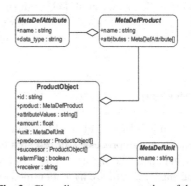

Fig. 2. Architecture model excerpt with business process, event, and data layer of NutriSafe introduced by Lamken et al. [5]

Fig. 3. Class diagram representation of the meta definition concept of NutriSafe introduced by Lamken et al. [5]

This infrastructure connects all actors in the supply chain, and each actor adds information to the blockchain. To build on this infrastructure, the data model of the product with the PCF as a new product attribute using the meta-model introduced by Lamken et al. [5] (see Fig. 3). We propose for this first option to carbon accounting a design that extends the existing data model such that all blockchain entries have this additional information. All relevant actors inside the supply chain provide data about carbon emissions for each product (see Fig. 2). Also, a smart contract is necessary to cumulate carbon emissions between the predecessor and successor of a product in the supply chain. The flow of information for food safety purposes and the PCF follows the same architecture. The information on production and distribution might serve as a meaningful parameter in buying decisions for consumers.

Corporate Carbon Footprints (CCF). The second option for implementing carbon accounting is the corporate carbon footprint (CCF). CCFs have an essential role in determining the greenhouse gas emissions according to the Paris agreement and the need for compensation. This part of the scenario is inspired by the EU ETS and its architecture depicted in Fig. 4. Independent national registries shape the EU ETS and each registry is linked with the European Union Transaction Log (EUTL) of the European Commission. The actors' roles are described as follows: First, each government must take an administrative part. Hence, each government manages the issuance of allowances, surrender of permits, the verification of reported emissions, and grants verification rights to trustworthy actors inside the registry. Second, an installation represents a site, which is emitting. The holder of an installation transfers permissions to other actors, receive allowances from the government, and issues credits e.g., by mitigation projects. For a digital infrastructure, this means that various actors are connected hierarchically. However, not many connections exist in this scenario. This structure is depicted in Fig. 4.

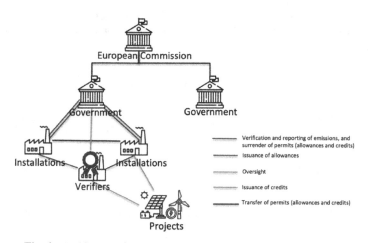

Fig. 4. Architecture for the centralized approach of the EU ETS [17]

Note that PCF and CCF are not independent of each other. The PCF of a product will rely to some extent on data that determine the CCF of the organizations involved. The PCF is related to the single steps in production and a CCF can serve as a proxy to PCFs when exact numbers are not known. Hence, the computation of PCF and CCF needs to be integrated.

The Implications for a Blockchain Infrastructure: The product carbon footprint can build on existing business transactions and, eventually a blockchain like the one we have established in project NutriSafe. The product carbon footprint can build on existing transactions and potentially has a high number of transactions; the corporate carbon footprint potentially needs a new infrastructure with fewer transactions. However, both need to be linked – to provide data in the blockchain and plausibility and correctness checks or auditing and certification.

4.2 Consortium Architecture

Public permissionless blockchains such as, e.g., Bitcoin being open for everyone and granting equal rights to all participants and transactions carry a minimal amount of usable payload. Implementing a blockchain-based EU ETS demands mechanisms: role-based access rights to sensitive data, separation of concerns in a channel-like topology of sidechains, (preferable) feeless transactions, and advanced transaction performance. According to these requirements, the findings mentioned by Braden [21], and considering our own experience from NutriSafe [4], we follow the ideas of private permissioned blockchains and rely on Hyperledger Fabric as our technology platform.

Establishing a productive private permissioned blockchain infrastructure requires the setup of a corresponding consortium. We analyze the possible relationships and motivations to join a consortium. Studying publications of the German Emissions Trading Authority (DEHSt) [2, 41, 46], architecture discussions for business models [47, 48], blockchain-based carbon markets [17, 22, 23, 33, 49], and documentation regarding the Paris Rulebook in practice [50], we identify three archetypes of carbon accounting consortia (see Fig. 5).

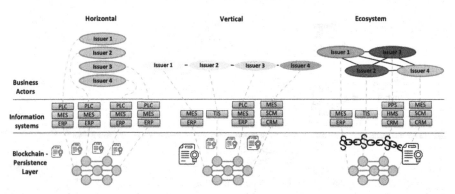

Fig. 5. Architectures of carbon accounting consortia by information systems, mitigation potential, and managing emissions shares

Horizontal Consortium. Actors in this consortium are in a similar field of business with the same kind of value-creating activities. The actors may compete in their business environment. They share the motivation to reduce the effort of accounting and report the CCF. Synergies in carbon accounting are leveraged by sharing data and collecting data on transactions to compute carbon footprints. Carbon accounting is a driver for horizontal integration.

Vertical Consortium. This consortium type collects different actors along a value chain. The mitigation potentials for the actors might differ. They coordinate to mitigate the joint PCF, i.e., by optimizing transportation according to PCF. Existing business relations inside the supply chain are the foundation for this type of consortium. Such a vertical consortium may provide a PCF as a value add to the customer. Sharing the effort for accounting and reporting the CCF is an additional motivation for the actors. This kind of interaction is a driver for vertical integration.

Ecosystem Consortium. CCF mitigation as a value proposition is crucial for this consortium type. The consortium contains actors with various information systems, interfaces, and different mitigation potentials. Traditional value activities and activities dedicated to mitigating the emissions complement each other. Examples for this kind of consortium could be, e.g., regions that promote their carbon emissions to the customer and other branding activities. Such a consortium might benefit from a way to manage emissions rights, e.g., through shares by tokens.

Implications for Blockchain Infrastructure. The business purpose of the consortium defines the kind of interactions necessary, the data model, and the blockchain infrastructure. A vertical consortium can build on existing infrastructures and information flows. The other consortium types need to build up new relations and dedicated infrastructure and may benefit from tokenization and smart contracts as technical means to automate, e.g., carbon accounting, compensation, or emissions trading.

4.3 Smart Contract Operations and Tokens

The design of smart contracts and tokens is an essential part of a blockchain to implement carbon accounting, compensations, or trading. This part of the article builds on the seminal paper on blockchain for carbon accounting by Richardson and Xu [17]. Tokens and processes for a future blockchain-based EU ETS implementation are proposed.

Table 1 summarizes the tokens and smart contracts with a brief description of Richardson and Xu [17] and our consideration for the coffee supply chain scenario.

Table 1. Processes according to [17] and our consideration for the demonstrator

Artefact	Description as stated in [17]	Consideration
Emission-token	*"1tCO₂e verified GHG emissions"*	Yes – by smart contract
Permit-token	*"Permit to emit 1 tCO₂e. Permits can represent both allowances issued by an authority, or credits granted by a verifier"*	Yes – by smart contract
Issuance of emissions	*"Emission tokens may be minted by any enterprise if a verifier co-signs the transaction as a true reflection of the enterprise's emissions"*	Yes – by smart contract

(continued)

Table 1. (*continued*)

Artefact	Description as stated in [17]	Consideration
Burn tokens	"*Emission tokens are burnt alongside an equal or greater number of permit tokens in a single transaction. This process also allows enterprises to voluntarily surrender excess permit tokens if they so choose*"	Yes – by smart contract
Role change	"*An authority can change the role of an enterprise, including promotion of an enterprise to verifier status or removal of an existing status*"	Not yet part of the storyline
Token exchange	"*Organizations can freely trade their permit tokens with the authority, which also acts as a liquidity provider*"	Not yet part of the storyline

E.g., the feature 'Issuance of Permit' is considered in the storyline of the demonstrator but not yet implemented as a smart contract. Features such as 'Role Change' are not part of the immediate scenario yet (Table 2).

4.4 Design Study "Demonstrator Coffee Supply Chain"

According to the presented archetypes of carbon consortia, we design the coffee supply chain as a vertical consortium (cf. Fig. 6) with actors, steps in value creation, information systems and blockchain as infrastructure.

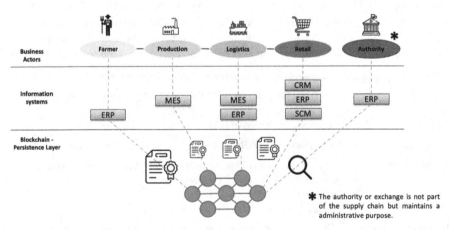

Fig. 6. The carbon accounting consortium for the coffee supply chain

The architecture of the information system in Fig. 6 contains a business actor layer, information system layer and the blockchain persistence layer. The business actors of our scenario are connected in the supply chain. Also, an authority actor is part of the scenario. The authority maintains an administrative purpose on the blockchain persistence layer. In Fig. 6 reported emissions are depicted with a document symbol.

Table 2. Scenario actors, annotated to the EU ETS taxonomy according to [17]

Actor	ETS Role	Description
Farmer	Enterprise (+Project)	A coffee farm or even a group of farms represented by a 'legal person', manages emissions reporting and emissions offsets from mitigations projects
Production	Enterprise (+Verifier)	A producer e.g., refines the coffee and reports operations emissions. The authority grants the producer verifier status. Hence, the producer is able to verify the emissions of the farms
Logistics	Enterprise (+Project)	Similar to the farm, the logistics actor takes the role of an enterprise which reports emissions. Emissions offsetting e.g., by fuel switching is possible
Retail	Enterprise (+Verifier)	Similar to the producer, the authority grants the retailer verifier status. Hence, the retailer reports its own emissions to the network and verifies emissions e.g., from its suppliers
Exchange/ Authority	Authority	An authorized exchange (e.g., the EEX [51]) or a governmental authority oversights the actors with verifier status. The authority also verifies emissions reporting and issues allowances to consortium

The subsequent section describes the design and implementation of the coffee supply chain demonstrator.

5   The Demonstrator

This section presents the demonstrator "Coffee Supply Chain". The technical basis for the implementation is Hyperledger Fabric 2.2 a framework for permissioned private blockchains. Hence, this chapter describes our design and implementation process of a private permissioned Blockchain-Demonstrator with Hyperledger Fabric. Note that all material of this demonstrator is published in a Github repository [52].

5.1   Architecture and Assembly

The setup (see Fig. 8) consists of five Raspberry Pi's, a network switch, two monitors, power supplies for each component, and a group of buttons as control elements. The

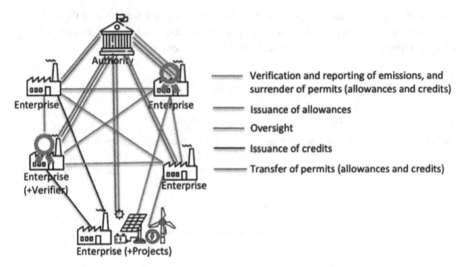

Fig. 7. Decentralized architecture and taxonomy for a blockchain-based EU ETS [17]

hardware is easily installed into a box (60 × 40 × 15 cm) and is therefore portable for events such as, fairs or conferences. The bill of materials (BOM) is attached in the projects' GitHub repository [52].

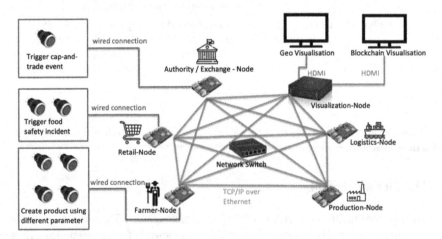

Fig. 8. Scheme of the demonstrator setup with the carbon accounting scenario actors

5.2 Interaction Concept and Visualization

The demonstrator aims to outline the technical feasibility of blockchain-based carbon accounting for a wider audience. Therefore, we introduce an interaction design to present various mechanisms inside the proposed carbon accounting scenario. The demonstrator deploys visual and haptic interfaces described in Table 3 and Fig. 9.

Table 3. Description for the numbered items in Fig. 9

No.	Description
1	Dashboard with geospatial and emissions data for each actor
2	2D-playground with the hardware nodes and background information's about the current scenario such as, activities of the actors or business relations
3	Monitor with a dynamic visualization of transactions from the blockchain
4	Changeable underground for depicting network topologies (e.g., implicating the peer-to-peer network)
5	Control panel with labeled buttons to trigger events
6	An instance of Hyperledger Explorer to easily access blockchain related data
7	A QR-Code leads to a website with data about the scenario. Further interactive functionalities such as, augmented reality is possible

A dashboard (1) based on the angular frontend framework is depicted in Fig. 9, it visualizes geospatial and emissions data, consuming input provided by a local MQTT broker. We use MQTT to ensure visualizations with a good performance, which fits for live demonstration purpose. Blockchain transactions on the Raspberry Pi cluster (4) are processed in a timeframe of approx. 30–60 s and a supply chain case may take up to six transactions. The blockchain transactions are depicted by Hyperledger Explorer (6) on a second monitor (3).

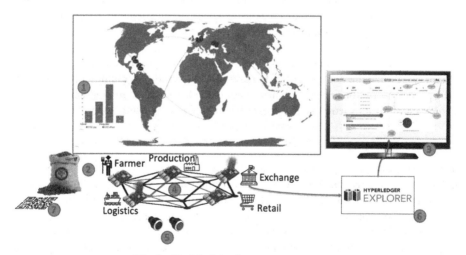

Fig. 9. Model of the demonstrator system

The control panel with buttons (5) allows starting events. The demonstrator enables to start the supply chain scenario for coffee from classical regions of origin, such as South America and Southeast Asia. A running supply chain case is depicted as coffee beans traveling across the different supply chain locations. An "event" button triggers a product incident and starts a tracing on the supply chain.

Fig. 10. The virtually decentralized demonstrator in action

The real demonstrator setup is depicted in Fig. 10 and shows the assembly of five computing nodes for five consortium actors (farmer, logistics, production, retail, and emissions exchange) of the coffee supply chain. Two displays are visualizing geospatial and emissions data (on the left screen) and transactional data on the blockchain (on the right screen). The energy supply, network infrastructure, and visualization node are in the grey box below the scenario playground. The buttons for interaction are on the lower part of the photo. Additional information about the scenario is grouped around the Hyperledger symbol on the scenario playground.

To allow a flexible modification of the existing scenario or the integration of a new system, we utilize the node-red platform and its flow-based programming paradigm to design a part of our business logic that is not embedded in a smart contract. Also, the integration of GPIO's from the Raspberry Pi is simplified by using node-red.

5.3 Implementation

Working with Hyperledger Fabric requires deep architectural knowledge, and setting up a customized network demands a lot of scripting work. Simplifying this process to demonstrate a bandwidth of scenarios, the tool Minifabric [53] is used in the demonstrator. Minifabric is an open-source project [54], which builds a layer of abstraction for Hyperledger Fabric and aims to reduce the effort for Hyperledger Fabric deployments. In contrast to a native setup of Hyperledger Fabric, Minifabric gathers all necessary parameters for setting up a network in one file. This configuration file is called spec.yaml [55], and following, we briefly describe its general structure.

The spec.yaml defines the network members as certificate authorities (CA), peers, and orderers. In the second part of the spec.yaml, additional parameters like custom endpoints are defined. Furthermore, a custom smart contract builder can be assigned to the network as an own Docker container. Minifabric starts the network based on this configuration file and separates the network members into different Docker containers.

The second use-case of Minifabric is the joining process of a single peer to an existing network. To start a single peer, it is only necessary to modify the spec.yaml, so only one peer is left. Table 4, in combination with Fig. 8, summarizes the basic steps for the joining process.

Table 4. Description of the steps in Fig. 11

No.	Description
1	To prepare the existing network for the joining process of a new peer, run the Minifabric command "channelquery". As a result, the channel configuration file will be created
2	Modify the spec.yaml on a different machine as described above and run the "netup" command. A single peer will be started
3	Copy the join request, which is created by the new peer, to the configuration file. After a majority of network peers have signed the new config file, run "channelupdate" to update the network. Join the single peer with the "nodeimport" command. Now the new peer is connected to the network and the order service but is not a member of the channel yet
4	Install the smart contract on the joined peer. After this, run the "approve" command on every peer, so the smart contract is approved. Now you can run the "commit" command to commit the smart contract. During this process the smart contract container on the new peer should be started. Run a simple "invoke" command to check if everything work as expected

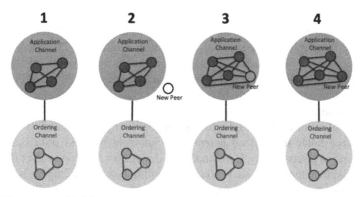

Fig. 11. The process of joining a new organization peer to an application channel, according to the notation introduced by Hoiss et al. [10]

The two usages of Minifabric described above illustrate how the framework simplifies the whole process of working with Hyperledger Fabric. This simplifies operations and deployment considerably.

5.4 Advanced Platform Support and Interfaces

Due to the requirement of a scenario with virtually decentralized nodes, we deploy the network peers across a cluster of devices. To meet the need for a cost-efficient design and to ease the reproduction of the demonstrator, we choose an ARM-based platform such as the Raspberry Pi. Furthermore, our decision is driven by the following considerations. First, most of today's consumer hardware is based on ARM processors, especially in IoT. Therefore, the demonstrator addresses a wide range of IoT-driven scenarios. Second, the bandwidth of open-source projects for ARM platforms combined with a network of edge nodes running a Hyperledger Fabric Blockchain shapes a promising ecosystem for developing distributed applications (DAPPS).

Because Hyperledger Fabric mainly provides precompiled Docker images for AMD64-devices, it is impossible to run Minifabric natively on ARM hardware. To solve this, we rebuilt the images first and resolved existing dependencies. After this, we integrate the new Hyperledger Fabric images and rebuild the CLI image of Minifabric. Our modifications make it possible to run Minifabric on any ARM64-based device such as Raspberry Pi. We contributed our implementation details [56] to the official Hyperledger Labs project [54] on GitHub. Currently, we run a multi-host network in our lab with five Raspberry Pi's and the MetaHL smart contract [57], which was created during the research project NutriSafe [4].

6 Conclusion and Future Work

This article presents considerations on the design of blockchain-based carbon accounting. The state-of-the-art analysis indicates a lack of guidance on designing blockchain and whether blockchain is a good choice as a technology for the use case of carbon accounting. To reflect on our design and potential next steps, we argue that there are three reasons why blockchain is a promising technology for carbon accounting:

1. **The architectural fit:** The bottom-up approach of Article 6.2 of the Paris agreement demands' integrity and transparency' and 'robust accounting' [1]. Decentralization, data integrity, and transparency are well-known implications of Distributed Ledger Technologies and Blockchain technology. Therefore, the architecture of blockchain-based implementation seems to be promising for collaborative, decentralized carbon accounting approaches.
2. **Potential of automation and digitalization:** Operating smart contracts on a trusted data source holds the general potential to automate business processes such as accounting of assets rapidly. Combined with devices for capturing sensor data, there is potential to automate manual carbon accounting tasks, including measuring real-world parameters. Tokens and smart contracts are "first-order citizens" of blockchain technology and provide the means to implement carbon accounting functionality.
3. **Security:** A key implication of blockchain technology is the security, availability, and integrity of data by the tamper-proof storing data using hash concatenation and avoiding colliding transactions by consensus protocols. The linkage of different carbon markets to reduce double accounting and other fraudulent actions is essential and will need efficient technical solutions. In this regard, cross-chain technologies

such as Polkadot [58] are promising approaches. The general question of scalability remains, depending on the utilized consensus protocols and types of blockchains.

The demonstrator of blockchain infrastructure for a coffee supply chain of artisan coffee illustrates the potential of blockchain beyond cryptocurrencies, money laundering, and the shadow economy. It is intended to explain operational cost efficiency and debunk the energy-consumption-of-blockchain-argument [59]. The demonstrator shows the integration of various functionalities: security, tracking, tracing, and carbon accounting. We argue that this will be needed for business cases of our approach. The demonstrator allows us to experiment with various technologies typical for IoT scenarios and Minifabric provides us functionalities to easily scale and adapt our infrastructure. Our design manages to refine our understanding of how to design lean systems and decentralized systems based on blockchain technology.

Future work in this regard focuses on the finalization of the demonstrator and its publication as an open-source kit [52], ready to be rebuilt by other institutions and to serve as a tool for validating blockchain-driven scenarios.

Acknowledgments. The Project LIONS is funded by dtec.bw–Digitalization and Technology Research Center of the Bundeswehr which we gratefully acknowledge. We want to thank our research partners from project LIONS for discussions, particularly Tim Hoiss, for his support with the NutriSafe code base, the coffee supply chain use case and his contributions to design and implementation.

References

1. UNFCCC: paris agreement, united nations framework on climate change. https://unfccc.int/files/meetings/paris_nov_2015/application/pdf/paris_agreement_english_.pdf. Accessed 04 Oct 2021
2. Schneider, L., et al.: Robust accounting of international transfers under article 6 of the paris agreement discussion paper (2017). https://www.dehst.de/SharedDocs/downloads/EN/project-mechanisms/discussion-papers/Differences_and_commonalities_paris_agreement2.pdf?__blob=publicationFile&v=4
3. World bank group: summary report: simulation on connecting climate market systems (English). https://documents.worldbank.org/en/publication/documents-reports/documentdetail/128121575306092470/summary%e2%80%90report%e2%80%90simulation%e2%80%90on%e2%80%90connecting%e2%80%90climate%e2%80%90market%e2%80%90systems. Accessed 17 Nov 2021
4. NutriSafe: NutriSafe - Sicherheit in der Lebensmittelproduktion und -logistik durch die Distributed-Ledger-Technologie. https://nutrisafe.de. Accessed 27 July 2020
5. Lamken, D., et al.: Design patterns and framework for blockchain integration in supply chains. In: IEEE International Conference on Blockchain and Cryptocurrency, ICBC 2021 (2021). https://doi.org/10.1109/ICBC51069.2021.9461062
6. Yaga, D., Mell, P., Roby, N., Scarfone, K.: Blockchain technology overview (2018). https://doi.org/10.6028/NIST.IR.8202
7. Bundesamt für Sicherheit in der Informationstechnik: Blockchain sicher gestalten. Bonn (2019)

8. Xu, X., et al.: A taxonomy of Blockchain-based systems for architecture design. In: 2017 IEEE International Conference on Software Architecture (ICSA), pp. 243–252 (2017). https://doi.org/10.1109/ICSA.2017.33

9. Marchesi, M., Marchesi, L., Tonelli, R.: An agile software engineering method to design blockchain applications. In: Proceedings of the 14th Central and Eastern European Software Engineering Conference Russia. Association for Computing Machinery, New York (2018). https://doi.org/10.1145/3290621.3290627

10. Hoiss, T., Seidenfad, K., Lechner, U.: Blockchain service operations - a structured approach to operate a blockchain solution. In: 2021 IEEE International Conference on Decentralized Applications and Infrastructures (DAPPS), pp. 11–19. IEEE (2021). https://doi.org/10.1109/DAPPS52256.2021.00007

11. Weking, J., Mandalenakis, M., Hein, A., Hermes, S., Böhm, M., Krcmar, H.: The impact of blockchain technology on business models – a taxonomy and archetypal patterns. Electron. Mark. **30**(2), 285–305 (2019). https://doi.org/10.1007/s12525-019-00386-3

12. Jensen, T., Hedman, J., Henningsson, S.: How tradelens delivers business value with blockchain technology. MIS Q. Exec. **18**(4), 221–243 (2019). https://doi.org/10.17705/2msqe.00018

13. Miehle, D., Henze, D., Seitz, A., Luckow, A., Bruegge, B.: PartChain: a decentralized traceability application for multi-tier supply chain networks in the automotive industry. In: 2019 IEEE International Conference on Decentralized Applications and Infrastructures (DAPPCON), pp. 140–145. IEEE, Newark (2019). https://doi.org/10.1109/DAPPCON.2019.00027

14. Catena-X automotive network e.V.i.G.: Catena-X automotive network. https://catena-x.net/en/. Accessed 15 Nov 2021

15. Dietrich, F., Ge, Y., Turgut, A., Louw, L., Palm, D.: Review and analysis of blockchain projects in supply chain management. Procedia Comput. Sci. **180**, 724–733 (2021). https://doi.org/10.1016/j.procs.2021.01.295

16. Schmiedel, C., Fraunhofer IPK: die hyperledger fabric-blockchain sorgt für datensicherheit in der additiven fertigung. https://doi.org/10.1007/978-3-030-75004-6_3. https://www.ipk.fraunhofer.de/de/publikationen/futur/futur-online-exklusiv/vertrauen40.html. Accessed 09 Jan 2021

17. Richardson, A., Xu, J.: Carbon trading with blockchain. In: Pardalos, P., Kotsireas, I., Guo, Y., Knottenbelt, W. (eds.) Mathematical Research for Blockchain Economy. SPBE, pp. 105–124. Springer, Cham (2020). https://doi.org/10.1007/978-3-030-53356-4_7

18. Eckert, J., López, D., Azevedo, C.L., Farooq, B.: A blockchain-based user-centric emission monitoring and trading system for multi-modal mobility. CoRR. abs/1908.0. (2019)

19. Baumann, T.: Blockchain and Emerging Digital Technologies for Enhancing Post-2020 Climate Markets (2018). https://doi.org/10.13140/RG.2.2.12242.71368

20. Al Kawasmi, E., Arnautovic, E., Svetinovic, D.: Bitcoin-based decentralized carbon emissions trading infrastructure model. Syst. Eng. **18**, 115–130 (2015). https://doi.org/10.1002/sys.21291

21. Braden, S.: Blockchain potentials and limitations for selected climate policy instruments (2019). https://www.giz.de/en/downloads/giz2019-en-blockchain-potentials-for-climate.pdf

22. Franke, L., Schletz, M., Salomo, S.: Designing a blockchain model for the paris agreement's carbon market mechanism. Sustainability **12**(3), 1068 (2020). https://doi.org/10.3390/su12031068

23. Schletz, M., Franke, L., Salomo, S.: Blockchain application for the paris agreement carbon market mechanism—a decision framework and architecture. Sustainability **12**(12), 5069 (2020). https://doi.org/10.3390/su12125069

24. Linux foundation: hyperledger fabric. https://www.hyperledger.org/use/fabric. Accessed 28 Dec 2021

25. Linux foundation: climate action and accounting SIG home. https://wiki.hyperledger.org/display/CASIG/Climate+Action+and+Accounting+SIG+Home. Accessed 18 Sep 2021
26. Energywatch Inc.: carbon accounting – everything you need to know. https://energywatch-inc.com/carbon-accounting/. Accessed 10 Feb 2022
27. Noelle Eckley Selin: carbon footprint. https://www.britannica.com/science/carbon-footprint
28. German Emissions Trading Authority (DEHSt): how does emissions trading work? https://www.dehst.de/EN/european-emissions-trading/understanding-emissions-trading/fundamentals/fundamentals_node.html. Accessed 29 Dec 2021
29. UNFCCC: data exchange standards for registry systems under the kyoto protocol. https://unfccc.int/files/kyoto_protocol/registry_systems/application/pdf/des_full_v1.1.10.pdf. Accessed 30 Jan 2022
30. European commission: EU ETS handbook. https://ec.europa.eu/clima/system/files/2017-03/ets_handbook_en.pdf. Accessed 30 Dec 2021
31. Abrell, J.: Database for the European Union Transaction Log. https://euets.info/static/download/Description_EUTL_database.pdf. Accessed 09 Jan 2021
32. Hearnehough, H., Kachi, A., Mooldijk, S., Warnecke, C., Schneider, L.: Future role for voluntary carbon markets in the Paris era (2020). https://www.umweltbundesamt.de/publikationen/future-role-for-voluntary-carbon-markets-in-the
33. Zhao, F., Chan, W.K.V.: When is blockchain worth it? a case study of carbon trading. Energies, 13 (2020). https://doi.org/10.3390/en13081980
34. Isermeyer, F., Heidecke, C., Osterburg, B.: Einbeziehung des Agrarsektors in die CO2-Bepreisung (2019). https://www.thuenen.de/media/publikationen/thuenen-workingpaper/ThuenenWorkingPaper_136.pdf
35. Lünenburger, B.: Klimaschutz und Emissionshandel in der Landwirtschaft (2013). http://www.uba.de/uba-info-medien/4397.html
36. Aakre, S., Hovi, J.: Emission trading: participation enforcement determines the need for compliance enforcement. Eur. Union Polit. 11, 427–445 (2010). https://doi.org/10.1177/1465116510369265
37. Lohmann, L.: Regulation as corruption in the carbon offset markets. In: Upsetting the Offset: The Political Economy of Carbon Markets. pp. 175–191. Mayfly Books, London (2009)
38. Frunza, M.C.: Fraud and carbon markets: the carbon connection (2013). https://doi.org/10.4324/9780203077399
39. Hermwille, L., Kreibich, N.: Identity crisis? voluntary carbon crediting and the paris agreement (2016)
40. Kreibich, N., Hermwille, L.: Caught in between: credibility and feasibility of the voluntary carbon market post-2020. Clim. Policy. 21, 1–19 (2021). https://doi.org/10.1080/14693062.2021.1948384
41. Schneider, L., Broekhoff, D., Cames, M., Healy, S., Füssler, J., La Hoz Theuer, S.: Market mechanisms in the paris agreement - differences and commonalities with kyoto mechanisms (2016). https://www.dehst.de/SharedDocs/downloads/DE/projektmechanismen/Differences_and_commonalities_paris_agreement_discussion_paper.html?nn=8596366
42. Müller, B., Michaelowa, A.: How to operationalize accounting under article 6 market mechanisms of the Paris agreement. Clim. Policy. 19, 812–819 (2019). https://doi.org/10.1080/14693062.2019.1599803
43. Hoiß, T., et al.: Design of blockchain-based information systems – design principles from the nutrisafe project. In: Clohessy, T., Walsh, E., Treiblmaier, H., and Stratopoulos, T. (eds.) "Blockchain beyond the Horizon" - Workshop at the European Conference on Information Systems (ECIS 2020) (2020)

44. Reimers, T., Leber, F., Lechner, U.: Integration of blockchain and internet of things in a car supply chain. In: 2019 IEEE International Conference on Decentralized Applications and Infrastructures (DAPPCON), pp. 146–151 (2019). https://doi.org/10.1109/DAPPCON.2019. 00028

45. Seidenfad, K., Hoiss, T., Lechner, U.: A blockchain to bridge business information systems and industrial automation environments in supply chains. In: Krieger, U.R., Eichler, G., Erfurth, C., Fahrnberger, G. (eds.) I4CS 2021. CCIS, vol. 1404, pp. 22–40. Springer, Cham (2021). https://doi.org/10.1007/978-3-030-75004-6_3

46. Füssler, J., Wunderlich, A., Kreibich, N., Obergassel, W.: Incentives for private sector participation in the article 6.4 mechanism. discussion paper (2019). https://www.dehst. de/SharedDocs/downloads/EN/project-mechanisms/discussion-papers/climate-conference-2019_1.pdf?__blob=publicationFile&v=4

47. Vogel, J., Hagen, S., Thomas, O.: Discovering Blockchain for Sustainable Product-Service Systems to enhance the Circular Economy (2019). https://aisel.aisnet.org/cgi/viewcontent. cgi?article=1295&context=wi2019

48. Gaiardelli, P., et al.: Product-service systems evolution in the era of Industry 4.0. Serv. Bus. 15(1), 177–207 (2021). https://doi.org/10.1007/s11628-021-00438-9

49. Kim, S.-K., Huh, J.-H.: Blockchain of carbon trading for UN sustainable development goals. Sustainability 12, 4021 (2020). https://doi.org/10.3390/su12104021

50. Greiner, S., Chagas, T., Krämer, N., Michaelowa, A., Brescia, D., Hoch, S.: Moving towards next generation carbon markets: observations from article 6 pilots. Freiburg (2019). https:// doi.org/10.5167/uzh-175360

51. European Energy Exchange AG: EU ETS Auctions. https://www.eex.com/en/markets/enviro nmental-markets/eu-ets-auctions. Accessed 07 Jan 2022

52. LIONS research project: carbon accounting demonstrator. https://github.com/LIONS-DLT/ lab-toolchain/tree/master/carbon-demonstrator. Accessed 07 Jan 2022

53. Li, T.: Minifabric: a hyperledger fabric quick start tool. https://www.hyperledger.org/blog/ 2020/04/29/minifabric-a-hyperledger-fabric-quick-start-tool-with-video-guides. Accessed 17 Nov 2021

54. Hyperledger Labs: Minifabric Repository. https://github.com/hyperledger-labs/minifabric. Accessed 17 Nov 2021

55. Li, T.: spec.yaml. https://github.com/hyperledger-labs/minifabric/blob/main/spec.yaml. Accessed 01 Jan 2021

56. Hyperledger Labs: create runningonarm.md #322. https://github.com/hyperledger-labs/min ifabric/pull/322. Accessed 28 Jan 2022

57. OTARIS interactive services GmbH: MetaHL Fabric. https://github.com/OTARIS/MF-Cha incode. Accessed 07 Jan 2022

58. Web 3.0 technologies stiftung: Polkadot. https://polkadot.network. Accessed 03 Jan 2022

59. Nakamoto, S.: Bitcoin: a Peer-to-Peer electronic cash system, 9 (2008). https://doi.org/10. 1007/s10838-008-9062-0

Applied Security and Privacy

A Platform for Offline Voice Assistants

Development of Assistant Applications Without Being Connected to Commercial Central Services

Jörg Roth[✉]

Faculty of Computer Science, Nuremberg Institute of Technology, Nuremberg, Germany
Joerg.Roth@th-nuernberg.de

Abstract. Smart speakers provide a convenient way to request information or control the smart home. Commercial devices require central services operated by large companies. As a result, many users are concerned about privacy and security. A solution could be to shift all involved software components to the end-user device. Even though we then cannot access the large variety of functions of commercial smart speakers, they often are sufficient for common applications such as weather forecast, public transportation timetables or to control smart home devices. Even though existing voice interaction platforms already provide basic functions such as wake word detection and speech recognition, a developer still has to put huge efforts to create smart speaker applications. In this paper we present the JabberBrick platform that significantly simplifies such developments.

Keywords: Smart speaker · Voice recognition · Privacy issues · App development

1 Introduction

Voice assistants are currently in fashion. So-called smart speakers such as Alexa or Google Assistant permanently listen to spoken input and provide answers to all-day questions. Third-party developers may create own assistant apps to extend the capabilities in arbitrary directions.

Commercial voice assistant platforms execute large portions of the entire answering process on central servers. For the input data flow, only wake word detection is executed on the home device. Digitally recorded speech is then transferred to servers that perform automatic speech-recognition (*ASR*), natural language understanding (*NLU*) and create the appropriate answer. This architecture has many advantages: the service provider can manage the complex computations centrally and is able to react on typical problems or extend the capabilities to also answer to new questions. If, e.g., many users get the wrong answer for a special question phrase, the service provider can centrally modify the respective response.

However, this approach has at least these caveats:

© The Author(s), under exclusive license to Springer Nature Switzerland AG 2022
F. Phillipson et al. (Eds.): I4CS 2022, CCIS 1585, pp. 49–62, 2022.
https://doi.org/10.1007/978-3-031-06668-9_6

- Users are not sure, the device only transmits recorded sounds *after* the wake word has been detected. As an extreme position, people are afraid, the device continuously transmits all sounds in the room.
- Users do not like sound recordings to be stored for long time periods. Large numbers of sound samples may enable the creation of good profiles of the user's voice and software may perfectly imitate a user's voice in the future.
- If the service provider is able to observe all voice interactions with a smart speaker, it may reveal personal habits or preferences.

Whereas some people are not even aware of such issues [7], many people consider privacy as the biggest problem when using such devices [4].

A solution could be to shift all central components to an offline smart speaker device. In this case, the device executes all steps related to speech recognition without the need to transfer personal speech data to a central instance. It should be noted that our notion of offline smart speakers does not mean to execute *all* tasks in an offline manner, but only components that are related to speech recognition. For, e.g., a weather forecast application, current weather data still may be taken from network services. However, the entire speech processing is executed on the smart speaker device.

If we apply this approach, we currently have to leave the market of commercial smart speaker platforms, as service providers want to have full control about the process. Fortunately, recent developments [2, 3] enable to set up offline assistants. However, they currently still leave many tasks to the application developer.

In this paper, we present the *JabberBrick* platform that simplifies the development of assistant apps for offline smart speakers.

2 The JabberBrick Platform

2.1 Architecture and Goals

In the JabberBrick platform not all components had been built from the scratch. *Voice interaction platforms* already provide basic building blocks for smart speakers, such as wake-word detection, automatic speech-recognition, natural language understanding and text-to-speech (TTS). Our platform is able to integrate these building blocks, provides additional components (see below) and offers an architecture as well as an API for developers. A typical interaction with the smart speaker is as follows:

- The wake-word detection permanently listens to a user-defined wake-word (e.g., '*Jarvis!*' or '*Hey Snips!*').
- Once the wake-word has been detected, a short sound is played to indicate, the user can now speak the question or command.
- ASR and NLU try to identify the most probable command. For this, a model was used. It was trained by sample sentences that contain variations of the same *intent*. So called *slots* mark variable parts of the commend, e.g., numbers, times, dates or members of fixed word lists (e.g., to indicate rooms or persons). As a result, a spoken command is mapped to one of multiple pre-defined intents with a list of slot values.

- JabberBrick now starts a session or continues a formerly started session. Sessions are structures to model dialogs with multiple commands/questions and answers.
- The tuple session/intent/slot-values is passed to a distribution system (here MQTT), that transmits the command to the respective app.
- The app that is responsible for this intent processes the request. It, e.g., looks for weather data or switches the light. It then formulates a spoken answer and creates visual output, if appropriate. In addition, it decides to terminate or continue a session.
- The TTS component now reads aloud the answer and the visual output is presented, if appropriate.

In this context, JabberBrick provides:

- an application framework that allows a developer to integrate arbitrary new apps into the runtime system;
- an utility library that simplifies the processing of slot values, e.g., to deal with timestamps, time intervals, or dates;
- the support of recurring tasks when mapping special slot values to raw data;
- the support to formulate answers, e.g., to create texts according to singular/plural ('*it rains 1 millimeter*', but '*it rains 2 millimeters*');
- components for rendering the visual output on the screen;
- utility components to get, parse und interpret data from external services (e.g., public transportation timetables, weather services).

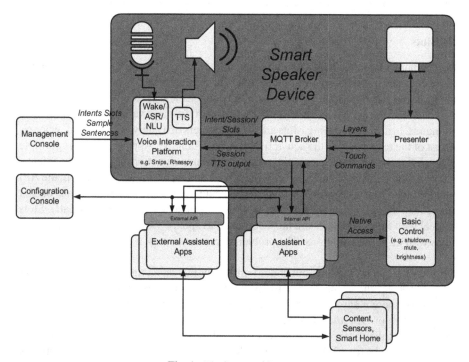

Fig. 1. Platform architecture

Figure 1 shows the overall architecture of the platform.

The most important component to configure the voice input flow is the *Management Console*. It usually is provided by the voice interaction platform and is accessed from a web browser. It is only required during development and can be deactivated after deployment. The *Configuration Console* is used to configure the assistants apps. If necessary, the apps offer a web interface where basic properties can be defined. E.g., for the public transportation timetable, the user can define the favorite departure station.

The *MQTT broker* [13] connects all further runtime components. MQTT is a light-weight technology that supports message transport and basic security features. It was built according to the publish-subscribe paradigm. There exist numerous implementations for MQTT (e.g., [5]) that easily can be exchanged.

A *Basic Control* component allows to access device-specific features. E.g., an app may shutdown the device, turn on and off the microphone, modify the loudspeaker's volume, modify the monitor's brightness or may play sounds. The *Presenter* is responsible for visual output and described in more detail in Subsect. 2.3.

The application developer accesses all features through an API. Apart from the basic control that only is accessible for internal apps, features are mapped to MQTT messages. As a result, assistant apps may also run on other devices connected to the network. To get further data, apps may use arbitrary ways to communicate during execution. A common way is to use REST Web service requests, as many publicly available information sources (e.g., weather forecast, public transportation timetables) provide a Web service API. For home automation, again MQTT is a common standard. Apps may use the broker installed on the device for this, to, e.g., access sensors, switches, motors or lamps.

2.2 Slots

Slots are parts of spoken texts that can be modified without changing the overall intent. E.g., if the user wants to set a reminder timer for 5 min, to set a timer is the *intent*, the time of 5 min the *slot* value. The distinction of intents and slots allows a developer to easily create different functions without to deal with the large variety of possible voice commands. In a wider meaning, slots are the parameters of a query or command, whereas the rest of the text specifies the actual function call (Table 1). Apps may handle multiple intents. E.g. set a timer and stop a timer are two different functions and thus two intents.

The developer should easily specify the format and type of slots. In addition, the API should provide functions to encapsulate and execute the respective computations on slot values. JabberBrick currently supports slots as described in Table 1 (lower half). Slots that deal with times and dates are most complex, as spoken words allow to express their values with different variations. The problem has many facets:

- Slot values can be missing, but should implicitly indicate a time. E.g., if the speaker wants to know the weather, he actually wants so know the weather *now*.
- Speakers know many symbolic expressions to indicate times and dates, e.g., '*noon*' for 12:00am or '*Tuesday*' for the date of next Tuesday;
- Speakers implicitly express granularity. E.g., if the speaker queries '*weather at noon*' the speaker asks for 12:00am. But '*weather in three days*' does not mean exactly '*in 72 h*' from now, but the whole day.

Table 1. Intent and slot examples

Intent	Examples sentences
Weather forecast	Tell me the weather (for) [Timer interval]
	What is the weather (for) [Timer interval]
	Give me a weather forecast (for) [Instant Time]
Set timer	Set the Timer to [Duration]
	Give me an alarm in [Duration]

Slot type	Examples
Cardinal number	1, 2, 3, 1000
String from a list	Living room, office, Jörg
Yes/No	Yes, no, correct, confirmed, wrong
Duration	10 min, 1 h, one and a half hour, 90 min
Instant time	Now, in five minutes, 8 o'clock, noon, next morning, in three days, on Monday
Time interval	This night, next week, next three hours, from Monday to Wednesday, next weekend, from 8 o'clock to 10 o'clock

- Speakers may ask both for points in time (even whole-day granularity) as well as for intervals. E.g., 'weather next week' asks for Monday to Sunday, but 'weather next Monday' only asks for one day.

The application developer does not want to deal with such questions. An application wants to receive a slot value with this information:

- indication of interval vs. point in time,
- timestamp or two timestamps (from, to) in computable formats,
- granularity (minute, hour, day, week).

Our platform computes this data automatically from spoken texts. Furthermore, it offers a number of functions, when such values have to be processed in applications, e.g., to iterate through intervals, or to find matches of entries in time intervals. The most complex functions deal with the opposite mapping of timestamps or dates to spoken texts. This often is required to confirm that the application properly recognized time expressions. If, e.g., the user asked for the weather forecast for the next day, the response may be 'Weather forecast for tomorrow: ...'. The TTS component is naïve in the way that it literally reads all texts that are passed. E.g., if the response contains '12:00', it could read 'twelve hours, zero minutes', or dependent on the TTS component, even does not recognize at all, this is time and may speak 'twelve colon zero'. To get sure to be read correctly, the app should (with help of our utility functions) directly pass 'twelve o clock' or much better 'noon' to the TTS component. The same problem occurs with durations (Table 2).

Table 2. Examples how durations could be expressed

Minutes	TTS text	Remark
1	One minute	Not '*one minutes*'
2	Two minutes	
60	One hour	Not '60 min'
61	Sixty-one minutes	Should not be expressed in hours
90	One and a half hours	Should not be expressed in minutes
120	Two hours	Not '*two hours and zero minutes*'

JabberBrick offers a lot of functions to perform the respective mapping according to the specific context. E.g., in German language, we have different articles for different Casus (e.g., '*noch eine Stunde*', '*in einer Stunde*'). This also has to be considered by the mapping functions to produce correct texts.

A certain drawback of this approach is the lack of slot types that accept *arbitrary* words. The current platform requires to know all possible words to express values beforehand. For numbers, times and dates there exists a large set of possible words, but it still is limited. There is no such slot type *any English word*. This is a serious problem, if an app, e.g., should present dictionary entries. Queries such as '*look up Wikipedia for [any noun]*' or '*remind me to tomorrow to [any phrase]*' are currently not within range with the current offline approach.

2.3 Visual Output

Visual output is important to illustrate spoken texts. Long messages such as the daily weather report, with, e.g., rain amounts for different hours are difficult to recognize, when the voice output is the only information channel.

For this, an assistant app *may* produce visual output. If the actual hardware does not have a monitor, the respective app also works, but visual output is ignored. Due to the usage in a smart speaker, there are several differences to existing GUI frameworks:

- We do not have a desktop system of overlapping windows. In contrast, we have a single window that displays the entire app content. The end-user is not able to explicitly swap between windows such as in desktop systems.
- The assistant apps should have reduced control about their visibility. They should pass priorities to the rendering system that finally decides what content will be displayed and how long.
- The API must provide rendering of contents across a network as an assistant app may not run on the smart speaker device.
- We need special dialog items not very common in traditional GUIs, e.g., some that show the current time.

 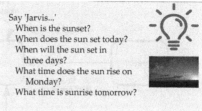

Fig. 2. Layers (time/calendar, left, advertisement for sunset information, right)

To support the developer to easily construct single-window-GUIs and to support the system to schedule contents according to rules, we developed the *Presenter* component. The most important entity is the *layer*. A layer can be roughly compared to a typical dialog frame of traditional GUIs, but is read-only and covers the entire screen. Each layer has a *structure* and *content*. Usually the structure is submitted once to the Presenter and then only content is updates. This in particular affects the usage across the network: once the structure is uploaded, subsequent calls only pass a list of content entries.

To control the display of layers, the app developer specifies priorities and timing configurations that allow the Presenter to schedule content:

- The priority is a number that orders the importance of this specific layer. It is considered, if multiple layer candidates are available for display.
- The app developer further defines duration and the maximum frequency (e.g., not more than once every 10 min). This is useful for advertisement layers (see below).

The end-user can define a profile, to affect these values. Moreover, he or she may define the layer that is displayed, if no other app offers content. This so-called *idle* layer is presented most of the time. Examples are the current time/calendar (Fig. 2, left) or the public transportation time table (see below).

A special type of layer is the *advertisement layer* (Fig. 2, right). An app may submit layers that are only displayed, when no other content was submitted for a certain time, i.e., recently no layer was brought to front and the current layer does not receive an update. In this case, the Presenter takes the advertisement layer that longest was not displayed. Advertisement layers may contain instructions for users to speak to apps, e.g., what are typical sentences. In addition, an app may show advertisement layers to provide information that may be interested to the user. The weather app, e.g., may frequently show the current weather conditions without explicitly asked.

To schedule the appearance of layers, the Presenter follows states (Fig. 3). These are affected by the scheduler, specific developer calls and timeouts. This supports the maximum flexibility and ensures that always the most important layer for a specific situation is displayed.

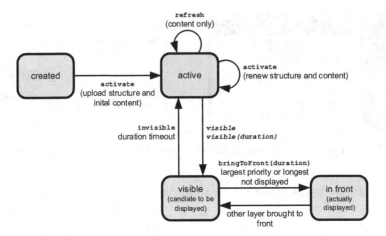

Fig. 3. State diagram to control visibility

Figure 4 shows the most important visual elements supported by the Presenter. In addition to typical GUI elements we have elements to express time. These are useful for the idle layer or timetables. The histogram is required to illustrate weather data, e.g., the amount of rain expected in the next days.

The largest degrees for configuration have text fields. In addition to typical settings (size, font, color, alignment etc.) there exist many methods that deal with texts that do not fit in the reserved space. The developer can configure the platform to cut longer texts, reduce the font size or display rolling texts. In the latter case, the presenter carries out the rolling in a predefined speed. Finally the developer can request the platform to perform an automatic hyphenation to display multiline texts.

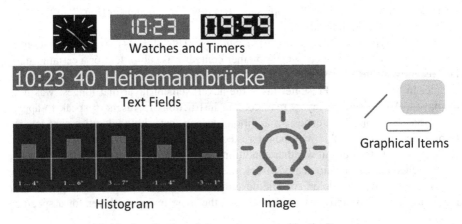

Fig. 4. A collection of elements supported by the Presenter

A final function of the Presenter is to provide a touch menu. Tabbing on the touch screen opens a full-screen dialog with a collection of buttons. The user can store frequently used requests here, e.g., to get the weather forecast of the next hours or mute or unmute the speaker. For repeated tasks it is often more convenient to use the touch function rather than speaking a command.

2.4 Security and Privacy Considerations

There exist several ways to attack smart speaker environments. This is because we have multiple components that are related to security and privacy, of which not all are fully under control by a developer or user. Generally, privacy in the context of smart speakers is considered as more complex than in other settings where users request computing services [6].

A first observation: as all computing components (apart from external apps) reside on the smart speaker device, basic network protection significantly simplifies the problem. E.g., in home environments, typically equipped with NAT function on the home router, potential attackers first must get access to the private network.

Assets that have to be protected are personal data of users, the home environment and the speaker device itself. In addition to attacks over the network, smart speakers can be attacked using voice commands. Any house guest can speak commands and thus is able to, e.g., influence the smart home environment [8]. This, however, is a problem of all smart speakers.

As an important goal, we achieved that no personal data (e.g., voice samples, commands) leave the home environment. We are sure that no service provider takes advantage of user's personal data. In addition, we do not have to consider attacks against commercial central services. The speaker's communication infrastructure is based on MQTT. We can rely on security mechanisms of MQTT brokers that are among others, client authentication with different mechanisms and payload encryption. With authentication we, e.g., avoid the integration of illegal content to be displayed by the Presenter. We further are able prohibit to subscribe to *all* MQTT topics, and, e.g., log all commands and responses.

Payload encryption is useful for external apps. Note that MQTT payload encryption only protects the communication with the platform. Further communication (e.g., to Web services, or to smart home components) cannot be protected by the platform, but require other mechanisms.

Two components are accessible from outside the device and are not protected by MQTT mechanisms: the Management Console and Configuration Console. Both components can be accessed by HTTP(S) and mainly provide a web page that can be controlled by a Web browser. The Management Console is part of the voice interaction platform, thus we cannot easily integrate protection mechanisms. In the current version, we simply shutdown both consoles after installation.

3   Sample Implementation and Evaluation

We developed smart speaker devices based on the JabberBrick platform in two versions: with and without display (Fig. 5). The basic computation component is a Raspberry

Fig. 5. Sample implementation (without display, left, with display right)

PI 3b. In addition, we need an array microphone, and for output, loudspeakers and an optional touch-screen monitor. The components for the non-monitor version cost about 90€ and an additional monitor approx. 40€.

As voice interaction platform we first used *Snips* [12], later *Rhasspy* [10]. The migration to Rhasspy was required, because of a change of the Snips business model: in 2020 its management console was closed for public use. As a result, existing implementations still run, but intent or slot configurations could not be changed anymore.

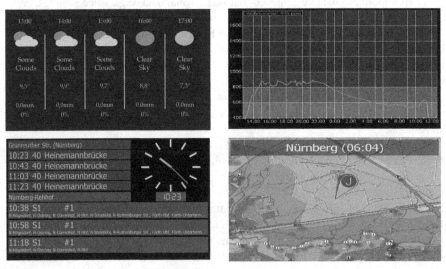

Fig. 6. Some assistant apps (weather forecast, upper left, CO_2 sensing, upper right, public transportation info, lower left, 'Where Is', lower right)

We developed a number of assistant apps that reflect a wide range of possible functions (Fig. 6) and cover frequently used applications with smart speakers [1]. The weather app provides information about general weather, sunrise/sunset, rain and temperature.

Typical queries are: '*how is weather tomorrow*' or '*amount of rain in the next 5 hours*'. The CO_2 app shows the current CO_2 indoor concentration. If it is higher than a pre-defined value, a warning is spoken. The public transportation timetable can answer questions about next departures of buses or trains. A timer app (not shown in the image) is a general reminder at a certain time and useful for, e.g., cooking.

As an example for an external app we developed 'Where Is?'. Family members that agreed to install the Zonezz apps [11] automatically transmit their current geographic position to a Zonezz server inside the home network. The server also runs a JabberBrick app, thus a user can ask for the respective position that will be displayed on a map.

To evaluate the usability, we collected the log file over 11 weeks of two devices used in a two-person household. In this time, the device was used for an average of 4.7 requests per day.

Table 3 shows the distribution of requests among the installed apps. Note that the CO_2 concentration app does not occur in the table as it was developed after this evaluation. Further note that on one device the public transportation timetable was configured as idle layer, thus users usually did not have to ask.

We further want to know, how successful the voice requests were and what failures occurred. Table 4 shows the statistics. An average of 1.4 voice transactions were required to finally fulfill a single request. That is considerably high. The largest contribution to multiple voice requests was a negative wake word detection: in more than one quarter of all requests, the wake word has not been detected and thus the user had to ask again. This is a serious problem. Common wake word detection components support a *sensitivity* parameter. However, setting it higher also means more false positive detections (see below).

In 16% the wake word was positively detected, but intent or slot were misunderstood. A very common problem was misinterpretation of numbers. E.g., in time duration slots, instead of '15 min' the slot '50 min' often was recognized. Also the confusions 55–15, 11–5, or 30–20 occurred, even they sound completely different in German. We also investigated the amount of unwanted actions (Table 5). It turns out, a wrong wake word detection (even with low sensitivity) often caused disturbance. Very often, only if people talk or if the radio was on, wake actions were triggered. Once ASR and NLU have been activated, they look for the most probable intent. Only if their probability was very low,

Table 3. Usage statistics of apps

App	Total count	Amount per day	Percentage
Timer	160	2.0	43.4%
Weather	140	1.8	37.9%
Where Is?	43	0.5	11.7%
Shutdown, Mute etc.	11	0.14	3.0%
Calendar, current Time	7	0.09	1.9%
Public Transportation Departure	4	0.05	1.1%
Saying of the Day	4	0.05	1.1%

Table 4. Statistics about intended usage

Property	Total count	Amount per day	Ratio to intended actions
Intended actions	369	4.7	100%
Total voice transactions	521	6.7	141.2%
Finally successful actions	358	4.6	97.0%
Wake word not detected	104	1.3	28.2%
Wake detected, but wrong interpreted intent or slot	59	0.76	16.0%
User gave up or used touch screen	11	0.14	3.0%

further steps are cancelled. In the lucky event, the device only produces two sounds (one for detected wake word, one for failure). This already disturbs users.

In the unfortunate case, an intent is generated and sent to an app. Here again two cases may occur: first, the app rejects the intent because of a mal-formed request. E.g., a user asks for a weather forecast too far in the future. This results in a spoken error message that also heavily disturbs users.

As a second case, a valid intent could incidentally be produced. This is a worst case, as the intent executes something unintentionally. If, e.g., the weather report of the next week is spoken, this takes a considerable amount of time, and caused the greatest disruption. It also happened once that a running TV causes the speaker device to shut down.

We also made a statistics about sound sources that caused unintended actions. However, these highly depend on the respective usage of such sources in a household. We thus do not show this statistics here. As a rule of thumb, nearly all sound sources that distribute spoken words (talking, video conferencing, TV, radio) are prone for false wake word or intent detection.

Table 5. Statistics about unintended usage

Property	Total count	Amount per day	Ratio to unintended actions
Total of unintended actions	412	5.3	100%
Wake word was detected but not an intent	310	4.0	75.2%
Wake word and intent detected, but app rejected because of mal-formed request	48	0.62	11.7%
Wake word and intent detected, app executed the request	55	0.71	13.3%

Table 6. Source lines of codes (SLOC) for selected components

App/Component	SLOC	Remark
Calendar, current Time	168	Watch and calendar sheet rendering are provided by the Presenter
Shutdown, Mute etc.	201	
Timer	461	
Public Transportation Departure	1862	1437 for Web service access (two sources for local transportation and trains)
Weather	3124	1393 for Web service access
Presenter	2983	
Support API	1236	Excluding standard libs and 3rd party libs, for e.g., JSON parsing

Finally we want to evaluate the implementation effort for creating apps. We used the source lines of code [9] (SLAC, i.e. code without comments and blank lines) for this (Table 6).

Not surprisingly the weather app was the most complex, as it covers a wide variety of usage scenarios. 45% were required to take the data from the Web service provider and to store it in a processable format. Also for the Public Transportation app, a large amount of code was spent to get the respective information from the service provider.

Further apps required only a very small amount of code, mainly for dialog control and generation of TTS output.

4 Conclusions

The JabberBrick platform significantly simplifies the development of offline smart speaker apps. We presented a successful implementation of device prototypes based on the Raspberry Pi. Different apps such as weather forecast, timer or public transportation timetable were implemented. Additional visual output is supported. As the voice processing is performed on the device and not shifted to a central service, we have significantly fewer privacy concerns. With the help of further security mechanisms (e.g., authentication of external apps), we are able to tailor the security demands to the respective scenario.

Currently, we perceive the following limitations with the approach. First, we cannot offer the large variety of apps compared to commercially managed smart speakers with their app stores. Second, some apps are not within range, because the approach requires all possibly spoken words to be known beforehand. This is, because for speech recognition, we have to train a model that is stored on a device with limited computational power. Apps such as 'Ask Wikipedia for …' or 'What are the opening hours of …' are impossible to develop as the slot values usually have unknown words.

Currently, the most important drawback is related to wake word detection that has a high rate of false positive and false negative. This results in many disturbances and multiple tries to place a command. Also the voice recognition sometimes failed to understand the given intent or slot. As a result, the JabberBrick prototype currently does not achieve the quality of commercial smart speakers.

References

1. Bentley, F., Luvogt, C., Silverman, M., Wirasinghe, R., White, B., Lottridge, D.: Understanding the long-term use of smart speaker assistants. Proc. ACM Interact. Mob. Wearable Ubiqui. Technol. **2**(3), 1–24 (2018)
2. Coucke, A., et al.: Snips voice platform: an embedded spoken language understanding system for private-by-design voice interfaces. arXiv:1805.10190v1
3. Dallmer-Zerbe, S., Haase, J.: Adapting smart home voice assistants to users' privacy needs using a Raspberry-Pi based and self-adapting system. In: 2021 IEEE 30th International Symposium on Industrial Electronics (ISIE), 20–23 June 2021 (2021)
4. Lau, J., Zimmerman, B., Schaub, F.: Alexa, are you listening?: privacy perceptions, concerns and privacy-seeking behaviors with smart speakers. Proc. ACM Hum.-Comput. Interact. **2**(CSCW), 1–31 (2018). https://doi.org/10.1145/3274371
5. Light, R.: Mosquitto: server and client implementation of the MQTT protocol. J. Open Source Softw. **2**(13), 265 (2017). https://doi.org/10.21105/joss.00265
6. Lutz, C., Newlands, G.: Privacy and smart speakers: a multi-dimensional approach. Inf. Soc. **37**(3), 147–162 (2021). https://doi.org/10.1080/01972243.2021.1897914
7. Malkin, N., Deatrick, J., Tong, A., Wijesekera, P., Egelman, S., Wagner, D.: Privacy attitudes of smart speaker users. Proc. Privacy Enhancing Technol. **2019**(4), 250–271 (2019)
8. Meng, N., Keküllüoğlu, D., Vaniea, K.: Owning and sharing: privacy perceptions of smart speaker users. Proc. ACM Hum.-Comput. Interact. **5**(CSCW1), 1–29 (2021). https://doi.org/10.1145/3449119
9. Nguyen, V., Deeds-Rubin, S., Tan, T., Boehm, B.: A SLOC Counting Standard, Center for Systems and Software Engineering, University of Southern California (2007)
10. Rhasspy Voice Assistant. https://rhasspy.readthedocs.io/
11. Roth, J.: Context-aware apps with the Zonezz platform. In: ACM MobiHeld 2011, Proceedings of the 3rd ACM SOSP Workshop on Networking, Systems, and Applications on Mobile Handhelds, Cascais, Portugal, 23 October 2011 (2011)
12. Snips, Sonos Announces Acquisition of Snips (2019). https://snips.ai/
13. Yassein, M.B., Shatnawi, M.Q., Aljwarneh, S., Al-Hatmi, R.: Internet of Things: survey and open issues of MQTT protocol. In: International Conference on Engineering & MIS (ICEMIS), 8–10 May 2017 (2017)

Consensus Algorithms in Cryptocurrency and V2X-IoT: Preliminary Study

Fatima Chahal[1], Dominique Gaiti[1], and Hacène Fouchal[2(✉)]

[1] LIST3N, University of Technology of Troyes, 12 rue Marie Curie - CS 42060,
10010 Troyes Cedex, France
{fatima.chahal,dominique.gaiti}@utt.fr
[2] CReSTIC, Université de Reims Champagne-Ardenne Moulin de la Housse,
BP 1039, 51687 Reims Cedex 2, France
Hacene.Fouchal@univ-reims.fr

Abstract. Globalization has had a profound impact on human life, resulting in the digitalization of many essential jobs. This development, of course, demonstrated the need to improve everything in the business world in order to satisfy the demands of the modern-day. In recent decades, there has been a clear need for a distributed database, and the Blockchain has proven to be an excellent solution. The Blockchain is a technology that allows for the storage of various types of transactions in connected blocks, with no way of deleting what has been entered on the ledgers, and therefore all business transactions are saved and secured. The consensus algorithm, which is responsible for confirming the blocks, sorting them, and ensuring everyone agree on them, is at the heart of the blockchain design. And, because blockchain is used in a variety of domains, the requirements change, and the consensus algorithm must accommodate these changes, which has resulted in the development of hundreds of algorithms. The goal of this study is to present the most useable algorithm in the cryptocurrency domain, as well as V2X communication, then, based on basic criteria, we compared these algorithms to evaluate which one is more efficient.

Keywords: Blockchain · Consensus algorithm · Cryptocurrency · Vehicle · V2X · IoT

1 Introduction

Since the Internet's global explosion, it has begun to integrate with all disciplines, including communication, education, medical, business, and currency. The demand for a distributed database system that overcomes long-distance limits and promotes work by providing a secure environment has increased, and researchers are working hard to create the finest answer for the world.

In 2008, the pseudonym *Satoshi Nakamoto* published a white paper where he (or they) described the **Blockchain**, and ever since a huge amount of studies direct to this domain, even though it is wasn't the first time to present, because, in 1991 *Stuart Haber* and *W. Scott Stornetta* publish a paper that presents a cryptographically based on blocks linked by chains [1]. With all of the advancements in the world, traditional databases could no longer meet business needs, where the need for multiple nodes in various locations has grown in recent decades, and the need to keep all nodes updated and containing the same digital information has become a priority, and blockchain was created to meet these needs. So the primary idea of blockchain is to give a distributed database, where we have **blocks** that hold a collection of data. A block, of course, has a limited storage space, so here is where the chain comes in, where each block is linked to the one before it, and this is how we maintain track [2]. And here comes the power of the blockchain, the decentralized system, where we can find blocks on different networks in different places but all connected at the same time, but we must be careful to avoid data redundancy in the blocks and not allow a malicious person to add a suspicious block, so if a bad actor tries to tamper with the network, the network must be strong enough to defend itself, and this is where the **consensus algorithm** comes in.

A consensus algorithm is a method for guaranteeing that all nodes on the network agree to add a new block to the blockchain. Since decentralization is the goal, the network will be designed as a peer-to-peer (p2p) network, with the majority of peers agreeing to add a new block. To do so, the main goal of the algorithm is to ensure that to add a trusted node to the blockchain, we must provide: reaching an agreement, collaboration, cooperation, equal rights for all nodes, and mandatory participation to all the nodes in the network [3]. Of course, the researcher creates a slew of algorithms, each with its unique set of features, to address certain demands in a specific domain. And it's apparent that cryptocurrency and vehicle-to-everything communication (V2X) are the two most popular industries where blockchains are employed, resulting in the invention and repair of new algorithms. This article presents the most well-known algorithms in both areas, such as PoW, PoS, PoB, and others in cryptocurrency, and PoL, PBFT, and others in V2X, and then compare them to evaluate these algorithms using certain key criteria that we have set, in order to conduct a primary study on them and determine their significance in each domain.

This paper is divided as follows. Section 2 will illustrate the most often used algorithms in the cryptocurrency domain, Sect. 3 will show another algorithm that is well-known in the V2X domain, and Sect. 4 will compare and discuss all of the algorithms to see based on different criteria the quality of these algorithms. Finally, there is a conclusion in the last part.

2   Consensus Algorithm in Cryptocurrency

The cryptocurrency was developed as a method for people to control their own money without having to rely on enterprises, banks, or governments, and their fees and controls are any type of currency that exists digitally or virtually and employs encryption to safeguard transactions. As a result of blockchain technology, all crypto assets are now stored on the blockchain and may be used without the involvement of a third party. As a result, the importance of consensus algorithms has increased in this sector, resulting in a range of algorithms. This section will describe how the most well-known algorithms function and where they are implemented.

2.1 Proof of Work (PoW)

The fundamental issue with the blockchain is that we need to prevent nodes from broadcasting blocks with the same information at the same time since this might harm the network and generate confusion by overloading it with redundant data. As a result, there is a requirement to agree on new blocks, demonstrating that the greater the number of nodes that offer their assent to a transaction, the more trustworthy and secure the network will be. Working without a disincentive may result in transactions being repeated, rendering the ledger ineffective. As a result, Proof Of Work (PoW) was invented to safeguard the ledgers, and it is now one of the most well-known algorithms in the cryptocurrency world. The concept is simple: the participant must properly solve a challenge (puzzle) in order to get the nodes' agreement to execute the activity. To learn more about how it works, we take a look at *Cynthia Dwork* and *Moni Naor*'s article, in which they propose a method for preventing DOS (denial-of-service) assaults and other network attacks (such as spam) by allowing the service requester to do specific activities. After a few years, *Markus Jakobsson* and *Ari Juels* presented POW in a paper based on Cynthia and Naor's work. In order to grasp the concept, Fig. 1 depicts the block structure in blockchains.

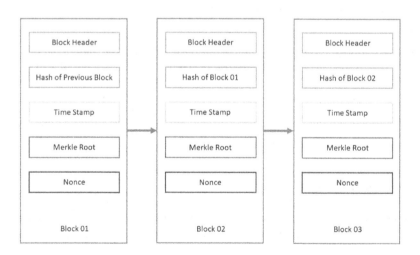

Fig. 1. Blocks structure

In general the concept is simple: we have Verifying nodes who are in charge of adding verifying transactions to the blockchain. In order to trust these nodes, they must prepare the block by including all necessary information (as shown in Fig. 1), such as version, size, timestamp, Merkle root, and, of course, the Prev-Hash (Hash of previous block) in order to keep in touch with the previous block, as well as the Nonce, which will contain the puzzle solution. The puzzle is a mathematical one that requires the node to guess a hidden value in order to solve it. After the block has been filled, it should be run via a hash function (SHA-256). If the output exceeds the difficulty level, the node must guess again; if not, it should broadcast the answer to the others in order to verify the block (check Prev-hash, Nonce,...), and if everything passes, they add the block to their chain and then resume the operation to guess a new puzzle [4,5].

Since its inception, PoW has been a very known algorithm in the cryptocurrency world and the most famous crypto in our decades are using it, like: **Bitcoin, Litecoin, Ethereum, Monero, Dogecoin, ...**

2.2   Proof of Stake (PoS)

Sunny King and *Scott Nadal* introduced another consensus mechanism called Proof of Stake (PoS) in 2012 [6], with the main purpose of reducing the energy usage that had skyrocketed due to the nodes that ran POW. The concept is simple: as the name implies, nodes stake a portion of their currency holdings to demonstrate their commitment, and one of them will choose the appropriate moment to solve the problem. As a result, the principle is identical to PoW, except that instead of running all of the nodes at the same time, one of them will be picked, preserving the blockchain's fairness. Of course, there are certain factors for selecting the next mining node, such as the size of the stake, as previously discussed, as well as the coin-age-based selection, and the randomization technique.

– **Coinage-based selection:** The concept is simple, the longer a validator candidate waits to be chosen, the more likely he is to be chosen as the new validator
– **Random Block selection:** That's correct, we claimed the next validator will be picked at random, but it's based on several criteria, such as 'lowest hash value' and 'largest stake', all of which can play a part in determining the next validator

As a result, in order to increase your chances to be the next miner, you should stake much more than the others.

PoS, like PoW, gained a lot of traction in the cryptocurrency world, and several cryptos began to incorporate it in their backends, the first of which was **Peercoin**, which is still in use today. **Nxt** also employs PoS for its research and development consensus [7].

2.3   Proof of Burn (PoB)

Many bitcoin researchers began to protest about PoW and PoS, both of which had numerous flaws that we were unable to conceal. And *Iain Stewart* is one of them who believes that "both proof of work and proof of stake utilize real resources that could be put to better use elsewhere". Because of that, he created the Proof of Burn in 2012 [8]. Proof of burn (POB) is a consensus technique that was developed as a solution to the PoW energy consumption problem or a PoW system that does not waste energy as it is well known. Its major activity is referred to as **"burn"**, and as the name implies, the participant should burn his money to demonstrate his devotion, and in exchange, his chances of being the next validator will increase. This approach works as follows: a miner candidate creates an unspendable address with his tag (a tag can be any kind of string). By doing so, the candidate will use less energy than if he were in PoW, while also ensuring that the network stays active and adaptable. The next step is to send the transaction's address to the validator, who will verify that everything is in order and that the coins delivered to the address have been burnt and are essentially unrecoverable. As a result, the miner receives a payment.

Many cryptos are requiring PoB in their backends, the most well-known of which being **Slimcoin**, which is based on Peercoin but employs PoB as its consensus mechanism and alternate mining/mining strategy. Another cryptocurrency that utilizes PoB is **TGCoin (Third Generation Coin)**, albeit it is no longer maintained or traded [9].

2.4 Proof of Importance (PoI)

In March 2015, a Singaporean group named **NEM (New Economy Movement)** saw the relevance of cryptocurrency wallets and decided to become involved, so they designed the Nano wallet and created a new cryptocurrency called **XEM**, as well as a new consensus technique called Proof of Importance (PoI) [10]. This method is based on a score of each member's importance in the blockchain network, which is why it's called Proof of Importance. Depending on the score, a person's chances of being chosen as the next miner may go up or down, or they may be kicked out of the network altogether, and several variables are used to compute the score. Here are some of the most important factors that might influence the score:

– **Net transfers:** This variable should represent the amount that has been spent in the last 30 days by the participant in order to do add a transactions
– **Currency vested:** This is the amount of cash the participant has invested in order to construct and add a new block to the network
– **Cluster nodes:** Some participants in this algorithm might aid others by giving them some of their score (vested) in order to assist them in becoming a miner; this action plays a role in calculating the important score, increasing it

Now it is clear that, the higher the score is the more trust the network has in this node's ability to verify transactions and mine. **Harvesting** is the name of the mining process in PoI, which differs from PoW and PoS in that it does not require a lot of machine power. Instead, each user creates a block that delegated harvesting to **Super Node (SN)**, which must meet the requirements. The prominence of the users who outsourced their harvesting to the SN determines the number of blocks an SN produces. Finally, the SN divides up the blockchain reward to users based on their relevance [11].

2.5   Proof of Capacity (PoC)

Proof of Capacity (PoC), which is also known as **Proof of Space (PoSpace)** and **Proof of Storage (PoStorage)**, is another consensus mechanism that is used to create new blocks. These names are reasonable because it is based on storage space. *Dziembowski et al.* stated the notion in their work in 2013, while *Ateniese et al.* did the same in 2014, with minor changes to the phrasing [12]. PoC is a blockchain consensus algorithm that governs the validity of new blocks. The technique is one of many available for determining which network member will be the next to produce a new block for the blockchain. The mechanism is considered to be particularly energy and resource-efficient, allowing it to be used by a broader audience. As a stake and deployment in the PoC consensus mechanism, participants give temporary storage space on their hard disk. Participants can use the network's memory to plot graphs from hashes. The more memory they set aside for plotting during the process, the more probable the next block will be generated. The node proves its commitment by validating the plotted hashes. If they are true, it can use them to demonstrate the capacity it has made accessible.

In the cryptocurrency industry, PoC has been further investigated, with **Signum** (formerly Burstcoin), **SpaceMint**, **Chia**, and **Spacemesh** being notable examples.

3   Consensus Algorithm in V2X Communication

The researchers establish a new element by combining the IoT (Internet of Things) and automotive domains, and what was a fantasy yesterday is now a reality, such as the driverless car. The autonomous vehicle is no longer a pipe dream; all of the major automobile manufacturers are working hard to enhance this type of vehicle and ensure that it has a high degree of security and usefulness. And in order to do so, the necessity for a decentralized database arose, and blockchain proved to be the ideal option. Of course, in order to operate optimally, the requirement for a consensus method emerged as well. So after looking at the most well-known consensus algorithm in the cryptocurrency sector in the previous section; this section will focus on the method that aids communications in the V2X industry and IoT.

3.1   Proof of Location (PoL)

The blockchain has recently gained a lot of attention for its efficiency and capacity to handle a range of decentralization-related concerns, if shortcomings are disregarded, its strongest advantage, consensus, may also be its greatest vulner-ability. As a result, it must be adjusted to the limitations of the system, and new algorithms must be created. The Proof of Location (PoL) consensus was created to allow solutions to be tailored to the constraints of V2X communications. A digital certificate that attests to someone's presence at a given geographic area at a certain time is known as Proof of Location. The decentralized nature of peer-to-peer networks offers more privacy by prohibiting central authorities from knowing both the physical location of users and the information they exchange. The Blockchain stores proofs of location. The following are some examples of PoL requirements: Every request or response must be signed with the sender's private key so that the receiver may use the public key to verify its integrity; the PoL check be done by using the System's Physical layer capabilities. A decentralized PoL method that allows automobiles to confirm their location to their neighbors even when they are outside of direct sensing range. The PoL technique used to investigate the detection performance and overhead for a platooning scenario. An investigation into the feasibility of constructing decentralized PoL without any infrastructure help using connection analysis and a realistic vehicle mobility data set [13,14].

3.2 Practical Byzantine Fault Tolerance (PBFT): Consensus Algorithm

In 1999, a new algorithm was published by *Miguel Castro* and *Barbara Liskov* under the name of Practical Byzantine Fault Tolerance (PBFT) algorithm [15].

The requirement for this technique has grown as the Byzantine Fault Tol-erance problem has grown, where there are numerous causes for failures and message manipulation when looking closer in the network, and this is unaccept-able in V2X communication where message correctness is critical. As a result, PBFT was dispatched to save the situation and offer a secure atmosphere.

All nodes in this network are connected, and the majority of nodes are trust-worthy and honest. To maintain the quality of algorithm function, one-third of all nodes in the system must be honest, else the system will be harmed. This approach can enable high-performance Byzantine state machine replication, han-dling thousands of requests per second with millisecond delay, and this is suited for IoT and communications between vehicles. Let us now go throw how it is work, PBFT is divided as shown in Fig. 2 into three phases: pre-prepare, prepare, and commit [16].

- **Pre-Prepare:** During this phase, the backup nodes get the request and develop a proposal (it is similar to filling some papers in order to submit a request in a formal way)
- **Prepare:** The nodes process the request in order to come to an agreement
- **Commit:** The nodes reply by expressing their agreement. They also perform the request twice to make sure they are getting the same results (and that to make sure that the consensus is high secure)

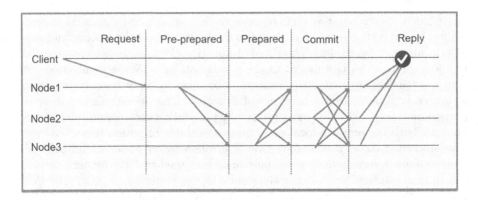

Fig. 2. PBFT

PBFT has proven highly effective for asking cars to retrieve consistent information and also enhancements thereof, such as Q/U, HQ, Zyzzyva, and Aardvark [17].

3.3   Proof of Authentication (PoAh)

Proof of Authentication (PoAh) is a lightweight block verification method that preserves the existing blockchain operating concept. PoAh's purpose is the same as any other algorithm: to authenticate the block to the blockchain in order to properly mine the block to the network. And this is the initial phase in the mining process, in which the miners trust the network's node, and should be aware that all nodes must contain and preserve identical records in order to monitor all transactions. The nodes that can be trusted are authenticated by T-Node (trusted node) in two steps: It should first authenticate the block with its source, then validate the block using T-Nodes. The ledger must be updated if everything works smoothly. If one of the miners makes a mistake, it will lose all of its trust value and revert to a regular node. For energy-efficient distributed secure communications and computing in the IoT, proof-of-authentication can replace the inverse hash calculation [18–20].

3.4   Proof of Eligibility (PoE)

Saunois, Geoffrey, et al. proposed the consensus algorithm PoE in 2020 with the goal of deciding on the same union of proposed values with a high probability that all the values proposed by the honest nodes belong to the decision [21]. There is a great need for an algorithm that is simple to implement and has a high degree of reaction in the IoT and V2X sectors, and this algorithm can serve both, which is considered a high request in the IoT domain in order to get proper communication between all the equipment [22]. Proof of Eligibility is a concept that helps to determine who is in charge of completing a task.

The purpose of this strategy is for all honest users of the asynchronous and permission less system to choose the same union of transactions in a finite and bounded number of rounds with a high probability. Aside from admitting a powerful adaptive adversary capable of corrupting entities in real-time, it must also accept a powerful adaptive enemy. Building a permission less blockchain will necessitate sequentially invoking a consensus instance with a sequence number. At the end of each round, the honest users must go through three primary phases: termination, agreement, and validity, and if all goes well, consensus is reached.

4   Comparison

In this section, Table 1 shows a comparison of all the algorithms discussed in the previous two parts; the criteria employed here are focused on the requirements of the world besides our own. Because this is merely primary research, the criteria we chose in this table are based on our interest in both areas and were picked subjectively. We believe that giving a score will be clearer than offering some scientific statistics that are based on genuine studies.

Table 1. Compare the algorithm The color scheme denotes how bad or good is the classification Green: represents to a good sign and it gives +1 to the score Orange: represents to a average sign and it gives 0 to the score Red: represents to a bad sign and it gives −1 to the score

		Criteria					
		Computing Time	Network Exchange	Convergence	Attack Resistance	Popularity	Score
Algorithms	PoW	Low	Medium	High	High	High	+2
	PoS	High	High	High	High	High	+5
	PoB	Medium	High	High	High	Medium	+3
	PoI	High	Medium	High	High	Medium	+3
	PoC	High	High	Medium	High	Medium	+3
	PoL	High	High	Medium	High	High	+4
	PBFT	High	High	High	High	High	+5
	PoAh	High	High	High	High	Low	+3
	PoE	High	High	High	High	Low	+3

First and foremost, the essence of any algorithm is its **computing time**, also known as running time, which represents the amount of time that this algorithm requires in order to produce its result, where we have a set of orders that must be processed by a computer, and in our comparison, we assume that all of the algorithms were run on the same computer, so their abilities are equal, The only variation that may alter the time is their own capabilities, which are depending on how they plan to reach a consensus. So, as previously stated, PoW is based on solving a puzzle, and as a result, its performance is based on the core of the computer, as well as the computing time counted the time of validator validation, and as a result, when compared to the others, PoW has the lowest capabilities, wherein compared to PoS it is so fast, where every 10 s this algorithm can produce a new block, whereas it takes 10 min in PoW, and although this may be fine in the cryptocurrency realm, but it is undesirable in the IoT, particularly in V2X, and as a result, PoL, PBFT, PoAh, and PoE are recognized for having quick time computing and are employed for that reason. And considering PoB, which is a combination of PoW and PoS, has middling capabilities when compared to other protocols. Since these algorithms are used in a decentralized system, their network speed is a high demand in both domains (even more so in V2X), so we looked at the capabilities of each algorithm in **Network exchange** column, and obviously, if one algorithm has a low capability, it will not be mentioned in this paper. The majority has a high level, but PoW and PoI have a medium level in comparison to the others because PoW has a lot of participants all around the world and that good it increase the security level but still affect its speed on the network, and PoI is only used now in NEM so it somewhat has its environment so it is should be more quality in this aspect. Of course, these algorithms will not work at the same level indefinitely; many factors, such as latency, node damage, and so on, can affect their efficiency. In the **Convergence** column, we tried to compare the algorithms and categorized them to see the fastest to recover like PoW, PoS, and all the others that have been rated High in the table where these algorithms have a large number of participant nodes that are scattered throughout a separate network, facilitating the recovery phase, which is different in the case of PoC and PoI, which are slower than the others. And since, the algorithms use the internet, there is a high risk of being attacked (DOS, Sybil attacks, etc.). As we mentioned in the **Attack Resistance** column, all of the algorithms in both domains have a high level of security, and it is not worth it to attack them and control the network because the costs would outweigh the benefits. We discussed the **Popularity** of the algorithms in the next column, where we can find the most famous one in each domain, taking into account that an algorithm in one major is also used in another, but when we categorized them in Sects. 2 and 3, we focused on the efficiency, where PBFT is also well-known in the cryptocurrency world, but V2X proved its efficiency and gave a remarkable result that deserves to be mentioned, just like PoC and PoL where each one is used in both domains. In cryptocurrency, however, PoW and PoS are the foundation for all other algorithms, and their popularity is enormous when compared to PoC, PoI, and PoB. PoAh and PoE, like PoL and PBFT, are highly useful in V2X applications, but because they are new, they are not as commonly utilized as the others. Finally, the **Score** column is just to present numerically the score of each algorithm to facilitate comparison, but we should be aware that a higher number does not necessarily mean a more efficient algorithm, because not all of the criteria are equal in importance. For example, let's compare PoL and PoΛH. By numbers, PoL has a score of +4, which is higher than PoAH's score of +3, but when we look at the criterion, the Low one for PoAH is popularity, which is less interesting than convergence for PoL, so if we're looking for a more efficient algorithm, we'll go with PoAh. As a result, we might conclude that the comparison is subjective, so the selection is relative to the application environment.

5   Conclusion

Digitalization has taken over the globe and begun to create new demands in areas where traditional databases are no longer capable of meeting them. The need for a decentralized database has become a constant, and Blockchain technology has emerged as the ideal solution. The consensus layer, which is considered the core of the blockchain, consists of numerous levels. The most essential is the consensus layer. In this layer, the researchers devised several algorithms, some of which were domain-specific and others which were more generic.

In this work, we focus on two areas: cryptography and V2X communication, and we describe the most well-known algorithms in both domains. Where we describe in the cryptocurrency domain how all of the Proof of Work, Proof of Stake, Proof of Burn, Proof of Importance, and Proof of Capacity are work besides give some examples of their applications, then in the V2X domain we presented all of the Proof of Location, Practical Byzantine Fault Tolerance, Proof of Authentication, and Proof of Eligibility. Then we did a global comparison of these algorithms based on some criteria like Computing time, network exchange, rate of convergence, attack resistance, and popularity, and we concluded that while there is no perfect algorithm, there is the best match algorithm in each domain. The next stage will be to add more criteria to acquire a better understanding of these algorithms, as well as execute simulations for these approaches to provide numerical results that will help categorization and enhance this initial study.

References

1. Nakamoto, S.: Bitcoin: a peer-to-peer electronic cash system. Decentralized Bus. Rev. 21260 (2008)
2. Nofer, M., Gomber, P., Hinz, O., Schiereck, D.: Blockchain. Bus. Inf. Syst. Eng. **59**, 183–187 (2017)
3. Bhardwaj, R., Datta, D.: Consensus algorithm. In: Decentralised Internet of Things, pp. 91–107 (2020)
4. Gervais, A., Karame, G.O., Wüst, K., Glykantzis, V., Ritzdorf, H., Capkun, S.: On the security and performance of proof of work blockchains. In: Proceedings of the 2016 ACM SIGSAC Conference on Computer and Communications Security, pp. 3–16 (2016)
5. Gupta, D., Saia, J., Young, M.: Proof of work without all the work. In: Proceedings of the 19th International Conference on Distributed Computing and Networking, pp. 1–10 (2018)
6. Larimer, D.: Transactions as proof-of-stake. Nov-2013 **909** (2013)
7. Stakefish, Proof of Stake: A Brief History, Medium, 14 September 2020. https://medium.com/stakefish/proof-of-stake-a-brief-history-4baa3effc917. Accessed 4 Mar 2022
8. Karantias, K., Kiayias, A., Zindros, D.: Proof-of-burn. In: International Conference on Financial Cryptography and Data Security, pp. 523–540 (2020)
9. Proof of burn, Bitcoin wiki, 15 January 2018. https://en.bitcoin.it/wiki/Proof_of_burn. Accessed 07 Mar 2022

10. Seth, S.: All About NEM (XEM), the Harvested Cryptocurrency, Investopedia, 26 January 2022. https://www.investopedia.com/tech/meet-nem-xem-harvested-cryptocurrency/. Accessed 07 Mar 2022

11. Komiya, K., Nakajima, T.: Increasing motivation for playing blockchain games using proof-of-achievement algorithm. In: Fang, X. (ed.) HCII 2019. LNCS, vol. 11595, pp. 125–140. Springer, Cham (2019). https://doi.org/10.1007/978-3-030-22602-2_11

12. Proof of space, Wikipedia, 13 February 2022. https://en.wikipedia.org/wiki/Proof_of_space. Accessed 07 Mar 2022

13. Boeira, F., Asplund, M., Barcellos, M.: Decentralized proof of location in vehicular ad hoc networks. Comput. Commun. **147**, 98–110 (2019)

14. Didouh, A., et al.: Novel centralized pseudonym changing scheme for location privacy in V2X communication. Energies **15**(3), 692 (2022)

15. Castro, M., Liskov, B.: Practical Byzantine fault tolerance. In: Third Symposium on Operating Systems Design and Implementation, New Orleans, USA (1999)

16. Oza, M.: Practical Byzantine Fault Tolerance (PBFT) the one Consensus to Master, Medium, 14 January 2019. https://medium.com/insatiableminds/practical-byzantine-fault-tolerance-pbft-the-one-consensus-to-master-400397f2b566. Accessed 08 Mar 2022

17. Rainer, B., Petscharnig, S.: Challenges and opportunities of named data networking in vehicle-to-everything communication: a review. Information **9**, 2078–2489 (2018)

18. Maitra, S., et al.: Proof-of-authentication consensus algorithm: blockchain-based IoT implementation. In: 2020 IEEE 6th World Forum on Internet of Things (WF-IoT). IEEE (2020)

19. Puthal, D., et al.: Proof-of-authentication for scalable blockchain in resource-constrained distributed systems. In: 2019 IEEE International Conference on Consumer Electronics (ICCE). IEEE (2019)

20. Puthal, D., Mohanty, S.P.: Proof of authentication: IoT-friendly blockchains. IEEE Potentials **38**(1), 26–29 (2018)

21. Saunois, G., et al.: Permissionless consensus based on proof-of-eligibility. In: 2020 IEEE 19th International Symposium on Network Computing and Applications (NCA). IEEE (2020)

22. Liu, H., et al.: A Byzantine-tolerant distributed consensus algorithm for connected vehicles using proof-of-eligibility. In: Proceedings of the 22nd International ACM Conference on Modeling, Analysis and Simulation of Wireless and Mobile Systems (2019)

Realtime Risk Monitoring of SSH Brute Force Attacks

Günter Fahrnberger$^{(\boxtimes)}$ (ID)

University of Hagen, Hagen, North Rhine-Westphalia, Germany
guenter.fahrnberger@studium.fernuni-hagen.de

Abstract. The Secure Shell (SSH) has served for years as the primary protocol to securely control networked remote devices. In particular, administrators of Linux and, to an increasing degree, also Windows operating systems with powerful rights capitalize on the speed and convenience of SSH. Consequentially, villains zero in on acquiring these mighty privileges, preferably by attempting a myriad of credentials until success or exhaustion. All known pertinent scientific resources limit themselves to compiling descriptive statistics or detecting such brute force attacks. The reviewed articles and papers neglect that each penetration attempt implies a differing hazard for an aim. This contribution bridges the gap by surveying relevant academical material and elaborating the blind spot of monitoring the risk of SSH brute force attacks in realtime. Beyond that, this document formally verifies the hazardously raised likeliness of SSH brute force attacks that knowingly or unwittingly use the same patterns as the passwords of their targets. Based on that, it presents a viable solution with a Condition Monitoring System (CMS) that monitors SSH brute force attacks and assesses their jeopardy in real time.

Keywords: Brute force attack · Monitoring · Nagios · Pattern detection · Risk monitoring · Secure Shell · SSH · Supervision · Surveillance

1 Introduction

Globalization has undoubtedly impacted many disciplines. For example, in computer science the global distribution of computing capacities (notably clouds) spatially separates computers from their users. Digital networks have pullulated to bridge this gap by exchanging traffic of distributed systems. Human clients mainly cause data transfers over such networks to access remote resources by dint of user interfaces. Despite the general popularity of Graphical User Interfaces (GUIs), especially system administrators consistently prefer text-based Terminal Users Interfaces (TUIs) for their daily labor. The usability of TUIs results from their swift and frugal representation of content.

In 1969, Teletype network (Telnet) emerged as one of the first protocols for textual remote access [26]. Its first usage happened five years later in 1974. The transmission of plaintext by Telnet entailed the quest for a secure successor.

F. Phillipson et al. (Eds.): I4CS 2022, CCIS 1585, pp. 75–95, 2022.
https://doi.org/10.1007/978-3-031-06668-9_8

Tatu Ylönen published SSH-1 as the first version of SSH in 1995 to provide encrypted command line accessibility to distant hosts. Security weaknesses spurred him to refine SSH-1 with the successor SSH-2 [21,38–41]. Apart from Telnet, SSH has also supplanted insecure data conveyance utilities, such as the File Transfer Protocol (FTP) [27], with its subsystem Secure File Transfer Protocol (SFTP). SSH has even ousted Berkeley r-commands like rlogin [14].

As particularly system administrators remotely operate machines, their accounts with administrative rights magically attract attackers. Even if an SSH Daemon (SSHD) inhibits direct logins to highly privileged roles, ordinary user accounts also lure hackers who hope for doable privilege escalation after successful intrusion.

The public availability of the utilized asymmetrical and symmetric cryptosystems for SSH has allowed the community to rigorously scrutinize their strength. Therefore, offenders commonly stand better chances by trying to guess credentials rather than to break well proven cryptosystems. During such so-called brute force attacks, they test different user name-password-combinations until they succeed by finding valid credentials or fail by exhausting all intended possibilities. In the narrower sense, brute force attacks try a multitude of combinatorial strings of a character set as passwords. In the broader sense, they iterate over all elements of a predefined set of frequently used passwords. Experts refer to the latter as dictionary attacks. Tools for brute force attacking range from simple, self-tinkered shell scripts over universal authentication crackers (exemplarily Hydra or Ncrack) to sophisticated penetration test frameworks (e.g. Metasploit [16]) and do not require very deep knowledge in Information Technology (IT). Hence, a respectable number of endangerers comes into consideration for such systematical attacks, starting with curious script kiddies and ranging to conscience-proof, professional or governmental actors. The holders of attacked SSH accounts decisively influence an attack's success with their configured secrets. Default and easily guessable passwords bestow a quick victory on intruders.

An SSHD by default records every unsuccessful login attempt in a log file. Aside from the aforementioned intrusion attempts, entitled users can also induce such log entries by mistyping their credentials. The scientific literature presently encompasses a plurality of approaches to distinguish systematic and accidental login failures. Some of them exclusively dedicate themselves to the SSH protocol. Regrettably, these publications lump all abortive logon tries as True Positives (TPs) together and, thus, merely evaluate their quantity rather than their quality. All citations ins Sect. 2 evidence the proposition in the previous sentence.

Since each password-guessing attempt differently threatens an SSH account, this paper proposes a host-based approach for the realtime risk monitoring of all miscarried authentications. It assumes that once the patterns of tried and real password resemble, subsequent brute force attacks with the same pattern impend with elevated probability and implicate a higher likelihood of guessing a correct password. For this purpose, simply observing failed authentication requests by origin, time, and user name does not suffice. Instead of that, this paper's remainder describes the manipulation of an SSHD to extract user names and password patterns of attempted logons, their contrasting juxtaposition with existing accounts, and proper alerting by a CMS. Shifting the defending line as close as possible to the attack origin(s) and pursuing a classical network-based detection at the firewall(s) or even the Internet Service Provider (ISP) fails because End-to-End (E2E) encryption of SSH hamstrings any password pattern comparison on intermediary equipment.

Subsequently to this introduction, Sect. 2 appraises merits and limits of available scholarly treatises about SSH brute force attacks. As they evenhandedly treat all TPs, Sect. 3 introduces the data collection for realtime threat-discriminating monitoring. Section 4 continues with a description of Key Performance Indicator (KPI) generation by contrasting the password patterns of missed logons with those of existent SSH accounts. Section 5 reports on the upshot of an experiment with different notification strategies, i.e. calculations of various pattern match maxima (thresholds) whose exceedances trigger notifications. Ultimately, Sect. 6 recapitulates this disquisition and recommends toeholds for promising future research.

2   Related Work

Citing all disquisitions about brute force attacks independently of any specific protocol would definitely go beyond the scope of this section. For that reason, it only focuses on those with unambiguous reference to SSH in chronological order. Many of them take advantage of machine and/or deep learning and strive for perfect classification of authentication tries into regular logins as True Negatives (TNs) or TPs and, thereby, for minimization of False Negatives (FNs) and False Positives (FPs). FNs mean cases of wrongly classified successful logins whereas FPs refer to falsely categorized logon errors. Misclassification primarily happens with network-related data since the analysis of ciphered SSH traffic turns out to be much more opaque than the inspection of plaintext host logs.

2008. Owens and Matthews choose the easy way with hosts-based data by tampering with their honeypots' SSH Daemons (SSHDs) in order to record the cleartext of all entered credentials and ignite statistical fireworks [24]. They prove that many brute force attacks rely on pre-compiled lists of user names and passwords. Furthermore, they identify weak credentials as potential Achilles heel that even renders brute force attacks against fully patched systems effective. The prospect of capturing administration privileges lets approximately a quarter of all logon attempts target the superuser role root in Owens and Matthews' investigation. A small number of slow motion and distributed attacks appears specifically designed to evade recognition by intrusion detection systems. Finally, the authors suggest safeguards for SSH as follows.

- Enforcement of strong passwords with password checking programs or libraries
- Avoidance of popular user names
- Disablement of logins via SSH for root accounts

- Binding of SSHDs to non-standard high ports
- Usage of Transmission Control Protocol (TCP) wrappers or iptables to block Internet Protocol (IP) addresses after repeated failed login attempts (anti-hammering)
- Usage of firewalls to restrict access to SSHD ports by source IP addresses
- Usage of port-knocking or single packet authorization to restrict access to SSHD ports
- Requirement of public-key authentication with passphrases in place of passwords

2009. Sperotto et al. train a flow-based Hidden Markov Model (HMM) with captured network traces to emulate the behavior of SSH brute force attacks [33]. They assume that a typical traced attack divides into scanning, brute force, and die-off phase. In the end, they conclude their publication with the intention to adapt their HMM for the detection of miscellaneous attack types against SSH and other protocols.

2010. Kenna showcases statistics about SSH brute force attacks in his survey [15]. It descries a subset of attacking hosts as botnet members (bots) that behave surprisingly predictable. For instance, their sleep periods between attacks or the interarrival time of unsuccessful logon attempts from all bots of a suspected botnet remain nearly constant. Botnets assure their survival by steadily trying to acquire new bots. For that purpose, they either disseminate baits (by way of example with phishing) and wait for infection or they actively conquer and assimilate their victims. For the latter, they usually scan the public IPv4 address space for prey. In accordance with Seifert, roughly 500 bot scanners suffice to reconnoiter the entire range 0.0.0.0/0 in one day [31]. Eventually, Kenna justifies the deployment of a DenyHosts service on all nodes of an organization to thwart obvious brute forcers [15]. Once blacklisted by one node, perpetual mutual synchronization of the ban list file */etc/hosts.deny* among all associated units baffles all further penetration efforts via SSH against any of them.

2011. McDougall et al. audit existent credentials with the support of network dictionaries to prevent SSH and FTP brute force attacks [22]. They consider default user names (such as admin, administrator, or device name) and common user name schemes (combinations of first and last names) as two worthwhile groups to be included in these dictionaries. In addition, they allude to the RockYou incident with the exposure of 32,603,388 user credentials that has occurred in 2009. Although the initial exploit has profited from a trivial Structured Query Language (SQL) injection vulnerability, it offers valuable clues to password favorites. A dictionary attack based on the top 5,000 passwords would result in a guessing rate of 0.9%.

2015. Najafabadi et al. apply four machine learning models on collected network traffic for the distinction between benign and malicious abortive SSH logons [23].

As login failures mostly happen because of malign intent, they additionally generate some innocuous events for training purposes of their classifiers, viz. simulate cases where legitimate users have forgotten their credentials. The protagonists figure out that the originally picked Netflow features have not satisfactorily discerned TPs and FPs. Thence, they introduce an aggregation of Netflows to extract appropriate features.

2016. Lee et al. compare the quality of firewall recordings of dropped packets and host logfiles for the detection of SSH brute force attacks in High Performance Computing (HPC) multi-user service environments [18,19]. They name their mechanisms Drop-Events Based Detection (D-EBD) respectively Fail-Logs Based Detection (F-LBD). Their contrasting juxtaposition attests F-LBD a lower attack recognition efficiency than D-EBD because the latter also finds SSH scanning attacks for example.

Almost the same author group evidences that a remarkable percentage of observed SSH brute force attacks follows human dynamic characteristics of a typical heavy-tailed distribution [20]. These invasive attempts imply persistence over an extremely long period from a relatively tiny amount of source IP addresses. Albeit predicting their future maleficent activities makes difficulties, mutually exchanging the IP addresses of such long-term culprits among partner organizations helps to impede malfeasant incidents.

Studiawan et al. take authentication logs from an Intrusion Detection System (IDS) called SSHCure, cluster the recorded SSH brute force attacks by means of weighted k-clique percolation, and visualize the output as graphs [34]. The writers admit that their proposed method sorely slows down at rising edge count. For this reason, they plan exploring other partitioning or community detection methods to optimize clustering.

2017. Yao et al. employ the both unsupervised machine learning algorithms Self-Organizing Map (SOM) and Association Rule Mining (ARM) for modeling, visualizing, and interpreting the behaviors of SSH brute force attacks [37]. They decide against supervised and semi-supervised machine learning due to the costliness of labeled traffic for their training in practice. The evaluation of Yao et al. corroborates the hypothesis that behavioral patterns of SSH brute force attacks significantly differ from those of normal SSH sessions.

2018. Faust analyzes SSH brute force attack vectors from a spatiotemporal standpoint in his master thesis [8]. He chiefly wants to figure out whether geography and/or daytime affect the risk of victimization by examining common and uncommon attack attributes and the variance of those values subject to location. Thereto, Faust deploys a Modern Honey Network (MHN) with one master and five slave servers. He disperses the latter to Bangalore in India, Frankfurt in Germany, London in England, San Francisco in the United States, and Singapore. During a three months long study phase, the city state in Southeast Asia turns out to be riskiest of the five cities for hosting since its local honeypot suffers from far the most invasion tries. The spot of a honeypot apparently makes the temporal attack structure predictable. Attacks more frequently take place on workdays and during workhours. On the basis of these findings, Faust derives tailored mitigation strategies against SSH brute force attacks for each of the five sites.

Sadasivam et al. describe a honeynet architecture to investigate all incurred SSH brute force attacks [30]. This includes stealthy ones that take long at low intensity to avoid discovery. Remarkably, most of the monitored vicious SSH traffic has less login tries per flow than in the past due to concealment objectives. For the sake of their examination, the scholars even permit successful attacks to a certain degree by deliberately setting insecure passwords. Two categories of persons ensue from these working logons. The first category comprises invaders who just break into the honeynet and, on this account, immediately terminate a connection upon accomplished logon. They probably share functioning credentials with fellows and/or other malefactors. The second class relates to more offensive interlopers who furthermore execute several shell commands, principally to infect their alleged quarry.

2019. Cao et al. come along with Continuous Auditing (CAUDIT) of SSH Servers to mitigate brute force attacks against them [2]. Their concept pursues the goal to automatically isolate hosts of a production network that shape up as vulnerable to such offenses. On that account, its developers route an enticing full class B network to an SSH-based honeypot that henceforth mimics a realistic server farm of 64k machines. CAUDIT replays all inbound logon tries of the honeypot on all productive nodes. Matching credentials lead to immediate blacklisting of the source IP address with the help of a Black Hole Router (BHR) and isolation of the target node because no authorized user would try accessing any of the luring class B IP addresses. In such a case of positive authentication, CAUDIT blacklists and isolates on the assumption of stolen credentials.

Shmagin criticizes the poor effectivity of pure host-based solutions against distributed SSH brute force attacks in large environments with hundreds or even thousands of interconnected computers since a brisk and perpetual exchange of currently banned sources among them emerges as sumptuous [32]. On account of this, he recommends to aggregate all relevant logs, analyze them with the aid of machine learning, and amalgamate all host-based firewalls to a uniformly acting firewall. He explains and contrasts the three techniques Naïve Bayes (NB), k-Nearest Neighbors (k-NN), and Decision Trees. Unlike similar academic work, he purposefully omits source IP addresses as feature. This permits generalizing all of them as feasible attack sources. At the end, Shmagin announces to test Support Vector Machines (SVMs) as another classifier and to process realtime in lieu of conserved data in future.

2020. Wu et al. reuse the previously presented honeypot of Cao et al. (that listens to a complete class B network [2]) with a longitudinal scrutiny of eleven billions SSH brute force attacks [36]. It discovers a 70% rate of persistent attackers who stand out by recurring IP addresses. The scientists also experience a rapidly escalating ratio of invasion attempts with purloined SSH keys. Moreover, they notice a globally coordinated botnet that spoofs millions of unique client versions. On those grounds, they advise blocking based upon anomalies instead of client signatures. Last but not least, they reveal a few human-supervised bots that only act during human working days and coruscate with more diverse devices and more ingenious attack strategies.

Hossain et al. deem all screened academic proposals about mitigation against FTP and SSH brute force attacks as inefficient [12]. Consequently, they focus on optimally ferreting the latter out by comparing the two Artificial Neural Networks (ANNs) named Long Short-Term Memory (LSTM) and Multilayer Perceptron (MLP) with the five machine learning classifiers Decision Table, J48, k-NN, NB, and Random Forest (RF). The four performance metrics Precision, Recall, F1-score, and Area Under the Curve (AUC) – Receiver Operating Characteristics (ROC) curve of the five models LSTM, Decision Table, J48, k-NN, and RF virtually equal each other by leaning toward score one while MLP and NB underperform with lower scores.

Hynek et al. address FP issues in prior related work by creating a model with greater accuracy and resilience against FPs [13]. For this, they utilize the five machine learning methods 5-NN, Adaptive Boosting Tree, C4.5 Decision Tree, NB, and RF on network-related data in their assessment. As in the recently cited treatise of Hossain et al. [12], NB again underperforms with the lowest accuracy. In contrast, Adaptive Boosting Tree outperforms with the highest.

2021. Wanjau et al. pursue the questions whether a deep learning model, on the one hand, can be elaborated that correctly detects SSH brute force attacks and, on the other hand, better performs than other machine learning models [35]. To this end, they extend the studies of Fernández and Xu [9] as well as of Kim et al. [17] by proposing an amalgamated IDS based on the supervised deep learning algorithm Convolutional Neural Network (CNN). Their CNN outplays Decision Tree, k-NN, Logistic Regression, NB, and Support Vector Machine (SVM) in terms of Accuracy, Precision, and Recall. Further, it trumps k-NN, Logistic Regression, and SVM concerning F1-score.

Park et al. complain about the absence of standardized procedures for analyzing logfiles of IT infrastructure to (re)act timely against security threats [25]. Aside from that, they advert to Internet routers that often lack in protection by separate devices. As solution, they proffer a model that extracts and fragments specific data from the router logs in order to detect indiscriminate SSH brute force attacks. Blacklisting the source IP addresses of all unsuccessful login tries may be an ineffective policy in the authors' opinion because one-time attacks and erroneously supplied credentials by ordinary users do not need countermeasures. On these grounds, the mechanism of Park et al. distinguishes between good-natured, suspicious, and iniquitous sources predicated on the strength, timing, and origin of recognized attacks. Even though the idea shows promise at first glance, it necessitates refinement with capabilities for realtime operation.

Raikar and Maralappanavar propose a Zeek IDS dedicated to Internet of Things (IoT) networks for security and resource conservation reasons [28]. Penetration tests supported by Hydra attest the proposal savings of 25% processing power, 40% electrical energy, and 10% memory utilization.

Hancock et al. make use of the same data set like Wanjau et al. [35] to track SSH and FTP brute force attacks down in big data [11]. They object to the absent transparency of the feature choosing by Wanjau et al. On account of that, comparing the outcome of both author groups fails. Hancock et al. pose two research questions. On the one hand, they ask themselves whether Decision Tree can classify brute force attacks by SSH, FTP, or a combination of both protocols with strong results and, to that end, obviate the necessity for more complex algorithms. On the other hand, they fathom the smallest number of machine learning features to achieve consistently paramount classification performance. The first question gets satisfyingly answered with metrics close to the theoretical optimum value of 1. The elaboration of the second question proves that Decision Tree models trained on data with only two independent variables perform similarly to those with more.

Summary. Since the itemized scholarly pieces in this section span over a couple of pages, Table 1 summarizes them and their goals. In spite of contributions with multiple aims, the rightmost column emphasizes each one's main objective. One reference dedicates itself to the auditing of login credentials, two references zoom in on modeling SSH brute force attacks, five predominantly compile statistics of them, and 13 concentrate on their detection. Unfortunately, none of them diagnoses the riskiness of sundry TPs for a victim, which lets the realtime risk monitoring in this contribution become indispensable.

Table 1. Summary of related work

Year	Authors	Title	Objective(s)
2008	Owens and Matthews	A Study of Passwords and Methods Used in Brute-Force SSH Attacks [24]	Host-based attack statistics
2009	Sperotto et al.	Hidden Markov Model Modeling of SSH Brute-Force Attacks [33]	Network-based attack modeling
2010	Kenna	Analysis of and Response to SSH Brute Force Attacks [15]	Host-based attack statistics
2011	McDougall et al.	Using an Enhanced Dictionary to Facilitate Auditing Techniques Related to Brute Force SSH and FTP Attacks [22]	Host-based auditing
2015	Najafabadi et al.	Detection of SSH Brute Force Attacks Using Aggregated Netflow Data [23]	Network-based attack detection
2016	Lee et al.	Brute-force Attacks Analysis against SSH in HPC Multi-user Service Environment [19]	Host- and network-based attack detection
2016	Lee et al.	A Denied-Events based Detection Method against SSH Brute-force Attack in Supercomputing Service Environment [18]	Host- and network-based attack detection
2016	Lee et al.	Heavy-Tailed Distribution of the SSH Brute-force Attack Duration in a Multi-user Environment [20]	Host- and network-based attack detection

(continued)

Table 1. (*continued*)

Year	Authors	Title	Objective(s)
2016	Studiawan et al.	Clustering of SSH Brute-Force Attack Logs Using k-Clique Percolation [34]	Host-based attack detection
2017	Yao et al.	Data Analytics for Modeling and Visualizing Attack Behaviors: A Case Study on SSH Brute Force Attacks [37]	Network-based attack modeling
2018	Faust	Distributed Analysis of SSH Brute Force and Dictionary Based Attacks [8]	Host-based attack statistics
2018	Sadasivam et al.	Honeynet Data Analysis and Distributed SSH Brute-Force Attacks [30]	Host- and network-based attack statistics
2019	Cao et al.	CAUDIT: Continuous Auditing of SSH Servers to Mitigate Brute-Force Attacks [2]	Host-based attack detection
2019	Shmagin	Utilizing Machine Learning Classifiers to Identify SSH Brute Force Attacks [32]	Network-based attack detection
2020	Wu et al.	Mining Threat Intelligence from Billion-scale SSH Brute-Force Attacks [36]	Host-based attack statistics
2020	Hossain et al.	SSH and FTP Brute-force Attacks Detection in Computer Networks: LSTM and Machine Learning Approaches [12]	Network-based attack detection
2020	Hynek et al.	Refined Detection of SSH Brute-Force Attackers Using Machine Learning [13]	Network-based attack detection
2021	Wanjau et al.	SSH-Brute Force Attack Detection Model based on Deep Learning [35]	Network-based attack detection
2021	Park et al.	Network Log-Based SSH Brute-Force Attack Detection Model [25]	Network-based attack detection
2021	Raikar and Maralappanavar	SSH Brute Force Attack Mitigation in Internet of Things (IoT) Network: An Edge Device Security Measure [28]	Network-based attack detection
2021	Hancock et al.	Detecting SSH and FTP Brute Force Attacks in Big Data [11]	Network-based attack detection

3   Data Collection

This section explicates the recording process of received credentials by a usual SSHD on Linux. A honeypot would more simply dump them, but experienced hackers could perceive and lose interest in it. The author of this scholarly piece also intends to exhibit the necessary system configuration's simplicity. Luckily, manipulations of such settings demand superuser rights. As a consequence, barely fraudulent system administrators and penetrators with escalated privileges can disclose unencrypted SSH user name-password-pairs in this vein.

/etc/ssh/sshd_config. Good practice demands the deactivation of root logins via SSH pursuant to one of Owens and Matthews' specified suggestions in Sect. 2 [24]. The configuration file of an SSHD */etc/ssh/sshd_config* implements this constraint by containing one or more of the following options.

- AllowUsers <Itemization of authorized user name(s) excludes root.>
- AllowGroups <Itemization of authorized group name(s) excludes root.>
- DenyUsers <Itemization of unauthorized user name(s) includes root.>

– DenyGroups <Itemization of unauthorized group name(s) includes root.>
– PermitRootLogin no

Insisting on at least one of these lines would deprive SSHD of logging all deciphered SSH passwords. Since the Pluggable Authentication Modules (PAM) offer an alternative possibility for the inhibition of root logons, the first four options can in lieu thereof be confidently commented out or deleted, the fifth switched on, and PAM enabled as hereinafter quoted.

– PermitRootLogin yes
– UsePAM yes

/etc/pam.d/sshd. The PAM configuration file of SSHD */etc/pam.d/sshd* requires two additional lines as subsequently shown.

– auth
  required pam_listfile.so file=/etc/ssh/deniedusers item=user onerr=succeed
  sense=deny
– auth sufficient pam_exec.so expose_authtok /root/sshd.bash

The first line refers to the file */etc/ssh/deniedusers* that contains all user names that shall be left without direct SSH accessibility. The second specifies the (executable) bash script */root/sshd.bash* that separately processes the password of every logon attempt.

/etc/ssh/deniedusers. Because */etc/ssh/sshd_config* must allow root logins in favor of comprehensive cleartext password recording, */etc/ssh/deniedusers* scotches them by comprising the superuser name as thereinafter jotted.

– root

/root/sshd.bash. The deployment of the executable file */root/sshd.bash* in the home directory of root protects it from inquisitive gazes and tampering by users without superuser power. The author of this paper has decided to hereafter showcase the original bash script including describing comments instead of pseudocode for convenient reproduction. In his humble opinion, too many scholarly publications comprise unreproducible pseudocode.

1. #!/usr/bin/bash
2. read PASSWORD # reads password from standard input
3. PATTERN=$(/usr/bin/echo -n ${PASSWORD} | /usr/bin/awk '{
   for (loop = 1; loop <= length($0); loop++) {if (substr($0,loop,1) ~ /[0-9]/)
   {printf "0"} else if (substr($0,loop,1) ~ /[A-Z]/) {printf "A"} else if (sub-
   str($0,loop,1) ~ /[a-z]/) {printf "a"} else {printf "_"}}
   }' | /usr/bin/sha512sum | /usr/bin/cut -d" " -f1) # extracts hashed pass-
   word pattern from entered password
4. SHADOW=$(/usr/bin/grep $̂{PAM_USER}: /etc/shadow | /usr/bin/cut
   -d: -f2) # reads password information for entered user name from
   /etc/shadow
5. TYPE=$(/usr/bin/echo ${SHADOW} | /usr/bin/cut -d$ -f2) # extracts
   hash type from password information
6. SALT=$(/usr/bin/echo ${SHADOW} | /usr/bin/cut -d$ -f3) # extracts
   salt from password information
7. if [-n "${PASSWORD}" -a -n "${SALT}" -a -n "${TYPE}" -a
   "$(/usr/bin/openssl passwd -${TYPE} -salt ${SALT} ${PASSWORD})"
   == "${SHADOW}"] # tests for correctly entered credentials
8. then # entered correct credentials
9. /usr/bin/grep -v "$̂{PAM_USER} " /root/shadow > /root/shadow- # copies
   all user names and password pattern hashes but current one from /root/shadow
   to /root/shadow-
10. /usr/bin/cp -f /root/shadow- /root/shadow # copies /root/shadow- to
    /root/shadow
11. > /root/shadow- # empties /root/shadow-
12. /usr/bin/echo "${PAM_USER} ${PATTERN}" >> /root/shadow # adds
    current user name and password pattern hash to /root/shadow
13. else # entered wrong credentials
14. /usr/bin/echo "$(/usr/bin/date '+%Y%m%d%H%M') ${PAM_USER}
    ${PATTERN} ${PAM_RHOST} ${PASSWORD}" >> /root/sshd.log #
    logs timestamp, user name, hashed password pattern, source IP address,
    and cleartext password to /root/sshd.log
15. fi # ends conditional construct
16. exit $? # exits with return code

In a nutshell, the bash script creates a pattern for an obtained password by
turning each contained digit to *0*, each uppercase character to *A*, each lowercase
letter to *a*, and each special character to _. Afterward, it hashes the password
pattern with the Secure Hash Algorithm 512 (SHA-512) [4]. Upon verifying the
gained credentials, the bash script appends the unaltered details (timestamp,
user name, source IP address, and plaintext password) as well as the hashed
password pattern of a failed login attempt to the log file */root/sshd.log*. It does
not document successful logons for privacy causes, but maintains correct user
names and their corresponding hashed password patterns in the file */root/shadow*
as comparative strings for the KPI generation in Sect. 4.

The motive for positioning the files *sshd.log*, *shadow*, and *shadow*-in the directory */root* resembles the location decision for *sshd.bash*. It goes without saying

that deceitful superusers can readily manipulate this bash script and trace genuine plaintext passwords. By the way, if Security-Enhanced Linux (SELinux) adamantly guards the operating system, the types of the four alluded files must transition from admin_home_t to

- passwd_exec_t for */root/sshd.bash*,
- tmp_t for */root/sshd.log*,
- and shadow_t for */root/shadow* and */root/shadow-*.

/etc/logrotate.d/sshd. The optional periodic rotation of */root/sshd.log* makes sense for two reasons. Firstly, the pattern comparison in Sect. 4 saves computing power because it merely has to trawl through a limited set of recent log entries. Secondly, this kind of compartmentalization allows targeted searches in individual time spans by means of unambiguously assigned data chunks. The following recommendation enforces daily rotation and a safekeeping period of 366 days that also covers leap years entirely.

```
1. /root/*.log
2. {
3. copytruncate
4. daily
5. missingok
6. notifempty
7. rotate 366
8. }
```

Once a restart of SSHD puts the described changes in this section into operation, */root/sshd.log* arises and grows with every miscarried login attempt.

4 KPI Generation

This section envisages the periodical generation of two Key Performance Indicators (KPIs) from an SSHD.

The first KPI termed as UNAME serves as baseline and counts all unsuccessful SSH logon tries for existing user names of the recent minute. Each of these counted attempts barely stands a minuscule chance of $P(\sigma = p) = \frac{1}{|\Sigma|^m}$ to succeed as per Theorem 1.

Theorem 1. *Let Σ denote a character set with cardinality $|\Sigma|$, let Σ^* denote the key space for SSH with $|\Sigma|^*$ possible elements, i.e. a countably infinite set of passwords, and let $H : \Sigma^* \rightarrow \Sigma^m | m \in \mathbb{N}$ denote a hash function.*

Then the image of H with $|\Sigma|^m$ different hash values determines the likelihood $P(\sigma = p) = \frac{1}{|\Sigma|^m}$ of guessing a password $p \in \Sigma^*$ with a randomly selected $\sigma \in \Sigma^*$.

Proof. Since nary a medium can store passwords of arbitrary length and for the sake of privacy, hash values with a predefined size persistently represent them.

This predetermination reduces a set of denumerably infinite passwords to $|\Sigma|^m$ different hash values. The guessability of a password $P(\sigma = p) = \frac{1}{|\Sigma|^m}$ ensues from the reciprocal of $|\Sigma|^m$.   □

The second KPI denominated as PWDPAT accumulates all abortive login attempts of the last minute whose user name-hashed password pattern-pairs comply with existent ones. Compared to UNAME, such a try's prospect of success improves to $P(\sigma = p) = \frac{1}{\prod_{i=1}^{l} |\Sigma_{j_i}|}$ according to Theorem 2. In the worst case of a purely numerical password $p \in \Sigma_{0-9}^l$, an adverse $\sigma \in \Sigma_{0-9}^l$ fulfills $PAT(\sigma) = PAT(p) = \underbrace{0 \cdots 0}_{l \text{ times}}$ and even succeeds with an auspicious likeliness of $P(\sigma = p) = \frac{1}{|\Sigma_{0-9}|^l} = \frac{1}{10^l}$. If an SSH brute force attack proceeds with $PAT(\sigma) = PAT(p)$, then PWDPAT does not wane. Quite the contrary, the odds of guessing p considerably rise.

Theorem 2. *Let $\Sigma_{\{0-9\}}$ denote the natural numbers from 0 to 9 with cardinality $|\Sigma_{\{0-9\}}| = 10$, let $\Sigma_{\{A-Z\}}$ denote the capital letters from A to Z with cardinality $|\Sigma_{\{A-Z\}}| = 26$, let $\Sigma_{\{a-z\}}$ denote the lowercase characters from a to z with cardinality $|\Sigma_{\{a-z\}}| = 26$, let $\Sigma_{\{SC\}}$ denote the set of employed printable special characters with cardinality $|\Sigma_{\{SC\}}|$, let $\Sigma = \Sigma_{\{0-9\}} \cup \Sigma_{\{A-Z\}} \cup \Sigma_{\{a-z\}} \cup \Sigma_{\{SC\}}$ denote the united character set with cardinality $|\Sigma| = |\Sigma_{\{0-9\}}| + \Sigma_{\{A-Z\}} + \Sigma_{\{a-z\}} + |\Sigma_{\{SC\}}| = 10 + 26 + 26 + |\Sigma_{\{SC\}}| = 62 + |\Sigma_{\{SC\}}|$, let $p = v_1 \cdots v_l \in \Sigma^l | l \in \mathbb{N}$ denote a password of length l, let*

$$PAT(v) = \Sigma \to \Sigma = \begin{cases} 0 & \text{if } v \in \Sigma_{\{0-9\}} \\ A & \text{if } v \in \Sigma_{\{A-Z\}} \\ a & \text{if } v \in \Sigma_{\{a-z\}} \\ - & \text{if } v \in \Sigma_{\{SC\}} \end{cases}$$

denote a pattern function for a sole character $v \in \Sigma$, let $PAT(p) = \Sigma^l \to \Sigma^l = PAT(v_1) \cdots PAT(v_l)$ denote a pattern function for p.

Then a witting or coincidental logon attempt with a haphazard password $\sigma \in \Sigma^l | PAT(\sigma) = PAT(p)$ stands a success probability of $P(\sigma = p) = \frac{1}{\prod_{i=1}^{l} |\Sigma_{j_i}|} | i \in \mathbb{N} \wedge 1 \le i \le l \wedge j_i \in \{\{0 - 9\}, \{A - Z\}, \{a - z\}, \{SC\}\} \wedge v_i \in \Sigma_{j_i}$.

Proof. The key space magnitude with passwords of length l, which share the right pattern $PAT(p)$, stems from the cardinalities of the character subsets that contain the constituent characters of p. The product of the l cardinalities $\prod_{i=1}^{l} |\Sigma_{j_i}|$ yields all combinatory password compositions. The inverse of this product $P(\sigma = p) = \frac{1}{\prod_{i=1}^{l} |\Sigma_{j_i}|}$ conforms to the probabilistic chain rule.   □

The preparation of both KPIs needs, on the one hand, the explicated modifications in Sect. 3 for an adequate ascertainment of all login tries and, on the other hand, the implementations in the remainder of this section.

/root/kpi.bash. Again on security grounds, the bash script *kpi.bash* resides in the path */root*. It accounts for the computation of both above-mentioned KPIs. Interested researchers may copy and directly run its program code below.

1. #!/usr/bin/bash
2. if ["$1" != "pattern"] # decides between both KPIs
3. then # decides for KPI UNAME
4. /usr/bin/cut -d" " -f1 /root/shadow | { while read USERNAME # reads all user names from */root/shadow*
5. do # iterates over all user names from */root/shadow*
6. REGEX="${REGEX}|$(/usr/bin/date -d "1 minute ago" "+%Y%m%d%H%M") ${USERNAME}" # assembles search pattern
7. done # ends loop construct
8. REGEX=$(/usr/bin/echo ${REGEX} | /usr/bin/sed 's/|//') # truncates leading pipe symbol from search pattern
9. /usr/bin/grep -Ec "${REGEX}" /root/sshd.log # evaluates KPI UNAME by applying search pattern on */root/sshd.log*
10. } # closes conditional construct for KPI UNAME
11. else # decides for KPI PWDPAT
12. { while read USERNAME PATTERN # reads all user names and hashed password patterns from */root/shadow*
13. do # iterates over all user names and hashed password patterns from */root/shadow*
14. REGEX="${REGEX}|$(/usr/bin/date -d "1 minute ago" "+%Y%m%d%H%M") ${USERNAME} ${PATTERN}" # assembles search pattern
15. done < /root/shadow # ends loop construct
16. REGEX=$(/usr/bin/echo ${REGEX} | /usr/bin/sed 's/|//') # truncates leading pipe symbol from search pattern
17. /usr/bin/grep -Ec "${REGEX}" /root/sshd.log # evaluates KPI PWDPAT by applying search pattern on */root/sshd.log*
18. } # closes conditional construct for KPI PWDPAT
19. fi # closes conditional construct

Executing */root/kpi.bash* without handing over any parameters calculates UNAME while specifying *pattern* as first parameter computes PWDPAT. In dependence on the chosen KPI, the bash script collects needful fields from */etc/shadow* and compiles a suitable search pattern. */usr/bin/grep* applies such a regular expression and straightly outputs the correspondent KPI.

/etc/snmp/snmpd.conf. Besides other bearers, the Short Network Management Protocol (SNMP) [3] suits the secure and lightweight transport of KPIs from an SNMP-capable node to a CMS. Their secrecy and integrity just persist with SNMPv3, the third version of SNMP [1]. Provided that an SNMP account with the user name nagios has been created, */etc/snmp/snmpd.conf* as the configuration file of an SNMP Daemon (SNMPD) must include the below-mentioned items.

- rouser nagios
- exec UNAME /root/kpi.bash
- exec PWDPAT /root/kpi.bash pattern

The foremost item grants harmless reading permissions to nagios while each of both others generates a retrievable Object Identifier (OID) per KPI. SNMPD sequentially allocates leaves of the subtree 1.3.6.1.4.1.2021.8.1.101, viz. 1.3.6.1.4.1.2021.8.1.101.1 to UNAME and 1.3.6.1.4.1.2021.8.1.101.2 to PWD-PAT. Since SELinux by default bars SNMPD from actions in root's home directory, its executable file */usr/sbin/snmpd* calls for relabeling from type snmpd_exec_t to bin_t.

Upon restarting SNMPD with the updated */etc/snmp/snmpd.conf*, a CMS may recall UNAME and PWDPAT.

5   Experiment

Most brute force attacks against publicly accessible SSHDs perpetually occur and normally target the superuser account root because it exists in every Linux operating system. UNAME incorporates all miscarried logon tries against present user accounts inclusive those against root. As a result, UNAME often takes nonzero values, which promptly renders it scientifically presentable.

By contrast, abiding by best practices and selecting a complex or long password certainly contributes to security, but dooms PWDPAT to zero level with rare outlying spikes. To make realtime risk monitoring with PWDPAT more demonstrative in this publication, root's genuine hashed password pattern in */root/shadow* gets replaced by a feigned one that provokes more matches. This step does not degrade system security because, on the one hand, */etc/shadow* remains unchanged and, on the other hand, the line with the entry root in */etc/ssh/deniedusers* forbids straight root access via SSH.

McDougall et al. mention an SQL injection attack in 2009 against the former United States (US) company RockYou in their report [22]. This event has revealed 14,344,392 distinct cleartext passwords of 32,603,388 customers in the famous text file *rockyou.txt*. Dictionary attacks essentially benefit from such a word list, but it also conduces to this disquisition. The both largest subsets of *rockyou.txt* comprehend 689,708 items (4.81%), whereof each consists of exactly eight lowercase letters, and 608,481 words (4.24%), which have the consistence of six lowercase characters in common. The members of the first subset correspond to the pattern $PAT(p) = aaaaaaaa$ and those of the second to $PAT(p) = aaaaaa$ in compliance with Theorem 2. Since 2021, a novel text file *rockyou2021.txt* with 8,459,060,239 leaked passwords has circulated on the Internet. Its two largest subsets coincide with those of *rockyou.txt*, though with swapped roles. 133,973,538 elements (1.58%) conform to the pattern $PAT(p) = aaaaaaaa$ and 308,915,776 (3.65%) to the pattern $PAT(p) = aaaaaa$.

Due to the higher relevance in the younger *rockyou2021.txt* and greater password guessability danger by shorter patterns, replacing the real hashed password pattern of root in */root/shadow* with the SHA-512 hash of $PAT(p) = aaaaaa$ for demonstration purposes seems to be an excellent choice.

With this adaption of */root/shadow* in operation, a CMS with an installed Nagios instance regularly polled UNAME and PWDPAT of a publicly exposed SSHD via SNMPv3 during January 2022. Since SNMPD recalculated both KPIs every minute with the execution of */root/kpi.bash*, the polling by the CMS likewise took place every 60 s.

A fixed (critical) threshold of zero for each KPI caused an exceedance for each nonzero measurement in agreement with the motto that every login failure matters. Beyond this, the CMS computed the three single dynamic (critical) thresholds and the three threshold pair selection techniques for each KPI that Fahrnberger compares in the youngest treatise of his trilogy about reliable Condition Monitoring (CM) of telecommunication services [7]. The subsequent listing temporally sorts and abstracts them.

- **Three sigma rule without prior outlier removal:** The (critical) threshold lies three standard deviations above the arithmetic mean of an unfiltered KPI history [5].
- **Three sigma rule with prior outlier removal:** The (critical) threshold lies three standard deviations above the arithmetic mean of an outlier-freed KPI history [5,6].
- **Maximal value:** The (critical) threshold adopts the maximum of an outlier-freed KPI history [5,6].
- **Tolerant approach:** The maximum of an unfiltered array with dynamical thresholds becomes the critical threshold and the median the warning threshold [5–7].
- **Balanced approach:** The maximum of an unfiltered array with dynamical thresholds becomes the critical threshold and the minimum the warning threshold. [5–7].
- **Strict approach:** The median of an unfiltered array with dynamical thresholds becomes the critical threshold and the minimum the warning threshold [5–7].

The CMS reckoned each of these listed dynamic thresholds by loading up to 52 historic values (depending on how many exist) that a KPI had assumed during the past 365 days. More precisely, the CMS incorporated those KPI values that it had fetched exactly a week ago, exactly two weeks ago, ..., exactly 51 weeks ago, and exactly 52 weeks ago. This period of a year best covers all conceivable attack seasons.

Irrespective of fixed or dynamic thresholds, not less than ten threshold exceedances at a stretch sufficed to precipitate a notification. This delaying retention time simulated the prevention of desensitizing the responsible staff by notifying short-term peaks. For instance, notifications in the wake of incorrectly entered credentials by eligible users or a modicum of veritable SSH brute force attacks could wreak such desensitization. Table 2 confirms the effectiveness of this deferring action for UNAME as well as Table 3 does for PWDPAT. Both tables display only value pairs whereof each pair's count of notifications clearly undercuts its counterpart with the number of threshold exceedances.

Table 2. Threshold exceedances/notifications of UNAME

	Warning	Critical
Fixed (critical) threshold of zero	N/A	22,924/1,032
Three sigma rule without prior outlier removal	N/A	3,695/22
Three sigma rule with prior outlier removal	N/A	4,323/24
Maximum value	N/A	3,359/17
Tolerant approach	845/21	1,010/16
Balanced approach	1,304/61	942/54
Strict approach	524/36	1,733/55

In virtue of Table 2, the amount of 22,924 attack phases against existing accounts during the 31 days long January with 44,640 min shows the omnipresence of SSH attacks. 1,032 of them even lasted longer than nine minutes whereby each generated a notification. The six dynamical threshold calculation approaches manifestly revised these figures downward because of their intelligent consideration of historical UNAME values. The tolerant technique still notified 16 conspicuously intensive attack series. Practically all of them aimed at the highly privileged root due to its allurement and no publicity of the other permitted user account names. UNAME demonstrates the terrifying numerousness of unsolicited (miscarried) access attempts via SSH rather than their quality.

Table 3. Threshold exceedances/notifications of PWDPAT

	Warning	Critical
Fixed (critical) threshold of zero	N/A	5,914/41
Three sigma rule without prior outlier removal	N/A	1,836/21
Three sigma rule with prior outlier removal	N/A	1,840/23
Maximum value	N/A	1,540/16
Tolerant approach	667/0	1,466/0
Balanced approach	685/1	1,510/1
Strict approach	16/0	4,354/22

The notifications of PWDPAT in Table 3 of course undershoot their counterparts of UNAME in Table 2 because the user names as well as password patterns of access tries have had to accord with right credentials to be tallied by PWDPAT. Astonishingly, in face of this tighter condition, 5,914 attack time intervals anyway bechanced. 41 of them spanned ten minutes or more. Exceptionally two threshold pair picking procedures ranked them as regularities. While the balanced technique yet triggered a warning and a critical notification, the tolerant remained completely silent. Figure 1 depicts PWDPAT during the observation period. A glimpse of it makes clear that the surge in the morning of January 19 precipitated both notifications of the balanced method. It lasted approximately five hours and did not exceed an average of 2.23 failed logon attempts per minute. A closer look in the log file unveiled a dictionary attack that had also comprised other password patterns than $PAT(p) = aaaaaa$. SSH brute force attacks in the narrower sense with a plethora of combinatorial strings of a character set did not befall during the considered month. Obviously, hackers seek rapid success with dictionary attacks and/or fear anti-hammering mechanisms that could spoil their party.

However, the experiment substantiates the effectuality of the introduced real-time risk monitoring approach against SSH brute force attacks because it even ferrets out dictionary attacks with their non-combinatorial property. Competitive mechanisms to the showcased and tested one in this treatise do not exist at its publication time to which comparisons could be drawn.

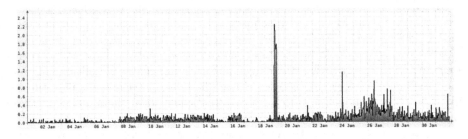

Fig. 1. Observation period of PWDPAT

6   Conclusion

This scholarly piece enriches the scientific world in several dimensions.

Firstly, it thoroughly surveys the present literature about SSH brute force attacks. Evidently, all appraised proposals hold them equally dangerous in lieu of differentiate their particular risks.

The second merit concerns Theorem 2 just as its proof and explanation. They altogether show the perilously increased incidence rate of SSH brute force attacks that wittingly or coincidentally use the same patterns as the passwords of their targets.

A suggestion for a CMS, which conducts realtime risk monitoring of SSH brute force attacks via SNMPv3, excels as the third achievement.

As fourth attainment, a successional experiment with an imitated feeble root password demonstrated its efficacy. The experimental SSHD never underwent genuine risk since even fitting SSH credentials induced denials because of respective SSHD settings. The trial proved the quantitative prevalence of SSH dictionary attacks over brute force attacks.

Notwithstanding all these accomplishments, they leave room for improvement. Along with the contrasting juxtaposition of patterns of tried and true passwords, the hamming distance between them might also deserve to be quantified as prospective risk metric [10,29].

To give a concluding example, contemporary CMSs generally poll KPIs from proprietary agents and/or plugins and merely resort to SNMP in case this software cannot be deployed. It bodes well to implement the suggested realtime risk monitoring of SSH brute force attacks with such agents and/or plugins.

Acknowledgments. Many thanks to Bettina Baumgartner from the University of Vienna for proofreading this paper!

References

1. Blumenthal, U., Wijnen, B.: User-based Security Model (USM) for version 3 of the Simple Network Management Protocol (SNMPv3). RFC 3414 (Internet Standard), December 2002. https://doi.org/10.17487/RFC3414
2. Cao, P.M., et al.: CAUDIT: continuous auditing of SSH servers to mitigate brute-force attacks. In: Proceedings of the 16th USENIX Conference on Networked Systems Design and Implementation, pp. 667–682. USENIX Association, February 2019. https://www.usenix.org/system/files/nsdi19-cao.pdf
3. Case, J.D., Fedor, M., Schoffstall, M.L., Davin, J.R.: A Simple Network Management Protocol (SNMP). RFC 1157 (Historic), May 1990. https://doi.org/10.17487/RFC1157
4. Eastlake, D., Hansen, T.: US Secure Hash Algorithms (SHA and SHA-based HMAC and HKDF). RFC 6234 (Informational), May 2011. https://doi.org/10.17487/RFC6234
5. Fahrnberger, G.: Reliable condition monitoring of telecommunication services with time-varying load characteristic. In: Negi, A., Bhatnagar, R., Parida, L. (eds.) ICDCIT 2018. LNCS, vol. 10722, pp. 173–188. Springer, Cham (2018). https://doi.org/10.1007/978-3-319-72344-0_14
6. Fahrnberger, G.: Outlier removal for the reliable condition monitoring of telecommunication services. In: 2019 20th International Conference on Parallel and Distributed Computing, Applications and Technologies (PDCAT), pp. 240–246, December 2019. https://doi.org/10.1109/PDCAT46702.2019.00052
7. Fahrnberger, G.: Threshold pair selection for the reliable condition monitoring of telecommunication services. In: Krieger, U.R., Eichler, G., Erfurth, C., Fahrnberger, G. (eds.) I4CS 2021. CCIS, vol. 1404, pp. 9–21. Springer, Cham (2021). https://doi.org/10.1007/978-3-030-75004-6_2
8. Faust, J.: Distributed Analysis of SSH Brute Force and Dictionary Based Attacks. Master's thesis, Saint Cloud State University, May 2018. https://repository.stcloudstate.edu/cgi/viewcontent.cgi?article=1083&context=msia_etds
9. Fernández, G.C., Xu, S.: A case study on using deep learning for network intrusion detection. In: 2019 IEEE Military Communications Conference (MILCOM), MILCOM 2019, pp. 1–6. IEEE, November 2019. https://doi.org/10.1109/MILCOM47813.2019.9020824
10. Hamming, R.W.: Error detecting and error correcting codes. Bell Syst. Tech. J. **29**(2), 147–160 (1950). https://doi.org/10.1002/j.1538-7305.1950.tb00463.x

11. Hancock, J., Khoshgoftaar, T.M., Leevy, J.L.: Detecting SSH and FTP brute force attacks in big data. In: 2021 20th IEEE International Conference on Machine Learning and Applications (ICMLA), pp. 760–765. IEEE, December 2021. https://doi.org/10.1109/ICMLA52953.2021.00126

12. Hossain, M.D., Ochiai, H., Doudou, F., Kadobayashi, Y.: SSH and FTP brute-force attacks detection in computer networks: LSTM and machine learning approaches. In: 2020 5th International Conference on Computer and Communication Systems (ICCCS), pp. 491–497. IEEE, May 2020. https://doi.org/10.1109/ICCCS49078.2020.9118459

13. Hynek, K., Beneš, T., Čejka, T., Kubátová, H.: Refined detection of SSH brute-force attackers using machine learning. In: Hölbl, M., Rannenberg, K., Welzer, T. (eds.) SEC 2020. IAICT, vol. 580, pp. 49–63. Springer, Cham (2020). https://doi.org/10.1007/978-3-030-58201-2_4

14. Kantor, B.: BSD Rlogin. RFC 1282 (Informational), December 1991. https://doi.org/10.17487/RFC1282

15. Kenna, C.: Analysis of and Response to SSH Brute Force Attacks, April 2010. https://citeseerx.ist.psu.edu/viewdoc/download?doi=10.1.1.587.8707&rep=rep1&type=pdf

16. Kennedy, D., O'Gorman, J., Kearns, D., Aharoni, M.: Metasploit: The Penetration Tester's Guide. No Starch Press, July 2011

17. Kim, J., Shin, Y., Choi, E.: An intrusion detection model based on a convolutional neural network. J. Multimed. Inf. Syst. **6**(4), 165–172 (2019). https://doi.org/10.33851/JMIS.2019.6.4.165

18. Lee, J.K., Kim, S.J., Hong, T.: A denied-events based detection method against SSH brute-force attack in supercomputing service environment. In: The 2016 International Conference on Security and Management (SAM 2016), pp. 351–352. CSREA Press, July 2016. https://worldcomp-proceedings.com/proc/p2016/SAM9761.pdf

19. Lee, J.K., Kim, S.J., Hong, T.: Brute-force attacks analysis against SSH in HPC multi-user service environment. Indian J. Sci. Technol. **9**(24) (2016). http://ischolar.info/index.php/indjst/article/view/134547

20. Lee, J.K., Kim, S.J., Park, C.Y., Hong, T., Chae, H.: Heavy-tailed distribution of the SSH brute-force attack duration in a multi-user environment. J. Korean Phys. Soc. **69**(2), 253–258 (2016). https://doi.org/10.3938/jkps.69.253

21. Lehtinen, S., Lonvick, C.: The Secure Shell (SSH) Protocol Assigned Numbers. RFC 4250 (Proposed Standard), January 2006. https://doi.org/10.17487/RFC4250

22. McDougall, R., Gillespie, N., Guster, D.: Using an enhanced dictionary to facilitate auditing techniques related to brute force SSH and FTP attacks. In: 44th Midwest Instruction and Computing Symposium (MICS). Midwest Instruction and Computing Symposium (MICS), April 2011. https://micsymposium.org/mics_2011_proceedings/mics2011_submission_10.pdf

23. Najafabadi, M.M., Khoshgoftaar, T.M., Calvert, C., Kemp, C.: Detection of SSH brute force attacks using aggregated netflow data. In: 2015 IEEE 14th International Conference on Machine Learning and Applications (ICMLA), pp. 283–288. IEEE, December 2015. https://doi.org/10.1109/ICMLA.2015.20

24. Owens, J., Matthews, J.: A Study of Passwords and Methods Used in Brute-Force SSH Attacks, February 2008. https://people.clarkson.edu/~jmatthew/publications/leet08.pdf

25. Park, J., Kim, J., Gupta, B.B., Park, N.: Network log-based SSH brute-force attack detection model. Comput. Mater. Continua **68**(1), 887–901 (2021). https://doi.org/10.32604/cmc.2021.015172

26. Postel, J., Reynolds, J.K.: Telnet Protocol Specification. RFC 854 (Internet Standard), May 1983. https://doi.org/10.17487/RFC0854

27. Postel, J., Reynolds, J.K.: File Transfer Protocol. RFC 959 (Internet Standard), October 1985. https://doi.org/10.17487/RFC0959

28. Raikar, M.M., Maralappanavar, M.: SSH brute force attack mitigation in Internet of Things (IoT) network: an edge device security measure. In: 2021 2nd International Conference on Secure Cyber Computing and Communications (ICSCCC), pp. 72–77, May 2021. https://doi.org/10.1109/ICSCCC51823.2021.9478131

29. Reed, I.S.: A class of multiple-error-correcting codes and the decoding scheme. Inf. Theory Trans. IRE Prof. Group **4**(4), 38–49 (1954). https://doi.org/10.1109/TIT.1954.1057465

30. Sadasivam, G.K., Hota, C., Anand, B.: Honeynet data analysis and distributed SSH brute-force attacks. In: Chakraverty, S., Goel, A., Misra, S. (eds.) Towards Extensible and Adaptable Methods in Computing, pp. 107–118. Springer, Singapore (2018). https://doi.org/10.1007/978-981-13-2348-5_9

31. Seifert, C.: Analyzing Malicious SSH Login Attempts, September 2006. https://www.symantec.com/connect/articles/analyzing-malicious-ssh-login-attempts

32. Shmagin, D.: Utilizing Machine Learning Classifiers to Identify SSH Brute Force Attacks, May 2019. https://scholarworks.wm.edu/honorstheses/1416

33. Sperotto, A., Sadre, R., de Boer, P.-T., Pras, A.: Hidden Markov model modeling of SSH brute-force attacks. In: Bartolini, C., Gaspary, L.P. (eds.) DSOM 2009. LNCS, vol. 5841, pp. 164–176. Springer, Heidelberg (2009). https://doi.org/10.1007/978-3-642-04989-7_13

34. Studiawan, H., Pratomo, B.A., Anggoro, R.: Clustering of SSH brute-force attack logs using k-Clique percolation. In: 2016 International Conference on Information Communication Technology and Systems (ICTS), pp. 39–42. IEEE, October 2016. https://doi.org/10.1109/ICTS.2016.7910269

35. Wanjau, S.K., Wambugu, G.M., Kamau, G.N.: SSH-brute force attack detection model based on deep learning. Int. J. Comput. Appl. Technol. Res. (IJCATR) **10**(1), 42–50 (2021). https://ijcat.com/archieve/volume10/issue1/ijcatr10011008.pdf

36. Wu, Y., Cao, P.M., Withers, A., Kalbarczyk, Z.T., Iyer, R.K.: Mining threat intelligence from billion-scale SSH brute-force attacks. In: Proceedings of Decentralized IoT Systems and Security (DISS) Workshop 2020, February 2020. https://www.ndss-symposium.org/wp-content/uploads/2020/04/diss2020-23007-paper.pdf

37. Yao, C., Luo, X., Zincir-Heywood, A.N.: Data analytics for modeling and visualizing attack behaviors: a case study on SSH brute force attacks. In: 2017 IEEE Symposium Series on Computational Intelligence (SSCI), pp. 1–8. IEEE, December 2017. https://doi.org/10.1109/SSCI.2017.8280913

38. Ylönen, T., Lonvick, C.: The Secure Shell (SSH) Authentication Protocol. RFC 4252 (Proposed Standard), January 2006. https://doi.org/10.17487/RFC4252

39. Ylönen, T., Lonvick, C.: The Secure Shell (SSH) Connection Protocol. RFC 4254 (Proposed Standard), January 2006. https://doi.org/10.17487/RFC4254

40. Ylönen, T., Lonvick, C.: The Secure Shell (SSH) Protocol Architecture. RFC 4251 (Proposed Standard), January 2006. https://doi.org/10.17487/RFC4251

41. Ylönen, T., Lonvick, C.: The Secure Shell (SSH) Transport Layer Protocol. RFC 4253 (Proposed Standard), January 2006. https://doi.org/10.17487/RFC4253

eHealth and Infrastructure

Emergency Evacuation Software Simulation Process for Physical Changes

Dan Wu$^{(\boxtimes)}$, Imran Shafiq Ahmad$^{(\boxtimes)}$, and Rachit Tomar

University of Windsor, Windsor, ON N9B3P4, Canada
{danwu,imran,tomarr}@uwindsor.ca

Abstract. Public safety mandate throughout of the world requires indoor public spaces such as schools, shopping malls, cinemas, sporting complex, etc. to have an emergency evacuation plan for a safe exit of the occupants. For many years, evacuation planning and development of safety measures are accomplished on the basis of simulation models available through various different software applications. While computer scientists are working on improving algorithms for software simulations, architect/builders are inventing various new structures/fixtures and measures to potentially save lives during an emergency. This paper proposes a process that creates a 3D base model of an evacuation systems to simulate physical changes such as retractable seats, movable walls etc., to evaluate their effectiveness before embarking on costly and time consuming physical changes in a given indoor environment. To develop our process, tools like Unity 3D and ©Autodesk Maya are used to simulate suggested changes. This proposed process is intended to provide planners/engineers and researchers a new perspective to work on simulating existing models with new recommendations or physical changes before committing on making such changes and evaluate their effectiveness when designing or renovating indoor public spaces.

Keywords: Emergency evacuation system · Public safety · Safety measures · Simulation model

1 Introduction

According to governmental regulations around the world, indoor public spaces are required to have complete safety measures and equipment in place for emergency procedures to ensure safety of people inside. In many cases, regulations require all indoor places to conduct practice drills to simulate emergency evacuation planning and be ready for such cases to ensure safety of all.

Throughout the world, fire appears to be the primary reason for most of the reported indoor tragedies resulting in loss of human life. In 1994, a fire in Karamay - China killed 325 people because of lack of emergency exits for crowd to get out [18]. A 2013 night club fire in Santa Maria - Brazil resulted in the death of 242 and injured at least 630 others because of exceeding the capacity limit,

F. Phillipson et al. (Eds.): I4CS 2022, CCIS 1585, pp. 99–115, 2022.
https://doi.org/10.1007/978-3-031-06668-9_9

thus, creating a shortage of emergency exits [6]. Another nightclub fire in West Warwick - United States in 2003 resulted in killing 100 people while injuring 230 others as most people headed for the front door among the four possible exits, resulting in blocking the exit and causing a stampede [16]. A cinema fire in Delhi - India in 1997 resulted in the death of 59 individuals trapped inside due to suffocation [4]. A garment factory fire in Karachi - Pakistan in 2012 resulted in the death of 289 people due to suffocation since all of the exits and windows were locked, preventing employees from getting out [14].

Such incidents could have possibly been prevented by using appropriate safety measures and guaranteeing safety protocols. Fire drills and other mock evacuations mostly fail to prepare general public for evacuations [22]. Thus, the development of safety policies based around such scenarios do not necessarily account for actual human behavior. However, different simulations can provide additional information for assessing safety policies to address various environmental and emotional effects [17]. Over the years, a large number of models for pedestrian simulation have been developed. Such simulations can be used in a variety of situations such as evacuation study in congested areas, etc. [7]. However, use of computer graphics to simulate such general phenomenon is still a difficult task since natural crowd is generally collective because of a "common purpose" or "mutual destination" that is shared by individuals [13].

For nearly two decades, companies are using simulation models/software for evacuation planning. Researchers are working on such simulation software to improve their efficiency by developing advanced algorithms with various conditional parameters. These simulation software allow to simulate various kind of emergency scenarios in order to observe, how such public spaces could be better designed, built, or renovated to avoid or at least minimize the loss of human life. Over the years, many different simulation software have been developed to provide designers with ways of forecasting evacuation times for different types of indoor environments such as multi-story buildings, concert venues, etc. A large number of simulation software for pedestrian simulation (a kind of crown simulation) have been developed in many disciplines such as robotics, computer graphics, evacuation dynamics, etc., that can be used to study various situations [17]. However, most of the available simulation software, work only in a predefined 3D environment, available within the software system. Additionally, none of these software provide a method/process to incorporate any possible physical changes or implement new safety measures in an indoor environment. Physical change in the context of this manuscript implies a change in the placement, orientation, organization, or configuration of physical components such as chairs, doors, walls, etc. in the indoor setting or environment that can potentially impact the occupants. For example, in a theater setting, walls are placed at fixed locations. However, if relocation of walls (movable walls) is allowed, this will become a physical change that will impact not only the dimension of the theater but will also allow free movement of individuals present in it without any collision with other individuals or objects such as chairs, etc.

This paper proposes a process for simulation software model of evacuation system. The proposed process is for an indoor environment to incorporate any possible physical change/measure before its actual implementation. This process is able to incorporate any possible physical changes or measures before they are actually constructed or implemented using Unity game development engine and Autodesk Maya. This process can be used for emergency planning and management as well as future research.

Rest of the paper is organized as follows. Section 2 provides a review of several different crowd simulation models and popular simulation software. In Sect. 3, we provide a discussion of our proposed methodology. Section 4 provides details of experiments and evaluation of the proposed process. Finally, Sect. 5 provides some concluding remarks.

2   Literature Review

As mentioned earlier, fire is a primary cause of most of the reported indoor emergencies/incidents throughout the world. These incidents primarily happened because either the safety measures were not strictly followed, or the indoor environment was not built with facilities to speed up the evacuation process.

For quite sometime, many different commercial entities and individuals are working on evacuation simulation models to study evacuation times and efficiencies during emergency situations. These simulation software provide a wide variety of features to simulate the required effects during emergencies and can be classified on the basis of techniques used as: (1) flow-based models [7], (2) agent-based models [1], and (3) activity-based models [21].

The primary focus of flow-based models is on the entire crowd as a single unit. This model is primarily used to estimate the movement or flow of a large and dense crowd in a given environment [24]. Agent-based models, on the other hand, are computer models to capture well defined behavior of active entities, known as agents, in a specific environment. The agents may represent individuals, homes, vehicles, machinery, products, or anything relevant to the system [1]. A well known example involving this technique is the computer game SIM-City in which individuals or other entities interact with each other and/or their environment. Activity-based models primarily focus on a set of daily patterns of activities of individuals. Such models predicts when, where, for how long, and with whom each activity may occur [21]. This paper is primarily based on proposing a software simulation process for evacuation using agent-based modeling technique.

Tables 1 and 2 provide a summary of 14 most popular and contemporary evacuation/simulation models on the basis of features and parameters they support. Note that the systems marked in Table 1 as "**" are commercial in nature and may provide consultancy services only.

In Table 1, the column "Agent Movement" shows how the indicated software moves occupants throughout a building. For most software, the user or modeling program generally assigns a particular unimpeded (low density) velocity to occupants. The more significant differences in the software occur when the occupants get closer, resulting in congestion within the environment. In this column, "Density" means the software assigns speed and flow depending on space density to people or populations. "Inter-person Dist." means a $360°$ "bubble", surrounds each individual, requiring a minimum distance from other occupants, barriers, and construction elements (walls, angles, handrails, etc.). "Empty grid cell" means an occupant does not migrate into a grid cell that is already occupied by another occupant. Therefore, the occupant waits for the next cell to become empty. If there are more than one occupant waiting for the sameg cell, then the model fixes the disputes that may occur by deciding which occupant moves first. "Conditional" means that movement throughout the building depends on environmental circumstances, structure, other evacuees, and/or fire condition with conditional models. Not much emphasis is put on congestion within the building for this designation alone. "Cellular automata (CA)" means that in this model, the occupants move through the simulated throw of a weighted die from cell/grid to another cell. In this model, all the agents behave as a single unit, e.g., if one agent dies, the others die due to the same effects such as a fire.

The column "Fire Data" in Table 1 describes whether the software allows the user to integrate the fire impacts into the simulation of evacuation. A software can integrate fire information in the following ways: (a) import fire data/results from another model, (b) enable the user to enter fire data throughout the evacuation at certain times, or (c) the model can have its fire model running simultaneously with the evacuation model. If the software cannot integrate fire data, it runs all simulations in non-fire mode. The aim to include such information is to evaluate occupants' safety, who move through degraded circumstances and to see how their conduct can be altered. "Y1" in this column means the model can import fire data, and "Y2" means the model has its own simultaneous fire element. The column "CAD" in Table 1 indicates whether the model allows import of CAD files.

Table 2 is included in a similar manner to describe additional capabilities of the above mentioned software. During an evacuation, as the evacuating occupants in the building move in one direction, emergency responders or other individuals may need to move in the opposite direction. This can lead to less width for the occupants of the building. The "Counter-flow" column in Table 2 indicates those software that can simulate counter-flow. In many cases, exit gates can be blocked. The "Exit block" column in this table indicates model's ability to allow user to simulate whether exits could be blocked or not. In a building fire, it is very likely that the environmental conditions caused by the fire will affect the occupants. Some software that incorporate fire capabilities allow to alter occupant's conduct depending on these fire circumstances. The "Fire conditions" column indicates if a model is capable of changing occupants' behavior owing to fire. The column "Toxicity" shows models that can mimic occupants' disability or death owing to toxic products from fire such as smoke or other chemical fumes. The column "Disdvantaged/Slow moving" indicates whether a model can simulate movement of physically challenged/slow moving occupants.

A survey of literature [7,17,22,24,25] indicates several agent-based crowd simulation models. Helbling et al. Social force model [7] uses the fundamental idea on how to apply agent-based approach to a crowd simulation. In this

Table 1. Comparison of existing models: For column "Purpose", "1" means any type of building, "2" means only specializes in residential buildings, "3" means specialize in public transport stations, and "4" means simulate buildings with only 1-route/exit.

Software model	Visualization	Purpose	Agent movement	Fire data	CAD
WAYOUT [19]	2D	4	Density	N	N
PEDROUTE** [3]	2D,3D	3	Density	N	Y
Simulex [8]	2D	1	Inter-person Dist	N	Y
FDS+Evac [12]	2D,3D	1	Inter-person Dist	Y2	N
Simwalk [20]	2D,3D	3	User Choice	N	N
buildingEXODUS [15]	2D,3D	1	Empty grid cell	Y1	N
Legion [2]	2D,3D	4	Inter-person Dist	Y1	Y
MassMotion [5]	2D,3D	1	Conditional	N	Y
PathFinder**	2D	1	Density	N	Y
ALLSAFE**	2D	4	User Choice	Y1	N
CRISP**	2D,3D	1	Empty grid cell	Y2	Y
EGRESS 2002**	2D	1	Cellular Automata	Y2	N
SGEM**	2D	4	Density	N	Y
EXIT89**	No	3	Density	Y1	N

Table 2. Special features comparison

Software model	Counter flow	Exit block	Toxicity	Disadvantaged/ Slow moving	Fire conditions
WAYOUT [19]	N	N	N	N	N
PEDROUTE** [3]	N	N	N	Y	N
Simulex [8]	Y	Y	N	N	N
FDS+Evac [12]	Y	Y	Y	N	N
Simwalk [20]	Y	N	N	Y	Y
buildingEXODUS [15]	Y	Y	Y	N	Y
Legion [2]	N	Y	Y	Y	Y
MassMotion [5]	Y	Y	N	Y	Y
PathFinder**	N	N	N	N	N
ALLSAFE**	N	N	N	N	Y
CRISP**	Y	Y	N	Y	N
EGRESS 2002**	Y	Y	Y	Y	Y
SGEM**	Y	Y	N	Y	N
EXIT89**	Y	Y	Y	Y	Y

model, authors apply the repulsion and tangential forces on each agent. As a result, the steering agent can avoid obstacles and other moving agents. However, every agent shares the same set of attributes without providing individual identity to agents. All agents navigate with the same moving speed which is not the same as the actual human crowd in which individuals move with different speed. Zavin et al. [25] proposed an intelligent automated fire exit guidance system using A* search algorithm. The guidance system not only guides the affected people through the safest optimal path, it also calculates the least crowded and the shortest path exits while considering the distance, endangered node, crowd distribution mechanism, etc. However, the proposed system is based only on a simulation of a sample floor plan of a building and ignores some real-world factors such as guided path for nearest fire exits, etc. Wong et al. [24] proposed a system to assist in rapid evacuation by calculating the optimum route for each local area with the idea to reduce congestion while maximizing the number of evacuees arriving at exits in each time span. Their system considers crowd distribution, exit locations, and corridor widths when determining optimal routes. It also simulates crowd movements during route optimization. As a basis, they expect the crowd to take different evacuation routes and arrive at respective exits at nearly the same time. If this is not the case, their system brings up-to-date routes or paths of the slower crowds. This system lacks simulation to model slow-moving or physically challenged individuals. Evacuation simulation in the airport domain needs additional characteristics beyond most simulations, including the distinctive behaviors of the first-time visitors who may not have complete understanding of the area or the measures and families who do not necessarily conform to frequently assumed pedestrian habits. Tsai et al. [22] proposed ESCAPES - a simulation tool for multi-agent evacuation that includes four main features: (i) distinct kinds of agents; (ii) emotional interactions; (iii) informational interactions; (iv) behavioral interactions. They use ESCAPES to model the international terminal of the Los Angeles International Airport (LAX).

On the basis of analysis of the impact of different factors on passenger's behavior under fire evacuation in metro station, Zhang et al. [26] have modeled facilities in a metro station such as gates, stairs, passageways, entrances and exits. They simulated the process of fire spread and the passenger evacuation scenarios by the model of cellular automata. Wagner et al. [23] present a prototype of a computer simulation and decision support system that utilizes the agent-based modeling to simulate crowd evacuation in a concert setting due to fire while allowing various disaster scenarios for testing with the aim of testing multiple scenarios and decision support for the planning and preparedness phase of emergency management in case of fire disasters at concert venues. The prototype is unique in the present literature as it is specifically intended to simulate a concert site setting such as a stadium or auditorium and is extremely configurable to allow user definition of concert venues with any arrangement of seats, routes, phases, exits and individuals as well as the definition of various fires with fire and smoke dynamics included.

These simulation software have various benefits as well as drawbacks. For example, these models can only work with a set of parameters that are predefined inside the software package. These software cannot import any file to add a new 3D environment into their software package. Therefore, any possible physical change/measures and new feature/parameter in technology that may come up in future cannot be implemented in these software. In the next section, we introduce a process for the development of software simulation for indoor environments that is capable of incorporating a variety of possible physical change/measures before their actual development/deployment.

3   Proposed Methodology

This section provides details of our proposed software simulation process. The proposed process is designed to evaluate any possible physical changes/measures to an indoor environment to check its effectiveness in case of an emergency for various different scenarios.

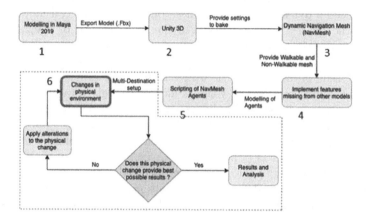

Fig. 1. Flowchart of proposed software simulation process

The flowchart in Fig. 1 depicts various techniques and software used in the proposed process. The highlighted part 6 depicts the main feature of the proposed process and allows to incorporate any possible physical change/measures which can help improving the evacuation time and efficiency. Subsequent paragraphs in this section provide a brief explanation of each of the important components in the flow chart.

To create a 3D indoor environment, we use Autodesk Maya. Autodesk Maya is a very popular and a leading 3D computer graphics application software that is capable of handling complete animation production pipeline and runs on all three major platforms, i.e., Microsoft Windows, MacOS and Linux. It is a 3D modeling and animation software and is capable of generating realistic special effects and high quality rendering through a set of menus. It provides a wide range of options to export created 3D models to other software systems. Since we use Unity in our next step, it allows us to export in ".fbx" format to achieve better stability of the created 3D model.

Unity is a cross-platform game engine. The navigation system in Unity enables us to easily incorporate powerful path finding capability to the characters/agents in games or simulations. Unity provides an intelligent surface called navigation mesh (NavMesh) for agents to move around. NavMesh for agents is a component which takes some selected waypoints and makes an AI agent patrol in the map. Therefore, to move the agent, we need to tell NavMesh to move an agent to a given destination. This is achieved by telling the agent to start calculating the simple path by using NavMesh for agents and the destination point. Once the calculation is finished, the AI agent begins to move along the path until it reaches its destination.

Path planning and navigation play an important and significant role in simulated virtual environments and computer games. However, while designing an emergency situation, we need a dynamic environment with dynamic obstacles (such as falling roof/wall) that can appear at any point in time. For such scenarios, we need a dynamic navigation mesh on which agents can move and find a path to the nearest exit. Intelligent dynamic relocation of agents requires addressing two main problems (i) how to discover the target, and (ii) how to move to the target location. These two problems are quite distinct but are closely linked. The issue of discovering the target is more global but static because it considers the whole environment whereas moving to a given target is more local and vibrant since every agent may look only at the direction it has to move and may know how to avoid collisions with other moving agents.

The navigation system is automatically built from the geometry of the scene to represent walkable areas (where the agent can stand and move). The locations are then connected to a top laying surface called the navigation mesh (or NavMesh for short). While defining the navigation mesh to provide walkable and non-walkable region, we must provide default parameters such as radius of an agent, its height, walking speed, etc.

As mentioned before, not all of the existing software models described in Tables 1 and 2 facilitate all of the necessary features. In the proposed process, not only we implemented additional features but also those of all of the mentioned software models. Crowd distribution is obtained through raycasting, a unity feature. At any given point in time, an agent casts a ray to determine how many other agents are proceeding to a particular door and to determine additional paths leading to the same door. The default entry of the raycast feature for every exit is put to the value equal to the 10% population for that scenario. If more than 10% of people are going to a single exit, the next person takes another nearest exit. For the "fire data" feature, the fire component in the existing systems is made available either through import or by implementing it in the proposed process. However, in our case, we prefer to implement it in the Unity 3D environment to obtain more accurate results. This allows us to check the number of casualties due to a fire. It should be noted that the fire also affects the behavior of the agents. The "exit block" feature is implemented by dropping random blocks of "concrete" from the top or any other area to block the exits in certain situations, thus, forcing the agents to consider another unblocked exit. For the "toxicity" feature, we consider choking of agents due to smoke, invisible gases, or other chemical fumes. This feature is implemented by setting the timer for agents to start choking, etc. If the agents are still inside the environment after the start of the choking time, it potentially leads to their death by choking. The "Disadvantage/Slow" moving feature is taken into consideration by very few of the existing models. However, we implement this feature by simulating agents on wheelchairs to simulate wheelchair-accessible doors and to give priority to such agents over normal agents.

After designing all of the main components mentioned in the workflow, an external file designed in CAD software (such as .fbx file in our case) can be imported into our process. This allows us to evaluate if the physical change may possibly create a difference in evacuation timing and efficiency. This can help designer and planning engineers to create prototypes of the physical changes outside the software model and import them to evaluate the impact of such physical changes.

4   Experimental Setup and Results

We developed and tested our software simulation process on an Intel based personal computer (PC) with a 3.3 GHz Intel Core i7 CPU, 32 GB DDR3 memory, and a 4 GB NVIDIA GeForce GTX 960 graphics card running Microsoft Windows 10 operating System. The display resolution is set to 2560 × 1440 pixels. Additional software used are: (a) Unity 3.1.4f1 Personal (64 bit) and (b) AutoDesk Maya 2019 (Educational version).

To control the environment, a user in our system is allowed to adjust certain parameters in a selection pane. This setup allows a user to evaluate the system against a given set of existing and newly proposed set of parameters. Some of these parameters are only valid for specific physical changes. For example, the parameter "Delay Chair Retract" is valid only when retractable chairs are present in the system. Similarly, "Use Glow Paint" will work only when "Glow-in-the-dark Paint" physical change/property is present in the system. On the other hand, some of these parameters such as simulation start time, NavMesh run speed, etc. are mandatory for all scenarios that have been discussed before and are part of our experiments.

4.1   Physical Changes

Simulation allows us to evaluate effectiveness of planned or designed physical changes/measures during an emergency situation before they are actually constructed/implemented. The physical changes/measures we simulate in our setup include retractable chairs (Fig. 2), extra staff members (Fig. 3), glow-in-the-dark paint (Fig. 4), and movable walls (Fig. 5). In case of an emergency, safety measures are also implemented in our experiments to simulate evacuation priority given to children and people with special needs. It is important to note that the proposed process is capable of simulating other physical changes that may appear in future and to evaluate their effectiveness in the same fashion.

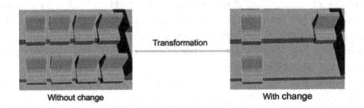

Fig. 2. Retractable seats

 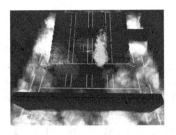 

Fig. 3. Assisting staff [9]   **Fig. 4.** Glow-in-the-dark paint [10]   **Fig. 5.** Movable walls [11]

To validate the proposed simulation process for indoor environments, we recreated the cinema hall fire scenario [4] as an example. This setup is shown in Fig. 6 and the model includes seating for 192 agents including 5 designated seats in the front for physically challenged individuals using wheelchairs. There are 4 exit doors and we created 101 agents for the simulation using dynamic navigation mesh for the movement of all occupants/agents. In our experiments, we simulated some specific features such as smoke, fire etc. that perhaps was likely the case during the actual emergency to provide a realistic emergency scenario. Through Unity scripting feature, agents are directed towards the nearest exit door.

We simulated all of the above mentioned physical changes/measures on individual basis as well as by creating their combinations. It is important to note that for each of the physical changes, as long as it is in the .fbx file produced by Maya, our approach could then further process it to see its effectiveness in an emergency situation. It should also be noted that none of the earlier reviewed software models can import a new 3D environment into their software package.

Fig. 6. Default cinema hall's setting created in Unity without any emergency

4.2 Experimental Results

This section provides results and discussions of our experiments on a cinema hall model for a set of scenarios with certain physical changes and/or measures and comparing the obtained results with that of the actual tragedy. In each simulation, we recorded the *evacuation time* (in seconds), *number of escaped agents*, and *number of dead agents* at the end of the simulation. Also, we counted the number of agents died due to a specific cause such as *Death by fire*, *Death by roof (falling debris)*, and *Death by choking*.

Our first experiment simulated a scenario with no emergency situation in the cinema hall. In this case, all of the 101 agents were able to get out of the cinema hall within 43.20 s and there was no casualty. It is probably worth mentioning that this first experiment is an attempt to model the Uphaar Cinema fire tragedy [4] assuming as if no emergency has happened.

4.3 Baseline Scenario 1

As mentioned earlier, the Uphaar cinema fire tragedy [4] resulted in the death of 59 individuals who were trapped inside the cinema and died primarily due to suffocation, choking, fire, blocked exits, pitch black darkness, etc. Figure 7 simulates what may have happened in the Uphaar Cinema on that day. Results of our simulation of this tragedy are shown in Table 3. After setting all the parameters, simulation using the proposed process provides similar results and showed the evacuation took 57.72 s and 49 agents died, essentially 2 less than the actual incident. The statistics reported in Table 3 are later used in other simulations to calculate percentage of improvements.

We consider the scenario presented in Fig. 7 and Table 3 as the *Baseline Scenario 1*. We simulated other scenarios by adding different physical changes to this baseline scenario and comparing results.

Fig. 7. Simulation depicting a possible scenario of the Uphaar Cinema on Friday, 13 June 1997

Table 3. Results for the Uphaar Cinema fire simulation in Fig. 7 - *the Baseline Scenario 1*

Total agents	Escaped agents	Dead agents	Time (s)	Death by fire	Death by roof	Death by choking
101	52	49	57.72	5	9	35

The Retractable Seats Scenario. The first physical change to the *Baseline Scenario 1* is the use of retractable seats, as shown in Fig. 8. In this simulation, only 16 agents died, and the remaining 85 agents took 47.86 s to safely escape. Some of the agents still died due to fire and falling roof/debris. However, death by choking is zero because the agents were able to exit quickly, before the spread of fire and presumably due to retractable seats. Result of this simulation are provided in Table 4. A comparison of these results with those of the *Baseline Scenario 1* shows a 17.08% reduction in the evacuation time and saving 67% (or 33) more lives due to the retractable seats.

Movable Walls Scenario. In this simulation, we simulated only the provision of movable walls in the cinema hall to see its effectiveness in saving lives. Results of this simulation are reported in Table 4 which also indicates 16.67% less evacuation time and 57% less number of casualties.

Fig. 8. Simulating retractable seats

The Retractable Seats and Movable Walls Scenario. After implementing these two physical changes individually, we simulate both of them together and the results are provided in Table 4 as well.

As can be observed from these 3 scenarios, evacuation was faster and there were less number of casualties, resulting in more lives being saved. These simulations show the effectiveness of the physical changes of retractable seats and movable walls.

Table 4. Results of simulations using retractable seats, movable walls, and both

Physical changes	Total agents	Escaped agents	Dead agents	Time (s)	Death by fire	Death by roof	Death by choking
Retractable seats	101	85	16	47.86	1	15	0
Movable walls	101	80	21	48.12	7	14	0
Retractable seats and Movable walls	101	85	16	38.50	1	15	0

4.4   Baseline Scenario 2

As mentioned earlier, due to an electrical short-circuit, the Uphaar Cinema hall was totally dark with no lit up emergency exit signs. In order to recreate this situation, we introduced a new scenario and called it *Baseline Scenario 2* while keeping the same cinema hall model and simulating darkness to indicate loss of electrical power due to short circuit, thus, making it hard for agents to find the nearest exit. In our simulation, we assumed that the short circuit happened 3 s after the start of simulation. Table 5 shows the result of simulation for this baseline scenario.

Table 5. Results of the simulated *Baseline Scenario 2*

Total agents	Escaped agents	Dead agents	Time (s)	Death by fire	Death by roof	Death by choking
101	6	95	53.98	13	6	76

In this simulation, we noticed that the agents were moving randomly as if they had no knowledge of the nearest exit. This created a situation similar to what may have been at the Uphaar Cinema. Not to any surprise, only very few agents were able to find their way out of the cinema hall, and most of them (95 out of 101) died inside In other experiments, like before, we simulated additional physical changes to this *Baseline Scenario 2*.

The Glow-in-the-Dark Scenario. First, we considered glow-in-the-dark paint to mark pathways as shown in Fig. 9. Results of this simulation are presented in Table 6. After implementing this physical change, only 17 agents died whereas it took 56.02 s for the remainder of the 84 agents to escape safely. Still some agents died because of both fire and/or falling debris. Glow-in-the-dark paint provided vital directions to the agents to escape safely, leading to only 4 deaths due to choking. Due to glow-in-the-dark paint, agents are able to get out rather than randomly moving around looking for the exits. By comparing results in Table 6 with those in Table 5, we can observe that although there is a 4% increase in evacuation time, the overall efficiency of the system still increased to 82.10% because 78(=84-6) lives are saved.

Extra Staff Scenario. The next physical change/measure that we experimented is that of considering availability of extra staff only while removing glow-in-the-dark paint from the simulation. As we can guess, the staff is expected to have training and better knowledge of the cinema hall layout, entry and exit points, etc. In our simulations, we added two extra staff members (i.e., agents) to direct other agents to the nearest exit and leave the building once everyone gets out. The results of this scenario are presented in Table 6 as well.

Fig. 9. Simulation using Glow-in-the-dark paint stripes

Table 6. Results of simulations using glow-in-the-dark stripes, extra staff, and both

Physical changes measure	Total agents	Escaped agents	Dead agents	Time (s)	Death by fire	Death by roof	Death by choking
Glow-in-the-dark stripes	101	84	17	56.02	9	4	4
Extra staff	101	63	38	59.84	1	7	30
Glow-in-the-dark stripes and extra staff	101	67	34	59.66	2	11	21

Results indicate that only 38 agents died, and it took 59.84 s for 63 agents to safely get out. Some of the agents still died due to fire and falling debris. Compared with glow-in-the-dark paint, the extra staff measure although resulted in fewer casualties but not quite as effective when compared with the original scenario. In this scenario, 30 agents died because of choking. These results lead us to the conclusion that the 10% increase in evacuation time is due to agents taking time to understand the staff. Although, the efficiency of the system increased by 60% because 63 lives were saved compared with the *Baseline Scenario 2*.

The Glow-in-the-Dark Paint and Extra Staff Scenario. Like earlier *Baseline Scenario 1*, we simulated a combination of both glow-in-the-dark paint and the extra staff together and the results are shown in Table 6 as well.

The results show that only 34 agents died, and it took 59.66 s for 67 agents to get out safely. However, some of the agents still died due to fire and/or falling debris. By comparing results, we can conclude that by using both of the physical change (glow-in-the-dark paint strips) and the safety measure (extra staff) together, the efficiency of the system is increased by 64% (more lives saved) while evacuation took 10% more time.

As can be observed from these 3 scenarios, these physical changes/measures dramatically reduce the fatality rate.

5   Conclusion

In the paper, we presented an emergency evacuation simulation process that can be used by researchers, designers, and engineers for design and implementation of new features and techniques to help reduce casualties during emergency evacuation scenarios. The process is capable of integrating new features and to simulate various level of details and crowd densities, even larger crowd sizes. And it is capable of dealing with a large number of parameters that can be used to simulate various scenarios and multiple environments with a large number of agents. This can allow researchers/planners/developers to observe effects of various situations in design/planning phase without the investments of time and money and analyze the effects of these changes to save the human capital.

References

1. Anylogic.   https://www.anylogic.com/use-of-simulation/agent-based-modeling/. Accessed 19 Mar 2022
2. Berrou, J.L., Beecham, J.: Calibration and validation of the legion simulation model using empirical data. In: Waldau, N., Gattermann, P., Knoflacher, H., Schreckenberg, M. (eds.) Pedestrian and Evacuation Dynamics, pp. 167–181. Springer, Cham (2007). https://doi.org/10.1007/978-3-540-47064-9_15
3. Buckman, L., Leather, J.: Modeling station congestion the PEDROUTE way. Traffic Engineering Control (1994)
4. Chakravarty, S.: Inquiry committee report exposes management's callousness behind uphaar cinema tragedy. India Today (2013). https://www. indiatoday.in/magazine/states/story/19970714-inquiry-committee-report-exposes-management-callousness-behind-uphaar-cinema-tragedy-830337-1997-07-14. Accessed 19 Mar 2022
5. Challenger, R., Clegg, C., Robinson, M.: Understanding crowd behaviours: practical guidance and lessons identified. The Cabinet Office Emergency Planning College (2009)
6. Darlington, S., Brocchetto, M., Ford, D.: Fire rips through crowded brazil nightclub, killing 233. CNN (2013). https://edition.cnn.com/2013/01/27/world/americas/brazil-nightclub-fire/index.html. Accessed 19 Mar 2022
7. Helbing, D., Molnar, P.: Social force model for pedestrian dynamics. Phys. Rev. E **51**(5), 4282 (1995)
8. Integrated Environmental Solutions, Simulex User Manual: Evacuation Modeling Software, Integrated Environmental Solutions Inc., March 2001
9. Illustration: Assisting staffs. https://www.dreamstime.com/illustration/. Accessed 19 Mar 2022

10. Illustration: Glow-in-the-dark paint. https://www.vmsd.com/content/photolumi nescent-egress-path-markings. Accessed 19 Mar 2022
11. Illustration: Moveable walls. https://www.becker.uk.com/movable-walls/. Accessed 19 Mar 2022
12. Korhonen, T., Hostikka, S.: Fire dynamics simulator with evacuation: FDS+Evac: technical reference and user's guide. Julkaisija - Utgivare - Publisher (2009)
13. Lu, G., Chen, L., Luo, W.: Real-time crowd simulation integrating potential fields and agent method. ACM Trans. Model. Comput. Simul. (TOMACS) 26(4), 28 (2016)
14. Neuman, S.: Pakistan factory fires kill more than 300. NPR (2012). https://www. npr.org/sections/thetwo-way/2012/09/12/160995406/pakistan-factory-fires-kill-more-than-300. Accessed 19 Mar 2022
15. Park, J., Gwynne, S., Galea, E., Lawrence, P.: Validating the building exodus evacuation model using data from an unannounced trial evacuation. In: Proceedings of 2nd International Pedestrian and Evacuation Dynamics Conference, Greenwich, UK, pp. 295–306. CMS Press, January 2003. ISBN 1904521088
16. Parker, E.: Station fire memorial to be dedicated may 21. The Provincial Journal (2017). https://www.providencejournal.com/story/news/2017/02/24/station-fire-memorial-to-be-dedicated-may-21/22090621007/
17. Pelechano, N., Malkawi, A.: Evacuation simulation models: challenges in modeling high rise building evacuation with cellular automata approaches. Autom. Constr. 17(4), 377–385 (2008)
18. Reuters: China 1994 fire killed 288 pupils as officials fled-expose. https://www. reuters.com/article/idUSPEK242373. Accessed 19 Mar 2022
19. Shestopal, V., Grubits, S.: Evacuation model for merging traffic flows in multi-room and multi-storey buildings. Fire Saf. Sci. 4, 625–632 (1994)
20. Steiner, A., Philipp, M., Schmid, A.: Parameter estimation for a pedestrian simulation model. In: Swiss Transport Research Conference, Ascona, Switzerland, 12 September 2007 (2007)
21. Sun, S.: Agent-based crowd simulation modelling for a gaming environment. Master's thesis, University of Windsor (2017). https://scholar.uwindsor.ca/etd/7399/
22. Tsai, J., Fridman, N., et al.: Escapes: evacuation simulation with children, authorities, parents, emotions, and social comparison. In: The 10th International Conference on Autonomous Agents & Multiagent Systems, vol. 2, pp. 457–464 (2011)
23. Wagner, N., Agrawal, V.: An agent-based simulation system for concert venue crowd evacuation modeling in the presence of a fire disaster. Expert Syst. Appl. 41(6), 2807–2815 (2014)
24. Wong, S.-K., Wang, Y.-S., Tang, P.-K., Tsai, T.-Y.: Optimized evacuation route based on crowd simulation. Comput. Vis. Media 3(3), 243–261 (2017). https://doi. org/10.1007/s41095-017-0081-9
25. Zavin, A., Anzum, F., Rahman, S.F.: Towards developing an intelligent fire exit guidance system using informed search technique. In: 2018 21st International Conference on Computer & Information Technology, pp. 1–6 (2018)
26. Zhang, X., Zhong, Q., Li, Y., Li, W., Luo, Q.: Simulation of fire emergency evacuation in metro station based on cellular automata. In: 3rd IEEE International Conference on Intelligent Transportation Engineering, pp. 40–44 (2018)

Context Information Management in a Microservice Based Measurement and Processing Infrastructure

Steffen Späthe[1]($\boxtimes$) , Florian Greulich[2], and Sebastian Apel[3]

[1] Friedrich Schiller University Jena, 07743 Jena, Germany
`steffen.spaethe@uni-jena.de`
[2] Sächsisches Landesgymnasium Sankt Afra, 01662 Meißen, Germany
`florian.greulich@afra.lernsax.de`
[3] Technische Hochschule Ingolstadt, 85019 Ingolstadt, Germany
`sebastian.apel@thi.de`

Abstract. Within a distributed software system for measuring and processing data streams, the services require knowledge to the contextualization of information. Using microservices in combination with a network of heterogeneous devices - as usual in an internet of things setting - requires the management of knowledge about integrated data and its context. Reference architectures suggest here the centralization of this knowledge management. This contribution deals with the question of how this knowledge can be structured and how to apply integration and processing services in a microservice architecture. The main focus here is on how data collection and context can be combined independently of the corresponding services and without influencing participating services. The result is a data model and a query language, which we used within the architecture to manage knowledge and used by integration and processing services. The result is evaluated based on scenario considerations in the internet of things setting, such as adding, replacing and removing devices while maintaining the context. Additionally, we provide an insight into the practical application of the approach in a realized microservice infrastructure for the management and optimization of a local smart grid.

Keywords: Microservice architecture · Internet of things · Measurement infrastructure · Context information

1 Introduction

Consider a network of small devices with various actuators and sensors. This network is known as the internet of things (IoT). The integration of these devices into a software system requires the handling of a large number of different and

F. Phillipson et al. (Eds.): I4CS 2022, CCIS 1585, pp. 116–135, 2022.
https://doi.org/10.1007/978-3-031-06668-9_10

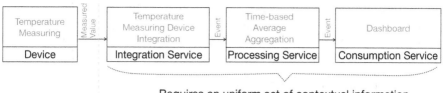

Fig. 1. Integration and processing of a temperature measuring device as an example

heterogeneous devices [22]. This software system has to process the corresponding communication protocols and data formats as well as the transformation into data streams in order to manage further processing.

Within such a software system we can differentiate between three types of services: (1) services that handle the integration of devices, (2) services that handle the processing of data streams and (3) services that handle the consumption of processed information [1,18]. These services build our so-called measurement and processing infrastructure. The services transfer events via data streams between each other. In order to map the integrated information from devices to data stream events – especially their origin, measurement time, value, and, unit, and other context information – knowledge is required.

The example use case shown in Fig. 1 is to integrate a temperature measuring device. There is a service that connects an external temperature device and generates a continuous data stream of temperature measurement events. Each event contains the measured temperature value, the time of measurement and an identification of the measuring instrument.

However, the integrated device is usually not aware of its place of use. In this case, the integration service needs to add additional information; the resulting event gets enriched. Further, if another service wants to determine the average over the last hour for these temperature events by location, it must know exactly how the integration service has enriched these events. Thus, each service within the software system must work on the same knowledge, in detail about contextual information.

If we realize such a microservice architecture based system, as motivated by our setup [3], then each resulting service in this architecture should be isolated, loosely coupled, independently deployable, resilient services [20, P. 27ff]. This distributed services setup raised the question of the management of context information regarding data streams. This management is essential because the use of context information in the services without management can lead to implicit dependencies. These dependencies endanger the principles of microservice architecture. Further, those implicit relationships are error-prone, and independent deployment of individual services can lead to asynchronicity in data understanding between various services. One service must provide application-specific configuration options, documentation maintained and deployments have to be instantiated accordingly – across all services of the software system.

Our presented approach aims to manage contextual information within a specific service within a microservice-based application. This consolidates and makes explicit the relationships between the integration, processing and visualisation tasks of a measurement and processing infrastructure. Therefore, we have to answer two questions: (1) how this context information for data streams could be structured and (2) how we offer information in such an architecture to other services. The approach reduces the number of implicit dependencies between services and strengthens the isolated development and deployment of individual services. The evaluation of this approach that we perform does not apply performance measurements, as these have a negligible impact on the execution of the individual services. Instead, we analyze the resulting service network using scenarios found in the context of IoT.

We organized the remaining paper as follows. In Sect. 2, we will go into detail on related work on IoT architectures, measurement infrastructures and microservice architectures. Section 3 deals with the challenge we want to address – a formal representation of what a typical approach would be. The following Sect. 4 presents our solution to manage knowledge in a distributed environment, and Sect. 5 provides the scenario-based analysis of our setup. The following Sect. 6 provides an insight into the experience gained and lessons learned when using this context information management in an implemented scenario. Finally, Sect. 7 discusses the outcome.

2   Related Work

The topics IoT, microservice architectures, measurement infrastructures and events, as well as time-series databases, are relevant for the consideration of related works.

Concerning microservice architectures literature on tenets, architectural style and definitions are available, as outlined by Zimmermann [23] and Newman [16]. The architecture beginnings date back to the "33rd Degree Conference" in Krakow (2012) on the topic "Microservices-Java, the Unix Way" by Lewis [14], the talk on "Micro-Service Architecture" by George at the Baruco (2012) [10] and the talks by Andrian Cockroft in the context of Netflix on their "fine-grained SOA". These styles and definitions apply in particular to the focus of sizing decisions, isolation, dependencies and interaction with other services. Further, there is a wide range of work on the topic of transforming legacy applications into the microservice approach. There is a range of work on mechanisms to break business logic into microservice candidates, as done by Chen et al. [7], and domain-driven design approaches for microservices, as done by Diepenbrock et al. [9]. In the context of our work, these approaches are of central importance. Especially concerning design decisions, such as how data sources are connected, and the scope of processing services.

In [18,19] Vianden et al. describe a reference architecture for enterprise measurement infrastructures. The architecture contains different levels of services for visualisation, processing and persistence, integration, transport and consumption of data. We also found comparable components in architecture descriptions in the context of IoT. For example, Brundu et al. describe an infrastructure based on IoT for energy management and simulation using a pool of services in combination with a messaging middleware to decouple them [6].

In addition to these insights, there are publications on the topic of IoT architectures, such as in Krčo et al. [12], Choudhary and Jain [8], Al-Fuqaha et al. [2] and Yang et al. [21]. These differentiate in possible approaches to the interaction between things, networking and software systems, as well as access points for end-users. Besides, traditional architecture approaches, also service-oriented, and distributed approaches get into focus. For example, once more, a microservice-based approach, as shown in Krylovskiy et al. [13]. Further, Microsoft provides a reference architecture for IoT [1] which differentiates between IoT devices as things, processing as insights and business integration as actions. This reference architecture states that "[i]nformation models describing the devices, their attributes and associated data schema are key for implementing solution business logic and processing" [1]. Further, this reference architecture gives OPC UA [11] as an example in the case of the "Industrial IoT scenario". OPC UA is a platform-independent, service-oriented architecture that allows transporting machine-related data as well as the semantic description of them. Another reference architecture is provided in Bauer et al. [5], which is "designed [. . .] for the generation of compliant IoT concrete architectures that are tailored to one's specific needs".

Finally, to look at the type of data to be considered along with the infrastructure, approaches to complex event processing, e. g., Luckham [15] with further architecture styles, event structures and processing of them; as well as databases focusing time series as done by Bader [4], are essential.

The realisation of a measurement and processing infrastructure is discussed as a current and challenging topic. This is according to our assessment of microservice architectures in this context. We notice that the challenges to address the implicit interrelationships have not been fully addressed. This applies in particular to the interdependencies on a knowledge level between the different services.

The distinction of our approach to IoT reference architecture and data models like OPC UA is substantial. The reference architecture and data model are aimed at the management of devices and the resulting data flows. We focus on labelling and understanding data streams, which consist of quite plain measurement data, outside the measurement device. The aim is to avoid implicit dependencies and the scattering of knowledge across different microservices.

3   Measurement and Processing Infrastructure

Before we look at the management of contextual information in Sect. 4, this chapter will describe how device integration and processing services mostly tend to look. Figure 2 shows an abstract measurement and processing infrastructure

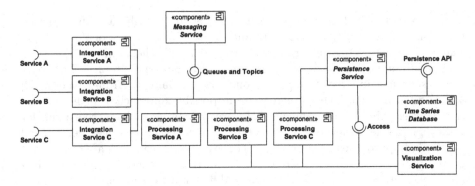

Fig. 2. Abstract visualization of involved components in a measurement and processing infrastructure

using a messaging middleware as a component to decouple individual systems. This architecture utilizes a message-oriented middleware and the measurement infrastructures motivated in Vianden et al. [18,19] and by Microsoft's reference architecture [1]. The architecture differentiates between the messaging middleware and abstract components for integration, processing and consumption, in this case, to persist and visualize the data streams. The integration services serve the connection of data sources. E. g., these can be connection endpoints of measuring instruments or external services which provide information. A messaging middleware decouples the integration services from the remaining services and subsequently enable event-based processing. The processing services use the events from the message service for analysis to create and publish new (higher-level) events, e. g., by using complex event processing concepts. Persistence services listen for events and store a subset (or all) of these events for downstream processing, e. g., for manual analyses and learning processes. Visualization services use stored content as well as events to visualize values and indicators.

3.1   Application in Integration Services

We used this abstract infrastructure in Fig. 2 in the following to describe the realization of integration services and processing services in our application case. Starting with the integration services, these act as a data transformer to overcome different system landscapes. Their primary task is the continued consumption of measurements of a data source. Each consumption activity records at execution time t, a quantity p of information so that $info_t^1, \ldots, info_t^p$ is available, where each $info$ describe abstractly a tuple $(time, key, value)$. In respect to a measurement, key is some measurement value identifier, $time$ is the time of measurement and $value$ is the value measured. Based on this input, the transformation can be described as function f to map $info_t^1, \ldots, info_t^p$ onto u different events $event_t^{m_1}, \ldots, event_t^{m_u}$ labelled by m (as in metric). Each $event$ is defined as a tuple $(time, value, tag^1, \ldots, tag^k)$, where $time$ is the time of measurement, *value* the measured value and $(tag^1, \ldots, tag^k)$ the so-called context information. For example, this can be an identifier of the described context, an identifier of the origin of the measured value, a unit, or the acquisition rate. This representation of events is related to events described by Luckham in [15, S. 88].

Regarding [15, P. 88], "an event is an object that is a record of an activity in a system". Within this definition of events, Luckham defines three aspects: form, significance and relativity. In our case, the form is mostly a measurement value, while the significance is related to the activity of our measurement infrastructure and the relativity is related to various analyses, forecasts and optimizations services. However, we describe the task for our integration services as the following:

$$f : (info_t^1, \ldots, info_t^p) \longmapsto (event_t^{m_1}, \ldots, event_t^{m_u})$$
$$with \quad info_t^q := (time, key, value)$$
$$event_t^{m_u} := (time, value, tag_1, \ldots, tag_k)$$

Please note, several events can result from one specific information $info_t^q$, but we do not consider the case where different pieces of information give rise to one event. A so-called metric (measured values of a time series) finally arises for $t_1, \ldots, t_n$ as $event_{t_1}^m, \ldots, event_{t_n}^m$.

As an example, we use a data source, which offers weather information, which we integrated. The input is a measurement of the individual current temperature, humidity and wind speed. A device called $Sensor_1$ collects measured values in the laboratory in Jena so that the service records the following values as input:

$$info_t = ((20{:}41, \text{temp-celsius}, \quad 5),$$
$$(20{:}42, \text{humidity-percent}, 42),$$
$$(20{:}43, \text{wind-speed-kmh}, 11))$$

As expected, something like this would be the result of the transformation:

$$event_t^{\text{temp}} = (20{:}41, \ 5, \ Sensor_1, \ Jena, \ °C)$$
$$event_t^{\text{humidity}} = (20{:}42, \ 42, \ Sensor_1, \ Jena, \ \%)$$
$$event_t^{\text{wind}} = (20{:}43, \ 11, \ Sensor_1, \ Jena, \ km/h)$$

The tags are related to the used device in tag^1, the location in tag^2 and the unit of the measured value in tag^3. It is conceivable to use more tags to capture, e.g., measurement frequency and exact location or point of use.

3.2 Application in Processing Services

Besides the integration of endpoints, the processing services used in the measurement and processing infrastructures utilizes these events. Their task is to transform a set of events from different metrics $m_1, \ldots, m_q$ that were recorded (or even measured) at different times $t_1, \ldots, t_q$ into one or more specific values, which in turn can be understood as events for different metrics $m'_1, ..., m'_r$ at the time t' in the system. We describe the processing service task like the following:

$$g : (event_{t_1}^{m_1}, ..., event_{t_q}^{m_q}) \longmapsto (event_{t'}^{m'_1}, ..., event_{t'}^{m'_r})$$

The example used before, going further, could be used in a processing step that aggregates events over time. In this example, we apply an aggregation function average to the temperature events at the location *Jena*. This stateful processing service thus consumes an event and delivers zero or one event as output. An output event is produced only if three or more temperature events have been processed in the last ten minutes, as shown below:

$$g_{avg}((20{:}42, 5, \text{Sensor}_1, \text{Jena}, {}^{\circ}\text{C})) \mapsto \emptyset$$
$$g_{avg}((20{:}43, 6, \text{Sensor}_1, \text{Jena}, {}^{\circ}\text{C})) \mapsto \emptyset$$
$$g_{avg}((20{:}44, 4, \text{Sensor}_1, \text{Jena}, {}^{\circ}\text{C})) \mapsto ((20{:}44, 5, \text{AvgSensor}_1, \text{Jena}, {}^{\circ}\text{C}))$$

Processing services usually need to know which events exist in data streams, which tags this event use, what they mean, and independently of this, the meaning of the measured value itself. Relations are implicit between the mapping of information in the integration service, the processing service (and the detection on specific tag combinations), as well as services to manage the visualization (selection of individual metrics, aggregation or grouping by tags) and the persistence. The relationships could be maintained, for example, by the configuration of a service, in which we describe a processing service precisely according to which metric and which tags it should use for searching. It would be conceivable to store this configuration decentralized.

To summarizing, currently, there are no relationships represented yet in a structured form, and this abstract infrastructure can not ensure the isolation of a microservice that handles integration or processing tasks. A further challenge is a differentiation between data collection and the assignment to a context, through which the measured value gains meaning. When a temperature sensor measures a temperature, the information is only valuable if it is known where it was measured - indoors or outdoors. Furthermore, in which reference system the value is determined and at which point of use the device is located. Only this contextual information enables the meaningful usage of the measured value in processing services. Conversely, for a context for which the measured value was collected, it is irrelevant with which device the value was measured. The Sen_1, which currently collects data in Jena, could be moved to somewhere else. A new device Sen_2 and a new integration service (especially if the data providing interface is different) must, therefore, be implemented in such a way that all context information is handled in the same way so that processing services are not affected by the replacement. We understand these relations and the associated context information as implicit. Changes to these affect more than one service and affect the independence of the services according to "Microservices' tenets" [23].

4   Context Information Management

To address the problems of establishing relations between measuring instrument and context, to add additional context information and to reduce implicit relations between different services we suggest to use shared context information. The challenge here is how this context information management service can structure its knowledge and how to formulate queries so that other services can benefit from it.

4.1   Context Information Data Model

The aim is to manage measurement devices and context information appropriately and to provide a query interface which offers other services access to this knowledge. The idea for organising this knowledge is to use a document-like structure. This structure captures attributes for different entities of the infrastructure. Documents in this model are entities in the described scenario - both measuring devices and the corresponding context. For example, a document could describe a house, a second document could describe a temperature measuring device, and a third document could describe the living room for which the temperature is measured.

Each document contains one or more attributes. It is uniquely identifiable as well as classifiable and manages a set of data sources or contexts of a data source. In the previous example, this means that the document describing the living room must be assigned a classification as room, as well as properties describing it, e. g., size or location and finally the reference to the data source to act as context.

We achieve classifiability by typing the documents. The so-called document templates describe the available attributes and permitted metrics of a document type. Documents, metrics and their tags are also described by templates to ensure that they use the same metrics across multiple documents and document types.

Figure 3 shows the complete data model. The representation differentiates between entity types for instances and entity types for templates, as well as three areas covering tags, metrics and documents for better readability. *TagTemplate*, *MetricTemplate* and *DocumentTemplate* describe the abstract representation. These specialize the entity type *Template* and are uniquely identifiable by their name. *AttributeTemplate* as a particular case describes available attributes for a *DocumentTemplate*. The *name* and *type* are defined. Additionally, the attribute defines if it is *required* or not. The *DocumentTemplate* requires marking one of the attributes as an identifying attribute (*idAttribute*). A document template can inherit from another template, cyclic inheritance is not allowed. The template utilizes inherited attributes and allows to use them as identifying attributes. The overwriting of attributes is allowed. An instance of *Document* must reference a *DocumentTemplate*. Further, the instance must assign values to required attributes that result from the template and its inherited. From the set of available metrics, an instance of *Document* can ultimately define whether it represents

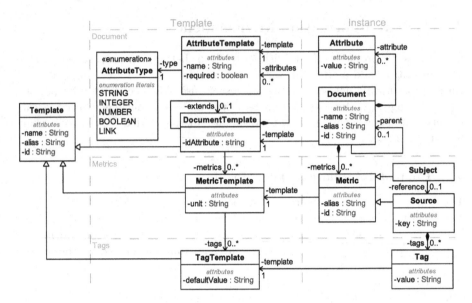

Fig. 3. Datamodel to describe documents related to source metrics and contexts

these as a context or as a source. For a metric as a data source, it is required to specify the associated naming of the value used by the measuring instrument (*key*) and to define the measurement related context information, e.g., device information. For a metric that represents a context, it is required to specify the link to the corresponding metric within the document structure. We can in turn organise the documents themselves in a hierarchy. Links between one document to other documents can be realized using attributes with the type *LINK* (compare Fig. 3).

The value of tags of instanced source metrics ultimately derives from the attributes of the document. It was necessary to implement a supporting syntax to support the filling of tags starting from the current document. Within colons, tags can specify the attribute name to which the content refers. For example, if the document has an attribute *SerialNumber* then the tag value *:SerialNumber:* can be used to use appropriate information in the metric. The *parent* prefix can be used to navigate up one level in the hierarchy. If the example document has a parent document with a *Location* attribute, a tag could use *:parent.Location:-:SerialNumber:*. It is possible to use the *parent* navigability multiple times, and alternatively, the attribute name of attributes of the type *LINK* can be used to reach linked documents.

Listing 1. Query syntax to access documents

```
name = < letter | digit >
document-template = name | "*" | "**" | ('"' string '"')
attribute-name = name | ('"' string '"')
attribute-value = name | ('"' string '"')
pair = attribute-name "=" attribute-value
attributes = "[" pair { "," pair } "]"
selector = document-template [ attributes ]
query = selector { "/" selector }
```

4.2   Application of the Context Information Data Model

So far we have focused on the data model. In the following, we will discuss how to apply this data model to the various services in the measurement and processing infrastructure. For practical utilisation, services need a way to address the information of the data model. We have decided to use a query syntax that supports the hierarchical and document-oriented structure. The query syntax is based on XPath [17] and allows you to select classified documents. Based on the parent relation, the documents form a directed graph. The aim of the query, as in the original XPath use case, is the conditional selection of a subtree, in our case a subgraph. The primary selection criterion of the subgraph is the classification of the documents. Secondary criteria are the attributes that can be added to limit the query result. Listing 1 shows this query syntax.

For example, a document template *Sensor* could exist with an attribute *SerialNumber*. It could be used to describe the document Sen_1, which references a document of the template *Location*. It would thus be possible to search for documents of type *Sensor*. The search could be restricted to documents with a specific serial number or assigned to a specific location via the parent relationship. The query *Sensor[SerialNumber="1"]* returns all documents of type *Sensor* with value *1* for attribute *SerialNumber*. The query *Location[City="Jena"]/Sensor[SerialNumber="1"]* returns all documents of type *Sensor* with attribute *SerialNumber 1* as children of a document with type *Location* with *Jena* as the value of attribute *City*. The result is a set of documents. These documents can be used (see Fig. 3) to correlate with the assigned metrics. Thus, the result is an abstract representation of the events $x_1, ..., x_s$ defined as the tuple $(key, m, tag^1, ..., tag^k)$; the link between the events of the data source and the metric is made using the metric identifier *key*.

Concerning the weather example from Sect. 3, it is therefore required to query what the integrated sensor has to measure. A query could be *Location/Sensor[SerialNumber="1"]* and the result would be a list of tuple $(key, m, tag^1, ..., tag^k)$:

((temp-celsius,	temp,	Sensor₁,	Jena,	°C),
(humidity-percent,	humidity,	Sensor₁,	Jena,	%),
(wind-speed-kmh,	wind,	Sensor₁,	Jena,	km/h))

Applying this context information and the query capabilities to the measurement and processing infrastructure services allows a simplification of the tasks within the service implementation. For integration services, Sect. 3 describes the transformation of information from external data sources as follows:

$$f : (info_t^1, ..., info_t^p) \longmapsto (event_t^{m_1}, ..., event_t^{m_u})$$

If we integrate the abstract representation of events $x_1, ..., x_s$ into the transformation, then a suitable $info_t^v$ should be found for each x_u, so that the following condition applies:

$$\forall u \in (1, ..., s) \exists v \in (1, ..., p) : \left(key_{x_u} = key_{info_t^v}\right)$$

This condition allows the generation of events as output of f for each u and v where the condition as mentioned above is $true$:

$$event_t^{m_{x_u}} = (time_{info_t^v}, value_{info_t^v}, tag_{x_u}^1, ..., tag_{x_u}^k)$$

In the case of processing services, the approach also applies. For this purpose, Sect. 3 defines function g, which describes the task the processing services perform in the infrastructure:

$$g : (event_{t_1}^{m_1}, ..., event_{t_q}^{m_q}) \longmapsto (event_{t'}^{m'_1}, ..., event_{t'}^{m'_r})$$

The context information management can be used here to query the metrics used as input and to get the abstract description $x'_1, ..., x'_i$. Here it may be necessary to limit the selection of metrics. This selection can be used to get input metrics $event_{t_1}^{m_1}, ..., event_{t_q}^{m_q}$. Further, another query can ask which metrics have to be generated as output and get $x''_1, ..., x''_o$, which can be used to get $event_{t'}^{m'_1}, ...,$ $event_{t'}^{m'_r}$. During processing, the service must ensure that the intermediate result is generated from the requested input. Like the input information in the case of integration services, this interim result can be described as aggregations $agg_{t'}^1$, ..., $agg_{t'}^p$ and each aggregation is defined as the tuple $(time, key, value)$. Based on the assignment between information and events in the case of our integration services, the assignment between $agg_{t'}^1, ..., agg_{t'}^p$ and event $event_{t'}^{m'_1}, ..., event_{t'}^{m'_r}$ can now be realised.

Finally, the context information management and its query options can be integrated into visualisation services to obtain metrics, correctly annotate and visually prepare them.

5   Scenario-Based Evaluation

To evaluate the data model and query mentioned in Sect. 4 we implemented them as a single microservice. This implementation offers the capabilities for administration and visualization of context information and related data streams as well as a REST API endpoint to send queries for requesting documents or metrics as described. During the following evaluation, we will discuss the impacts of this approach on a range of scenarios required in an IoT related setup:

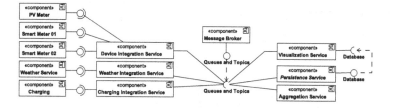

Fig. 4. Exemplary setup for a software system for processing sensor data

1. *Scenario: Add a new device, with a set of sensors*
   The scenario can be specialized in two directions: a new device with a known communication protocol and data format, as well as a new unknown device. If a new unknown sensor is integrated into the system, an adapter must be implemented that understands the communication protocol and data format and converts it to a suitable internal format during integration so that other services can further process it.
2. *Scenario: Replacement of a (broken) device with a comparable*
   Data streams and events from a specific endpoint are related to a context - a temperature sensor captures the temperature for a particular location. If the sensor fails and is replaced, the data source changes, but usually not the context.
3. *Scenario: Modification of the device context*
   Change the context of a device, e.g., by replacing the existing device.
4. *Scenario: Implementation of a new data stream processor*
   A new processor implementation consumes one or more data streams, analyzes them, and produces one or more new data streams.

In the following, the scenarios are considered based on the criteria development effort, independent development of the individual service (refer to microservice architecture) and isolated and fail-safe execution. Each scenario is examined without using a central administration of context information (WOM, see Sect. 3) and with using a context information management (WIM, see Sect. 4). Before the actual scenario evaluation, however, an example setup is described in the following, which represents a microservice architecture using the context information management services implemented.

Exemplary Setup. In order to discuss the scenarios mentioned, we use the following exemplary setup. The setup is shown in Fig. 4, and is based on a local smart grid setting which includes one photovoltaic meter, two smart meters, a service for weather information and a charging point for an electric vehicle. The exemplary setup connects each device via one of the three integration services. The photovoltaic meter and the two smart meters are connected via one integration service since this one can access their information by using the same provided interface. The setup includes an aggregation service, which calculates energy consumption by aggregating measurement values over a period of time.

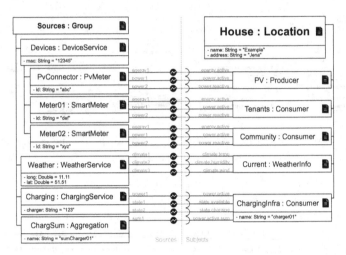

Fig. 5. Instanced data model representing the context information. An object diagram served as a baseline, whereby the document templates function as classes and interfaces are used to represent metric sources, the use of interfaces symbolises contexts that refer to a source metric.

For the consumption of information, the example uses a visualization and persistence service. The persistence service stores some of the events for temporal processing. The visualization service presents current events and past information read from the persistence service.

Based on the document model introduced for our context information management, the structure shown in Fig. 5 can be derived for this example. The object diagram uses instances for the documents. The underlying document templates, presented as class names, are not described in detail here. If a document provides metrics as a source, the visualization uses the symbolism of an interface. If a metric refers as a context to a source, the visualization uses the symbolism of the interface usage. The diagram in Fig. 5 groups all documents of a location and shows on the left side the installed sensors and on the right side a structuring of reality. In the example, several meters for energy production and consumption are used, as well as two service endpoints for weather information and charging infrastructure usage. The related contexts describe the photovoltaic system, the charging points and the consumers of energy (the tenants and the community consumption).

The structure shown in Fig. 5 instantiates a house using the template *Location*. This house gets various devices assigned - for example, the instance *Meter01* with the ID *def* described by using the template *SmartMeter*. Also, a corresponding *Tenant* describes the measured value using the template *Consumer* and gives it a similar context.

Scenario: Add a New Device, with a Set of Sensors. We have to divide this scenario into two specialisations: first, add a new device with a known communication protocol and data format, and second, add a new device with the unknown protocol. Generally, we assume that an integration service integrates several devices. It would be conceivable that a service integrates precisely one device, but this setting is of no importance in the following consideration.

Starting with the specific scenario of a completely new device, whose communication protocol and data format is unknown, the following section describes the development of the software system necessary for the realization of the WOM and WIM scenario. In comparison to Fig. 4 we assume that we add the *Charging* device, and we realize the component *Charging Integration Service*.

In the case of WOM, it is necessary to implement a new integration service to handle the communication protocol and data format. In the scope of the integration, it is necessary to extract and prepare the information necessary for further processing, as well as to sufficiently label information for subsequent processing by adding source and context information. The labelled and enriched events are to be transformed into a system internal data format and published accordingly, e.g., via a message-based middleware, as shown in Fig. 4. The information necessary for transformation and enrichment must be managed inside the service. The more independent integration services exist, the more independently managed information pools emerge.

When using a CIM, related to the WIM scenario, the realization of the service is also necessary. In this case, however, it is not necessary to manage the required data itself, but to extract all available information. When transforming incoming information, it is required to identify the data source and to query the CIM accordingly. In detail, the available information is deserialized and then transformed into a list $info_t^1, ..., info_t^p$ of tuples $(time, key, value)$ (according to Sect. 3). For example, an installation *12345* and meter *abc* as source identification result in a query like *DeviceService[mac= "12345"]/*[id= "abc"]* which is used to address the subtree, that provides the required metrics. The result of this request is used to generate the events, internally to be published, based on the pool of available information and finally to published them for further processing, e.g. via a message-based middleware.

The second specialization of this scenario addresses the case of a known sensor type. In the case of WOM, this requires modifications to the integration service, especially if there is a difference in the information to be extracted. It would be conceivable to cover such cases in the implementation of the service and to new devices in the future by individual configurations. In the case of WIM, no modifications to the service itself are necessary. The new device just has to be created in the CIM and linked to a corresponding context. The integration service would recognize the new device within the next information query, like *DeviceService[mac= "54321"]/*[id= "xyz"]*, and thus receive the new transformation response.

Scenario: Replacement of a (Broken) Device with a Comparable. When a device is replaced, the identification characteristics of a data stream change, but not the context. In this case, we assume that the replaced device corresponds to the same design. Otherwise, the scenario for adding a new device would apply.

Concerning WOM, the development effort depends on what has been provided in the individual integration service for configurable enrichment capabilities. If configuration capabilities exist to handle identification and mapping to the context, the correction is sufficient. If not, the maintainer must change the implementation. Replacement would thus be feasible without affecting other services and would only require modifications to the integration service. It would even be conceivable that no mapping to a context-identifying characteristic would be performed, in which case the data streams would only be available to the processing services under the device and source identifiers. In this case, the exchange of a device would influence all services related to the data streams. An independent deployment would not be possible.

Related to WIM, the maintainer must modify the data model via the configuration backend. Here a new device must be configured and linked to the original context. As in the previous scenario, the integration service would make a request to the CIM with characteristics of the device as usual and thus receive the transformation information. No changes to the services are required.

Scenario: Modification of the Device Context. In addition to replacing devices, we assume the possibility of changing the associated context. This context modification happens, for example, when measuring installations change their point of use. In the example in Fig. 4, a smart meter could be assigned to a new tenant.

In WOM case, it is required to adjust the enrichment via a configuration, if any exists, or to modify the implementation, as in the scenario of Sect. 5. Similarly, if no context identifying characteristic is transported in the data stream, repositioning the device would affect all services involved in the processing process. At least one service would have to be adapted, in extreme cases several, to apply the changes across the processing chain.

Concerning WIM, it would be necessary to modify the linking via the data model. Requests against CIM using identifying features of the device would subsequently lead to new transformation information. The integration or processing services do not have to be adjusted. The changes can be made without affecting the system execution.

Scenario: Implementation of a New Data Stream Processor. This scenario describes adding a new processing service. The example in Fig. 4 shows an aggregation service that aggregates the consumption generated by charge points over a defined time window. For this purpose, the *Consumer* consumes assigned data streams (see Fig. 5), and publishes new assigned data streams with the original context.

In the case of WOM, this requires a connection to the data stream via a message-based middleware. The events have to be filtered according to the conditions, for future modifications the filter is to be realized configurable. The resulting data streams that result from the aggregation have to be published in the message-based middleware. The decision must be made as to how the context of the incoming data stream applies to the outgoing data stream. The development and deployment of the processing service is possible independently of other services. However, it must be provided in the implementation how, if necessary, changing incoming and outgoing data stream descriptions can be adjusted to meet future requirements.

Regarding the WIM scenario, a query against the CIM is necessary. For example, a specific consumer can be queried with *Consumer[name= "charger01"]*. The result would contain all metrics related to this context. By configuring the metrics to be processed, requesting services can limit the selection. Further, another query has to be made to get the resulting metrics. Here, each key (see Sect. 4) describes a possible aggregation result. Our example of an aggregation service can calculate the *sum, max* and *min* and *average* (also keys) from the input metric over a definable time window. Using *sum, max* and *min* and *average*, the mapping to the parameter to be determined can be realized, and a similar event can be generated. The use of the central CIM allows independent service development and deployment.

6   Experiences and Lesson Learned

The CIM is available as a single microservice and can be integrated into measurement and processing infrastructures. The implementation is available as an open-source project[1], can be integrated into existing infrastructures and allows the adaptation of integration and processing services to use the CIM service.

The service was realized as part of our project work to implement a measurement and processing infrastructure for a local smart grid in a dense area. This setup includes local energy production, energy supply for tenants, car-sharing with electric vehicles, private and public charging infrastructure as well as the optimization of the overall system to maximize the use of renewable energies, which means the reduction of energy consumption from the upper-level power grid. The entire architecture comprises multiple services to realize integration, processing, optimization, persistence and visualization. The CIM service enables the independent development of individual services and easier adoption to changing technical settings. The context information management service avoids implicit shared knowledge between the individual integration and processing services of the infrastructure. Some experiences gained from applying this CIM approach and the service adoption into our infrastructure is presented below.

Integration services using the CIM service demonstrate lower maintenance and the ability to manage relationships between data sources and context externally. Even if the initial development costs and the technical complexity of the services increase, the advantages outweigh the disadvantages in the long run. Existing, implicit dependencies are brought to the surface and are made explicit.

---

[1] https://github.com/winner-potential/masterdata

Previously scattered knowledge is brought together in one place, making it easier to maintain.

A declarative data model that can be adapted at runtime instead of a fixed programmed explicit one increases flexibility and speed of adaptation. This is particularly valuable for development and proof-of-concept setups. On the other side, adopting this concept requires a lot of abstraction skills and understanding of meta-models. This can be a challenge when working with undergraduates.

Runtime performance was not a critical aspect when using the CIM service in our setting. There are two ways to integrate this CIM service into other services. First, queries are formulated for each incoming information during the integration processing as on-demand requests. Secondly, build up a local cache by caching responses or requesting mappings in advance, and update this cache at regular intervals. Combining authentication and query, our current setup results in about 100 ms for processing two HTTPS-based REST-API requests. With caching enabled the effect on the throughput of the data stream processing was negligible.

The implementation of the query and caching mechanisms in each microservice results in a lot of duplicate code. So by implementing a client library that can be used in the services, the usage of a CIM service becomes more convenient to the development team.

The development environment requires an endpoint to handle the requests for the service to be implemented. Developers' unawareness of an expected instance of the data model could be a hurdle in the development. This hurdle has to be compensated with clean project setups that provide a ready-to-run dev environment and thus create a usable instance of the data model - as this is true for all development of distributed systems.

Further, information from the CIM service could be used, e.g., to produce visualizations of data streams for end users. With the dynamic data model, the capability of referencing documents to each other and the navigation by the query language, it is possible to implement further dynamic application scenarios.

7   Discussion

The resulting context information management enables the data stream related knowledge. In the following, we will discuss the results in the context of fail-safety, alternative approaches and processing services.

Using a context information management, integration and processing services can make use of shared knowledge and incorporate it into their processing logic. In this way, the dispersion of knowledge and reliance on implicit assumptions can be avoided. One risk that arises with this approach is the "single point of failure". In our view, this problem can be reduced by setting up the service redundantly, which increases reliability. The knowledge itself is usually not subject to constant changes, so using local caches reduce this failure risk even more. In our case, information was added or changed quite irregularly. This happened, for example, when new measuring devices were installed or new services for integration or processing were added. In addition, if the query results were appropriately saved, the entire system would be able to continue working if the knowledge base fails. The service can usually be used in such a way that the latest queries are valid as long as no new query can be executed.

Besides the reliability and the single point of failure, the discussion about the differentiation of service configuration and knowledge management is interesting. During the model design and the web service implementation, it was discussed whether the knowledge could be transferred to each service via a specific configuration. In principle, if the configuration is provided in a structured and universal way for all services, the answer would be yes. In that case, a structuring of the configuration would have taken place, which in our case would be fundamentally similar to the model presented. The result would be a centralized configuration file that all services use with a permanent structure. Thus, the presented approach would be equivalent.

An alternative approach would be to embed knowledge in individual configurations of individual services. In this case, we slide into the problematic situation outlined at the beginning. Knowledge management must take place along the configuration chain of each service implicitly. If a name or an identifier of a measured value changes, all related services are affected.

The last point of discussion concerns processing services. During implementation and application, it becomes apparent that the use of the knowledge base seems possible with the theoretical approach. Our practical implementation and application show that the use of a knowledge base based on the presented approach is feasible. To extend the usefulness, however, an extension of the query language is conceivable if necessary, for example, to request even more precise addressing of documents or metrics of a document.

8   Conclusion

Measurement and processing infrastructures implemented with a microservice architecture contains loosely coupled services that realize integration, processing, visualization and persistence tasks. Due to the increasing number of implicit shared knowledge resulting from the meaning of the measured values, the independent development of individual services was not ensured. For the design of clear responsibilities and dependencies, a service for the management of context information for data streams was implemented in the measurement and processing infrastructure and discussed through frequently occurring scenarios in this domain. As shown in different scenarios and our practical experience, we are therefore able to design integration services that understand the domain-specific language of the services to be integrated, have a deep understanding of the knowledge management service, and bring the information from both sources together. The context of a measured value that enters the system in this way is no longer decided in the service itself.

Additionally, downstream processing services can make use of the same knowledge and realize processing such as aggregations or predictions. This approach reduces coupling between the processing and integration services. Through clean management of knowledge and separation of sources and contexts, even the exchange of measuring instruments is possible without modifying services related to the data streams. Through this management of context information and architectural decisions, we were able to sharpen the microservice principles in the case of application and ensure the independent development of individual services.

References

1. Microsoft azure IoT reference architecture (2018)
2. Al-Fuqaha, A., Guizani, M., Mohammadi, M., Aledhari, M., Ayyash, M.: Internet of things: a survey on enabling technologies, protocols, and applications. IEEE Commun. Surv. Tutor. **17**(4), 2347–2376 (2015). https://doi.org/10.1109/COMST. 2015.2444095. ISSN 1553–877X
3. Apel, S., Hertrampf, F., Späthe, S.: Microservice architecture within in-house infrastructures for enterprise integration and measurement: an experience report. In: Hodoň, M., Eichler, G., Erfurth, C., Fahrnberger, G. (eds.) I4CS 2018. CCIS, vol. 863, pp. 3–17. Springer, Cham (2018). https://doi.org/10.1007/978-3-319-93408-2_1
4. Bader, A.: Comparison of Time Series Databases. Diplomarbeit, Institute of Parallel and Distributed Systems, University of Stuttgart, Stuttgart (2016)
5. Bauer, M., et al.: IoT reference architecture. In: Enabling Things to Talk, pp. 163–211, Springer, Berlin, Heidelberg (2013). https://doi.org/10.1007/978-3-642-40403-0_8
6. Brundu, F.G., et al.: IoT software infrastructure for energy management and simulation in smart cities. IEEE Trans. Ind. Inf. **13**(2), 832–840 (2017). https://doi.org/10.1109/TII.2016.2627479. ISSN 1551–3203
7. Chen, R., Li, S., Li, Z.: From monolith to microservices: a dataflow-driven approach. In: 2017 24th Asia-Pacific Software Engineering Conference (APSEC), pp. 466–475, December 2017. https://doi.org/10.1109/APSEC.2017.53
8. Choudhary, G., Jain, A.K.: Internet of things: A survey on architecture, technologies, protocols and challenges. In: 2016 International Conference on Recent Advances and Innovations in Engineering (ICRAIE), pp. 1–8, December 2016. https://doi.org/10.1109/ICRAIE.2016.7939537. ISSN 5090–2806
9. Diepenbrock, A., Rademacher, F., Sachweh, S.: An ontology-based approach for domain-driven design of microservice architectures. In: Eibl, M., Gaedke, M. (eds.) INFORMATIK 2017, pp. 1777–1791. Gesellschaft für Informatik, Bonn (2017)
10. George, F.: Micro-service architecture, talk at Barcelona Ruby Conference (2012)
11. International Electrotechnical Commision: OPC unified architecture - part 1: Overview and concepts, IEC TR 62541–1 (2016)
12. Krčo, S., Pokrić, B., Carrez, F.: Designing IoT architecture(s): a European perspective. In: 2014 IEEE World Forum on Internet of Things (WF-IoT), pp. 79–84, March 2014. https://doi.org/10.1109/WF-IoT.2014.6803124
13. Krylovskiy, A., Jahn, M., Patti, E.: Designing a smart city internet of things platform with microservice architecture. In: 2015 3rd International Conference on Future Internet of Things and Cloud, pp. 25–30, August 2015. https://doi.org/10.1109/FiCloud.2015.55
14. Lewis, J.: Micro services - java, the unix way, talk at 33rd Degree Conference (2012)

15. Luckham, D.: The Power of Events - An Introduction to Complex Event Processing. Addison-Wesley, 2nd (edn.) (2002)
16. Newman, S.: Building Microservices. O'Reilly Media (2015). ISBN 978-1491950357
17. Robie, J., Dyck, M., Spiegel, J.: XML path language (XPath) 3.1. W3C recommendation, W3C, March 2017. https://www.w3.org/TR/2017/REC-xpath-31-20170321/
18. Vianden, M., Lichter, H., Steffens, A.: Towards a maintainable federalist enterprise measurement infrastructure. In: 2013 Joint Conference of the 23rd International Workshop on Software Measurement and the 8th International Conference on Software Process and Product Measurement, pp. 63–70, October 2013. https://doi.org/10.1109/IWSM-Mensura.2013.20
19. Vianden, M., Lichter, H., Steffens, A.: Experience on a microservice-based reference architecture for measurement systems. In: 2014 21st Asia-Pacific Software Engineering Conference, vol. 1, pp. 183–190, December 2014. https://doi.org/10.1109/APSEC.2014.37, ISSN 1530–1362
20. Wolff, E.: Microservices: Flexible Software Architectures. Addison-Wesley (2016). ISBN 978-0134602417
21. Yang, Z., Yue, Y., Yang, Y., Peng, Y., Wang, X., Liu, W.: Study and application on the architecture and key technologies for IOT. In: 2011 International Conference on Multimedia Technology, pp. 747–751, July 2011. https://doi.org/10.1109/ICMT.2011.6002149
22. Zanella, A., Bui, N., Castellani, A., Vangelista, L., Zorzi, M.: Internet of things for smart cities. IEEE Internet Things J. 1(1), 22–32 (2014). https://doi.org/10.1109/JIOT.2014.2306328. ISSN 2327-4662
23. Zimmermann, O.: Microservices tenets. Comput. Sci. Res. Develop. 32(3), 301–310 (2017). https://doi.org/10.1007/s00450-016-0337-0. ISSN 1865-2042

A Web Architecture for E-Health Applications Supporting the Efficient Multipath Transport of Medical Images

Kibriya Inamdar, Oormila Ramanandan Kottayi Pilapprathodi, Jopaul John, Markus Wolff, Marcel Großmann, and Udo R. Krieger[✉]

Fakultät WIAI, Otto-Friedrich-Universität,
An der Weberei 5, 96047 Bamberg, Germany
udo.krieger@ieee.org

Abstract. New advanced e-health applications are required to support the effective processing of diagnostic and therapeutic healthcare protocols in modern societies. Looking at the work flow handled by the consulted medical staff in the first level of a medical treatment chain such as family doctors, an effective treatment usually requires the processing of pre-recorded medical images of a patient during the first diagnostic phase. We consider the development of a Web server architecture that offers the transport of medical images by an Android application and illustrate its design by a realized PACS prototype. The effective data transport of medical images is realized by a multipath-QUIC protocol which is integrated into a DICOM proxy server. Its further development can integrate other fog computing systems which support additional interconnected e-health applications employed by a consortium of users in a medical treatment process.

Keywords: e-Health · DICOM · Android applications · Multipath-QUIC

1 Introduction

Nowadays, new advanced e-health applications are required to support the effective processing of diagnostic and therapeutic healthcare protocols in a modern society as the pandemic has recently shown. Looking at the work flow handled by the medical staff in the first level of a medical treatment chain such as family doctors, an effective treatment usually requires the processing of pre-recorded CT and/or MRT images of a sick person during the first diagnostic phase. These applications provide an important domain within the rapidly evolving Internet-of-things and the related cloud and fog computing concepts, cf. [1,14].

Considering a single patient, this set of digital medical images such as X-rays, CTs, MRTs, PETs and others is generated during a first diagnostic phase within a radiological analysis department by sophisticated imaging devices [24]. The latter produce these images in a standardized format based on the Digital

© The Author(s), under exclusive license to Springer Nature Switzerland AG 2022
F. Phillipson et al. (Eds.): I4CS 2022, CCIS 1585, pp. 136–152, 2022.
https://doi.org/10.1007/978-3-031-06668-9_11

Imaging and Communications in Medicine (DICOM) standard [21]. This NEMA standard describes numerous details about the structure, storage, and transport of such medical images and their corresponding data files. The number of these medical images is increasing rapidly, promoting the need to upgrade both storage and retrieval systems [4, 16, 25]. Normally, a recorded set of DICOM compatible images contains additionally a lot of medical metadata and information on the collection of these images, i.e., a patient's image set is normally quite large and commonly its size is more than 100 MB as it may contain more than 100 images.

The DICOM format [21] ensures that medical images comply with high quality standards which allow a precise diagnosis and interpretation. Using teleradiology, in principle these images can be sent by different methods from one location to another one. As these images are large in size and number regarding a single patient, it is difficult to transmit such a large amount of medical data along existing communication networks with relatively low bandwidth, in particular along the last link, if it is a wireless one. Considering the data transfer between medical units at different sites in a standard treatment process, for this reason the images are often transferred by means of storage devices such as DVDs. Even in today's modern Internet environment incorporating wired and wireless network infrastructures this handling is still a day-by-day standard.

Experiments of loading such a DICOM image set via a cellular network into a Web application that is using a browser with Android OS [12] show that the actual loading time is rather high. The resulting latency to depict such a DICOM image by a Web browser rendering the transferred medical data generates an intolerable delay in the view of medical professionals. The latter personnel normally needs these images instantly when they are examining and giving advice to a treated patient. Hence, the efficient transfer of requested DICOM compatible images from a remote storage server to a potentially mobile Web client at the distant treatment site constitutes a serious technical problem as the medical staff can only provide a very limited time slice for each patient. Hence, the current way of transferring DICOM compatible images by client-server oriented, Web based e-health applications using a standard HTTP protocol stack is impractical and requires effective improvements of the related protocols.

In our study we have developed a Web based image retrieval architecture for a requested medical image set. It uses an Android based client to retrieve and render a remotely requested series of DICOM compatible images. Our architecture incorporates a standard Orthanc server [16] storing these medical images. Considering the image transport along the Internet, we apply the new multipath-QUIC transport protocol [5]. The latter is enhancing the well established Quick UDP Internet Connection (QUIC) protocol [15]. It has been designed to support transport and session services for HTTP similar to TCP with TLS on top of UDP. Multipath-QUIC [5] has the ability to exploit different paths which exist between a sender and a receiver and provides bandwidth aggregation and a seamless network failover. We use an existing implementation of multipath-QUIC by the programming language Go [11]. The client side of the e-health application has been developed using Android [12]. The latter is a popular open source software system based on Linux and primarily designed for touch screen mobile devices such as smartphones and tablets. The DICOM server side of our Web application has been developed using Python [22]. Using Go, we have built and integrated the required multipath-QUIC client and multipath-QUIC server with the developed client-server based Picture Archiving and Communication System (PACS) architecture to transfer the DICOM compatible images.

The paper is organized as follows. In Sect. 2 we present the foundations of digital imaging and communication techniques for e-health applications based on the current medical standard DICOM. In Sect. 3 we describe an enhanced PACS architecture for the medical image transfers using a proxy server that is interconnected with a DICOM cloud infrastructure. In Sect. 4 we discuss our versatile Web-server architecture for the efficient multipath transport of medical images to an e-health app. Finally, some conclusions are presented.

2   Foundations of Digital Imaging and Communication Techniques for e-Health Applications

Nowadays, digital images are generated in medical applications during a diagnostic investigation by sophisticated technical devices. The latter imaging systems generate the required medical images of high resolution such as X-rays, CTs, MRTs, and PETs, in a standardized image format, cf. [24]. It is normally based on NEMA's Digital Imaging and Communications in Medicine (DICOM) standard [21]. This NEMA standard which partly overlaps with other areas of medical informatics has been developed with an emphasis on diagnostic medical imaging as practiced in radiology, cardiology, pathology, dentistry, and ophthalmology. It is used in image based therapies such as interventional radiology, radiotherapy, and surgery, cf. [16]. It primarily facilitates the interoperability of Picture Archiving and Communication Systems (PACS) claiming a DICOM conformance in a multi-vendor environment. However, DICOM by itself does not guarantee this interoperability in a straightforward manner in all use cases [21]. However, the DICOM technology and its related tools are also applicable to a much wider range of image and non-image related information exchange processes needed in today's clinical infrastructures, veterinary, and medical research.

2.1   The Scope of the Medical Imaging Standard DICOM

Regarding the handling of medical images, DICOM [21] is currently the major global standard. It covers the processing, communication, and management of medical images and their related metadata. In particular, DICOM facilitates the interoperability of medical image processing equipment by specifying

- a set of processing, viewing, and networking protocols followed by those image generating devices claiming a DICOM conformance,
- the syntax and semantics of commands and associated information that can be exchanged by these DICOM protocols,

- a set of media storage services obeyed by those DICOM compatible systems, as well as a file format and a medical directory structure to facilitate the access to these images and related meta information stored at DICOM servers,
- and additional information which must be supplied with an implementation if DICOM conformance is claimed.

However, the DICOM standard does not specify

- the implementation details of any standard feature in a DICOM compatible system,
- the overall set of features and functions expected from a Picture Archiving and Communication System, which is implemented by an integration of a group of DICOM compatible devices,
- a testing and validation procedure to assess an implementation's conformance to the DICOM standard.

These shortcomings are handled by additional software systems and processes which have been developed by equipment providers and software developers in the last decades. In our current research perspective we shall focus on a lightweight, open source software development regarding this PACS/DICOM environment, cf. [16,17].

2.2 Objectives and Use Cases of a Medical Image Transfer

Medical professionals normally want to request and display the recorded medical images of a patient during a consultation phase in a timely manner without any significant delays or waiting times regarding the image rendering by an app. In this way, they are able to give their patients a fast, accurate diagnosis. Normal use cases include scenarios where a medical professional wants

- to retrieve relevant DICOM compatible images via standard end devices, e.g. a laptop, an Android tablet or even Android phone,
- to be able to search for DICOM images using a unique image identifier of a patient, the *PatientID*, on a server storing these images,
- to zoom into a specific DICOM image such that one can see specific details or get a general overview on the image,
- to use a medical Web application supported either by a wired in-house communication network or WiFi network, or by both types.

The DICOM protocol inherently targets primarily the intranet of a single hospital, not the Internet or the cloud. Thus, its protocols may be blocked by an outbound firewall. Furthermore, although the DICOM data exchange protocol supports TLS encryption, this feature is rarely enabled. Depending on the type of an e-health application, one can, of course, leverage the HTTP protocol in this context. Such Web-based protocols are easier to work with, can be transparently encrypted by HTTPS, and are compatible with a multiple-hospital scenario.

Regarding the processed DICOM objects of a medical study stored at a DICOM server like Orthanc [16,17], the diagram depicted in Fig. 1 illustrates the hierarchy of a patient's data set. Each study includes a set of a series of medical images. Each series is in turn a set of image instances, where the latter is a synonym for a single DICOM compatible file. The DICOM standard arranges the associated identifiers *StudyInstanceUID*, *SeriesInstanceUID* and *SOPInstanceUID* to be globally unique. Thus, it is mandatory for two different image generating devices not to generate the same identifiers, even if they are manufactured by different vendors. An Orthanc server exploits this rule to derive its own unique identifiers.

However, even if the *PatientID* must be a unique index within a given hospital, it is not guaranteed to be globally unique. This means that different patients' image recordings at different hospitals might share the same *PatientID*.

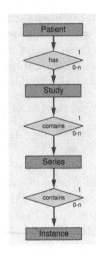

Fig. 1. Data hierarchy of a DICOM object (cf. [21])

A recorded collection of DICOM compatible images contains a lot of medical information about a specific patient's physical state and additional metadata. Such a patient's image set is normally large and commonly sized more than 100 MB as it may contain more than 100 images. Currently, loading such an image set along a communication network between a PACS server storing the required data and a client retrieving the latter reveals that the actual downloading period may be quite high. Medical professionals need these images instantly when they are examining a patient and giving advice. Thus, an experienced high latency may constitute a severe QoE problem as there is only very limited time for each patient during a medical consultation. Therefore, it can be concluded that the current way of transferring DICOM images by means of a standard client-server architecture employing a HTTP-TCP protocol stack is not a very practical approach and may not be effective by itself.

3 An Enhanced PACS Architecture for the Transfer of Medical Images

A classical Picture Archiving and Communication System (PACS) for medical images and their related e-health applications normally incorporates a client-server model. The PACS services include an easy access to a patient's reports and images, enhanced analysis viewing, and a chronological data management, among other functions. Such a PACS environment should be both user friendly and developer friendly. Examples of a PACS server include DCM4CHE and Orthanc, among others, cf. [16,17]. Examples of PACS clients are provided by 3D Slicer, Horos, DWV, and others, cf. [9].

In our approach we first follow the distributed image processing concept of Jodogne [16,17] and enhance a standard PACS by a proxy server and a client-centric improvement of its medical imaging application to manage the required image transfer to a mobile device more efficiently, see Fig. 2.

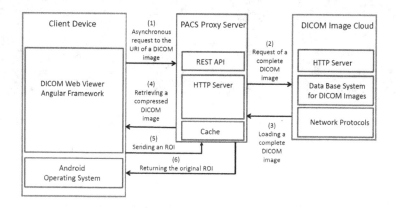

Fig. 2. An enhanced PACS architecture for the medical image transfer

The mobile client with such a new designed Web application embedded into Android can request the image data from the used Orthanc proxy server (1) using its REST API as interface. We can store these medical images that are retrieved from an attached cloud server or an interconnected DICOM image server infrastructure in the cloud (2, 3) by means of the DICOM network protocols in the cache of this proxy server. The latter can also change the format, split images into smaller blocks, the tiles, and compress those parts, cf. [16,18,21]. Then the proxy can handle related retrievals from its cache and reply to compressed image requests of a client (4) which are invoked by such an initial lightweight request (1) for an object of interest (ROI). On a user's ROI enquiry to show the full sized DICOM format of an image block, the proxy can also deliver this larger original object (6) from the cache (see Figs. 4, 5).

Similar to Jodogne's approach [16], our distributed DICOM system offers in this way some specific PACS proxy services regarding stored DICOM objects, and arranges the image access of the mobile client on top of Android to the specified DICOM proxy server as well as the related data transport more effectively than a classical PACS model.

Considering Web viewers and visualization tools for DICOM images, the DICOM Web Viewer (DWV) [9] is a widely adopted standard open source PACS client that can be used as Web based DICOM image viewer. Its advantage is that it accepts files both in a DICOM file format *.dcm* and a *.jpeg* format. Moreover, it has some advanced functions, e.g., paning, that allows the user to zoom into the images, draw, which is used to plot a line from one point to another one in a DICOM image (-these lines can be labelled and classified using titles

142   K. Inamdar et al.

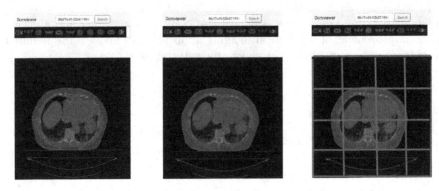

Fig. 3. Compressed version of the image in the Android app

Fig. 4. Original version of the image in the Android app

Fig. 5. Conceptional view on tiles splitting of an image in the Android app

and can be used for distance measurements in an image-), and window/level-windowing, also known as grey-level mapping, contrast stretching, histogram modification or contrast enhancement. It determines a process in which a CT image greyscale component of a DICOM image is manipulated via incorporated CT numbers. Performing this manipulation will change the appearance of the picture to highlight particular structures [24]. The window level is usually measured in Hounsfield units [20].

The widely adopted DWV-Angular [10] is a Web package based DICOM viewer that inherits these functionalities. As it is written in Angular CLI [2], it can be adopted by many popular operating systems for smart devices like Android [12] and iOS due to the availability of advanced Web browsers on top of these operating systems. We have used this Web programming and application framework for the Android app to realize a first prototype of the mobile client for a DICOM image retrieval in the described enhanced PACS model shown in Fig. 2.

Regarding this enhanced PACS architecture, the client uses this Android app as Web API to access the proxy server and employs unique predefined URIs as basic reference to the images and their tiles (see Figs. 3, 4 and 5). In Fig. 3 we show a compressed version of such a DICOM image. In our approach the images are displayed as 4 × 4 up to 7 × 7 grid in a tile structure using the Grid Layout Manager and Recycler View in Android. Whenever a particular region of an image area is selected in the compressed picture, the corresponding original image part is automatically loaded. Figure 4 shows the original version of the fully loaded DICOM image arising from that one in Fig. 3.

The image data are specified in terms of sub-blocks of a DICOM instance, called tiles (see Fig. 5), that are encoded as separate subframes. The latter are split up at the proxy server and transferred as compressed tiles to the client after they were requested by the Web application encoded by Angular. It is embedded within the Android application to support the use cases of mobile users. There the tiles are represented as a matrix of HTML canvases. Each canvas gets a binding to a click event in our JavaScript code. Such a click, when fired, triggers a related JavaScript method that identifies the particular canvas and loads the corresponding original tile from the proxy server. Thus, tiles without useful information don't require to be loaded what can reduce the bandwidth demand. In this manner, we could save between 25% up to 39% of the transport bandwidth for the considered 4×4 and 7×7 grid structured images in some studied cases.

However, in this first client-centric PACS realization the data are sent along a TCP transport layer which can potentially cause long transfer times and high end-to-end latency. Considering the actors like doctors, these long waiting times provide a bad user experience and cause a loss of productivity. As doctors are likely to have an adequate number of patients during their daily medical round, it is essential that they can request these DICOM images associated with a patient at hand in a fast way. It may not always be possible to achieve this goal so easily using the sketched transport architecture of the PACS proxy.

4   A Versatile Web-Server Architecture for the Efficient Multipath Transport of Medical Images

Considering the DICOM proxy architecture for new e-health applications running on top of a client-server micro-service model, it is our key objective to present a server-centric extension of the sketched PACS model and its proof-of-concept realization in this section. This improvement is achieved by integrating a more efficient transport protocol stack. Therefore, the new design can support the use of mobile Web applications of medical professionals in local treatment units more efficiently. As before, the latter personnel is assumed to require the retrieval and transport of medical images stored in an associated accessible DICOM server in a cloud as quickly as possible.

The associated Web server system comprises local clients running Android apps that get access to a DICOM proxy server. The latter issues retrieval requests to a PACS image server like Orthanc storing medical data in conformance with the DICOM standard, see Fig. 6. The task of this extended DICOM proxy server, now implemented by Python [22], is to handle the DICOM requests from the client side and to process and save the requested DICOM files retrieved from a remote DICOM server or DICOM cloud. Then the latter image data are transferred as retrieval response back to the clients.

4.1   The Transport of Medical Data Along a Multipath-QUIC Route

Normally, a client-server architecture for Web applications applies a standard protocol stack employing a HTTP/1.1 or HTTP/2.0 application protocol on top of TCP as transport protocol. Recently, the transition to HTTP/3.0 has been

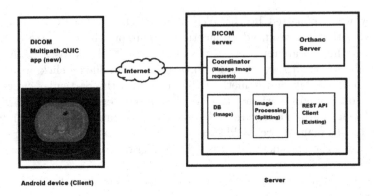

Fig. 6. Client-server architecture of the DICOM system enhanced by a multipath transport protocol

prepared which offers the use of QUIC as enhanced version of a UDP transport protocol with additional flow and congestion control functionalities [11,15], see Fig. 7.

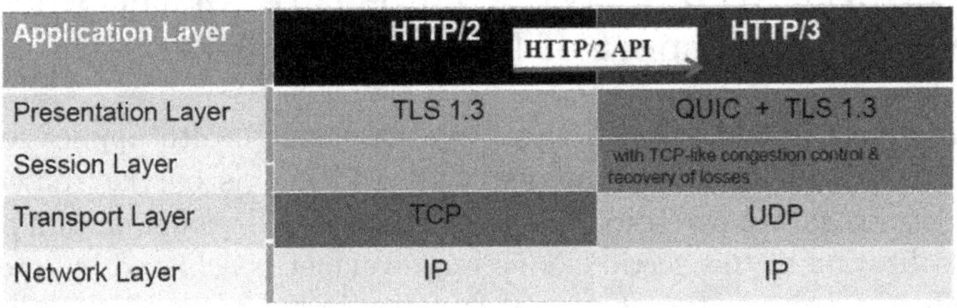

Application Layer	HTTP/2	HTTP/2 API	HTTP/3
Presentation Layer	TLS 1.3		QUIC + TLS 1.3
Session Layer			with TCP-like congestion control & recovery of losses
Transport Layer	TCP		UDP
Network Layer	IP		IP

Fig. 7. HTTP/2.0 and HTTP/3.0 architectures of a communication system with TCP or QUIC based data transport

However, it is to be expected that either communication stack cannot provide the transport performance that is required for an efficient, mobile e-health application with retrieved medical image data. Therefore, one may consider existing multipath variants of the TCP or QUIC protocols at the transport layer [5]. The objective of our advanced server-centric PACS architecture is to mitigate these transport problems by improving the data transfer of DICOM images over a communication network. As QUIC is derived from the lightweight UDP protocol and more efficient than TCP, we have determined to integrate the multipath-QUIC (MPQUIC) protocol for the data transport of medical images in e-health applications. The related transport protocol stack is depicted in Fig. 8.

Multipath-QUIC [5] is basically a natural extension of the QUIC protocol at the transport and session layers. QUIC [15] achieves already performances improvements compared to TCP. Additional improvements are gained by the concept to multiplex several QUIC/UDP connections introducing an adequate

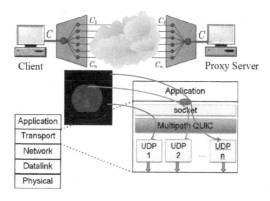

Fig. 8. Multipath-QUIC transport protocol stack (see also [5])

session functionality, cf. Fig. 8. By multipath-QUIC the medical data can now be transferred simultaneously along $n > 1$ established paths with their capacities $C_1, \cdots, C_n$. This scheme has several advantages including the aggregation of the bandwidth $C = \sum_{i=1}^{n} C_i$, failure resiliency and an easier failover in the case when one part of the underlying network fails. Given all these benefits, it is also quite likely that it can effectively support a DICOM image transfer scenario both reducing latency and improving the throughput.

Therefore, it is the objective of this second part of our proof-of-concept PACS study to produce a working prototype of a DICOM proxy server architecture with a multipath-QUIC component regarding the data transfer of sliced DICOM compatible images. Regarding the overall client-server architecture of the realized Web application, we have developed a new transport service using the programming language Python. It consists of DICOM related functionalities, like the communication with the Orthanc background server that stores the retrieved medical images, cf. [16]. Furthermore, the functionality to split up DICOM images into smaller tiles as well as certain caching functions have been provided as before, see Sect. 3. These basic functions are required for an effective transport of the large medical data sets along a pre-established multipath-QUIC route between the Python-server as DICOM proxy endpoint and an Android client retrieving these DICOM files, see Fig. 6.

Compared to the client-centric PACS model shown in Fig. 2, this new server-centric prototype consists of an extended native Android e-health application, which implements a multipath-QUIC client. It requests the data of a DICOM image from the corresponding multipath-QUIC endpoint in the proxy server. The latter is based on a server application written in Python which contains the sketched image processing functionality, like compressing the images and splitting them up into tiles, etc. It also interfaces with the associated Orthanc server which stores and manages the DICOM images in the background. An overview of this new client-server architecture with its multipath-QUIC stack is depicted in Fig. 9.

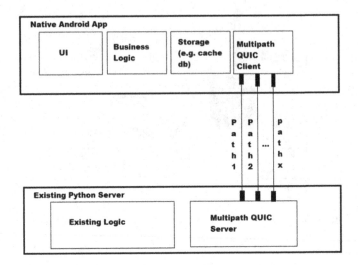

Fig. 9. Multipath-QUIC architecture of the communication subsystem

Regarding the new transport architecture, multipath-QUIC is not implemented from scratch, but an already existing implementation [5,11] in the programming language Go has been used. It can be accessed by Python ctypes [23]. First, a library from the multipath-QUIC Go code has been created in C-shared mode. When the code is executed for the first time after the start of the Python server application initiated by the client's request, then a listener of the multipath-QUIC server is spinned up, see Fig. 9. Thereafter and whenever an additional request arrives, a method to transfer the data to the multipath-QUIC client is executed.

In order to verify whether it is feasible to use this favoured approach identified during our analysis phase, i.e., basing the implementation of the data transport onto the existing multipath-QUIC Go code as proof-of-concept, the sketched approach has been assimilated with the previous enhanced PACS model of Fig. 2. To integrate the DICOM server application and the multipath-QUIC functionality at the transport layer, a coordinator component has been realized. It provides the interface between the existing functionality of the application and transport layers and processes the retrieval requests in such a way that a retrieved DICOM image can be transferred along an established multipath-QUIC route. Furthermore, the coordinator can check whether the requested image tiles of a requested DICOM image are already in the server's local transport buffer. In this case, the multipath-QUIC sender can use these elements. The associated Orthanc storage server is only contacted, if the required images are not locally available. This policy can save unnecessary round trips and, thus, further improve the transport performance of requested medical data sets. This implementation verifies the possibility to actually access the sketched network protocol stack by the Go code, which is then called via the Android application and the Python server application. The prototype proves the feasibility of our advanced transport concept. Hence, the selected PACS/DICOM design approach can be used with the multipath-QUIC Go-implementation in the sketched e-health scenarios.

Moreover, we have figured out that the multipath-QUIC protocol can provide large benefits. As it is assumed that the Orthanc server and the DICOM proxy server are either located on the same machine or being connected by a high-speed network, it is sufficient to limit the usage of multipath-QUIC to the corresponding connection between the Android e-health application and the Python-proxy server in our new design.

4.2   Functionality of the DICOM Proxy Server

The major task of the DICOM proxy server in the PACS architecture of Fig. 6 is to handle the retrieval requests invoked at the client side, to process and to store the corresponding DICOM objects that are actually retrieved from the DICOM server realized by Orthanc and, finally, to respond to the client's request by transferring the appropriate DICOM objects.

If a DICOM object is not available in the cache of the proxy server, it is retrieved at the associated Orthanc server side or a cluster of DICOM servers. After retrieving the DICOM compliant object in a byte format from the Orthanc server, it is the proxy server's main job to convert splitted DICOM images into a *.jpeg* format and to compress them afterwards (see also [18]). Then the proxy server can handle the consecutive requests from the client side regarding the original DICOM images or their optional resizing.

The image retrieval process works as follows. Whenever the proxy server receives a client's request with a specified patient identifier *PatientID*, the server checks if the *PatientID* key is present in its local database. If it is present there, the associated data can be sent back to the client. However, if the *PatientID* key is not found in the cache, the proxy server has to load the requested object from the associated Orthanc server. The latter server then provides the required DICOM file set.

Considering the implementation of the described system, the main functionalities at the proxy server side comprise the following functions:

1. to split the images into tiles with a specified $n * n$-format, $n \in \{4, \dots, 7\}$,
2. to save the processed image and its compressed tiles into a related database as local cache site, and
3. to prepare the transfer of the corresponding objects to the requesting client.

Regarding the implementation, the general-purpose programming language Python [22] has been used since it can be easily customized to the used Web frameworks and apps to build the designed Web server system with the proper tools and libraries such as Django [6] or Flask [27]. In particular, the Django REST-framework [7] which combines Django with a REST architecture [8] has been used. This approach can easily help to separate the client and server sides and, in turn, supports the portability and scalability of the designed architecture.

After the proxy server has downloaded the required DICOM files from the Orthanc server, it converts these DICOM files into corresponding files with a *.jpeg*-format to prepare their further transport. Regarding our implementation these image files in *.jpeg*-format are compressed with the help of the Python package Pillow (PIL) [3]. As PIL does a lossy *.jpeg*-compression, the image size is drastically reduced. For instance, a DICOM file with a size of 80 MB is reduced to 7 MB during such a *.jpeg*-conversion. These compressed image blocks are then ready for a fast client access and can be transferred to the client side by the applied multipath-QUIC transport protocol stack of the Web server architecture.

When the client selects any of these received images for viewing, the *.jpeg*-compliant image is loaded into the user's app. This transmission approach saves a large amount of bandwidth and reduces the latency time of a response to the medical object request. For this purpose the image is divided into multiple subparts, i.e., the tiles, on which the compression has been performed. When the client send the first request, the lowest resolution files are returned. Once the user clicks on any of the thumbnail images the better version of the still compressed *.jpeg*-tiles are sent back. Now if the user wants to see the original image of any part, he/she can simply click on the particular part and the corresponding original tile is finally transferred back to the client.

4.3   Client Realization by a Multipath Compatible Android App

Regarding the developed client-server architecture for the DICOM image retrieval and transfer in Fig. 6, the new client side has been developed using an Android system [12] and the programming language Go [19]. This selection is reasonable for the described e-health scenarios since Android is a versatile open source, Linux based software system designed for mobile touch screen devices such as smartphones and tablets. Regarding the development of an Android app, one can implement it by the Angular [2] framework and further embedded the Angular application as WebView into the Android system as shown in Sect. 3. However, this approach cannot be used in combination with multipath-QUIC, as Angular [2] applications are a subset of JavaScript applications which, in general, cannot access the networking stack of a browser directly. But such an access scheme would be necessary to use the developed multipath-QUIC API.

Therefore, it has been necessary to implement a completely new native Android application compared to the previous one of Sect. 3. To support multipath-QUIC, two possible approaches have been identified: either to use the existing multipath-QUIC implementation [5,11] in the language Go, which might be the simplest solution, or to use the Cronet library applied by Chromium on Android [13]. In the first case, one needs to check whether the Go code is able to access the used Android network stack. In conclusion, accessing the network layer functionality is no problem at all. However, as Cronet has only implemented QUIC (cf. [11,13]), but not multipath-QUIC, this second case has been disregarded in our implementation.

Regarding the development of the new client application, Android version 11 is used here. Go is a statically typed, compiled programming language that provides a high performance in networking and concurrency scenarios [19]. Therefore, it has been employed in the multipath-QUIC implementation [5]. The front-end design of the new Android application is very similar to the previously developed Angular Web app in Sect. 3. The existing multipath-QUIC implementation [5] written in Go is also used for our network communication stack. Furthermore, the Go tool gobind [26] is applied to generate an Android archive file from the multipath-QUIC Go-client. This archive is then used in the Android application, to fetch the image data from the proxy server. All the client-server communication takes place by means of this Go code. The search box uses an input text string to load the medical images of a patient using the *PatientID* as key. This request is issued by the Go-client. Then this client establishes the multipath connection with the Go-endpoint as counterpart in the proxy server and requests data via the multipath-QUIC implementation. If the related *PatientID* key has been found, all the available compressed image data in *.jpeg* format that belong to the patient are returned to the client side. These image data are stored in the cache of the application and immediately displayed as thumbnails or references. Whenever the user clicks on a particular thumbnail, then corresponding image tiles are loaded by the Go code as before.

4.4 Effective Medical Object Retrieval and Communication by an e-Health Application

The message sequence diagram in Fig. 10 depicts the prototypical communication flow between the various components of the resulting enhanced client-server PACS architecture. An e-health application based on the Android app first requests the required medical data at the proxy server using a patient's identifier. This request is passed by the multipath-QUIC client which is invoked at the communication layer by the related DICOM image request. Using the Go implementation of multipath-QUIC, a corresponding connection with the

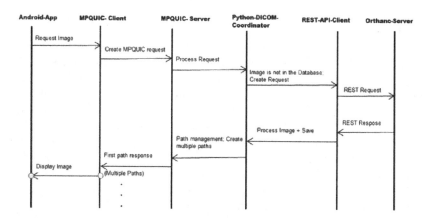

Fig. 10. Message flow of a proxy server retrieval regarding a DICOM image transfer

addressed multipath-QUIC server that is residing at the backend of the e-health application is then established. This medical data request is finally lifted to the application layer of the Python-proxy server. The latter validates the request and looks for the requested data in the associated medical database. If the data are not present in this cache of the proxy, they are fetched from the interconnected Orthanc server using a REST request. In this way, the required date become available at the proxy side locally for the invoked data transfer. Then this cached data are transferred to the client application by the multipath-QUIC server using multiple QUIC/UDP paths. Once the data are received at the multipath-QUIC client, they are rendered and displayed by the Android e-health application.

5   Conclusions

Nowadays, new advanced e-health applications are required to support the effective processing of the implemented diagnostic and therapeutic healthcare protocols of a modern society as the pandemic has shown, see also [14]. A classical Picture Archiving and Communication System (PACS) for medical images and their related e-health apps incorporates a client-server system based on the DICOM [21] standard and Android Web clients, cf. [4,16,17].

In our study we have shown how such a PACS architecture can be enhanced by a DICOM server that manages the medical image transfer and uses a set of reformatted, compressed tiles of an original image to speed up the retrieval and transport processes. Furthermore, we have designed a Web server application that offers the effective transport of these medical image data by means of a multipath-QUIC [5] protocol. It is integrated into the PACS architecture of a proxy server storing the retrieved DICOM images. We have implemented the designed architecture by a prototype with an integrated multipath-QUIC transport layer which has been realized by the programming language Go, see [11]. Our experiments have revealed the feasibility of the developed enhanced PACS architecture and its benefits. Further performance studies are needed to evaluate the full potential of the developed multipath-transport method for retrieved DICOM images.

The realized prototype still has some weaknesses such as a lack of encryption with regard to the data transport and the data-in-rest of a transferred DICOM image in the stack. These deficiencies might violate compliance regulations like HIPAA and GDPR for such sensitive medical data. Thus, a more advanced security and privacy policy must be integrated into the developed protocol stack and a strong verification of the resulting code is required after that as well.

Moreover, the applied QUIC Go project [11], which provides the basis of our applied multipath-QUIC [5] Go coding scheme, has recently added some technical support for HTTP/3.0. It should be checked whether these API enhancements can also be ported to a multipath-QUIC scheme to support the presented DICOM application scenarios. Furthermore, a study of the proposed multipath transport concept is currently realized in a real industrial context of medical image analysis. After its completion comprehensive measurement studies will be executed to reveal its performance compared to the single-path approach realized by current PACS systems. All these issues shall become a subject of our future research.

References

1. Aazam, M., Huh, E.-N.: Fog computing and smart gateway based communication for cloud of things. In: 2014 International Conference on Future Internet of Things and Cloud (FiCloud), pp. 464–470, August 2014
2. Angular - The modern web developer's platform. https://angular.io/
3. Clark, A., et al.: Pillow. https://pillow.readthedocs.io/en/stable/
4. Cornerstone Project: Medical Imaging, Simplified. https://cornerstonejs.org/
5. De Coninck, Q., Bonaventure, O.: Multipath QUIC: design and evaluation. In: Proceedings of the 13th International Conference on Emerging Networking EXperiments and Technologies, CoNEXT 2017, pp. 160–166 (2017)
6. Django Software Foundation: Django. https://www.djangoproject.com/
7. Encode OSS Ltd.: Django REST framework. https://www.django-rest-framework.org/
8. Fielding, R.T.: REST: architectural styles and the design of network-based software architectures. Doctoral dissertation, University of California, Irvine (2000)
9. GitHub Project: DWV - DICOM Web Viewer. https://github.com/ivmartel/dwv
10. GitHub Project: DWV-angular. https://github.com/ivmartel/dwv-angular
11. GitHub Project: A QUIC implementation in pure Go. https://github.com/qdeconinck/mp-quic
12. Google: Android. https://www.android.com/
13. Google: Documentation for app developers. Developer Guides, Cronet. https://developer.android.com/guide/topics/connectivity/cronet/reference/org/chromium/net/CronetEngine
14. Islam, S.M.R., et al.: The internet of things for health care: a comprehensive survey. IEEE Access 3, 678–708 (2015)
15. Iyengar, J., Thomson, M.: QUIC: a UDP-based multiplexed and secure transport. Internet draft, draft-ietf-quic-transport-04, June 2017. https://datatracker.ietf.org/doc/rfc9000/
16. Jodogne, S.: The Orthanc ecosystem for medical imaging. J. Digit. Imaging 31(3), 341–352 (2018). https://doi.org/10.1007/s10278-018-0082-y
17. Jodogne, S.: Orthanc - the free and open-source, lightweight DICOM server. Orthanc Labs, Visé, Belgium. https://www.orthanc-labs.com/, https://www.orthanc-server.com/
18. Kaur, H., Kaur, R., Kumar, N.: Lossless compression of DICOM images using genetic algorithm. In: 2015 1st International Conference on Next Generation Computing Technologies (NGCT), pp. 985–989, September 2015
19. Kincaid, J.: Google's go: a new programming language that's Python Meets C++. TechCrunch. Retrieved, vol. 29 (2010)
20. Mah, P., Reeves, T.E., McDavid, W.D.: Deriving hounsfield units using grey levels in cone beam computed tomography. Dentomaxillofacial Radiol. 39(6), 323–335 (2010). pMID: 20729181
21. National Electrical Manufacturers Association, NEMA PS3/ISO 12052. Digital Imaging and Communications in Medicine (DICOM) Standard (2017). https://www.dicomstandard.org/

22. Python Software Foundation: Python. https://www.python.org/
23. Python Software Foundation: ctypes - A foreign function library for Python. https://docs.python.org/dev/library/ctypes.html
24. Seeram, E.: Computed Tomography - Physical Principles, Clinical Applications, and Quality Control. Elsevier, Amsterdam (2015)
25. Tahmoush, D., Samet, H.: A new database for medical images and information. In: Horii, S.C., Andriole, K.P. (eds.) Proceedings of SPIE 6516, Medical Imaging 2007: PACS and Imaging Informatics, 65160G, pp. 140–148. International Society for Optics and Photonics (2007)
26. The Go Project: Documentation - Binding Go. https://godoc.org/golang.org/x/mobile/cmd/gobind
27. The Pallets Projects: Flask. https://palletsprojects.com/p/flask/

Smart Mobility and Routing

Understanding Human Mobility for Data-Driven Policy Making

Jesper Slik[1]([✉]) and Sandjai Bhulai[2]

[1] Pon, Stadionplein 28, 1076 CM Amsterdam, The Netherlands
jesper.slik@pon.com
[2] Vrije Universiteit Amsterdam, De Boelelaan 1111,
1081 HV Amsterdam, The Netherlands

Abstract. This study aims to identify the patterns of behavior which underlie human mobility. More specifically, we compare commuters who drive in a car with those who use the train in the same geographic region of the Netherlands. We try to understand the mode choices of the commuters based on three factors: the cost of the transport mode, the CO_2 emissions, and the travel time. The analysis has been based on data consisting of travel transactions in the Netherlands during 2018 containing over half a million records. We show how this raw data can be transformed into relevant insights on the three factors. A large difference is observed in terms of CO_2 emissions and cost, a minor difference in speed. Besides, the computation of congestion shows intuitive results. These results can be used to stimulate behavioral change proactively and to improve trip planners.

Keywords: Travel behavior · Mobility transactions · Highway sensors · Carbon emissions · Travel times · Data analysis

1 Introduction

Commuting long times and distances has become a regular part of the daily routine for most people. How people travel to work is in part a function of personal preference, which has been discussed in terms of comfort in the vehicle, addressing issues such as temperature, air quality, noise, vibration, light, and ergonomics [2]. However, the mode choice also reflects contextual factors [8], including economics – the cost and acceptability of different commuting modes due to travel times and CO_2 emissions.

The continued expansion of commuting distance and time in cars has obvious environmental consequences as it relies on fossil fuels. Pollution generated by cars has health consequences for travelers [5,11]. Commuting can also be stressful, and the duration of the trip contributes to the stress experienced by workers [4,12]. There are few studies that have looked at commuting experiences for mass transit commuters. Singer et al. [9] found increased stress on crowded trains. Indices of

Table 1. Mobility transactions dataset, sampled and containing fictive values because of data privacy agreements

Type	Start_ts	End_ts	Start_city	End_city	Distance	Duration	CO$_2$
Car	10/03/2018 07:45	10/03/2018 08:24	Utrecht	Wageningen	49	39	7.02
Train	28/11/2018 08:32	28/11/2018 09:20	Zandvoort	Amsterdam	27	48	0.16
Train	09/04/2018 16:51	09/04/2018 17:37	Amersfoort	Zwolle	66	46	0.4
Car	09/07/2018 14:00	09/07/2018 14:36	Beilen	Groningen	52	36	8.71
Car	21/01/2018 07:45	21/01/2018 08:33	Wijchen	Den Bosch	39	48	6.82

stress were reduced when train commutes were improved by route changes that shortened commuting time and enhanced predictability of the trip [12].

Few studies have directly compared riders across modalities, such as train versus car commuting. Based on available information, one might predict that car commuting is less preferable than train commuting, particularly because of differences in predictability and effort, both of which have been linked to stress [3,7]. For example, the vagaries of traffic and sudden onset of accidents or other kinds of traffic jams make driving times for the commute to and from work unpredictable, especially in densely populated major metropolitan areas. Driving also requires constant attention and effort – more so as conditions worsen. Trains are likely to be more predictable and less effortful as a mode of travel.

On the other hand, driving may afford a higher level of control for the driver. The driver has more ability to influence the time of departure, route, and road speed. Williams et al. [13] found that drivers in the UK had higher levels of perceived control than those using other transit modes. Past research in other situations also indicates that control may be an important factor in mode choice [6]. Car commuting affords a higher degree of control over social interaction, a critical aspect of privacy. Indeed, if drivers do have higher levels of perceived control than do train commuters, driving may be a more preferred mode of travel.

In this paper, we compare commuters who drive in a car with those who use the train in the same geographic region of the Netherlands. We try to understand the mode choices of the commuters based on three factors: the cost of the transport mode, the CO$_2$ emissions, and the travel time. For this purpose, we use a rich dataset of mobility transactions by employees of a private company. We show how to transform the data into relevant insights, such as congestion, to calculate the three above-stated factors. This allows us to compute relevant statistics by predicting travel mode choice. This predictive model, in turn, can be used for policy making and better network decisions.

2   Problem Formulation

The focus of this study is on understanding human travel behavior when it comes to using the car and the train as travel modalities. Our approach is to compare how the modalities train and car differ in terms of CO$_2$ emissions, cost, and travel time.

Fig. 1. Usage of the train throughout the weeks of the year, relative to the average number of transactions per week

We analyze two rich datasets: mobility transactions and highway sensors. Both collect data based on real-life events through human interaction. The first challenge is that the data cannot be used directly for analysis. We show that one should carefully transform the data to avoid biases in the analysis. Another challenge is to quantify congestion when traveling from A to B, based solely on highway sensors. We develop a methodology to address both these challenges.

After we have transformed the data, we provide an analysis on the differences in human behavior to explain why a modality choice between train and car is made. This result can be used to predict modality choices, and we show how they can be used in practice through a use case.

3 Methodology

We present various methodologies for answering our research questions. First, we analyze a rich dataset containing mobility transactions. Hereafter, we explain how to process and combine statistics related to congestion.

3.1 Mobility Transactions

We first analyze a mobility data set that is unique in its kind. It has been made available for analysis under strict conditions by a private company providing mobility to its customers through a mobility card. The data contains mobility transactions that are registered through automated systems. In this section, we describe its origin, show how to process such data, and present various statistics originating from an exploratory analysis.

As in [10], the full dataset contains over half a million mobility transactions from over a thousand employees originating from various companies and offices in the Netherlands. The data analyzed concerns a period of one entire year 2018. Amongst other statistics, we know the transport type, start and end date and

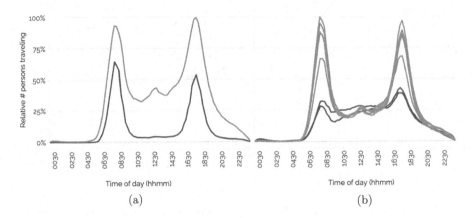

Fig. 2. People traveling simultaneously: (a) split by car (grey) and train (blue); (b) split by weekdays and colored by working days (grey) and weekend (blue) (Color figure online)

time, start and end location, distance, duration, and costs of each transaction. In this paper, we focus on a processed dataset containing trips with transport types 'car' and 'public transport' only. Regarding the public transport transactions, an additional unique characteristic of the data is that the timestamps concern historic check-in and check out timestamps. Thus, all possible real-life delays, such as malfunctions, transfers, leaves on the rails, and walking time from the entrance to the trains are taken into account.

Table 1 shows a representative sample of the most important columns in the dataset, containing fictive values because of data privacy agreements. Each record in Table 1 shows a mobility transaction. The 'type' specifies the modality used to travel: car or train. The transaction starts at timestamp 'start_ts' and ends at timestamp 'end_ts'. The starting location is given by 'start_city' and the destination location by 'end_city'. The last three columns display the statistics on this transaction: the distance measured in kilometers ('distance'), the duration in minutes ('duration'), and the CO_2 emissions measured in kilograms ('CO_2'). The CO_2 emissions are estimated through our own analysis, which is described in the last paragraph of this section.

The raw data needs to be processed before it can be used to answer our research question. Most importantly, we need to apply the appropriate filters. As the data is gathered through automated systems, it contains transactions that we do not wish to analyze. First, we filter out short trips. Most car trips are short, as a new trip is registered each time the engine is turned on or off. Also, for public transport, in the Netherlands, some stations cannot be traversed without checking in and out at each entrance. Thus, trips that have a duration (in time) shorter than a threshold are filtered. Second, we filter trips having a highly similar start and end location. These trips are difficult to analyze, as it is challenging to determine the true destination or purpose of the trip. Third,

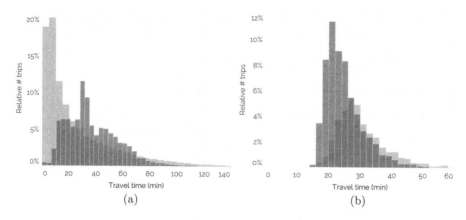

Fig. 3. Distributions of travel duration split by car (grey) and train (blue): (a) amongst all transactions; (b) amongst transactions between Utrecht and Amersfoort (Color figure online)

we filter car trips starting and ending at gas stations. We do not see these trips as the intended start or end locations of the users. They are forced to visit gas stations in order to reach their destination. Also, some gas stations are not accessible by public transport. In addition to filtering, we apply a correction on the start and end locations of trips by public transport. The raw locations will always be at stations. However, these are not the actual start and end locations of the travel. We correct these locations by sampling a random address within the area that is reachable within ten minutes by bike. Afterward, we re-compute the travel time and distance using an API.

After gathering and processing the raw data, we can explore the data. We start by looking at the usage of the train. Figure 1 shows the relationship between the week of the year and the relative number of transactions by train. The percentage is relative to the mean number of train transactions per week. A clear relationship can be observed between the train usage and the weeks containing holidays. In the first week of the year, the train usage is at a low level of −22%. The weeks containing the spring holidays, summer holidays, and the Christmas holiday all show a train usage lower than −20%. Interestingly, around November and at the beginning of December, the train usage is relatively high. This might be explained by poor weather conditions or a relatively low number of holidays during these weeks.

Next, we take a closer look at the time of the day at which people travel. For each transaction in our dataset, we know the timestamp of the start and end. Therefore, we can derive the number of people that are traveling at any minute of any day. Figure 2 shows the results of this exercise. On the left (a), it shows the relative number of people traveling during the day split by car (grey) and train (blue). On the right (b), it shows the same information split by days during the week (grey) and days during the weekend (blue). The numbers are relative to the maximum. In both graphs, high peaks can be observed during

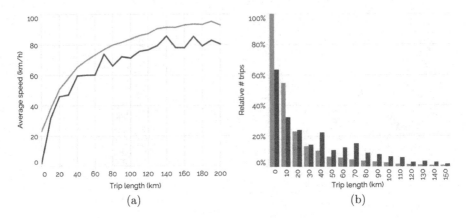

Fig. 4. Interaction between transport type and speed, for car (grey) and train (blue): (a) interaction between trip length and average speed; (b) interaction between trip length and number of trips (Color figure online)

typical commuting hours. However, clear differences are visible between trips by car and train. A much larger number of people are traveling during the middle of the day, and a small peak can be observed after lunch. Besides the graph split by train and car, large differences are visible amongst days in the week. On the weekend, fewer people travel during commute hours. Next to these differences, the number of people traveling is the largest on Tuesday, the smallest on Sunday and during the workweek the lowest on Friday.

Figure 3 compares the distribution of travel duration for car and train transactions. On the left (a), we see that cars are more frequently used for relatively short trips. In contrast, trains are generally used for relatively long trips. This could be explained by the fact that the car might be faster. However, the right graph (b) seems to reject this hypothesis. The travel time distribution for both train and car between two specific cities in the Netherlands is shown here. The cities are Utrecht and Amersfoort, both located in the center of the Netherlands. Between them, the travel time distribution of the train is smaller than that of the car.

To further investigate the interaction between transport type and speed, we explore two relations: that between trip length and speed; and that between trip length and the frequency of occurrence. Figure 4 shows these graphs, for both car (grey) and train (blue). If we want to approach answering the question of which transport type is fastest, we need to consider both. On the left, we overall see an increasing relation between trip length and average speed. Also, the average speed of the train always lies below that of the car. On the right, we see a different distribution of trip length for both transport types. The car is often used for relatively short trips, whereas the train is used for relatively long trips. Thus, if we would simply compare the average speed of all car transactions with all train transactions, we would get a biased result.

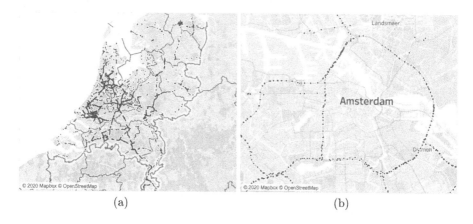

(a)   (b)

Fig. 5. NDW measurement sites: (a) in the Netherlands; (b) surrounding Amsterdam

Lastly, we combine transactions in our dataset to estimate the carbon footprint in terms of CO_2 emissions. Different transport types have different carbon footprints. Regarding public transport, these figures are publicly available. In the Netherlands, through [1]. However, for car transactions, these figures depend on a range of factors, such as the engine, driving behavior, car weight, or outside temperature. This makes it more difficult to quantify the footprint. However, the full dataset contains fuel-related transactions. Each re-fuel of a car is stored as a transaction, containing the volume and type of fuel used. Using these statistics, we can estimate the amount of fuel burned for each car transaction in the full dataset. We join this to the mobility transactions dataset, hereby creating the CO_2 column. This can be translated towards kilograms of CO_2.

3.2   Congestion

Congestion is a factor that affects travel time. Depending on the location of the congestion and the route, this might have a large or minor influence. Still, in [10], we have shown that overall there is a relation between the departure time and the expected travel time. Thus, if we want to make network-related decisions, we need to measure and quantify congestion. In this section, we describe how to process measurements related to congestion on roads.

In the Netherlands, the Nationale Databank Wegverkeersgegevens (NDW) tracks the speed and volume of cars by using more than 37,000 sensors on federal roads. These statistics are made available publicly through their data portal on a minute level. Figure 5 visualizes these measurement sites. On the left (a), most measurement sites in the Netherlands are shown. On the right (b), the sites within Amsterdam are shown. When closely studying the sites within Amsterdam, we can see these are tied to a road segment, thus, being specific for a certain direction of traffic flow. This allows us to compute statistics on both a micro and macro scale. Our goal is to quantify congestion on the road at a specific time,

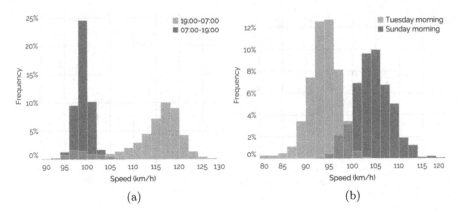

Fig. 6. Differences in observed speed values depending on: (a) time of day; (b) day within week

between two specific locations, and in a certain direction. To do so, we need to process this data appropriately.

The main challenges in processing the NDW data are finding relevant sites and determining a congestion level for each site. Finding relevant measurement sites is challenging as there are thousands of sites. However, we are only interested in those sites covering the traveled route. We filter the relevant sites by fitting a rectangle between the start and end coordinate of the corresponding trip. Depending on the trip length, the width of the rectangle is adjusted. We only consider sites positioned inside the rectangle. Next, we filter these sites on having a direction within a threshold of 90° of the general trip direction. We can determine the direction of the traffic that the site is measuring because we know the ID and location of the next site on the road segment.

Determining a congestion level for each measurement site is a challenge as well. The sites can be located at different road types with different speed limits. To further complicate this, the speed limit can vary throughout the day. Thus, we cannot directly take the velocity of the traffic as a statistic of congestion. Instead, we first derive the distribution of speed measurement values for each site. This can be dependent on the time of the day. Using these distributions, we can convert each measurement value to a congestion score by comparing it to the location of its corresponding distribution.

Figure 6 visualizes the distribution of observed speed values, split by two different dimensions. On the left (a), it is split by time of day, and on the right (b), it is split by day of week. Both graphs display observed values by a unique measurement site. Whilst the differences on the right graph can be explained through congestion, those on the left cannot. On the left, it is a site placed on a Dutch highway having a different speed limit during the night. This limit is enforced through trajectory speed control, so drivers are hesitant to exceed it. Remarkably, during the night, some vehicles still drive at the same speed as the one allowed during the day. This could be explained by limits on certain

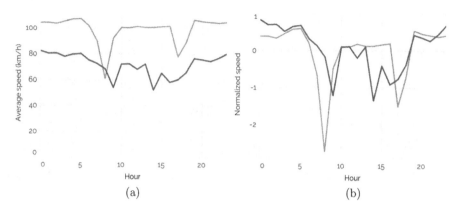

Fig. 7. Observed (a) vs normalized (b) speed values by measurement sites having a speed limit of 100 km/h (grey) and 80 km/h (blue) (Color figure online)

vehicles (e.g., heavy trucks) or due to habit. The graph on the right (b), displays the observed values on a measurement site that is sensitive to traffic jams. It compares speed values observed on Tuesday morning with those observed on Sunday morning in November. We observe that the speed values on Tuesday seem much lower than those on Sunday, which is intuitive as more people travel on Tuesday morning (Fig. 3).

Figure 7 visualizes the result of normalizing the observed speed values. It compares two measurement sites in different parts of the country having a different speed limit. One has a limit of 100 km/h (grey), the other a limit of 80 km/h (blue). If a trip traverses both sites, we need to consolidate both, despite these differences. The normalized speed values seem to achieve this. We observe that during the night and the middle of the day, the normalized values are highly similar for both sites. Both are close to, or slightly above 0. This is intuitive as the observed values lie close to the speed limit. The speed values hardly exceed, but often lie underneath this limit, thus, we expect a slightly positive normalized speed. During rush hours, we observe some differences. Those are intuitive as well, as they directly are a result of the raw data values.

4 Results

This section highlights our most important findings from analyzing the mobility transactions and congestion data sets.

Figure 8 compares the mobility transactions of cars and the train through three different statistics: CO_2 emissions, cost, and speed. We observe a significant difference in terms of CO_2 emissions. Compared to a car, the train hardly emits CO_2. When taking into account well-to-tank emissions, this difference grows even larger. Regarding cost, the train is more expensive when looking at variable cost. However, when including fixed costs, the train has a lower cost per kilometer. Looking at speed, we observe that both transport types are relatively close.

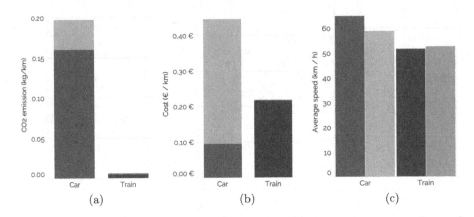

Fig. 8. Comparison of car (grey) and train (blue) through: (a) CO_2 emission by tank-to-wheel (dark) and well-to-tank (light); (b) cost by variable (dark) and fixed (light); (c) speed outside (dark) and during (light) rush hour (Color figure online)

The car is slightly faster than the train. The differences during rush hour are most prominent. The speed of the car decreases during rush hour, whereas the speed of the train increases. This is likely explained by congested roads and a higher number of trains scheduled during rush hour.

Remarkably, the total cost (variable + flexible) of the car is twice as high as the cost of the train. The variable cost is the leading cause, consisting of more than €0.30 per kilometer. When making a fair comparison between car and train, we think both factors should be taken into account. Besides, the observed difference in speed hardly changes looking at both transport types. This might be because we average over the whole country, so local differences might be larger. The observed difference in CO_2 is extreme, however, it conforms with our expectations.

Figure 9 shows the result of computing the congestion between two locations. It compares the normalized speed (low speed indicates high congestion) amongst the hours within a day. All days in 2018 are averaged in making this graph. The measurement sites taken into account lie between two cities in the Netherlands: Amsterdam and Almere. The normalized speed is computed in both directions, from Amsterdam to Almere (blue) and from Almere to Amsterdam (grey). We focus on these cities because a large part of the inhabitants of Almere work in and commute to Amsterdam. This effect is visible in the computed congestion. Traffic heading towards Amsterdam is congested during both morning and evening rush hours, whereas traffic heading towards Almere is only congested during the evening rush hours.

5   Use Cases

The data analyzed in this research and the corresponding results can be used for predicting the modality choice of individuals. Understanding the relation

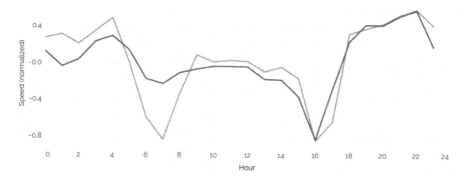

Fig. 9. Quantifying congestion: congestion from Amsterdam to Almere (blue) and from Almere to Amsterdam (grey) split by hour of the day (Color figure online)

between CO_2, cost, and time and modality choice allows us to do so accurately. In [10], we did so with a 97% accuracy. This is largely based on the same mobility transactions dataset, enriched with a generic dataset regarding reachability features, which quantify how well the network of a modality is developed. Interestingly, the main predictors of this model are the reachability features, more so than specific travel times. Additionally, the travel type (commute or personal) showed to have a large influence on travel mode choice. The reliable predictions of this model can help users in their decision-making. For example, we can send proactive messages to notify users of alternative travel modes, or we can increase the visibility of relevant travel modes in travel planners.

If the user allows us, we can notify him/her of alternative travel modes. This can be relevant because users might lack the knowledge, construction or traffic jams are anticipated, or because of policymakers wanting to stimulate behavioral change. In all cases, we only want to send notifications to users with a certain probability of adjusting their behavior. For instance, if a company wants to stimulate train usage to its employees, they could notify all people within a certain distance or travel time from their respective office. However, this ignores the relation between other modalities. It could be that for an individual, the travel time using the train is 25 min and 10 min by using the car. These users will have a relatively low probability of traveling by train. On the other hand, there might be users having 40 min of travel time using the train and 30 min using the car. The second group of users would have a higher probability of traveling by train. The model estimates these probabilities, including more statistics than travel time, and helps select relevant users for behavioral change.

Besides proactively stimulating behavioral change, we can use our data and results to improve trip planners. These face the challenge of displaying the most relevant modalities to their users. Using our insights, we can adjust the visibility of travel modes based on the estimated probability they will be chosen. Currently, we can balance train and car. In the future, we can extend the analysis to include more forms of mobility by including shared concepts such as bikes, scooters, or cars.

6 Conclusion

In this research, we have developed methods for handling data sets containing mobility transactions and congestion. In our opinion, we have shown promising results for different use cases. Still, our methodology can be further improved. In this section, we further discuss our findings and highlight potential improvements to our methodology.

Our results comparing train and car mobility concerning CO_2, cost, and speed require some side notes. First of all, we assume car trips are executed with one person at a time. We could apply a general correction, however, we have little data to make an educated guess. Therefore, we left the statistics as is. Regarding the CO_2 emissions, all our transactions in the dataset are based on data from 2018. Given the electrification in the automotive industry, we expect this to impact the emissions. Tank-to-wheel emissions might decrease, however, the emissions due to producing an electric car might increase because of the battery production. Finally, we realize that the historic data introduces a bias regarding speed. For example, transactions that would take an extremely long time with public transport might not be executed, hence not showing up in our dataset, thereby not influencing public transport speed in our analysis.

We see the most significant potential for improvement in the methodology to measure congestion. This can be done in both selecting relevant measurement sites and in better interpreting the speed values coming from them. We can improve on selecting sites between an origin and destination by integrating a routing API to give us exact routes between them instead of fitting a rectangle. Having these routes, we can focus only on the sites covering them. As a result of this, we would reduce the number of measurement sites we take into account.

Further, we can better interpret the speed values resulting from each measurement site by considering the speed limit on the corresponding road segment. Currently, we implicitly derive this speed limit by analyzing the distribution of observations from a specific measurement site. However, if a road segment is often heavily congested, this might influence our derived limit.

Besides these methodological improvements, it would be relevant to incorporate data on more modalities than the train and the car. The mobility transactions dataset already contains more modalities, however, these volumes are too low to draw conclusions. For example, its structure is set up also to incorporate trips done by shared scooters or shared cars. As these services become more common, we might be able to observe a behavioral change in some scenarios towards these modalities. Additionally, the Netherlands is well known for its usage of bicycles. Little data is generated on those, as they do not contain sensors and it hereby requires manual effort to register when and where these trips are made. Given the electrification in the bicycle industry, we do expect more data to be generated in the future. Electric bicycles can generate data through sensors, such as their motor, lights, lock, or anti-theft location modules.

Finally, the study could be expanded with interviews or a survey in which commuters can deliver input directly themselves. In our data, for example, it might still be the case that certain users did not have a choice between different modalities. Perhaps, they were only compensated in such a way they could only consider one of the choices. Besides, there could be practical circumstances, like lending the car to a relative, which might influence the choices. Besides, when setting up such a survey, one could ask on which incentives the commuters themselves might consider for changing their behavior.

References

1. Lijst emissiefactoren, totale lijst (2020). https://www.co2emissiefactoren.nl/lijst-emissiefactoren
2. Da Silva, M.G.: Measurements of comfort in vehicles. Meas. Sci. Technol. **13**(6), R41 (2002)
3. Evans, G.W., Lercher, P., Meis, M., Ising, H., Kofler, W.W.: Community noise exposure and stress in children. J. Acoust. Soc. Am. **109**(3), 1023–1027 (2001)
4. Evans, G.W., Wener, R.E.: Rail commuting duration and passenger stress. Health Psychol. **25**(3), 408 (2006)
5. Frumkin, H.: Urban sprawl and public health. Public Health Rep. (2016)
6. Glass, D.C., Singer, J.E.: Urban stress: experiments on noise and social stressors (1972)
7. Kluger, A.N.: Commute variability and strain. J. Organ. Behav.: Int. J. Ind. Occup. Organ. Psychol. Behav. **19**(2), 147–165 (1998)
8. Schade, J., Schlag, B.: Acceptability of urban transport pricing strategies. Transport. Res. F: Traffic Psychol. Behav. **6**(1), 45–61 (2003)
9. Singer, J.E., Lundberg, U., Frankenhaeuser, M.: Stress on the train: a study of urban commuting. Psychological Laboratories, University of Stockholm (1974)
10. Slik, J., Bhulai, S.: Transaction-driven mobility analysis for travel mode choices. In: Proceedings of the 11th International Conference on Ambient Systems, Networks and Technologies (ANT), pp. 169–177 (2019)
11. Wener, R., Evans, G.W.: Transportation and health: the impact of commuting. In: Encyclopedia of Environmental Health, pp. 400–407. Elsevier Inc. (2011)
12. Wener, R.E., Evans, G.W., Phillips, D., Nadler, N.: Running for the 7: 45: the effects of public transit improvements on commuter stress. Transportation **30**(2), 203–220 (2003)
13. Williams, G., Murphy, J., Hill, R.: A latent class analysis of commuters' transportation mode and relationships with commuter stress. In: Fourth International Conference on Traffic and Transport Psychology, Washington, DC (2008)

Research on Detecting Similarity in Trajectory Data and Possible Use Cases

Moritz Peter Weber[1,2]([📧]) [ID] and Ilenia Salvadori[2] [ID]

[1] University of Applied Sciences Jena, Carl-Zeiß-Promenade 2, 07745 Jena, Germany
[2] Data in Motion Consulting GmbH Jena, Kahlaische Str. 4, 07745 Jena, Germany
info@datainmotion.de

Abstract. Today's road traffic is extremely complex and its management offers many opportunities for improvement. By determining similarities among different tracks, it should be possible to reduce congestion times, for example by suggesting car-sharing within the different
participants. Traffic data could also be analyzed based on similarity calculations, in order to recognize possible future dangerous situations in
advance and to prevent them through a warning system. With this work
an attempt has been made to identify similar tracks based on different
criteria, in such a way to build the basis of a more complex system,
which could potentially address different use cases within the road traffic system. In the following sections, the use cases are first described in
more detail and existing possible solutions are examined. The main topic
of geographic similarity is then presented, as it represents the common
ground for all the considered use cases. Other potentially useful parameters are discussed. The whole analysis is finally introduced, which compares two different approaches and studies their potential to be included
in a real application. The results and methods that could be further
investigated are then presented, together with the importance of 5G
technology.

Keywords: Similarity · Machine learning · Deep learning · Big data
analytics · 5G/6G technologies and ad-hoc mobile networks

1 Motivation and Use Cases

The daily occurring traffic flow is a very complex system nowadays. Various
participants such as cars, pedestrians, cyclists, trams, trains, and many others
interact with each other at any time to get from A to B. So, it happens that
some road users start their journey within the same area and also have a close
destination, even if the two routes may differ. Being able to determine similar
routes by studying tracks from different users can help avoid traffic congestion,
for example by identifying possible commuters. This data can be analyzed to
provide information on whether the commute would be more suitable at a different time, or to find commuters in the vicinity who also drive the same or

F. Phillipson et al. (Eds.): I4CS 2022, CCIS 1585, pp. 168–184, 2022.
https://doi.org/10.1007/978-3-031-06668-9_13

a similar route and thus offer them opportunities for car-sharing, saving then money on fuel and helping protect the environment.

Predicting future traffic flow using data collected at one intersection could also improve the traffic management system, by foreseeing possible congestion and helping to adjust traffic light signal plans accordingly.

Due to the very complex traffic system and to the fact that drivers are subjected to mistakes, driver-related causes of accidents are not rare. Looking at the statistics in Fig. 1, it's clear that there are problems that could be avoided with modern technology [1].

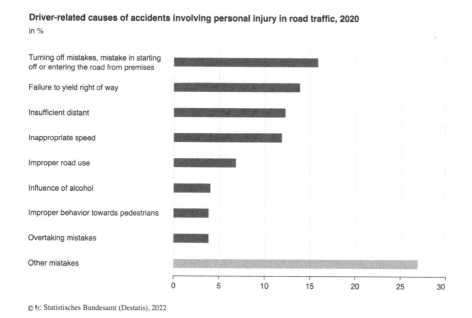

Fig. 1. Driver-related causes of accidents involving personal injury in road traffic, 2020 (on a total of 264499 accidents) [1]

Reducing these numbers can not only make traffic flow more relaxed for everyone involved, but it can also save lives. Being able to predict the traffic flow and collecting data from the different road participants, one can develop an alert system that will warn drivers of possible dangerous situations. An example of such critical circumstances is, for instance, when traffic lights are off or not functional; if there was an application that can alert drivers approaching the intersection about other drivers or pedestrians reaching the same area, it could warn them in real time.

Collecting multiple tracks from the same user can help foreseeing in which direction he is most likely to go, allowing the system to send alerts only for the concerning parts of the intersection. Of course, for such an application the understanding of two similar tracks is not enough. However, this study can serve as a basis for much more complex use cases.

Solution approaches for all these use cases share the same basis, geographic similarity. In the following, the meaning of this term is discussed, and the study to identify similar tracks based on that is analyzed. The process and results of this research should be accounted as a preliminary study for the named use cases.

2   Similarity Detection

2.1   State of the Art

For accomplishing the named use cases it is necessary to be able to understand and calculate the concept of similarity, meaning when two road tracks can be considered similar, and how to assert their similarity in terms of different criteria. There are several subgroups of ways to measure similarities in data [3,5,7,8,10–13,15,16]. Similarity-based metrics, distance-based metrics, and other various methods were researched. However, after extensive investigations and testing, none of them was suitable for the aforementioned use cases. Reasons for this were, e.g., that they are not efficient enough for the complex use cases, that problems occur when there are different lengths and thus a different number of coordinates, or that the method only uses single values in our data sets and does not understand the meaning of the data, e.g., when the coordinates of two routes are close to each other or have the same start and end points. Also, some have referred to completely different subject matters, such as text analysis. In the following section, the study of possible new solutions to identify similar road tracks is described.

2.2   Geographic Similarity

In order to develop a system to use as a fundamental for all the previously described use cases, a definition for similarity and how it should be evaluated in the application is necessary. There are a variety of different definitions and methods to capture similarities in data. In this work, the focus is on geographic similarity, since it has been considered the basis for all the use cases. To illustrate the concept of geographic similarity, in Fig. 2 an Open Street Map screenshot displaying two routes between the cities of Weimar and Jena is shown [14].

As can be seen at first glance, there is not only one route from the start point to the destination. This is not a novelty, but due to the multitude of different highways, country roads, or similar, there are of course various possibilities of route selection.

As first step to study geographic similarity, it should be found out how similar these routes are to each other or to routes that, for example, go in a completely different direction, share just some small but identical route segments, or also even have a different destination. What is immediately obvious, just from the

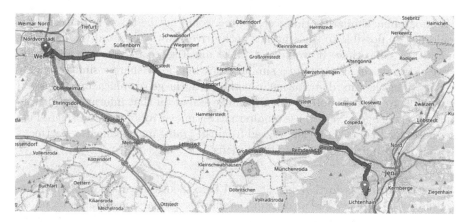

Fig. 2. Example tracks with same start point and end point (Jena - Weimar) [14]

fact that they share the same start and end point, is that they must be relatively close to each other, if the criterion of the shortest connection is considered and no other detours are included. Considering as similarity criteria just the start and end points, one should expect the tracks from the example to have a high level of similarity. On the other hand, if more points along the track are considered, the level of similarity would be lower, since they do not share all the geographic points.

2.3   Parameters Description

Depending on the use case one wants to consider, there are different parameters that should be taken into account in addition to the mere geographic coordinates, to assert similarity among tracks. In the following the different metrics necessary to describe the previously mentioned use cases are presented.

Coordinates
For the foundation of geographic similarity, firstly the focus is only on the geographic coordinates. These are chosen because they represent a route geographically. Of particular importance are the coordinates of the start and end point of a track, because these allow us to check whether two commuters share the same journey. However, it can be still useful to compare all coordinates of a track to determine whether two commuters just share a part of the route, which can still result in a car-sharing suggestion.

Time
If instead, the focus is on which route has been traveled at the same time of the day, then it would be important to take into account the time distribution. This parameter is especially important for the commuter's use case. Imagine two drivers who take a similar route or share some parts every day. From a geographical point of view, their tracks would be categorized as similar using

pure geographic similarity. However, if time would not be taken into account, it would not be possible to say whether both drivers always started their journey around the same time. It would not make much sense to suggest car-sharing between two drivers that share a similar track but don't share a similar time.

Analyzing the time distribution, together with the geographical one, it should be possible to identify potential traffic jams. Based on that information drivers could also get suggestions to use an alternative time or route to avoid them. Furthermore this kind of data can be used from the traffic management department in order to optimize traffic light signal plans.

Speed
Adding the speed as further metric could help identify traffic jams in a more accurate way. Suppose the algorithm classifies as similar some tracks based on coordinates, time and speed; analyzing then the speed profile one can find out whether at some point along the road the speed value was very low or close to zero, which could be an indicator for a traffic jam.

Bearing
Having access to the bearing information at a certain location could be useful to predict turning points at intersections in case of ambiguity. If we consider, for instance, intersections in which, from the same lane, one can both go straight or turn right. Being able to use data from previously traveled tracks by the same user could potentially exploit the bearing information to know where the driver in the current situation is most likely to go. This could help in predicting and preventing dangerous situations in traffic.

In the following analysis only geographical coordinates are taken into account, as geographic similarity represents the basis even for the most complex use cases.

3   Data Analysis

3.1   Data Collection

The track data for the following studies are collected using two methods. On the one hand, a self-developed mobile application is used to save all the previously described metrics every second while driving a route. However, this requires a lot of effort if a large amount of tracks are immediately needed, such as it is the case for these studies. To compensate for that, a rudimentary track generator was internally developed, which creates a sample of tracks around a certain area.

3.2   Preprocessing Data and Statistical Approach

Before developing any kind of algorithm, it is necessary to understand the data and to discover and recognize possible correlations among the different variables in play. Furthermore, it is important to get a feeling of the data and what results or details can be already expected using simpler or statistical methods.

The first used dataset consists of a sample of 10 tracks from Gera to Jena, recorded with the previously mentioned mobile application.

Due to the interest in the geographic similarity, the speed dependency is removed, by normalizing the tracks in such a way they look like if they were all traveled at 50 km/h. Further, a χ^2 approach is used to get a quantitative similarity result. One of the collected track is taken as if it were a new track entering the system, while the others play the role of historical data. The χ^2 value is calculated between the new track and all the others. The lower the χ^2, the most similar the tracks are. The final result of this first approach is shown in Fig. 3. On the y-axis the $\sqrt{latitude^2 + longitude^2}$ is shown, while on the x-axis there is the time at which we would have reached the corresponding y-value if the track was traveled at 50 km/h. As you can see from the plot, the route that lies in the same direction and passes through the same regions of the test route (track 0) has received a lower χ^2 value, while the route in the opposite direction has received a higher χ^2 value, which helps to order the tracks according to geographic similarity.

In a real-world application, a lot more data has to be handled, which would result in a lot of computational time for such an algorithm. This because every point along the track is evaluated with all the others in the rest of the tracks. To study even more complex correlations which are needed for some of the use cases, algorithms are necessary that would be able to handle both more data and more variables.

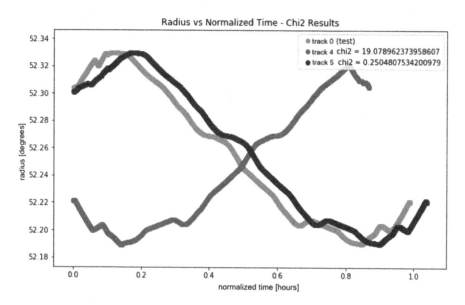

Fig. 3. Track visualization after removing speed dependency (y-axis: radius $= \sqrt{latitude^2 + longitude^2}$; x-axis: time at which we would have reached the corresponding value if the track was traveled at 50 km/h)] [19]

3.3   Machine Learning Approach: K-Means

To create a system that can handle more data and can deal with more variables, some machine learning algorithms are tested. The first one is the K-means clustering algorithm.

The same sample of 10 tracks recorded by the mobile application is used for this analysis.

Instead of focusing on the whole track, the geographic similarity has been defined in three different ways, based on:

- **Start Point** = tracks with a similar start point should belong to the same cluster;
- **End Point** = tracks with a similar end point should belong to the same cluster;
- **Combined Start and End Point** = tracks with a similar start point and end point should belong to the same cluster.

The start and end points are simply the pair of latitude and longitude coordinates at the time the track starts and at the last recorded time for that track. The method then tries to split the data into different clusters, in such a way that data belonging to the same cluster are closer to their cluster center than to the other cluster centers [4]. To achieve this practically, a determination of the optimal number of clusters is necessary, because an incorrect number of clusters could skew the results. For example, if the prediction causes a smaller number of clusters, tracks that should belong to two different clusters will instead be placed in the same cluster [4]. To calculate the optimal number of clusters, there are several methods; the Elbow method [17] and the Average Silhouette method [18] are the most common. For this study the decision was to use the Average Silhouette method because the Elbow method does not always work promisingly, especially if the data to be processed is not very clustered [6].

The results for the first two cluster variants (start point and end point) can be seen in Fig. 4.

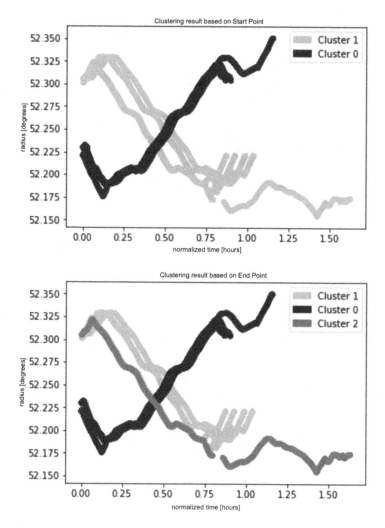

Fig. 4. Clustering based on start point (upper panel) and end point (lower panel) [19]

Tracks belonging to different clusters has been drawn in different colors, which is also highlighted and labeled with the corresponding cluster in the legend. It can be seen exactly which routes have been classified into which category based on their course. For the use cases of this project, both the start and end point of a track have to be combined to identify possible commuters, for instance. The combined results of the previous two clustering form a combined clustering selection. The result is shown in Fig. 5.

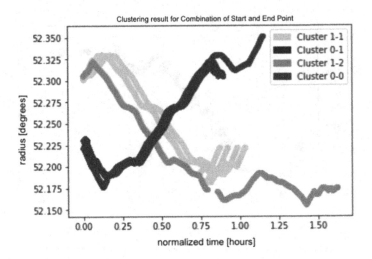

Fig. 5. Clustering based on start and end point (combined point cluster) [19]

The created method now can classify tracks in different clusters, based, for the moment, on the start and end point of the track, and the combination of them. This clustering algorithm can serve as a basis, allowing to identify groups of similar tracks. When a new track comes into the system, then, the most similar group can be determined, and within that group, one can implement an additional clustering, or even a χ^2 approach, to find the most similar track to the given one.

Depending on the similarity criteria, it is just important to find the right variables according to which clustering of the data should be based. One of the most important additional metric for all the described use cases is the time. In the following subsection a study is presented, using the K-means algorithm and accounting for both geographical start and end points, together with the starting time.

3.4   Adding Time Dependency

For this analysis, a sample of 2000 generated tracks is used: half of them from Jena to Erfurt and the other half from Weimar to Jena. A starting time has then been assigned to each track, in such a way that half of the tracks from Jena to Erfurt and Weimar to Jena starts at 7 am, while the other half starts at 11 am. The clustering then uses as variables the start point, the end point, and the starting time. Again the Average Silhouette method is used to find out the optimal number of clusters.

The accuracy of the algorithm can be computed, by looking at how well it performs with some new tracks. For this purpose, 200 newly created tracks between Jena-Erfurt and Erfurt-Weimar are used. The method takes a new set of tracks and tries to predict them into a cluster. The prediction is given in terms of the probability that a track belongs to a certain cluster. The accuracy is the highest among these probabilities. The testing process includes two sets of new tracks. One with similar and one with different starting times with respect the tracks used for training the clustering algorithm in the first place. The results are shown in Fig. 6.

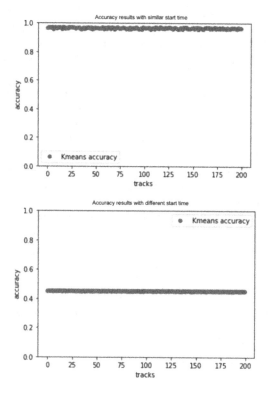

Fig. 6. Accuracy results for tracks with a similar (upper panel) and different start time (lower panel) with respect to the sample used for training the model [19]

Looking at the upper panel, in which tracks with similar starting times with respect to the training sample have been used, there is very high accuracy in the forecast. The K-means algorithm can therefore sort the new tracks very well into clusters. However, this is kind of expected since the tracks do not differ from the ones used at the beginning. In contrast, looking at the plot with different starting times, accuracy has now dropped significantly and is concentrated in the 0.4–0.5 range of the scale. This is an indication that the tracks probably belong to a non-existent cluster. This is a good result, because it demonstrates that with such an algorithm, it could already be identified, when a new track comes in, if the existing clusters describe it well, or whether it is necessary to add another cluster and rebuild the model.

In the next section another approach, using neural networks this time, is tested and compared to the clustering algorithm.

3.5   Neural Network Approach

Other tests have been done using a neural network algorithm, and results are compared to the ones obtained by the K-means algorithm previously described. Neural networks were chosen as alternative to the clustering algorithms, which show some limitations. As described in [9], for instance, the standard K-means clustering algorithm can only represent clusters that are linearly separable in pairs.

One of the main differences between these two approaches is that clustering is a form of unsupervised learning, in the sense that data is provided without any label, and the algorithm divides by itself the data into different categories. On the other hand, neural networks are usually used as a supervised learning algorithm, meaning one has to provide labels for each data point.

For this study the data set consists of 3000 generated tracks with three different sets of start and end points: Jena to Erfurt, Erfurt to Weimar, and Weimar to Jena. These start and end points are referred to as *features* in the following discussion. There are then four features per track (latitude of start and end point and longitude of start and end point). To provide labels for each data point, tracks have been first classified through a clustering algorithm.

The first step is to center the data at zero. Normalizing the data is important because this corresponds to a higher learning speed in practice, for example, by making sure that the input values tend to come from a smaller range of values. This can avoid errors like numerical overflow, which can occur when the computer works with very small or very large numbers [2].

The next step is then to divide the data into training and test sets. The data has been then split into two subsets of 2400 and 600 entries, respectively. The data for each subset has been shuffled and then randomly selected.

The creation of a neural network and especially the search for the optimal setup can be very complex. After hitting different approaches, a final version has been found.

The accuracy of this neural network algorithm is then compared to the one from the previous K-means clustering. For this purpose different kind of tracks have been generated, in such a way to have a sample of very similar tracks with respect to the ones used during training, as well as a sample of slightly different and drastically different ones.

The first comparison is shown in Fig. 7. For that, 100 tracks for each of the following combinations of start and end points have been used: Jena-Erfurt, Erfurt-Weimar, Weimar-Jena.

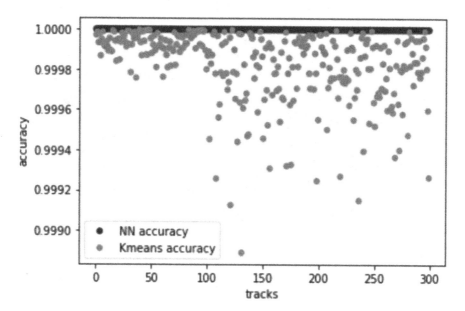

Fig. 7. Results of clustering with K-means and neural network (similar tracks with respect to the training sample) [19]

For this first test, no different predictions were made by the two algorithms, meaning that both the K-means and the neural network came to the same outcome for all tracks. Looking at the accuracy of the predictions, the neural network not only delivers very good and accurate results on average, but it has also a constantly better accuracy with respect to the clustering algorithm.

The second step is to compare predictions with slightly different tracks with respect to the ones used for training the model, as shown in Fig. 8, where 300 generated tracks, equally split among Erfurt-Jena, Weimar- Erfurt and Jena-Weimar. This is done to check how both methods respond to new data. This step is important to get a feeling of how suitable both methods would be for real-world use cases and how well they would perform.

Compared to the first step, some changes are identifiable. The accuracy for the K-means method is slowly decreasing and no longer has values in the very upper scale range for the accuracy. The neural network instead changed a lot. Now, it does not have a 100% or nearly 100% correct accuracy but is distributed like the K-means algorithms on different levels of the scale. This means that the neural network can now also make its decisions somewhat less accurately, which can be because it knows too little training data or that the tracks are more difficult to classify. But in general, it still works very well. In this case, some tracks were classified in different clusters from the two methods. There is an average of 21.47% of tracks for which the K-means algorithm and the neural network are in disagreement when predicting the belonging cluster. This result

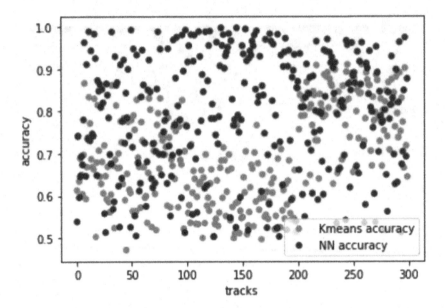

Fig. 8. Clustering with K-means and neural network (slightly different tracks with respect to the training sample) [19]

can still be used as an indication that the new track is probably belonging to a new category for the ones used for training the models.

The third step examined an even more extreme case. The test data is now using combinations that the two approaches do not know yet. For that, tracks from Gera-Dresden and Dresden-Gera have been used. The result for this scenario can be seen in Fig. 9.

This time, an average of 50% of the tracks get a different result from the two approaches. Much more interesting is the plot. The K-means algorithm has continued to decrease his accuracy and can only determine the correct cluster with an approximate 50% chance. But this is rather an indicator that the tracks perhaps do not fit into any of the previous clusters, as it is indeed the case. Completely different is instead the behavior of the neural network. Its accuracy is now completely at 100%, which means that it was able to cluster all-new tracks unambiguously. Even if the testing process would be repeated with again another 100 tracks with even more different parameters, the result would be the same. Not knowing anything about the test tracks used, one could conclude that the neural network approach is performing much better than the K-means. However, this is not true. The test tracks used belong to completely different categories with respect to the ones used to train the models. While the K-means algorithm can give us an indication about this, by classifying the new tracks in one of the known categories with very low accuracy, this is not the case for the neural network algorithm, which seems simply to assign one of the known labels to the new track with an accuracy of 1. To conclude, as being able to be warned

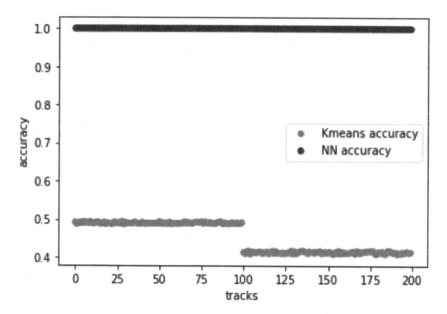

Fig. 9. Clustering with K-means and neural network (completely different tracks with respect to the training sample) [19]

by the algorithm when a completely different track from the ones already stored comes in is an important part of the system this study wants to put in place, the K-means algorithm looks much more promising in this sense. To keep working with a neural network, the found issue needs to be accounted for and avoided with perhaps some kind of infrastructure.

4   Results and Outlook

4.1   Achievements

With this study, a common ground was found for a variety of use cases which address different situations within the road traffic system. The concept of similarity in traffic data has been described, and the important parameters for the considered use cases have been discussed. In addition to a preliminary statistical analysis, aimed to find out the geographic similarity among road traffic data, two main approached have been found, that can be used as a foundation for further research. On the one hand, a clustering algorithm based on K-means, and, on the other hand, a neural network model. Both methods have their advantages and disadvantages for solving the problem.

Both of them seem to perform quite well when tracks belonging to already known categories are analyzed. Of course, to address the complexity of the presented use cases and to be able to work in a real environment, a more convoluted infrastructure that includes all necessary steps and automates them will be needed. For example, a K-means clustering algorithm could be put on top of the neural network model, since, as it has been seen, it can recognize when a new track does not belong to any existing cluster. This could work automatically as a circuit. Such a system could work with the current acquired knowledge in a real environment.

However, it is also worth mentioning that it is not necessarily the best solution, but there may be better approaches. Other methods could focus on image classification and map and analyze the similarity of tracks by the means of a previously specially created grid system. Also, the use of several other metrics, like the speed and the bearing, would be an additional step to take into account and test to address entirely the proposed use cases.

Within this study, an issue with neural network was found, as they seem not to be able to perform anomaly detection. In this regard, a further point of investigation could be the neuralization-propagation technique (NEON) [9]. This is a framework that deals in more detail with why a certain data point was assigned to a certain cluster. The cluster assignments should therefore be explained efficiently and reliably based on input characteristics. Through cluster mappings that can be explained by input features, NEON might be a possible starting point to develop an approach that could solve the current problem.

4.2 Advantages of Modern Technologies

In addition to the other methods that can be further examined, it is also important to consider which technologies could support the proposed approaches. One possibility would be the use of 5G technology, which would bring an enormous advantage, especially to those use cases which need a close to the real-time response. Let's consider in more detail the use case which treats with avoiding dangerous situations in traffic. As first step one would need to create a way of identifying conflicting areas on the road system. If we consider, for instance, an intersection, conflicting areas would be directions that cross each other. Then, the system would need to know the position of the user periodically, in such a way to determine in which area he is located, and to send him alerts about users approaching areas which are in conflict with his own, and, at the same time, to send alerts to the other users about him approaching the intersection. Combining that with the 5G technology enables us to access the data in real-time.

In addition to this, it would be helpful to receive real-time data from public transports that can also warn other participants. Receiving immediate information from street detectors that are installed at major intersections can also be used to detect positions more accurately. Collecting even real-time traffic light data can reduce the alerts to useful ones, and receiving data from environmental sensors can help trigger the alerts more reasonably.

The mobile standard 5G plays an important role in this context as it is the real-time transmission for all these data sources. Nowadays, everyone has their smartphone with them. This means it can be optimally used for tracking the necessary data. For other sources from which we want to get information, like street detectors or public transports, the transmitting devices can be also equipped with 5G.

Gathering this big amount of data is also necessary to keep improving the model using the historical and collected information. Understanding this plus the opportunity to compare it with present data, it should also be possible to predict the most sensitive intersections and the time intervals during which dangerous situations can most likely occur.

While collecting this data, of course, in a real-world deployment scenario, it is important to remember that the participants' location data is private. A system that works in a real environment must therefore also necessarily deal with data protection. This was left out for the time being, but it is an important matter to address before deploying such a system.

5 Conclusion

In this paper, some use cases of interest for the daily road traffic were presented and a common basis for their solution was found. Two main approaches for detecting and classifying trajectories data based on geographic similarity have been analyzed. Their performance have been compared and their potential deployment in a real system has been discussed. Further possible next steps and opportunities for improvements were described, as well as the importance of the 5G technology and its advantages for some of the use cases.

References

1. Statistisches Bundesamt. How to choose the optimal number of clusters for K-Means Clustering? (2022). https://www.destatis.de/EN/Themes/Society-Environment/Traffic-Accidents/_Graphic/_Interactive/traffic-accidents-driver-related-causes.html. Accessed 25 Mar 2022
2. Burkov, A.: Machine Learning Kompakt - ALLES WAS SIE WISSEN MÜSSEN. mitp Verlag (2019). ISBN 978-3958459953
3. Diallo, A.: [Draft] dynamic time warping algorithm for trajectories similarity (2020). https://alphasldiallo.github.io/dynamic-time-warping-algorithm-for-trajectoriessimilarity/. Accessed 10 Jan 2022
4. Géron, A.: Hands-On Machine Learning with Scikit-Learn, Keras, and TensorFlow - Concepts, Tools, and Techniques to Build Intelligent Systems. O'Reilly Media, Inc., Sebastopol (2019). ISBN 978-1-492-03261-8
5. Glen, S.: Jaccard index/similarity coefficient from StatisticsHowTo.com: elementary statistics for the rest of us! (2016). https://www.statisticshowto.com/jaccard-index/. Accessed 05 Jan 2022
6. Gove, R.: Using the elbow method to determine the optimal number of clusters for k-means clustering (2017). https://bl.ocks.org/rpgove/0060ff3b656618e9136b. Accessed 15 Jan 2022
7. OpenGenus IQ. Minkowski distance (2021). https://iq.opengenus.org/minkowski-distance/. Accessed 05 Jan 2022
8. Janoska, Z.: Trajectory similarity calculation using dynamic time warping. n.d. https://rpubs.com/janoskaz/10351. Accessed 13 Jan 2022

9. Kauffmann, J., et al.: From clustering to cluster explanations via neural networks (2019). https://doi.org/10.48550/ARXIV.1906.07633, https://arxiv.org/abs/1906.07633

10. Luber, S.: Was ist geospatial analytics? (2020). https://www.bigdata-insider.de/was-ist-geospatialanalytics-a-945606/. Accessed 06 Jan 2022

11. Lüthe, M.: Calculate similarity—the most relevant metrics in a nutshell (2019). https://towardsdatascience.com/calculate-similarity-the-most-relevant-metrics-in-a-nutshell-9a43564f533e. Accessed 04 Jan 2022

12. Magdy, N., et al.: Review on trajectory similarity measures. In: 2015 IEEE Seventh International Conference on Intelligent Computing and Information Systems (ICICIS), pp. 613–619 (2015). https://doi.org/10.1109/IntelCIS.2015.7397286

13. Mahavar, V., et al.: Optimum route planning of a city using GIS technology. https://www.researchgate.net/publication/332446199_OPTIMUM_ROUTE_PLANNING_OF_A_CITY_USING_GIS_TECHNOLOGY. Accessed 13 Jan 2022

14. Open Street Map. Route planning for the journey from Ernst-Abbe Hochschule Jena, Germany to Weimar, Germany (2022). https://routing.openstreetmap.de. Accessed 25 Mar 2022

15. Müller, M.: Dynamic time warping. In: Müller, M. (ed.) Information Retrieval for Music and Motion, vol. 2, pp. 69–84. Springer, Heidelberg (2007). https://doi.org/10.1007/978-3-540-74048-3_4

16. Murayama, Y.: Progress in Geospatial Analysis. Springer, Heidelberg (2012). https://doi.org/10.1007/978-4-431-54000-7. ISBN 978-4-431-54000-7

17. Sarkar, T.: Clustering metrics better than the elbow-method (2019). https://towardsdatascience.com/clustering-metrics-better-than-the-elbow-method-6926e1f723a6. Accessed 02 Feb 2022

18. Shetty, R.: How to choose the optimal number of clusters for K-means clustering? (2019). https://www.kaggle.com/getting-started/101093. Accessed 23 Jan 2022

19. Weber, M.P.: Research on detecting similarities in trajectory data: technical approaches and practical use-cases. Bachelor thesis, University of Applied Sciences Jena (2021)

Misbehavior Verification on Cooperative Intelligent Transport System

Emilien Bourdy$^{(\boxtimes)}$ (iD), Marwane Ayaida, and Hacène Fouchal

Université de Reims Champagne-Ardenne, CReSTIC, Reims, France
{emilien.bourdy,marwane.ayaida,hacene.fouchal}@univ-reims.fr

Abstract. Cooperative Intelligent Transport System is a branch of the Vehicular Ad-Hoc Network, where all messages are used to improve safety of users. Since these messages are sent clearly, anyone could send false messages, and anyone could track a user. To overcome these problems, messages are signed with a certificate, which guarantee their authenticity and integrity. Furthermore, these certificates enable a pseudonym mechanism for the privacy. However, if a malicious node joins the system with a valid certificate, we need to detect it, and revoke it from the system. Some works already exist on the detection and reporting of misbehavior. However, how can we manage a node making fake report to untrust honest nodes? In this paper, we propose to add a verification with the neighborhood after the reception of misbehavior report in order to avoid any misuse of this mechanism.

Keywords: Intelligent transport systems · Misbehavior detection · Security

1 Introduction

Nowadays, more and more Intelligent Transports Systems (ITS) use Vehicular Ad-Hoc Networks (VANET) in order to improve the security and the safety of the vehicular users in Cooperative-ITS (C-ITS). In Europe, cooperative messages, e.g., Cooperative Awareness Message (CAM) [3] (application-like beacons), Decentralized Environmental Notification Message (DENM) [4] (event messages), and Beacons [5], are sent clearly to be fully cooperative [6]. As a consequence, anyone can send or receive everything. This implies that anyone can send false data, modify data when forwarding messages and potentially track users. To prevent this, a certificate mechanism is used with the support of Public Key Infrastructure (PKI). Using these certificates, users sign their messages and so authenticity and integrity are ensured. Furthermore, certificates include a pseudonymisation mechanism, which guarantee privacy [6].

However, what can we do, if a malicious node is recognized using its certificate authority? This malicious node will have a valid pool of certificates and will be able to send false data in the network for a certain duration.

F. Phillipson et al. (Eds.): I4CS 2022, CCIS 1585, pp. 185–195, 2022.
https://doi.org/10.1007/978-3-031-06668-9_14

In this paper we will propose to help to remedy this problematic, with a system of report/review of malicious nodes. The report of malicious node will be same as in [14]: when a node detects a malicious node, it will make a report and send it to a misbehavior authority (MA). Our improvement is made by adding a reviewing step in order to confirm the report. Indeed, if we do not make this review, anyone could create report incriminating any honest node.

This paper is organized as follows. In Sect. 2, we will see how malicious nodes are detected within the C-ITS. In Sect. 3, we will detail our proposal of the improvement on how to untrust malicious nodes. In Sect. 4, we will present some application scenarios of our proposed methodology. In Sect. 5 we will demonstrate the efficiency of our methodology using a custom simulation to evaluate its impacts on the system. Finally, Sect. 6 will conclude this paper.

2   Related Works

In this section, we will first present some type of attacks, and then, how they could be detected and how attackers may be untrusted/revoked by the system.

2.1   Type of Attacks

Despite the fact that the certificates and the pseudonym mechanisms are used in C-ITS in order to guarantee the integrity, the authenticity and the privacy, many attacks are still possible. For example, jamming, false data injection, replay, routing or Sybil attacks can be performed [13].

Jamming attack is launched by the attacker in order to disrupt the used wireless channel. This type of attack can be used in Cooperative Adaptive Cruise Control (CACC) [7] in order to limit the efficiency and, possibly, to cause accidents. In CACC, the first vehicle is the one that is actually driven by a human or autonomously. It sends messages to its following vehicles. Following vehicles will be guided by the leader. When an attacker disrupt these communications, the followers can not know how to drive.

False data injection is when an attacker sends false information like a blocked road, traffic jam, emergency braking, etc. As for jamming attack, this type of attack may be used in CACC [8,12], but also with autonomous vehicles. Indeed, if a vehicle receives a false emergency braking warning from the one in front of it, it will also brake and potentially may cause traffic jam or even accident.

Replay attack and routing attacks are used to replay messages in order to disrupt the network, and its routing protocol in multi-hop routing. In single-hop, replay attack is easily identified because of the timestamp is used in every message [16], and duplicate packet detection is also considered in the European standard [5]. However, in multi-hop routing, the attacker may deviate the message, or launch a black-hole attack [9].

Finally, Sybil attack is when a node simulates other users [10]. It is similar to data injection and routing attack. The force of Sybil attack is to use the pseudonym mechanism to simulate the other nodes. This type of attack is one of most studied attack [11,17].

2.2   Detection and Prevention

To detect an attack, we have different solutions that we divide into four categories according to the survey of Rens Wouter van der Heijden et al. [13], and CaTch detectors from Joseph Kamel et al. [15].

The four categories are Node-Centric Misbehavior Detection (behavioral and trusted-based), and Data-Centric Misbehavior Detection (consistency and plausibility).

Behavioral node-centric detection methods use patterns and does not consider data semantics. Trusted-based ones assume that most of the nodes are honest, with a specific vote schemes to revoke attackers.

Consistency data-centric detection approaches use the relation between the packets to correlate the validity of data. Plausibility detection ones use models to verify data, by checking that they are compliant with the given models.

Finally, CaTch detectors mechanisms use the range tolerant approaches to improve the misbehavior detection and separate them from a sensor mistake.

When an attack is detected, in [14], authors propose a method to report the attack or the sensor misbehavior. They defined a format for the report to be sent to a Misbehavior Authority (MA). The MA can untrust an attacker or send it a message to prevent it from a sensor problem in order to recalibrate it.

3   Our Proposed Method Description

As discussed in Subsect. 2.2, in [14], the authors use a MA to untrust an attacker or to warn a user that his sensors need to be calibrated. But they can not manage fake reports sent by an attacker who want to untrust an honest node.

In this paper, we propose to extend this approach with more steps to enhance its performances. In some C-ITS projects [1,2], ITS stations (ITS-S) use a hybridization mechanism between the ITS-G5 channels and the cellular network by sending CAMs in both networks. By doing this, they send their position to an entity, denoted a National Node (NN), which is able to send events to the ITS-S using a tile system (OSM tile for example) in order to cover non-G5 covered areas.

In our proposed methodology, the MA could send a request to ask for the neighborhood of any vehicle from the NN. This neighborhood will be used in order to send a review to the reporter and its neighbors about the suspicious one. By doing this, the reporter is notified that the MA is taking care about the potential reported threat. Moreover, the reporter's neighbors are aware that there is a potential threat, and in return they send a testimony to the MA. After that, MA can decide if the reporter made effectively a real report or misuse the system to send a fake report.

When the MA decides to reject a station, it is made temporarily, and the rejected station will be back if it stops its malicious behaviour. Of course, if the rejected station continues his misbehavior, the MA will reject it forever after a certain predefined threshold. When the MA rejects a station, all linked certificates will be revoked, and so, if the malicious node wants to change its pseudonym, it needs to be registered multiple time to the same PKI; thus switching to an other certificate generated from the same private key will fail since its key was revoked.

Theses behaviors are described in Algorithms 1, 2 and 3. Algorithm 1 is used by the misbehavior node detector, Algorithm 2 by the MA, and Algorithm 3 by its neighbors.

Algorithm 1. Algorithm used by the misbehavior detector

1: detection of a misbehavior
2: $report \leftarrow createReport()$
3: send $report$ to MA
4: wait for acknowledgement

Algorithm 2. Algorithm used by the misbehavior authority

1: receive $report$ from id_report
2: **if** $id\_report \in banned\_id$ **then**
3:     send review to id_report
4: **else**
5:     $id\_mal \leftarrow report.id\_malicious$
6:     **if** $id\_mal \in banned\_id$ **then**
7:         increase id_mal banishment time
8:     **else**
9:         $neighbors \leftarrow id\_report$ neighborhood
10:        **for all** $id \in neighbors - \{id\_mal\}$ **do**
11:            send review to id
12:        **end for**
13:        $nb\_yes \leftarrow 0$
14:        $nb\_no \leftarrow 0$
15:        **for all** $id \in neighbors - \{id\_mal, id\_report\}$ **do**
16:            **if** answer $= YES$ **then**
17:                $nb\_yes \leftarrow nb\_yes + 1$
18:            **else if** answer $= NO$ **then**
19:                $nb\_no \leftarrow nb\_no + 1$
20:            **end if**
21:        **end for**
22:        **if** $nb\_yes > TH\_MAL$ **then**
23:            add id_mal to $banned\_id$
24:        **else if** $nb\_no > TH\_REPORT$ **then**
25:            add id_report to $banned\_id$
26:        **end if**
27:    **end if**
28: **end if**

Algorithm 3. Algorithm used by the misbehavior reviewer

1: receive review from MA
2: $id\_mal \leftarrow review.id\_malicious$
3: $attack \leftarrow review.attack\_type$
4: send $is\_attack(id\_mal, attack)$ to MA

Adding these few steps has many advantages:

1. in case of malicious node detection by an ITS-S, the neighborhood is alerted and can be watchful;
2. a malicious node will not be able to reject an other ITS-S;
3. if an ITS-S makes one mistake in its algorithm or due to sensors defaults, it will not be rejected forever.

As for blockchain systems, this methodology has flaws. If the attackers are the majority of the system, they can untrust honest nodes by confirming the review of other malicious ones.

4 Scenarios

In order to demonstrate the three previous advantages, we propose in this section the execution of three situations.

4.1 Malicious Station Detected

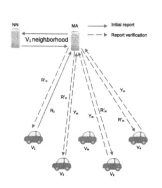

(a) Scenario 1: V_1 catches V_m

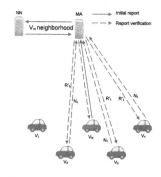

(b) Scenarios 2 and 3: V_m tries to blacklist V_1

Fig. 1. Illustration of scenarios

The first considered scenario is the simplest one: a malicious station (V_m) is detected by another station (V_1). V_1 sends a report to the MA. MA gets the neighborhood of V_m in the OSM tile. MA notifies all the stations in this tile except the malicious one. V_1 will not reply to the MA and only considers the message from MA as an acknowledgment of the consideration of the threat by it. The other stations will monitor V_m and check if it is a malicious station and agree. When MA has sufficient data to discriminate V_m, it will blacklist it (Fig. 1).

4.2 Malicious Station Tries to Blacklist Honest Stations

The second considered scenario consists in a malicious station (V_m) trying to incriminate a regular station (V_1). V_m sends report to the MA. MA gets the neighborhood of V_1 in the OSM tile. MA notifies all the stations in this tile except V_1. V_m will not reply to the MA and only considers the message from MA as an acknowledgment of the consideration of the threat by the MA. The other stations will monitor V_1 and check if it is a malicious station and disagree. MA will add V_m in the suspicious database, and inform the other stations to not take into account its MA reports during a moment. If V_m continues to make fake reports before the end of its blacklisting period, MA will send acknowledgement only to the V_m in order to let it think that it is still considered as valid. If V_m continues to make false reports before the end of the blacklisting period, MA will blacklist it forever.

4.3 Regular Station Makes Sometimes False Positives

The third considered scenario consists in a regular station (V_r) trying to incriminate a regular station (V_1) because of a one time error in it's monitoring algorithm. V_r sends report to the MA. MA gets the neighborhood of V_1 in the OSM tile. MA notifies all the stations in this tile except V_1. V_r will not reply to the MA and only considers the message from MA as an acknowledgment of the consideration of the threat by the MA. The other stations will monitor V_1 and check if it is a malicious station and disagree. MA will add V_r in the suspicious database, and inform the other stations to not take its MA reports into account during a moment. After the expiration of the blacklisting duration, if V_r has not send other false reports, it will be reintegrated to the regular process.

5 Simulation and Evaluation

5.1 Simulation

In order to evaluate our methodology, we build our custom simulation. In this simulation, we can set few parameters:

- M: is the percentage of malicious nodes from all the involved nodes in the simulation,
- D: is the probability for a node to detect a malicious one,
- Y: is the probability that a non-malicious node answers YES to a review to confirm it,
- T the percentage of YES answers needed to banish a malicious node.

For more simplicity, we set N, the probability that a non-malicious node answers NO to a review to deny it, to $Y - 15$.

From its definition, M is proportional to the number of vehicles, and so, we fixed Nb as the number of all the vehicles to the arbitrary value of 200, which represents a high concentration of vehicles in a city. Finally, each scenario can not have more than 1000 iterations to avoid infinite loops. Beyond this value, we suppose that the network changes a lot, because of velocity of VANETs and we are in another simulation.

The simulation works as follows: a step run all non-malicious nodes. Each node i will look for all nodes m if it is a malicious one. If m is malicious node, i has $D\%$ of probability to catch it. If i does not catch m, it continues to monitor the other nodes. Otherwise, its state pass from DETECTION to REPORTING. The other nodes pass from state DETECTION to REVIEWIG. In REPORTING state, the node waits and passes to DETECTION state. In REVIEWING state, i has $N\%$ of probability to reply NO, $Y + factor$ % of probability to reply YES and the rest to be SUSPICIOUS. The $factor$ is a number started at 0, incremented by 5 each time a same node that will not select YES result because i becomes more and more suspicious. If a reviewer has already answer YES for a MA reporting node, it will always answer YES. When all the nodes have complete their steps, we compare if the number of $YES > T$. If it is the case, m is banned. Finally, to be more pessimist, in the simulation, a node i can not detect more than one node per step.

5.2   Evaluation

Table 1 shows the different values used for the parameters, with a combination of 15 210 scenarios.

Table 1. Values used for the parameters

Parameter	From	To	Step
M	5	25	5
D	20	80	5
Y	20	80	5
T	0	85	5

For each scenario, we recorded the average time (number of steps) to detect a node, and for each step, we recorded the number of station who answered NO, $SUSPICIOUS$, and YES, the number of malicious nodes that are still in the system, and time since last banishment.

With these simulations, we were able to evaluate the impact of each parameter in terms of average time to detect a malicious node, the time needed to detect the all malicious nodes, and the impact in the awareness of the threat in the system. Table 2 shows for each varying parameter, the other fixed values that we selected to launch the simulation. Figure 2 shows the duration needed to detect a malicious node and all malicious nodes; while Fig. 3 shows the average of stations who answered *YES*, *NO* and *UNKNOW*.

Table 2. Values used for the evaluation

	M	D	Y	T	Figure
M	N/A	40	40	50	Figures 2a and 3a
D	20	N/A	40	50	Figures 2b and 3b
Y	20	40	N/A	50	Figures 2c and 3c
T	20	40	40	N/A	Figures 2d and 3d

Figure 2 shows that the duration needed to detect one malicious node is very close to the value of T. The more we have malicious nodes, the less time is needed to catch one of them. D and Y has no major impact on duration needed to detect one malicious node, because of the number of honest nodes against the malicious ones. If D is small, as we have more honest nodes than malicious nodes, the probability to detect a malicious node is higher and the reviewing step will be triggered. For the same reasons, if Y is low, T will be easily reached by the honest nodes. Finally, for the same reasons, the overall time needed to detect all malicious nodes is highly impacted by T and M. One can notice from these figures that the average time needed to detect a node stills approximately close to 2.5 steps.

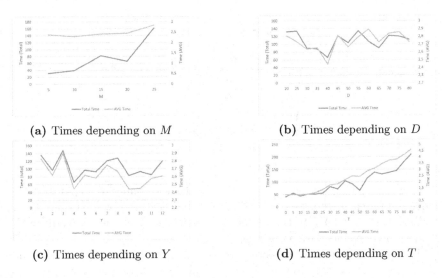

(a) Times depending on M

(b) Times depending on D

(c) Times depending on Y

(d) Times depending on T

Fig. 2. Times to detect malicious nodes

Figure 3 shows that we do not need to have many YES replies in order to detect malicious nodes, and thus, only the T has an influence on the banishment result. Indeed, when a node catches a malicious one, it will retry to untrust it, and so the others who did not identify the malicious nodes as wicked will be more and more suspicious. Note that we consider that the malicious nodes are in the NO section, and so, except for the Fig. 3a, 20% of the NO are malicious nodes. Finally, we can see that a majority of the nodes are suspicious. So, they will use malicious messages with more care.

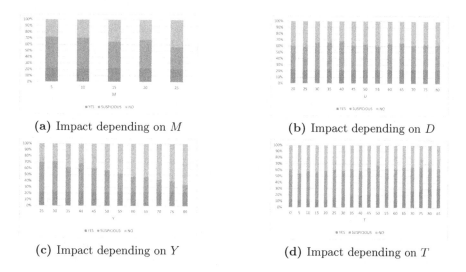

(a) Impact depending on M

(b) Impact depending on D

(c) Impact depending on Y

(d) Impact depending on T

Fig. 3. Impact in the environment seen by the nodes

6   Conclusion and Future Work

In this paper, we noticed that in C-ITS environment, we need to ensure authenticity, integrity and data privacy of users. To do that, we use the PKI mechanism, which manages the certificates used by vehicles to sign their data, while guaranteeing the integrity and authenticity of them, and also ensuring a pseudonymisation mechanism for privacy. If someone, who is already trusted by the PKI, is a malicious node, we have to detect it. A lot of works are related to the attack detection based on Node-Centric Misbehavior Detection (behavioral and trusted-based), Data-Centric Misbehavior Detection (consistency and plausibility) [13], or range tolerance [15]. The work in [14] proposes a method using a MA to untrust/revoke it.

Our methodology is an extension of this previous one, with the addition of a review to the reporter's neighborhood. By doing this, we can prevent them from the impact of the attack, and they can confirm or not if the attack is really launched to the MA and may also discredit the reporter if needed. While allowing not permanently untrusting a false reporter, someone making a one-shot mistake due to its sensors, it will be trusted again, and a real attacker with false reports will be untrusted longer and even forever.

In the next steps of this work, we will define the review ASN.1 definition. With this definition, we will be able to really implement the methodology and the three associated scenarios. The target scenarios will be then evaluated either by simulation or by real implementation.

References

1. C-roads project. https://www.c-roads.eu/platform.html. Accessed 11 Nov 2021
2. Intercor project. https://intercor-project.eu/. Accessed 11 Nov 2021
3. Intelligent transport systems (ITS); vehicular communications; basic set of applications; part 2: Specification of cooperative awareness basic service, April 2019
4. Intelligent transport systems (ITS); vehicular communications; basic set of applications; part 3: Specifications of decentralized environmental notification basic service, April 2019
5. Intelligent transport systems (ITS); vehicular communications; geonetworking; part 4: Geographical addressing and forwarding for point-to-point and point-to-multipoint communications; sub-part 1: Media-independent functionality, January 2020
6. Intelligent transport systems (ITS); security; security header and certificate formats, October 2021
7. Alipour-Fanid, A., Dabaghchian, M., Zhang, H., Zeng, K.: String stability analysis of cooperative adaptive cruise control under jamming attacks. In: 2017 IEEE 18th International Symposium on High Assurance Systems Engineering (HASE), pp. 157–162 (2017). https://doi.org/10.1109/HASE.2017.39
8. Amoozadeh, M., et al.: Security vulnerabilities of connected vehicle streams and their impact on cooperative driving. IEEE Commun. Mag. **53**(6), 126–132 (2015). https://doi.org/10.1109/MCOM.2015.7120028
9. Azees, M., Vijayakumar, P., Jegatha Deborah, L.: Comprehensive survey on security services in vehicular ad-hoc networks. IET Intell. Transp. Syst. **10**(6), 379–388 (2016). https://doi.org/10.1049/iet-its.2015.0072
10. Douceur, J.R.: The sybil attack. In: Druschel, P., Kaashoek, F., Rowstron, A. (eds.) IPTPS 2002. LNCS, vol. 2429, pp. 251–260. Springer, Heidelberg (2002). https://doi.org/10.1007/3-540-45748-8_24
11. Hamed, H., Keshavarz-Haddad, A., Haghighi, S.G.: Sybil attack detection in urban VANETs based on RSU support. In: Iranian Conference on Electrical Engineering (ICEE), pp. 602–606. IEEE (2018)
12. van der Heijden, R., Lukaseder, T., Kargl, F.: Analyzing attacks on cooperative adaptive cruise control (CACC). In: 2017 IEEE Vehicular Networking Conference (VNC), pp. 45–52 (2017). https://doi.org/10.1109/VNC.2017.8275598
13. van der Heijden, R.W., Dietzel, S., Leinmüller, T., Kargl, F.: Survey on misbehavior detection in cooperative intelligent transportation systems. IEEE Commun. Surv. Tutor. **21**(1), 779–811 (2018)
14. Kamel, J., Jemaa, I.B., Kaiser, A., Urien, P.: Misbehavior reporting protocol for C-ITS. In: 2018 IEEE Vehicular Networking Conference (VNC), pp. 1–4. IEEE (2018)

15. Kamel, J., Kaiser, A., ben Jemaa, I., Cincilla, P., Urien, P.: CaTch: a confidence range tolerant misbehavior detection approach. In: 2019 IEEE Wireless Communications and Networking Conference (WCNC), pp. 1–8. IEEE (2019)
16. Schmidt, D., Radke, K., Camtepe, S., Foo, E., Ren, M.: A survey and analysis of the GNSS spoofing threat and countermeasures. ACM Comput. Surv. (CSUR) **48**(4), 1–31 (2016)
17. Yao, Y., et al.: Multi-channel based Sybil attack detection in vehicular ad hoc networks using RSSI. IEEE Trans. Mob. Comput. **18**(2), 362–375 (2018)

Smart Cities and Standardization

A Multi Service Capacitated Facility Location Problem with Stochastic Demand

L. J. Kim[1,2], F. Phillipson[2,3]([envelope]) [ORCID], and R. S. Wezeman[2]

[1] Erasmus University, Rotterdam, The Netherlands
[2] TNO, The Hague, The Netherlands
frank.phillipson@tno.nl
[3] Maastricht University, Maastricht, The Netherlands

Abstract. This paper considers the problem of identifying optimal locations for wireless service installations in smart cities. The problem is modelled as a facility location problem with multiple service types, known as the Multi Service Facility Location Problem (MSCFLP). Given a set of potential facility locations and demand point data, the goal is to identify at which locations the facilities should be opened, and which demand points should be serviced by each open facility in order to minimise costs. In this study, the demand quantities at each demand point are assumed to follow a probability distribution. An adaptive neighbourhood search heuristic is proposed in order to find a good solution to the problem, where the stochastic demand was translated to a deterministic capacity constraint. The heuristic iteratively improves the service allocations in sub-regions of the problem instances, starting from an initial feasible solution. The results show that the heuristic is able to find good solutions within very short time. Furthermore, we assessed the handling of the stochasticity by the model. Its performance is assessed by means of simulation, and results show that this approach works well in various scenarios of traffic models.

Keywords: Smart city · Facility location problem · Adaptive large neighbourhood search · Wireless service distribution · Stochastic demand

1 Introduction

The Multi Service Capacitated Facility Location Problem (MSCFLP) is a generalisation of the Capacitated Facility Location Problem (CFLP). In the CFLP, there is a set of customers with individual demand for a single product that need to be satisfied. The customers are denoted as demand points. There are multiple locations where facilities can be opened such that they can service the demand points. The locations where it is possible to open a facility are called access points. Once a facility has been opened at an access point, the location is called

© The Author(s), under exclusive license to Springer Nature Switzerland AG 2022
F. Phillipson et al. (Eds.): I4CS 2022, CCIS 1585, pp. 199–214, 2022.
https://doi.org/10.1007/978-3-031-06668-9_15

a service point. These facilities have a capacity on the amount of service that can be delivered. The MSCFLP allows for multiple types of service, handled by the same service point. The problem consists of deciding where to open facilities such that the costs are minimised. Two types of costs are incurred: the setup costs for an access point to be prepared to be a service point, and the installations costs to equip a prepared service point with a device. In this study, we model the problem of distributing multiple wireless service installations across a smart city as a MSCFLP. The demand points correspond to households and other users who have devices that need connection. As access locations, lampposts are considered. Instead of a limit on how much service a facility can deliver, we have a limit on the number of connections to devices one installation can make.

The CFLP is in general NP-hard, meaning it becomes quickly unfeasible to solve large problem instances within reasonable time. The problem without capacity restrictions per facility, the Uncapacitated Facility Location Problem (UFLP), can be shown to be NP-hard via reduction from the Set Cover Problem (SCP), which is one of Karp's 21 NP-Complete problems, as listed by Karp [3]. The UFLP is a relaxation of the CFLP of the capacity restrictions, and is thus not more difficult than the CFLP. As a CFLP is a special case of the MSCFLP where the number of services equals 1, hence the complexity of the MSCFLP is NP-hard.

Often in a facility location problem, a demand point only needs to be covered once by a (single) service point, with no uncertainty in demand. Instead of this scenario, in our case each demand point has a certain level of demand for various services that needs to be fulfilled, possibly by multiple service points. As mentioned, demand is modelled as number of devices requiring connection. For example, imagine one demand point has a smartphone, smart television and two laptops that need internet access. The demand for the service Wi-Fi corresponds to four connections for this demand point. The demand is discrete valued, since it is not possible to have a fraction of a device in need of service. We assume that the demand is not deterministic but has an underlying probability distribution. The assumption of a normal distribution is used, but other distributions such as the Weibull distribution, which can take a similar shape as the normal distribution with the correct choice of parameters, may also be fitting candidates.

This gives us a 'Multi Service Capacitated Facility Location Problem with Stochastic Demand' (MSCFLP-SD). Where Facility Location Problems are well studied in general [6], the research in MSCFLP is more scarce. One of the earliest mentions of a multi-service instance is looked into by Suzuki and Hodgson [11]. A single source model is described, where a service point can offer three types of human services. The number of facilities that are opened is decided beforehand. Demand is described as a discrete set of demand points which need to be covered.

In the case of wireless services with only fixed location opening costs and installation costs, the distance between service and demand points are irrelevant as long as the demand point is within range of the service point(s) it is serviced by. Papers on this topic are from Veerman et al. [12], Hoekstra et al. [2] and Vos et al. [14]. They all give heuristic approaches for solving the MSCFLP using deterministic demand. An exact formulation for a similar MSCFLP with stochastic demand is presented by Verhoek [13]. It attempts to satisfy the demand at a given reliability level by incorporating it into a constraint in the mathematical program. The problem studied in this paper resembles that of Verhoek [13], whose exact approach suffers of high computation times. This topic therefore still requires further research in order to find methods that deliver good solutions within feasible time, which is the subject of this paper.

We start this paper, which is based on the master's thesis of the first author [4], with the problem as formulated by Verhoek [13] and proposes a heuristic approach based on neighbourhood search as presented in papers as Chyu and Chang [1]. Local search methods are generally very fast and can easily deliver intermediate solutions, but have less guarantee on optimality. In Sect. 2 we define the MSCFLP-SD in detail. In Sect. 3 we propose the 'Adaptive Large Neighbourhood Search with Exact Subproblems' (ALNS-ES) for this problem and show the computational results in Sect. 4. Not only the performance of the heuristic are shown, but also how well the stochasticity is handled, in Sect. 5. We end with some conclusions and ideas for further research.

2 Mathematical Model

In this section, the mathematical model describing the problem at hand is presented. Table 1 shows the notation of sets, parameters and variables that are used to describe the base mathematical model respectively. The problem to solve can then be defined as a Mixed-Integer Programming (MIP) Problem:

$$\min \quad \sum_{u \in S} \sum_{j \in L} c_j^u x_j^u + \sum_{j \in L} f_j y_j, \tag{1}$$

$$s.t. \qquad x_j^u \le y_j \qquad\qquad \forall j \in L, \forall u \in S, \tag{2}$$

$$\sum_{i \in D^u} z_{ij}^u \le N^u x_j^u \qquad \forall j \in L, \forall u \in S, \tag{3}$$

$$P(\sum_{j \in L} z_{ij}^u \ge d_i^u) \ge \alpha \qquad \forall i \in D^u, \forall u \in S, \tag{4}$$

$$x_j^u \in \{0,1\} \qquad\qquad \forall j \in L, \forall u \in S, \tag{5}$$

$$y_j \in \{0,1\} \qquad\qquad \forall j \in L, \tag{6}$$

$$z_{ij}^u \in \mathbb{N} \qquad\qquad \forall \{i,j\} \in \mathbb{H}^u. \tag{7}$$

Table 1. List of variables, sets and parameters

Variable	Description
y_j	$\begin{cases} 1 & \text{if service point } j \text{ is opened,} \\ 0 & \text{otherwise} \end{cases}$
x_j^u	$\begin{cases} 1 & \text{if service point } j \text{ is equipped with service type } u, \\ 0 & \text{otherwise} \end{cases}$
z_{ij}^u	Numerical value representing the number of connections to devices for service type u provided by service point j to demand point i

Set	Description and Indices
S	The set of services: Wi-Fi (1), Alarm (2), Telecommunication Network (3), $u \in S$
L	The set of potential service locations, $j \in L$
D^u	The set of demand points for service u, $i \in D^u$
$\mathbb{H}^u$	Combinations of (i,j) for which demand point i can be reached by service point j with service type u

Parameter	Description
f_j	Fixed cost of opening service location j
c_j^u	Cost of installing service type u at service point j
d_i^u	Demand for service type u at demand point i
N^u	Service capacity for one installation of service type u, in number of connections available
α	Reliability level to meet demand
μ_i^u	Mean number of wireless devices in a household i requiring signal service type u
σ^u	Standard deviation of number of wireless devices per household requiring signal service type u

Equations (1) to (7) describe the basic MSCFLP. The problem minimises the total costs for opening the required access points to become active service points and the costs incurred to install the wireless services on to these points, summarised by (1). The constraints in (2) only allow service installations to be equipped in places which are open to be active. At the same time, it also ensures that only one installation of service type u can be made at location j, since the value of y_j is bounded from above by 1. The constraints in (3) make sure that an installation cannot deliver a signal to more devices than it is compatible with. The demand requirement is enforced by the constraints in (4), meaning that with probability $\alpha = 0.95$ in this study the constraint are met. Finally, the constraints in (5), (6) and (7) define the space of the decision variables. All variables in our model are considered to be integer valued, because the demand and service units are measured in number of devices. Notice that the variables z_{ij}^u can only exist in case demand point i can be reached by signal type u from service point j. In order to decrease the number of unnecessary variables and constraints, we define a separate set $\mathbb{H}^u$. The set $\mathbb{H}^u$ contains all combinations $\{i, j\}$ where the demand point i is within signal range of service point j for service type u.

Currently, the constraints in (4) contain a probability term which cannot be directly implemented into a solver. However, it is possible to rewrite constraints (4) into a more easily implementable form. We use a method for modelling with uncertain variables in case of the normal distribution. Postek [8] explains that "a safe way to implement our 95% constraint satisfaction requirement is to make sure that the 95% quantile of this random variable is less than or equal to b_i", where the random variable in our case is the demand level at each demand point. Given that $d_i^u \sim N(\mu_i^u, \sigma^u)$, we can derive a similar relation. This simplifies the probability containing constraint into a linear constraint which is comparable to the case of deterministic demand. In the linear transformation of random variable d_i^u, a 'constant' of $\sum_{j \in L} z_{ij}^u$ is deducted. Following [8], we can enforce constraints (4) using the following reformulation instead:

$$\mu_i^u + q_{0.95} \sqrt{(\sigma^u)^2} \leq \sum_{j \in L} z_{ij}^u. \tag{8}$$

The notation $q_{0.95}$ refers to the 95th percentile of the standard normal distribution. By doing this, we have translated the stochastic constraint into a deterministic one.

3   Solution Approach

As mentioned previously, the results from [2,13] show that solving the whole mathematical model using an exact approach is expected to result in undesirably long computation times for large instances. However, the results of [2], who uses the same mathematical model, suggest that the model solves in very short time in case of small instances. The exact evaluation took less than 1 s for less than 100 access locations (and around double the amount of demand points) with a 0.0% optimality gap, and for around 100 access locations a solution with a <5% gap was found within 1 s. Using this observation and the idea of neighbourhood search, we propose an Adaptive Large Neighbourhood Search with Exact Subproblems (ALNS-ES). In this section, we briefly introduce the concept of Adaptive Large Neighbourhood Search, followed by details on the ALNS-ES algorithm.

3.1   Adaptive Large Neighbourhood Search

In Large Neighbourhood Search (LNS), as presented by Shaw [10], an initial solution is gradually improved by alternately destroying and repairing the solution. The ALNS heuristic, introduced by Ropke and Pisinger [9], extends the LNS heuristic by allowing the use of multiple destroy and repair methods within the same search process. It belongs to the class of very large scale neighbourhood search algorithms [7]. This method explores a much bigger search space compared to generic local search methods which modify a small part of the solution. It keeps track of a current best solution by evaluating the objective values of found neighbourhoods.

Which destroy and repair methods are used at each turn are determined by probabilities of choosing a certain method pair, which are adjusted throughout the algorithm after each iteration. The probabilities of being selected depend on chances of success in improving the solution in the past iterations. The algorithm continuously explores neighbourhoods that are found via successive uses of destroy and repair methods, until a stopping criterion is met. There are two commonly used stopping criteria: the number of iterations and the number of consecutive iterations performed without finding an improvement.

3.2   Adaptive Large Neighbourhood Search with Exact Subproblems

The ALNS-ES algorithm uses the ALNS framework with a simulated annealing component, tabu search and two types of objective values. A solution is a set of open access points with service allocations, connecting service points with demand points, that satisfies the demand requirements of the problem instance. An overview of the whole algorithm is given by Algorithm 1.

We now take a look at the steps in Algorithm 1. In order to start the search process, we need to define a starting point. The starting point is a feasible solution which is not necessarily (and most likely not) optimal. An initial feasible solution is found using a constructive heuristic denoted as *constructiveHeuristic()*. In practice, the design of the constructive heuristic is not of importance as long as it is able to deliver a feasible allocation.

Next, the created initial solution undergoes a iterative destruction and reparation process. ALNS-ES uses two destroy methods. The destroy methods are denoted as $destroy_k()$ in Algorithm 1, with $k = 1$ or $k = 2$.

The first type of destroy method chooses a main demand point i_M randomly and removes all of its current connections to service points. For each disconnected service point, its links to all other demand points are also destroyed. The motivation behind this destroy method is that it is perhaps possible to find more efficient allocations within a certain sub-network, and doing it for many sub-networks can get the solution closer to the optimal allocation for the whole region. The results of Hoekstra [2] for running the SSH for small instances suggests that if we make our sub-regions contain around 100 access locations, they can be solved in very little time.

The second destroy method chooses a random service point j_M and destroys all links between several service points and their corresponding demand points that are close to j_M. The 300 service points closest to j_M are identified (or the maximal amount of service points in case the problem instance contains less than 300 service points in total) in the instance initialisation step and a number of them are disconnected. Again, this number is expected to lie around 100 and is taken equal to the value in the first destroy method such that solution repair times remain similar. The motivation behind this selection of service points is that after the repair method, the demands served by j_M can be taken over by the service points near j_M such that j_M can be closed.

In both destroy methods, the starting points i_M and j_M are picked randomly. It can occur that the same service or demand point is selected multiple times almost consecutively by chance, causing the algorithm to repeat unnecessary iterations which return the same result. In order to avoid such behaviour, a tabu list is employed for both the selection of i_M in the first destroy method and j_M in the second. Once a point has been selected, it is put in a tabu list which the algorithm does not choose as i_M or j_M for the next 100 iterations.

The main difference between this destroy methods is that in the first destroy method, some service points within the considered sub-region around i_M may not be disconnected, whilst in the second destroy method all service points within a certain distance of j_M are disconnected. Which of these two destroy methods are to be employed depends on a probability p_k for method k. The probability is described by (9).

$$p_k = \frac{w_k}{w_1 + w_2}. \qquad (9)$$

The weight of selecting a certain destroy method w_k is updated as:

$$w_k = \delta w_k + (1 - \delta)\Psi. \qquad (10)$$

The δ is a decay parameter with a value between 0 and 1. The Ψ is an outcome of a score function which is determined as:

$$\Psi = max \begin{cases} 20, & \text{if the new solution is the best obtained so far in terms of costs} \\ 15, & \text{if the new solution is better than the current solution in terms of balance} \\ 10, & \text{if the new solution is accepted} \\ 5, & \text{if the new solution is not accepted} \end{cases} \qquad (11)$$

Weights are initialised to be 10 in the default case for both methods such that a solution accepted in the simulated annealing process does not increase the initial weight of the destroy method used. Initially we will use $\delta = 0.9$ based on the analysis in [4].

Both destroy methods are followed up by the same type of repair method, denoted by $repair()$ in Algorithm 1. The two destroy methods result in incomplete solutions with demand points which are either completely or partially not satisfied and service points that are completely disconnected from their previous customers. Recall that we have made the stochastic demand element deterministic using (8), therefore our instance has known individual demand values per demand point. For partially unsatisfied demand points, it can be easily calculated how much demand is unsatisfied by looking at how much service was provided to them before destruction, and subtracting it from their total demand. Then we solve the MIP problem as described in Sect. 2 using a MIP commerical solver, but for the smaller sub-regions, resulting in the 'Exact Subproblem' part of the approach. A time limit of 5 s is enforced for the MIP subproblem, such that the theoretical maximum running time for the solely solving the subproblems is 25 min. In a case where the demand points and service points selected for the subproblem make it difficult for the exact IP to be solved to optimality, there are two options. The first is that the IP has found a feasible IP solution, which may not be optimal, but is the best solution so far. The subproblem then returns this solution as the best solution found. The other is that the IP has not been able to find a feasible IP solution. In this case, the IP does not return a solution and the algorithm reverts to the current solution before destruction. In practice, most subproblems are solved within 500 ms, and almost all subproblems are solved within 1 s.

After we have repaired a solution, we need to assess whether the new solution is better than the current best candidate. We use two criteria to determine whether a newly constructed solution is 'better' than the previous one. The first and foremost one is of course, the total costs. Note that in our model, costs are only incurred for the opening of an access point, and the single installation costs of a service at an opened access point. In other applications of LNS, there often exists other costs that are incurred for the supply of service from a service point to a demand point. For example, in Chyu and Chang [1], there exist transportation costs from a service point to a demand point. In these cases, the total costs often differ between two solutions which use the same number of facilities. This is not applicable to our problem and we use a secondary measure of solution quality. We define a new measure 'balance' of a solution, which indicates how well distributed the service load is across the service points. In order to assess this measure, let's say we have a set of L^* service points which have undergone change in an iteration of the algorithm. The service points in L^* are ordered in descending order of amount of service provided. Then, we take a look at the top and bottom 20% in the ordered list. Denote the collection of service points in the top 20% as L_{top}, and L_{bot} for the bottom 20%. We then define the measure 'Balance' for a set of service points as in (12). Since we would like have an even spread the service intensity if possible, a low value of this criterion is preferred.

$$Balance = \sum_{i \in D^u} (\sum_{j \in L_{top}} z_{ij}^u - \sum_{j \in L_{bot}} z_{ij}^u). \tag{12}$$

Given these two criteria, the current best solution is updated if the neighbour solution being explored returns a lower value in either one. Furthermore, a simulated annealing framework is used in order to allow for sufficient exploration of neighbourhoods that may not deliver improvements in the earlier iterations but possibly can in later ones. Simulated annealing allows for neighbourhoods which are not accepted according to the previous two acceptance criteria to still be accepted with a certain probability. This probability p_{accept} depends on the difference in criterion values between the neighbour solution and the current best solution Δ, and a temperature T, as in (13). Δ_c corresponds to the difference in cost criterion and Δ_b to the difference in balance criterion. We consider both probabilities corresponding to differences in both total costs and balance, and take the bigger probability of the two as the acceptance probability. The temperature T is adjusted every time the simulated annealing process is called. Using a cooling parameter ι, after each call T is updated to $\iota \cdot T$. The temperature is determined separately for the two criteria, distinguished as T_c for the cost criterion and T_b for the balance criterion. Cooling scheme ι is a parameter between 0 and 1 which controls how fast the probability of acceptance decreases, and set to 0.95 in this research.

$$p_{accept} = max\{exp(\frac{-\Delta_c}{T_c}), exp(\frac{-\Delta_b}{T_b})\}. \tag{13}$$

The ALNS-ES performs neighbourhood searches per service type, starting with the service type with lowest range. This is because it is most likely that the locations that need to be opened are the least flexible for services with low range. After the algorithm has terminated for a type of service, the opening costs f_j of opened locations in the solution are set to 0 for the next service type. The explained steps are performed for a maximum of 300 iterations for each service, and maximally 100 consecutive iterations without improvement.

Algorithm 1: ALNS-ES

Initialize costs f_j, c_j, demand points D^u, service points L;
Sort services types S in ascending order of service range;
for $u \in S$ **do**
    Initialize temperatures T_c, T_b, cooling ι and probability weights w_k.
    noChange $\leftarrow$ 0;
    $tabu_1 = \emptyset, tabu_2 = \emptyset$;
    initialSolution $\leftarrow$ constructiveHeuristic();
    bestSolution, currentSolution $\leftarrow$ initialSolution;
    while *Stopping criteria not met* **do**
        Choose destroy method destroy$_k$() with probability p_k;
        neighborSolution $\leftarrow$ destroy$_k$(currentSolution,$tabu_1$,$tabu_2$);
        neighborSolution $\leftarrow$ repair(neighborSolution);
        if *Better cost solution found* **then**
            currentSolution $\leftarrow$ neighborSolution;
            bestSolution $\leftarrow$ currentSolution;
            noChange $\leftarrow$ 0;
        else
            if *Better balance solution found* **then**
                currentSolution $\leftarrow$ neighborSolution;
                noChange $\leftarrow$ 0;
            else
                $p_{accept} \leftarrow max\{exp(\frac{-\Delta_c}{T_c}), exp(\frac{-\Delta_b}{T_b})\}$
                if *Solution accepted* **then**
                    currentSolution $\leftarrow$ neighborSolution;
                    noChange $\leftarrow$ 0;
                else
                  noChange $\leftarrow$ noChange + 1;
                end
                $T_c \leftarrow \iota T_c$;
                $T_b \leftarrow \iota T_b$;
            end
        end
    end
    update w_k;
end
return bestSolution;
update f_j;
end

---

4   Results

4.1   Data and Problem Instances

This study uses location data in two major cities of the Netherlands: Amsterdam and Rotterdam. Public lampposts are assumed to be viable access points. We use three (imaginary) service types, which will serve as example: 'Wi-Fi', 'Alarm' and 'Telecommunication Network'. The Wi-Fi service provides internet access to devices connected to it. The Alarm service is a new service designed to keep track of bicycle theft. If a bicycle is mounted with a special smart lock, this service detects whether any of them are being broken. An alerting sound is made if any are detected. The Telecommunication Network service is designed to work just like cell towers: they deliver signals to mobile devices such that calls can be made between users. The Telecommunication Network service may not only used by residents at the households, but also everyone else who is at the demand points, e.g., guests and bypassers. The three services all have different signal ranges as well as maximum number of connections per installation.

Table 2 shows the number of available access points $|L|$ and number of demand points $|D^{all}|$ per problem instance. These are found by selecting small regions of the cities of which we have the location data, and taking all recorded public lampposts as access points and addresses as demand points that are in the subarea spanned by the region coordinates.

For each demand point, the number of inhabitants is simulated using the proportions in Table 3[1], which contains the proportions of various household sizes in the Netherlands.

Table 2. Instance dimensions

Instance	$|L|$	$|D^{all}|$
Amsterdam 1	110	306
Amsterdam 2	1728	3479
Amsterdam 3	3322	4529
Amsterdam 4	6200	8545
Amsterdam 5	18487	11147
Rotterdam 1	1227	1715
Rotterdam 2	2005	2956
Rotterdam 3	10660	14542

---

[1] www.cbs.nl.

Table 3. Proportions of household sizes in Netherlands 2020 (source CBS)

Persons	Households	Proportion
1	3079778	0.38
2	2610601	0.33
3	938515	0.12
4	407592	0.05
5+	961314	0.12

Table 4. List of preset parameter values with constant installation costs

Parameter	Preset value
α	0.95
f_j	1000
c_j^u	350 $u = 1$, Wi-Fi 150 $u = 2$, Alarm 500 $u = 3$, Telecommunication Network
N^u	45 $u = 1$, Wi-Fi 50 $u = 2$, Alarm 62 $u = 3$, Telecommunication Network
μ_i^u	8 $\quad$ size $= 1$, $u = 1$, Wi-Fi 11 $\quad$ size $= 2$, $u = 1$, Wi-Fi 12 $\quad$ size $= 3$, $u = 1$, Wi-Fi 14 $\quad$ size $= 4$, $u = 1$, Wi-Fi 15 $\quad$ size $= 5+$, $u = 1$, Wi-Fi $1.35 \cdot size$ $\quad u = 2$, Alarm $size + 10$ $\quad u = 3$, Telecommunication Network
σ^u	2 $u = 1$, Wi-Fi 1 $u = 2$, Alarm 3 $u = 3$, Telecommunication Network
c_o^u	950 $\quad u = 1$, Wi-Fi 1000 $u = 2$, Alarm 1200 $u = 3$, Telecommunication Network
π^u	2 $\quad u = 1, 2, 3$

In Table 4 an overview of all parameters is given. The term '$size$' indicates the number of inhabitants in demand point i. Setup costs are assumed to be equal across all access locations and in all three scenarios. Installation costs have been decided based on Vos [14]. Capacities N^u are based on literature, and expected to be equal across all access locations. The demand mean parameters μ_i^u are designed such that for different service types, the shape of expected demands vary depending on the size of the household. The standard deviation values σ^u in Table 4 are default values used to evaluate the ALNS-ES performance for Table 5. The occupancy penalties c_o^u are set to arbitrary values that are lower than and close to f_j.

4.2   ALNS-ES Results

In this subsection we discuss the performance of the ALNS-ES heuristic compared to an exact approach on the same problem. The exact approach is implemented as the MIP described in Sect. 2. We take a look at the differences in optimal cost objective, balance objective and the computation time taken between the two methods. Table 5 displays the ALNS-ES results for the base problem for the instances in Table 2. For each service type, the algorithm was run for 300 iterations. The column 'Costs' denotes the cost objective and 'Balance' denotes the balance objective, summed over all service types. The runtime for the algorithm is given under the 'Time' column, which gives the run time in seconds. The last column describes the percentage of available access locations that are opened to be active service locations, with in brackets the exact number that are opened.

Table 5. Computational results base setting

Instance	Costs	Balance	Time (s)	% Open (num)
Amsterdam 1	182250.0	0.0	428	89.1 (98)
Amsterdam 2	2177800.0	70.0	639	70.3 (1215)
Amsterdam 3	2835350.0	58.0	2665	47.5 (1579)
Amsterdam 4	5385550.0	256.0	2850	48.5 (3009)
Amsterdam 5	7783350.0	1610.0	3024	25.3 (4679)
Rotterdam 1	1039500.0	21.0	414	46.1 (566)
Rotterdam 2	1812250.0	53.0	2505	49.4 (991)
Rotterdam 3	9501500.0	684.0	3029	51.2 (5459)

Table 6 shows the results of attempting to solve the problem with an exact approach. The ILOG CPLEX package has been used in order to solve the linear program with a 1% gap tolerance. The column 'IP solution' denotes the cost objective returned by CPLEX within the given time limit, which has been set to 12 h. The superscript LB indicates that CPLEX was not able to find a feasible integer solution in the given time using its branch and bound framework. Instead, it returns an objective on the lower bound that is expected over all unexplored nodes in the tree. Column 'IP Time' shows the time it took in order to solve the program in seconds. A dagger indicates that the program stopped after it hit the time limit. If the corresponding IP solution has no superscript, this indicates that the IP solution value is the best found integer solution so far. The column

'IP Gap' denotes the difference between the current upper and lower bound in the solution tree upon termination. As long as this gap is not equal to 0, a found integer solution most likely does not correspond to the optimal solution. The column 'Difference' shows the percentage difference in cost objective between the found IP solution and the ALNS-ES heuristic solution, with a negative difference denoting that the heuristic solution had a lower cost than the best solution found by the IP. Lastly, the 'Time Difference' column denotes the difference in computation time between the exact approach and ALNS-ES heuristic in seconds. A positive difference indicates that the exact approach was solved in a shorter time, whilst a negative difference means that the ALNS-ES heuristic was faster. The instances Amsterdam 4, Amsterdam 5 and Rotterdam 3 could not be evaluated exactly with an IP solver due to memory limitations. Looking at Table 6, we see that except for the smallest instance Amsterdam 1, the ALNS-ES finds a good solution within a much faster computation time than the exact method.

Table 6. Comparison with IP results for small instances

Instance	IP solution	IP time (s)	IP gap	Difference	Time difference (s)
Amsterdam 1	182400.0	13	0.54%	−0.08%	+417
Amsterdam 2	2096800.0	24163†	0.47%	3.86%	−24664
Amsterdam 3	2719604.2^{LB}	43205†	-	4.25%	-
Rotterdam 1	1035000.0	3059	0.10%	0.43%	−470
Rotterdam 2	1779850.0	14645	0.07%	1.82%	−14207

5   Assessment of Handling Stochasticity

Equation 8 transforms the stochastic model into a deterministic model. Here we want to assess whether this indeed captures the stochastic behaviour and whether the 95% constraint satisfaction requirement is met. For this, we use the ALNS-ES method to plan the infrastructure and use simulation to test this solution.

To simulate the stochastic behaviour, we use an ON-OFF traffic model [5]. We assume a certain number of time periods. Demand points are not expected to need service in every single time period. For this, we define two states a demand point can be in regards to a service type u: 'ON' and 'OFF'. In state OFF, the demand point is not in need of service. In state ON, the demand point has a certain level of demand for service type u. The length of the OFF period is drawn from the exponential distribution with rate λ, such that average time is $\frac{1}{\lambda}$. Once a demand point is in state ON for a certain service type, the number of consecutive periods that the status remains ON is drawn from an exponential distribution with rate η. After this time, the demand point returns to state OFF. Afterwards, the transition time to the next ON period is drawn and the process continues until it has reached the total number of periods.

This two state traffic model can be seen as a Markov chain with transition rates λ and η. The fraction of time a demand point is in state ON, given by (14), which can be interpreted as the probability that a demand point is in state ON in the Markov Chain:

$$Probability\ demand\ point\ is\ in\ state\ ON = \frac{\lambda}{\lambda + \eta}. \tag{14}$$

When a demand point is in state ON, the demand is assumed to be constant, μ'^u. This is chosen such that

$$\mu^u = \frac{\lambda}{\lambda + \eta} \cdot \mu'^u, \tag{15}$$

where μ^u equals the average demand from (8).

In this study, several combinations of values for λ and η are explored. These parameter values have direct influence on the mean and variance parameters used in the simulation model, and therefore the performance results are expected to vary per combination. Explored values are set between 0 and 1 for both parameters. Several combinations are explored as below in Table 7. The 'OFF' and 'ON' columns give a quick summary of the expected behaviour of the traffic simulation.

Table 7. Explored combination of (λ, η)

Scenario	λ	η	OFF	ON
1	0.7	0.15	Short	Long
2	0.8	0.6	Short	Short
3	0.8	0.3	Short	Regular
4	0.4	0.2	Regular	Long
5	0.5	0.5	Regular	Regular
6	0.5	0.7	Regular	Short
7	0.3	0.5	Long	Regular

We apply our Poisson traffic model to our ALNS-ES solution by taking the connections made by the algorithm between demand points and service points. Demand point i can only be serviced by the service points $j \in L$ that have $z_{ij}^u > 0$. Which service point is used, is during the simulation determined by optimisation of the allocation problem for each time period.

For instance (λ, η) we evaluate how much of the simulated demand could be successful handled by the allocation solution. Demand is dropped in case there is not enough capacity available. We use the number of time periods where we encounter a shortage in capacity as a reliability measure for the solution, defined by R, where P denotes the total number of time periods that have been simulated:

$$R = 1 - \frac{\sum_{t=1}^{P} \sum_{u \in S} \sum_{j \in L} I_{\{d_{jt}^{u*} > 0\}}}{\sum_{u \in S} P \times |L_{open}^{u}|}. \tag{16}$$

The term $I_{\{d_{it}^{u} > 0\}}$ denotes an indicator function having value 1 if there is any capacity shortage d_{it}^{u*} for service type u at demand point i during period t, else 0. The term $|L_{open}^{u}|$ in the denominator denotes the number of access points that are open for service type u. The calculation of R does not take the amount of capacity shortage into account whenever it occurs, only the frequency of a shortage happening.

A value close to 1 indicates a high reliability level. It is of interest whether R approaches the $\alpha = 0.95$ reliability threshold as predefined in the ALNS-ES algorithm. This is because substantially, the constraints (4) describe that the demand satisfaction requirement is to be held in $\alpha \cdot 100\%$ of all scenarios, independent of the degree to which the constraint is violated in the remaining $(1 - \alpha) \cdot 100\%$.

For the assessment, two instances are used of medium and large size: Amsterdam 3 and Amsterdam 5. Table 8 shows the R values. We compare the calculated R values to see if in this setting they match up to the reliability criterion $\alpha = 0.95$ which has been used to obtain solutions from the stationary equivalent. The columns correspond to combinations of (λ, η) listed in Table 7.

Table 8. Traffic model: free allocation with constant demand

Instance	1	2	3	4	5	6	7
Amsterdam 3	1.0	0.980	1.0	1.0	0.985	0.954	0.969
Amsterdam 5	1.0	0.984	1.0	1.0	0.986	0.964	0.974

For (λ, η) cases 1, 3 and 4 with free allocation, R equals 1.0, which is very high and even suggests that our solution may be too conservative. However, for other cases, like 6 and 7, R is only just above the required α. We note the in these cases we have a low value for the fraction value $\frac{\lambda}{\lambda+\eta}$. For higher fraction values $\frac{\lambda}{\lambda+\eta}$, the ALNS-ES algorithm insures its solution for higher demand values since it implies that demand points are expected to be in status ON often.

6 Conclusion and Further Research

In this paper, we explored the method of using an ALNS-ES heuristic on the Multi Source Capacitated Facility Location Problem with stochastic demands that have been translated into deterministic variants. The problem involved identifying a best set of available access points to open in order to satisfy the demands in the most cost efficient manner. A model was designed which found a solution satisfying demand with a 95% level of certainty. Comparing the heuristic results to the best solutions found with an exact analysis for small instances showed that the heuristic is able to deliver good solutions in much shorter time.

Afterwards, we assessed the handling of the stochasticity by the ALNS-ES heuristic. In overview, the ALNS-ES performs well in terms of the proportion of total demand quantity satisfied. However we saw differences between instances with low expected demand per time period caused by low transition rates λ compared to η and the other instances. They remained however, above the criterion of 0.95.

For future work, we recommend to look at the precise relationship between λ, η and α. Also it would be of interest to introduce a relation between demand and distance to the service point, as in reality, for some services, capacity depends on the distance between demand point and service point.

References

1. Chyu, C.C., Chang, W.S.: Multi-exchange neighborhood search heuristics for the multi-source capacitated facility location problem. Ind. Eng. Manag. Syst. **8**(1), 29–36 (2009)
2. Hoekstra, G., Phillipson, F.: Location assignment of capacitated services in smart cities. In: Renault, É., Boumerdassi, S., Bouzefrane, S. (eds.) International Conference on Mobile, Secure, and Programmable Networking, vol. 11005, pp. 192–206. Springer, Heidelberg (2019). https://doi.org/10.1007/978-3-030-03101-5_17
3. Karp, R.M.: Reducibility among combinatorial problems. In: Miller, R.E., Thatcher, J.W., Bohlinger, J.D. (eds.) Complexity of computer computations, pp. 85–103. Springer, Boston (1972). https://doi.org/10.1007/978-1-4684-2001-2_9
4. Kim, L.J.: A Multi service capacitated facility location problem with stochastic demand. Master's thesis. Erasmus University Rotterdam (2021)
5. Marvi, M., Aijaz, A., Khurram, M.: On the use of on/off traffic models for spatio-temporal analysis of wireless networks. IEEE Commun. Lett. **23**(7), 1219–1222 (2019)
6. Melo, M.T., Nickel, S., Saldanha-Da-Gama, F.: Facility location and supply chain management-a review. Eur. J. Oper. Res. **196**(2), 401–412 (2009)
7. Pisinger, D., Ropke, S.: Large neighborhood search. In: Gendreau, M., Potvin, J.Y. (eds.) Handbook of metaheuristics, vol. 146, pp. 399–419. Springer, Boston, MA. (2010). https://doi.org/10.1007/978-1-4419-1665-5_13
8. Postek, K.: Optimization under uncertainty: lecture notes, **5** (2019)
9. Ropke, S., Pisinger, D.: An adaptive large neighborhood search heuristic for the pickup and delivery problem with time windows. Transp. sci. **40**(4), 455–472 (2006)
10. Shaw, P.: A new local search algorithm providing high quality solutions to vehicle routing problems. APES Group, Dept of Computer Science, University of Strathclyde, Glasgow, Scotland, UK 46 (1997)
11. Suzuki, T., Hodgson, M.J.: Multi-service facility location models. Ann. Oper. Res. **123**, 223–240 (2003). https://doi.org/10.1023/A:1026183515320
12. Veerman, B., Phillipson, F.: Multi service modular capacitated facility location problem for smart cities. In: Lüke, K.-H., Eichler, G., Erfurth, C., Fahrnberger, G. (eds.) I4CS 2019. CCIS, vol. 1041, pp. 97–108. Springer, Cham (2019). https://doi.org/10.1007/978-3-030-22482-0_8
13. Verhoek, M.: Optimising the placement of access points for smart city services with stochastic demand. Master's thesis. Groningen University (2017)
14. Vos, T., Phillipson, F.: Dense multi-service planning in smart cities. In: International Conference on Information Society and Smart Cities (2018)

The Role of a Data Marketplace for Innovation and Value-Added Services in Smart and Sustainable Cities

Rebekka Alvsvåg, Anthony Bokolo Jr.(ID), and Sobah Abbas Petersen(✉)(ID)

Department of Computer Science, Norwegian University of Science and Technology,
Trondheim, Norway
rebekka.alvsvag@gmail.com, {anthony.j.bokolo,sap}@ntnu.no

Abstract. In this era of digitization, data is seen as the new oil due to the abundance of data generated from Internet of Things (IoT), social media and other platforms. Although prior studies have explored the challenges and opportunities that may arise in using these data to provide value added services, few studies explore how data from public, private and commercial data owners in smart cities and communities could enhance data reuse, sharing and collaboration among the different stakeholders. This study employs the system design approach to develop a data marketplace prototype, which provides data to create value-added services that could improve the lives of citizens. The prototype is developed for easy sharing, trading and utilization of available data for innovative services through collaboration. Qualitative data was collected using semi-structured interviews from experts in academia and industry to validate the concept of a data marketplace. Findings from this study reveal that the data marketplace prototype is useful, easy to use and supports data trading in smart cities.

Keywords: Information systems · Data marketplace · Iterative prototyping · System design · Smart sustainable cities · Expert evaluation

1 Introduction

The amount of global data reached 59 zettabytes (ZB) of data in 2020 and is expected to reach 149 ZB by 2024 according to Statista.com [1]. With the abundance of data, new challenges and opportunities arise. Internet of Things (IoT), sensors, social media and other systems generate enormous amounts of data and most of it is not utilized [2, 3]. The data has potential to aid stakeholders and enterprises with decision making, improving user experiences and increase revenues through leveraging on the data [4, 5]. To make this possible, there is a need for easy sharing and trading of the available data. This gives rise to the concept of a smart city data marketplace. The concept of a data marketplace has been discussed in the context of smart cities [6, 7]. In a complex environment, such as a city or a neighborhood, there are many challenges and opportunities where an open data marketplace could support to provide value-added services to the citizens [8].

© The Author(s), under exclusive license to Springer Nature Switzerland AG 2022
F. Phillipson et al. (Eds.): I4CS 2022, CCIS 1585, pp. 215–230, 2022.
https://doi.org/10.1007/978-3-031-06668-9_16

Data has for long been identified as a tradeable good [9]. In 1998, the term data marketplace was probably first used by Armstrong and Durfee [10], who modelled trading of information between digital libraries, focusing on the motivation and behavior of participants and identifying factors that affect interactions and cooperation in a network. The literature reports several concepts that address the needs for making data available and sharing of existing data. Concepts such as *data brokerage* were conceptualized, where a data brokerage is an idea that provides the means for citizens to take control of their own data and manage who has access to it and how they could use it, by allowing citizens to make their data available in a controlled manner [11]. *Data exchange* is another term used to describe similar ideas as that of a data brokerage. Similarly, *data hubs* have appeared to provide a single on-line presence and point of access to datasets, providing a central arena where data could be gathered, managed and exposed in a consistent manner [12, 13]. The city of Copenhagen, in Denmark, considers *data platforms* as a foundational pillar for smart, sustainable and livable cities. While these concepts provide possibilities for users to share their data and exercise control over the data, the concept of a data brokerage is still immature and lacks clear use cases for data owners to assess the potential users and value of the data [14].

The concept of *Open Data* has become central in sharing and reusing data in smart cities and communities, where data is made freely available, often by cities or other public organizations, and available for anyone to use [11]. Open Data can help cities to understand how they operate. However, they are often infrastructure-centric and of low value [11], and only a small amount of available data from cities and public authorities are Open Data. While there is a lot of interest around Open Data and data brokerages that could be useful for several actors to deliver services, there is a lack of clear use cases for both data providers and data consumers, to leverage on available data and develop innovative services for the benefit of a community; e.g. in Copenhagen, many users experienced difficulty in accessing and using data from their data platform [14].

A concept that has been quite central in the discussions related to data in the context of smart cities and communities is *open data ecosystems*, which describe loosely coupled networks of actors, or stakeholders, that consist of data providers, open data users (direct data users or service developers) and open data service end-users [15–18]. The need for enhancing the current notion of Open Data is thus essential to facilitate the numerous stakeholders to be active in sharing and using data. It is also important to support collaborative networks of public and private stakeholders for the provision of innovative and value-added services to citizens and in communities, based on existing data and data-based services and applications. Furthermore, it has been noted that an arena for increasing the understanding between both the data provider and user perspectives and mediating structures are important to enhancing data sharing [17].

In this paper, we present a prototype of a data marketplace where the stakeholders in an open data ecosystem, within a city or a community, could connect and share their data. This research aims to contribute to the understanding of the role of a data marketplace and design a smart city data marketplace based on use case scenarios, using ideas from the service design approach [19].

There are numerous definitions and descriptions of a data marketplace. A common understanding of a data marketplace could be as a platform through which data could be purchased or sold [9]. A data marketplace is also defined as a multi-sided platform that matches data providers and buyers and facilitates business data sharing among enterprises [20]. In smart cities and communities, data marketplaces make it easy for data buyers to find new and relevant datasets, and for the data sellers, it makes it easy to create value and perhaps make money from their data. Findings from the literature, e.g. [3], explore the idea of a data marketplace for scientific data and show some of the potential benefits of such a platform. Furthermore, a data marketplace provides good storage, neutral third-party platforms to motivate data enhancement, offers technical services such as data organization, cleaning [21], and enforces data ownership which is important towards ensuring data governance [22].

Presently, findings from the literature suggest that there are no clear definitions of a data marketplace that are widely used [23]. Additionally, there are fewer studies that explored data marketplaces in smart cities in the Norwegian context. The main goal of our research is to explore the role of a data marketplace in a smart city from the perspectives of several stakeholders from academia and industry. An iterative research and development approach has been adopted to develop a prototype of a data marketplace. An expert evaluation has been conducted and the qualitative data as feedback was received from the participants for evaluation of the developed data marketplace prototype.

The remainder of this paper is arranged as follows. Section 2 provides a literature review. Section 3 describes the method. Section 4 describes the smart city data marketplace prototype. Section 5 describes the evaluation results. Section 6 presents the discussions. Finally, Sect. 7 is the conclusion.

2 Literature Review

This section provides an understanding of the overview of a data marketplace, presents the challenges and benefits of a data marketplace and summarizes the needs for a data marketplace for smart cities and communities.

2.1 Overview of Data Marketplace

There are several definitions of a data marketplace in the literature. Researchers such as Schomm, Stahl and Vossen [9, 24] defined a data marketplace as a platform on which anybody (or at least a great number of potentially registered clients) can upload and maintain data sets. Another interesting definition was presented by Spiekermann [9, 24], which stated that a data marketplace can be understood as a digital platform on which data products are traded [23]. Data marketplaces are also facilitated by cloud-computing, and these data marketplaces offer a convenient single, logically centralized point for buying and selling data [25].

Conceptually, data marketplaces are multi-sided platforms, where a digital intermediary connects data providers, data purchasers and other complementary technology providers [26]. Similar to online marketplaces, a data marketplace is a platform that enables convenient buying and selling of products - in this case data [27]. Findings from the literature review show that there are studies related to data marketplaces, but only a few of these studies report on specific implementations of data marketplace prototypes such as i3 [7], Datapace [28], Wibson [29], IOTA Data Marketplace [30], IDMoB - IoT Data Marketplace on Blockchain [31], and Prodatamarket [32]. Examples of smart city data marketplaces are found in Stockholm [33]; a decentralized data marketplace for smart cities [7], and a decentralized marketplace for machine to machine (M2M) economy for Smart cities [21]. Features found in existing data marketplaces include searching for datasets and data providers, comparison of data providers and recommendation of datasets, e.g. Datarade [34].

Additionally, in the Norwegian context, Roman et al. researched Norwegian data marketplaces [32]. Their research was linked to the Prodatamarket which aimed to provide a data marketplace that sells and shares specific data from the building domain. Another study by Ulversøy and Fiskum [35] examined the privacy of individuals in decentralized data marketplaces.

2.2 The Need for a Data Marketplace

Open Data refers to data that can be used freely, redistributed and re-used by anyone. A study by Barns explores the trends of Open Data portals in urban governance [36]. Many Open Data portals, such as those of Singapore, Australia, and Canada, use the open source CKAN data management system [37]. Open Data portals can be an important inspiration for designing data marketplaces.

Open Data from cities is very limited and the amount of data available as Open Data is not enough to realize value out of them. To be able to create real value out of data, there is a need for citizens and organisations to make their data available [38]. This requires a means for organizations and citizens to manage and control their data. Data marketplaces provide interactions between data providers and data users, and could incorporate policies for transactions, support business models and services and other support functions [39]. Data marketplaces can reduce the barriers for access and interactions among the data providers and data users, as well as reduce the cost through a technical infrastructure that facilitates reuse of data.

Currently, data is scattered across different platforms, and it is hard to find and may have different access mechanisms. A single place and mechanism to access data can save money and time for the users [9]. Furthermore, literature suggests that the research and development in the area of data marketplaces have concentrated on the technological and technical infrastructure aspects of a data marketplace rather than the service aspects [20]. Thus, the service aspects such as possible business models, the social dimensions and the collective value of data marketplaces to a community or a business ecosystem around data-dependent services remains to be explored.

However, there are fewer studies that focus on the trend towards decentralized data marketplaces within smart cities and communities for supporting innovation and value-added services through collaboration among different stakeholders. Hence, there is a need for a study that identifies the role of a data marketplace, how the stakeholders could interact with and through such a data marketplace and, indeed, the possible scenarios where a data marketplace could be useful for a community.

2.3 Challenges and Benefits of Data Marketplaces

The main challenges and trends in the data marketplace domain as suggested in the literature, e.g. [24, 27, 40], are many. One of the main challenges is that stakeholders find it difficult to *assess the value of a dataset*. While there is a need for high quality data, the quality of data is a subjective aspect that is difficult to generalize. It is important to build trust among the sellers and the buyers and the ownership of data can often be a difficult legal issue. *The security of data storage and transactions* are challenging. Challenges also arise due to *privacy related legal issues* and *compliance to GDPR*, the General Data Protection Regulations of EU. And it has been seen that it is difficult to remain in the data trading market as many data marketplaces come and go.

A data marketplace enables buyers to easily find new and relevant datasets, and for the data sellers, it provides an opportunity to earn money from their data. Findings from [3] identified several benefits of data marketplaces. Data becomes more accessible, becomes easier to discover and compare datasets, rate and comment about datasets. Data marketplaces could provide innovative business models for data trading and reward the different stakeholders such as the data providers and consumers. They could be a neutral third-party platform that could provide efficient and secure data storage, protect data ownership and motivate data enhancement. Data marketplaces could also offer technical services beyond trading data, such as data organization and cleaning.

Furthermore, an increasing amount of innovative and value-added services rely on the availability of data, which can be resource intensive in terms of physical infrastructure, such as sensors, and the storage of data [6]. The possibility to share or make existing data accessible to a larger group of stakeholders and consumers and the platform for more data producers and consumers to meet virtually would lead to a more sustainable approach to creating value from existing data.

3 Method

An iterative research and development approach has been adopted to develop a prototype of a data marketplace. There were four system design iterations, where each iteration included *requirement specifications, design, prototyping and evaluation*, as shown in Fig. 1.

The design phase was inspired by ideas from service design [19], such as the descriptions of personas and customer journeys. In addition, ideas from Enterprise Architecture (EA) modelling were used to identify the functionalities of the data marketplace. There were no customer or predefined requirements for the project which required extra efforts to investigate and understand the related topics of data trading and specify relevant requirements. Hence, the service design approach was adopted for the requirements and design phases. The Personas approach consists of developing fictive representations of potential customers or users of the data marketplace. Customer journeys were developed to examine a service available from the data marketplace from a customer's or a user's perspective and involved creating flow diagrams that show all the steps that a customer needs to take to perform a specific task. An example of a customer journey for the smart city data marketplace could show all the steps that were needed to upload a new dataset (see Fig. 4).

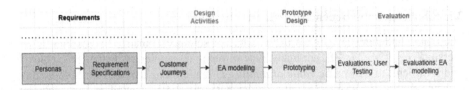

Fig. 1. Iterative design, development, and evaluation process

The *implementation* comprises of the rapid prototyping approach employed to design the system. The prototyping was done in *Figma,* which is a tool for designing interactive prototypes [41]. The functionalities of the data marketplace were designed based on the personas and customer journeys. In the first system iteration the most important functionalities were designed, such as the pages to search for data and upload data. The full stack development of a working data marketplace was considered, but it was not an objective of this study, which was conducted within the scope of a Master's thesis [42]. The features that are implemented in the current version of the prototype were aimed at evaluating the overall concept and hence some of the details such as specific data formats and the data management process are not described.

After developing the prototype, *user testing sessions* were used as an important part of the iterative prototyping process to rapidly identify logical errors, flaws in the user experience, bad choices of names or symbols and to obtain feedback from users about what they like and didn't like, and what could be improved. After the user testing, the *suggested improvements were implemented.* After four iterations, the final evaluation was based on the expert evaluation method, which is described in detail in Sect. 5. A detailed description of the design process, the personas and customer journeys are beyond the scope of this paper, and we have focused on the data marketplace prototype and the expert evaluation.

4   Data Marketplace Prototype

The rapid prototyping approach was chosen since it was a suitable approach for designing a prototype of the data marketplace, to get a more concrete idea of how the design and user experience of such a platform could look like before developing the actual system. The data marketplace was designed as a web-based platform, where users could search for data, upload their data to share, sell and buy data. The main page of the data marketplace is shown in Fig. 2. The main page, or the homepage, also displays the current trending datasets, the ones that are most requested for, news, features, success stories and some statistics related to the data marketplace. Users are able to log in and create their profiles (top right corner of the page).

In the rest of this section, we will describe the main functionalities of the data marketplace, using screenshots of the Figma prototype. The user is able to search for a dataset using search filters as shown in Fig. 3. The search results show the total number of datasets that meet the search criteria, and for each result, information about the format of the data, if it is Open Data or the price for the dataset and other information related

Fig. 2. Data marketplace prototype - the main page (homepage)

to the data, metadata, are provided; see the bottom part of Fig. 3. If the required dataset is not available, the user is able to request a dataset.

Fig. 3. Data marketplace prototype - search and request for datasets

The customer journey for buying a dataset is shown in Fig. 4. To buy a dataset, the user must first find the required dataset by using the search functionality. The user is able to download a test dataset to check if that is what is needed before purchasing it. Then, the user can add the dataset to the "*cart*" as in other market or shopping-based platforms and then proceed to a payment mode. This is shown in Fig. 5. The user is able to obtain additional information about the dataset such as the publisher of the data, when the data was last updated, the price of the dataset as well as the different pricing models, e.g., monthly subscription, and payment modes that are available, e.g., smart contracts.

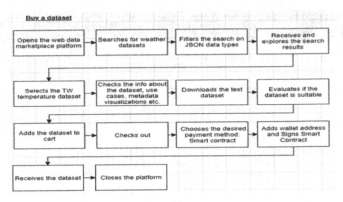

Fig. 4. Customer journey to buy a dataset in the data marketplace

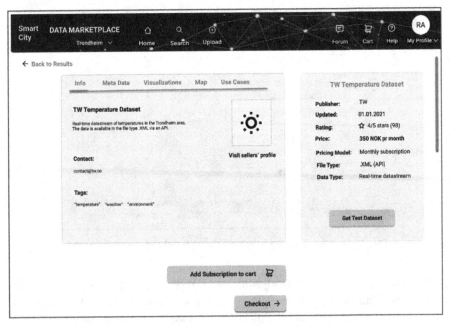

Fig. 5. Data marketplace prototype – screenshot for buying a dataset

Emphasis was made on supporting metadata about each dataset, which would facilitate data sharing and search. Furthermore, functionality was added to share use cases for datasets as this was identified as a major limitation of current data sharing platforms, e.g. [38]. Users are able to obtain an overview of the datasets that they had uploaded and how much they have sold. Most importantly, users are able to start a discussion forum to interact and share information and knowledge with other users of the system, see Fig. 6. The forum is a place for the users to discuss topics related to datasets and get tips and suggestions from the community. This functionality has been designed with the intention of facilitating knowledge sharing and trust building among the stakeholders of the community, which was also identified as an important service to motivate the use and participation by the stakeholders [17]. Such functionality indeed supports the creation of a social structure for interaction and to create shared pieces of identity among the users.

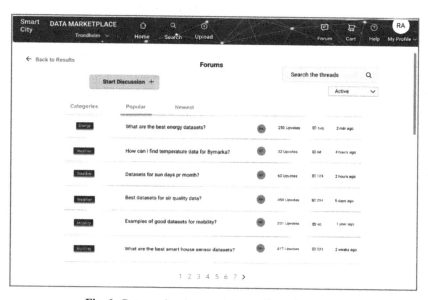

Fig. 6. Data marketplace prototype – discussion forum

5 Evaluation

The expert evaluation method was used to evaluate the data marketplace prototype by experts in the domain. The evaluations were conducted individually with each expert. The eleven experts were first asked some questions about demographic information and their prior knowledge about data marketplaces. An overview of this data is shown in Table 1. In this phase of the evaluation, the experts were also asked to describe in their own words, their perception of the concept of a data marketplace.

The participants were recruited from the researchers' network of contacts from research and industry. Several of the experts are also partners of the EU H2020 Lighthouse project Positive City Exchange (https://cityxchange.eu/). The main criterion for the choice of the experts is their experience with data in the context of their work. The participants represented the education and research sector, the bank and finance sector, the energy sector, the marine biology sector, the software development sector and the crypto currencies sector. These are very relevant sectors for a data marketplace. The experts were asked to indicate their level of prior knowledge about data marketplaces on a scale of 1–5, where 1 was the lowest and 5 was the highest. Experts 1–3 reported that they did not have much prior knowledge, i.e., level 1. The mean value of prior knowledge among the other 8 experts (experts 4–11) is 3.5. The participants consisted of 72,7% males and 27,3% females.

Table 1. Demographics of the participants in the user and expert evaluations

ID	Age Group	Role	Industry Sector	Prior knowledge (1 = lowest, 5 = highest)
Expert 1	20–29	Marine Biologist	Marine sector	1
Expert 2	20–29	Software Developer	IT sector	1
Expert 3	20–29	Student	University	1
Expert 4	20–29	PhD Scholar	University	2
Expert 5	40–49	System Architect	IT sector	5
Expert 6	40–49	Senior Researcher	University	3
Expert 7	40–49	Head of Technology Infrastructure	IT sector	4
Expert 8	30–39	PhD Scholar	University	3
Expert 9	30–39	Senior Data Scientist	Finance sector	4
Expert 10	30–39	Software Engineer	Finance sector	3
Expert 11	30–39	Lead Machine Learning Engineer	Energy sector	4

The experts were then provided user stories, similar to user scenarios, that they could try on the data marketplace. They were asked to perform tasks such as search for a dataset, request for a dataset, upload a dataset or find metadata about a dataset. Observations were made when the experts performed the tasks. A set of user stories were tested out by the experts, and they were encouraged to think aloud.

This was then followed by a semi-structured interview and a set of questions. Data was collected using semi-structured interviews as this approach allowed for follow-up questions and interactive and in-depth insights about the responses from the experts. Most of the experts were Norwegian and therefore the interviews were carried out in Norwegian. The interviews focused on understanding the experts' definition of a data marketplace and the scenarios that they thought data marketplaces would be useful for. The final part included obtaining feedback from the user testing and suggestions for improvements of the prototype, in addition to questions related to their preferred payment method (traditional or smart contracts) and missing features or elements in the prototype.

The interviews during the expert evaluations were recorded with audio and video recordings, in addition to written notes. The participants received an information letter about the expert evaluations including a consent form to provide permission to make recordings and write about their profiles, feedback, and suggestions. The expert evaluation approach was chosen since it provides opinions and needs from potential expert users of a data marketplace, as well as expert knowledge about smart contracts and decentralized applications.

5.1 Results

The questions asked during the evaluation were inspired by the Technology Acceptance Model (TAM) [43], which provides a framework for evaluating the perceived usefulness, perceived ease of use and the intention to use the artefact, in this case the data marketplace. The following 5-points Likert scale was used for evaluating the usefulness and ease of use: 1 = Very low level, 2 = low level, 3 = neutral, 4 = high level, 5 = very high level.

Fig. 7. Results from the expert evaluation of the data marketplace prototype

Figure 7 depicts the radar diagram of the mean values from expert evaluations. The experts' answers illustrate how the experts rate the perceived usefulness and ease of use of the prototype. Furthermore, their intention to buy data professionally, to buy data privately, sell data professionally, sell data privately and to recommend the data marketplace to others and also shown. The results as seen in Fig. 7 suggest that the prototype is useful, easy to use, supports buying data professionally, buying data privately and selling professionally, selling data privately.

A number of descriptions of a data marketplace were provided by the experts. One described it as a marketplace for selling computers as the word "data" could mean a computer in Norwegian. Several of the experts also described it as a trading or exchange platform for data, similar to the FINN (www.finn.no). One expert also saw it as "*a portal where one could pick and use or buy or rent data within a specific domain*". Some experts described it as a website while others referred to it as a platform. One expert described it as "*a place for exchange of large volumes of data*"; interestingly only one expert referred to the volume of data that could be supported by the data marketplace. One of the experts provided quite a detailed description: "*A common area where data can be offered as a product, a bit like a data product and it can be different licenses and different ways to share, can be based on membership etc., and there are many business models on the marketplace and it can also be completely open data where everyone contributes to it, a bit like the type of charity data, and it can be linked to it can be public who do it and also, consortia, it comes in many forms I think*". Another expert described it as a "*place where data providers and those who want to obtain data meet, a bit like the app store*". A data marketplace specific to a smart city was described as one that perhaps focused on specific types of data available in a city such as sensor data and IoT, real-time data, traffic data, energy related data and data that describes an infrastructure.

During the interviews, the experts identified several scenarios where a data marketplace would be useful. It can be a place where researchers could discover data easily; there is an abundance of research data, yet it is not so easy to find. It could help people find different kinds of data. A data marketplace could support sharing of data within and across projects and indeed help people sell their data. It can help to visualize data consumption patterns. Some of the scenarios that were mentioned that are of particular relevance to communities were that it could support services to offer for the city, provide insight to startups and create innovation. Some of the services identified were the management of waste efficiently using data and monitoring energy consumption.

6   Discussion

Qualitative data was collected to validate the data marketplace prototype. The experts were asked to describe a data marketplace in their own words. Based on the findings from this study, a smart city data marketplace is very similar to a general data marketplace, besides the fact that the data comes from the city. Examples of the data sources are IoT sensors, citizens and businesses or private enterprises in the city. The new proposed definition of a smart city data marketplace is as follows:

> "*A smart city data marketplace is a digital platform for easy selling, buying and sharing of data that mainly come from smart city data sources such as internet of things (IoT) sensors, citizen and business data from the smart city*".

The findings from the expert evaluations outline that the majority of the experts had no problems performing the test user stories or scenarios on the data marketplace prototype. However, one of the experts experienced difficulty in performing them. The user testing showed that the experts would like to have more metadata on the dataset information page to make it easier to evaluate if the data fits their own requirements. All the experts were able to find the metadata, map and use cases related information, but they had some suggestions for more information they would like to have in the different sections to make it easier to assess if the dataset is a good fit or not for their project. In the second iteration, the experts suggested that it would be nice to have a way to "request for a dataset", if a user did not find what they were looking for. Thus, in the third iteration, a "request a dataset" button was added, and all the experts were able to find this button. They mentioned it was a good option for the platform. Two of the experts were able to find the upload dataset page without problems. One expert tried to find the upload dataset option under *My profile* and suggested that it might be better to call it sell instead of upload to make the navigation clearer. One of the experts would like to have examples of how to fill in the fields in the register new dataset pages.

All the experts were able to find the Homepage and find the success stories, one of the information options available from the Homepage. The experts also contributed suggestions for improvements. Some of the improvements suggested were focused on the technical interoperability such as the support for Application Programming Interfaces (APIs). However, some of the suggestions focused on the quality of the data and supporting the participation, e.g., the use of smart contracts to verify the quality of the data; to include information on policies and GDPR, and not too restrictive copyright rules; facilitate crowdsourcing of data for datasets and include rewards for participants.

Generally, most of the experts liked the design of the prototype and said it was modern, intuitive and very easy to use. Most of the experts would choose traditional payment methods over smart contracts and crypto currencies, but said it was nice to have both options available, especially for the future.

7 Conclusion

This paper presents a prototype of a data marketplace for smart cities and communities. The main goal of our research was to explore the role of a data marketplace in smart cities and communities, for creating value out of data and supporting innovative value-added services. Going beyond the common understanding of a marketplace, where people could sell and buy things, in this case data, this data marketplace prototype identified some of the limitations of existing data sharing and exchange platforms and enhanced the concept by supporting knowledge and experience sharing among the users. The aim of the design was to provide a means for enhancing the reuse and sharing of data among the citizens of a community.

This study contributes to the literature on smart city data marketplaces by proposing a definition of a smart city data marketplace. Findings from this study suggest that a smart city data marketplace is a digital platform for easy selling, buying and sharing of data that mainly comes from smart city data sources such as Internet of Things (IoT) sensors, citizen and business data from the smart city. The data marketplace prototype was developed based on ideas from service design and evaluated through semi-structured interviews with experts from academia and industry to validate the design and the developed prototype. The prototype was evaluated by eleven experts and the overall results of the evaluation indicate a positive response to the work. Findings from the expert evaluation reveal that the prototype is useful, easy to use and can be utilized in making cities smarter.

This study shows possible solutions for a design of a data marketplace for a smart city or a community, with the potential to enhance the functionality as well as adapt the functionality to meet the users' needs, for example, sharing of user experiences, discussion forums and traditional payment methods or smart contracts with crypto currencies. The main limitation of this work is that the current expert evaluation focused on the basic functionality of a data marketplace, such as searching, registering, uploading and buying datasets and to obtain the experts' perceptions and views of a data marketplace rather than evaluating the functionality that is particularly focused on the community. Hence, the evaluations do not provide explicit feedback on the functionality that is designed to support the non-technical aspects of a community data marketplace, such as the use cases or the discussion forum. Hence one of the areas of our future work would be to evaluate these functionalities in more detail. Future work will also involve improving the developed prototype based on the feedback from the expert evaluations and collecting additional data.

Acknowledgements. The authors would like to thank the participants of the evaluation studies for their time and valuable feedback. Part of this work was funded by the EU H2020 Smart City project + CityxChange, grant agreement 824260.

References

1. Mlitz, K.: Global datasphere: Unique replicated data ratio. (2021) https://www.statista.com/statistics/1185888/
2. Anthony Jnr, B., et al.: API deployment for big data management towards sustainable energy prosumption in smart cities-a layered architecture perspective. Int. J. Sustain. Energ. **39**(3), 263–289 (2020)
3. Ghosh, H.: Data marketplace as a platform for sharing scientific data. In: Munshi, Usha Mujoo, Verma, Neeta (eds.) Data Science Landscape. SBD, vol. 38, pp. 99–105. Springer, Singapore (2018). https://doi.org/10.1007/978-981-10-7515-5_7
4. Lawrenz, S., Rausch, A.: Dont buy a pig in a poke - a framework for checking consumer requirements in a data marketplace. In: 54th Hawaii International Conference on System Sciences (HICCS). p. 4663 (2021)
5. Jnr, B.A., et al.: Big data driven multi-tier architecture for electric mobility as a service in smart cities. Int. J. Energy Sect. Manag. **14**(5), 1023–1047 (2020)
6. Petersen, S., Pourzolfaghar, Z., Alloush, I., Ahlers, D., Krogstie, J., Helfert, M.: Value-added services, virtual enterprises and data spaces inspired enterprise architecture for smart cities. In: Camarinha-Matos, Luis M., Afsarmanesh, Hamideh, Antonelli, Dario (eds.) PRO-VE 2019. IAICT, vol. 568, pp. 393–402. Springer, Cham (2019). https://doi.org/10.1007/978-3-030-28464-0_34
7. Ramachandran, G.S., Radhakrishnan, R., Krishnamachari, B.: Towards a de-centralized data marketplace for smart cities, In: IEEE International Smart Cities Conference (ISC2), IEEE. p. 1–8 (2018)
8. Salminen, M., A metadata model for hybrid data products on a multilateral data marketplace, in Faculty of Information Technology, University of Jyväskylä , p. 81 (2018)
9. Schomm, F., Stahl, F., Vossen, G.: Marketplaces for data: an initial survey. SIGMID Rec. **42**(1), 15–27 (2013)
10. Armstrong, A.A., Durfee, E.H.: Mixing and memory: emergent cooperation in an information marketplace, In: Proceedings of the International Conference on Multi Agent Systems 1998, pp. 34 –41 (1998)

11. Lea, R.: The case for a smart city data brokerage. In: Rodger Lea (2020)
12. Lea, R., Blackstock, M.: City hub: a cloud-based iot platform for smart cities. In: IEEE 6th International Conference on Cloud Computing Technology and Science. IEEE: Singapore. pp. 799–804. (2014)
13. Lea, R.: Smart City Datahubs – an innovation ecosystem enabler. City of Vancouver Open Data News: UrbanOpus - People, Data & The Future of Cities (2015)
14. Lea, R.: Smart City Data Brokerage: lessons from Copenhagen, in Rodger Lea. (2019)
15. Ahlers, D., Wienhofen, L., Petersen, S., Anvaari, M.: A smart city ecosystem enabling open innovation. In: Lüke, K.H., Eichler, G., Erfurth, C., Fahrnberger, G. (eds.) Proceedings of the Innovations for Community Services: 19th International Conference, I4CS 2019, Wolfsburg, Germany, June 24–26, 2019 , pp. 109–122. Springer International Publishing, Cham (2019). https://doi.org/10.1007/978-3-030-22482-0_9
16. Oliveira, M.I.S., Lima, G.D.F.B., Lóscio, B.F.: Investigations into data ecosystems: a systematic mapping study. Knowl. Inf. Syst. **61**(2), 589–630 (2019). https://doi.org/10.1007/s10 115-018-1323-6
17. Smith, G., Ofe, H.A., Sandberg, J.: Digital service innovation from open data: exploring the value proposition of an open data marketplace. In: 49th Hawaii International Conference on System Sciences (HICSS). Hawaii, pp. 1277–1286 (2016)
18. Tammisto, Y., Lindman, J.: Open data business models. In: 34th Information Systems Seminar in Scandinavia (2011)
19. Holmlid, S., Björndal, P.: Mapping what actors know when integrating resources: towards a service information canvas. In: Morelli, N., De Götzen, A., Grani, F. (eds), ServDes 2016, Copenhagen, Denmark (2016)
20. Abbas, A.E., et al.: Business data sharing through data marketplaces: a systematic literature review. J. Theor. Appl. Electron. Commer. Res. **16**(7), 3321–3339 (2021)
21. Musso, S., et al.: A decentralized market-place for m2m economy for smart cities. In: IEEE 28th International Conference on Enabling Technologies: Infrastructure for Collaborative Enterprises (WETICE), pp. 27–30 (2019)
22. Muschalle, A., et al.: Pricing approaches for data markets. In: International Workshop on Business Intelligence for the Real-Time Enterprise. Springer, Berlin, Heidelberg, pp. 129-144 (2021)
23. Spiekermann, M.: Data marketplaces: trends and monetisation of data goods. Intereconomics **54**(4), 208–216 (2019). https://doi.org/10.1007/s10272-019-0826-z
24. Stahl, F., Schomm, F., Vossen, G.: The data marketplace survey revisited (no. 18). ercis working paper. In: Ercis Working Paper, European Research Center for Informations Systems (2014)
25. Balazinska, M., Howe, B., Suciu, D.: Data markets in the cloud: an opportunity for the database community. Proc. VLDB Endowment **4**(12), 1482–1485 (2011)
26. Eisenmann, T.R., Parker, G.G., Van Alstyne, M.W.: Opening Platforms: How, When and Why? eBusiness & eCommerce (2008)
27. Lawrenz, S., Sharma, P., Rausch, A.: The significant role of metadata for data marketplaces. In: International Conference on Dublin Core and Metadata Applications, pp. 95–101 (2020)
28. Draskovic, D. Saleh, G.: Decentralized data marketplace based on block-chain. White Paper (2017)
29. Travizano, M., et al.: Wibson: a decentralized marketplace. In: SIGBPS 2018 Workshop on Blockchain and Smart Contract, San Francisco, CA, USA (2018)
30. IOTA. (IOTA Foundation). https://data.iota.org. Accessed 26 Feb 2022
31. Özyilmaz, K.R., Doğan, M., Yurdakul, A.: IDMoB: IoT data marketplace on blockchain. In: Vrypto Valley Conference on Blockchain Technology (CVCBT), pp. 11–19. IEEE (2018)
32. Roman, D., et al.: proDataMarket: a data marketplace for monetizing linked data. In: Proceedings of the CEUR Workshop (2017)

33. Välja, M., Ladhe, T.: Towards smart city marketplace at the example of stockholm. In: 48th Hawaii International Conference on System Sciences (HICCS), pp. 2375-2384. IEEE Computer Society: HI, USA (2015)
34. Datarade. https://datarade.ai/. Accessed 24 Mar 2022
35. Ulversøy, E., Fiskum, M.J.: Ensuring and preserving the privacy of individuals with a decentralized data marketplace. In: Department of Computer Science, Norwegian University of Science and Technology (2018)
36. Barns, S.: Smart cities and urban data platforms: designing interfaces for smart governance. City Cult. Soc. **12**, 5–12 (2018)
37. CKAN. The open source data management system (2021). https://ckan.org/. Accessed 26 Feb 2022
38. Lea, R.: Smart City Copenhagen: key lessons from the Head of City Data, Winn Nielsen, Urban Opus: People, Data & the Future of Cities (2016)
39. Zuiderwijk, A., et al.: Elements for the development of an open data marketplace. In: Conference for E-Democracy and Open Governement, pp. 309–322 (2014)
40. Koutroumpis, P., Leiponen, A., Thomas, L.D.: The (unfulfilled) potential of data marketplaces. In: ETLA Working Papers. (2017)
41. Figma. Figma the collaborative interface design tool (2021). https://www.figma.com/. Accessed 26 Feb 2022
42. Alvsvåg, R.: A Concept for Smart City Data Marketplace using Enterprise Ar-chitecture and Service Design Approaches, Norwegian University of Science and Technology (2021)
43. Davis, F.D.: Perceived usefulness, perceived ease of use, and user acceptance of information technology. MIS Q. **13**(3), 319–339 (1989)

Challenges of Future Smart and Secure IoT Networking

Dirk Von Hugo[1]([✉]), Gerald Eichler[1] [ID], and Behcet Sarikaya[2]

[1] Technology and Innovation, Deutsche Telekom AG, 64295 Darmstadt, Germany
{dirk.von-hugo,gerald.eichler}@telekom.de
[2] Dallas, TX 75001, USA
sarikaya@ieee.com

Abstract. Upcoming future telecommunication networks will have to provide reliable, secure, and high-quality connectivity between highly diverse devices and a plurality of service and content provider domains, using ideally compatible inter-operable fixed and mobile converged access technologies. Today, the majority of actual communication requests and user applications is initiated by both, human beings via personal handheld devices, and a plethora of types of machines. This are smart devices as sensors, watches, household appliances etc., and setting up the so-called Internet of Things. The amount of the latter will increase. New device types will emerge steadily and may span up a new market very well comparable to that of traditional human-centric communication, especially in view of the current vision to meet challenges to mankind as climate change, endemic diseases, unequal distribution of wealth and health in a global scale by means of digitalization and Information and Communication Technology.

To enable ease of operation at affordable costs for secure automatic deployment, upgrade, and maintenance of IoT, new models are required also for bootstrapping, authenticating, and subsequently authorizing a device during network attachment procedure, even without demanding specific and potentially complex or error-prone customer activity.

This contribution evaluates typical use cases and describes the problem space including underlying key issues related to sensing technologies and intelligent data analysis, but also measures to improve, e.g., reliability and resilience. The concepts investigated by different standard developing organizations are reviewed, and a set of open challenges and research topics are identified.

Keywords: 5G · Authentication · Heterogeneous networks · IoT · LoRa · Security · Radio sensing

1 Introduction to IoT Networking

1.1 Motivation and Related Research Projects and Initiatives

Regarding today's global challenges as addressed by United Nations (UN) in terms of sustainable goals (SDGs) or by European Union (EU) to make economy more green, digital, fair, and resilient, the contribution of worldwide available next generation telecommunication networks as the 5th generation of mobile systems (5G) and other Information and Telecommunication Technologies (ICT) is generally acknowledged [1]. The International Telecommunication Union (ITU) has set up agenda *Connect 2030* for Global Telecommunication/ICT Development'.[1] It is focusing on the goals in terms of growth, inclusiveness, sustainability, innovation, and partnerships to help to reduce poverty and hunger, boost health, create new jobs, help mitigate climate change, improve energy efficiency, and make cities and communities more sustainable by providing means to deliver high-quality goods and services in e.g., health care, education, finance, commerce, governance, agriculture, etc. while most areas inherit from connected appliances with the Internet of Things (IoT). A breakdown of selected application use cases where IoT and smartphone Apps contribute roughly equally to carbon emission savings thanks to ICT (avoiding ten times as much compared to own produced amount) was provided by GSMA for 2018[2] as shown in Fig. 1. As stated in [2] the increasing number of participants in different digital networks, and the depth of connection among them, demands for protection of the identity (people and objects) and the authenticity and integrity (data, algorithms and documents) of participants in these networks.

IoT, connected vehicles, distributed AI systems, energy networks, and digital learning platforms are such networks required for successful digital transformation in urban and rural communities, which have to be secured to allow for trust in these networks. Currently, only a minor amount of off-the-shelf IoT products provides encryption. Regarding the massive deployment and the fact that such devices will become part of everyday life in the future the scope for attack will broaden – while encryption and application of other security measures can make the use of IT considerably safer. In cellular networks, such authentication traditionally utilizes subscriber specific chip cards, whereas for local radio connections as attachment to WiFi routers, generally a user interaction in terms of, e.g., username/credential provision is required today. The need for much simpler and cost-efficient procedures resulted in approaches based on detecting and recognizing characteristic signals via, e.g., video/audio/haptic sensors, i.e., camera, microphone, or a touch-sensitive surface besides radio-based sensing of shapes or gestures.

Research is ongoing on various aspects of use cases as e.g., in the project System for *Monitoring Infants in Low-resource Environments* (SMILE)[3]. It is addressing inequity in coverage, inadequate human resources, and weak infrastructure, by exploring the potential of solutions for 'wearable IoT' to remotely monitor and capture several parameters and data for detecting and preventing many health conditions thus replacing and/or complementing infrequent, clinic-based measurements with unobtrusive, continuous sensing, monitoring, and assessment of necessary information.

Another recently kicked-off project is *Trust in Home: Rethinking Interface Design in IoT* (THRIDI)[4] using a Human-Data Interaction (HDI) Framework [3]. It is to explore data protection in smart homes in terms of

---

[1] URL: https://www.itu.int/en/mediacentre/backgrounders/Pages/connect-2030-agenda.aspx.

[2] URL: https://www.gsma.com/betterfuture/wp-content/uploads/2021/04/Mobile-Net-Zero-State-of-the-Industry-on-Climate-Action.pdf.

[3] URL: https://www.brunel.ac.uk/research/projects/system-for-monitoring-infants-in-low-resource-environments/.

[4] URL: https://spritehub.org/2022/02/07/thridi-trust-in-home-rethinking-interface-design-in-iot/.

- Legibility: transparency of data collection at home,
- Agency: control over personal data considering the multi-party use of home devices,
- Negotiability: changing relationships and managing control over personal data at home.

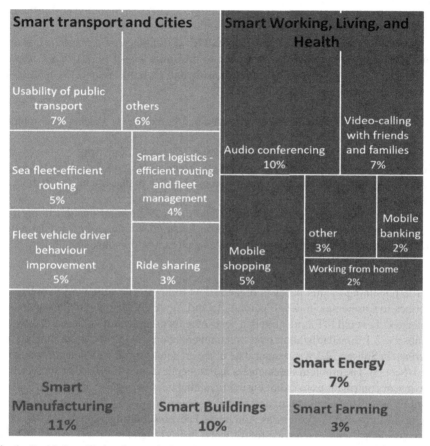

Fig. 1. Enabled avoided carbon emissions by IoT and smartphones according to GSMA in 2018

Several aspects of IoT with respect to connected vehicles for efficient transportation of goods, smart traffic control within urban areas, and digital farming in terms of intelligent agricultural machines in rural areas have been investigated in project *5G NetMobil*[5] [4]. A challenge here is provision of broadband wireless access over vast rural regions to close the digital gap. Applications and opportunities for future rural wireless communications cover a variety of areas, including residential welfare, digital agriculture, and transportation as off-road platooning of farming machines [5].

---

[5] URL: https://docbox.etsi.org/Workshop/2019/201903_ITSWS/SESSION04/ERICSSON_ MUEHLEISEN.pdf.

Connected Intelligent Transport Systems (C-ITS) and other Vehicle-to-Anything (V2X) applications towards autonomous driving may start not on public roads but in restricted environments as Campus areas as e.g., investigated in the research project *5G-based autonomous logistics*[6], which pursues the goal of researching autonomous transport. Autonomous Guided Vehicles (AGV) moving within an industrial environment helping to improve e.g., manufacturing processes [6] in framework of Industrial IoT (IIoT) require real-time transmission. The results of such research should be transferable to other areas of application.

Next Generation Internet of Things (NGIOT) [7] initiative is representing several projects and related initiatives, which work to maximize power of IoT in a European scale and has identified several IoT domains with high economic impact [8] in the focus of both industry and several communities:

- Energy Management (smart grids for demand-based power pricing and routing, preventing blackouts),
- Manufacturing (predictive maintenance, smart processing, logistics),
- Transportation (traffic jam predictions, optimal route calculation and vehicle tracking),
- Smart Cities & Communities (smart homes, disaster management, environmental monitoring),
- Healthcare (monitoring, assisted living, smart medical apparatus manufacturing),
- Smart Food & Farming (remote monitoring, data collection, automated farming), Retail (optimization of the supply chain), as well as new domains, including,
- Media, Insurance, Safety, and Defense.

The remaining of this paper is organized as follows: The following Subsect. 1.2 describes IoT use cases in detail, pointing to specific features required. Out of arising challenges of overall IoT as identified in Sect. 2 the focus on security issues is elaborated in Subsect. 2.1. Standardization work, recommendations and best current practice are described in Subsect. 2.2 whereupon state of the art solutions for authentication are provided (Sect. 3). The problem statement for IoT authentication is discussed in Subsect. 3.1. A review of contributions to radio sensing for authentication is given in Subsect. 3.2 followed by IP related architecture and protocol issues (Subsect. 3.3). Section 4 handles specific features of IoT systems as Automatic Packet Reporting System (APRS). The paper concludes with exemplary future work in R&D required (Sect. 5) so that the promise of IoT can be inherited in future deployments.

1.2 IoT Use Cases

As seen above, the IoT landscape is very diverse and heterogeneous, ranging from highly specialized devices and machines in IIoT deployed in dedicated areas, to low-cost sensors for massive roll-out in customers' homes and large-scale environments – as addressed by 3GPP, e.g., with Slice/Service Type (SST) massive Machine Type Communication (mMTC). Based on the specific use cases, the requirements deviate in terms of processing power and energy consumption of the things, data rate and quality parameters of the connectivity (error resilience, transmission delay, etc.).

---

[6] URL: https://wvsc.berlin/en/5g/.

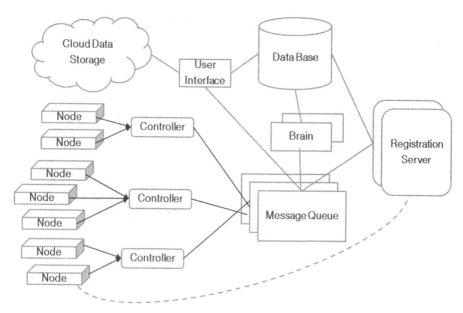

Fig. 2. High-level RIPE Atlas infrastructure (according to https://labs.ripe.net/)

Community IoT networks e.g., The Things Network (TTN)[7] are often built on Low-Power/Range Wide Area Networks (LoRaWAN)[8] technology, which is suited for IoT projects requiring high security and optimal performance. The technology provides long range low power wireless connectivity for devices, as, e.g., smart meters and other long range sensor applications like public security, agriculture, leak detection, disaster precaution, gas- and water metering, street lighting applications, etc. LoRaWAN projects requiring ultra-secure end-to-end (E2E) encryption combined with robust functionality, providing available security features and optimized LoRaWAN stack for best performance, integrated antenna together with sensors attached via SoC-based configurable analog and digital blocks ensuring easy and direct connection for any application. A more detailed overview on Automatic Packet Reporting System (APRS), enabling the amateur radio operator community to contact at anytime, anywhere (locally and globally), and via any device (including IoT sensors) any other member via global callsign-to-callsign messaging, bulletins, objects, email and voice, can be found in Sect. 4.

As another community IoT network may be seen RIPE Atlas (https://atlas.ripe.net/) by help of which the forum of European IP Networks Réseaux IP Européens (RIPE) Network Coordination Center (NCC) has built a global Internet measurement network of probes measuring Internet connectivity and reachability in real time. Provided by measurements at 10,000 probes hosted by individuals the Internet community can access RIPE Atlas data for use in terms of analyses of, e.g., the impact of Superstorm Sandy on Internet traffic routing, and for comparing response times of DNS servers. The collected data are inserted by so-called brains, i.e., higher level components, with access to the

---

[7] The Things Network. URL: https://www.thethingsnetwork.org/.

[8] URL: https://lora-alliance.org/.

central cloud data storage, into the specific Data Base. The RIPEstat User Interface for information service on Internet data/statistics provides access to the data. More information is available at RIPE websites.[9]

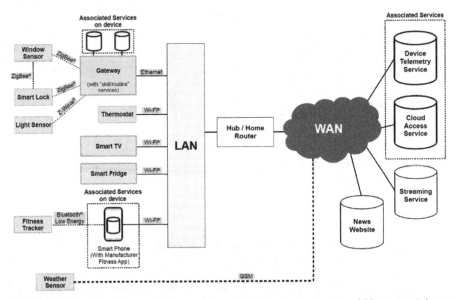

Fig. 3. Exemplary depiction of heterogeneity of IoT implementations within a smart home (Source: ETSI [11])

As shown in Fig. 2, the RIPE probes have to access after installation via decentral controllers and a Message Queue cluster asynchronously the Registration Servers with pre-installed material (predefined keys and addresses) in a flexible manner. These servers (acting as AAA servers) provide the probes' key to the controller, and vice versa (i.e., the controllers' one to the probe) before the probe can authenticate and connect to its assigned controller. All communication via this connection happens using Secure Shell Protocol (SSH) with port forwarding bi-directionally using individual SSH keys, session keys, and allocated ports to assure security and privacy. SSH is specified as a protocol for secure remote authentication and other secure network services over an insecure network relying on underlying lower layer (e.g., transport) protocols providing integrity and confidentiality protection. [9] describes the corresponding protocol framework and public key, password, and host-based client authentication method.

Whereas the examples above describe quite homogeneous structure of the IoT system, the area of the smart homes and/or the inclusion of those homes within the smart city exhibits different characteristics. An increasing number of devices, machines, and sensors, ranging from low-cost off-the-shelf home appliances as smoke detectors to complex control items for heating may all or partly be connected to the home IoT generating large amounts of data. Sometimes it is demanding for real-time processing, analyzing,

---

[9] URL: https://labs.ripe.net/author/kistel/ripe-atlas-probes-as-iot-devices/.

and decision making (associated services), managed centrally or de-centrally as depicted for a typical scenario in Fig. 3.

2 Overall IoT Challenges

As discussed in [7] the heterogeneity of IoT devices and the dynamic management of legacy and new devices and services poses especially challenges. In general, IoT devices, which may be deployed both in a highly distributed manner in rural areas to be connected via long-range technology but also in a dense urban environment with massive numbers per area via local short-range radio shall be seamlessly connected across multiple technologies and various domains. Interoperability requirements call for standardized solutions while the inherent decentralized structure demands new solutions in terms of control, monitoring, efficient routing and traffic shaping. How to deal with massive amount of data and real-time requirements in terms of intelligent data analytics, edge cloud computing, and software defined networking will be major task. Without being connected to the electric grid and operated in a stand-alone manner for years, power efficient operation of the device function and the connectivity solution is essential. Both massively deployed and single high-performance devices demand for reliable operation, flexibility and scalability, ease of use and convenience, global reach and, last but not the least, privacy and security in a per-design manner to really improve the users experience and not create additional burden. As result of the analysis, an overview on all identified IoT challenges will be provided in Sect. 5, while in the following the focus will be on countermeasures related to security.

2.1 IoT Security

Since IoT devices shall in general operate without continuous human assistance and create, collect, and often exchange sensitive data, they are prone to attacks and have to cope with different security issues. The aim to develop a trusted IoT ecosystem in view of billions of IoT devices powered by trillions of chips fueling a wide range of applications and IoT services is related to the key challenge of evolving trusted IoT solutions and data sharing in a fragmented supply chain, which requires supply chain security, traceability, and trust in the data. Trusted business alliances are needed for E2E solutions in the IoT value chain to minimize cost and risks from vulnerabilities and maximize the value of trusted ecosystems.

The overall aspects of security in IoT range from device security to secure connectivity via the IoT system to prevent all levels of attack and the typical assured privacy and integrity of the user data. In the layered view, security on access and transport networks as well as the core has to be granted all levels. Secured information transmission at physical and MAC layers provide link-layer security, network layer security in terms of use of IETF Security architecture and protocol (IPSec) as specified in RFC 4301 [10] and encryption of IP packet content, whereas an E2E security on application level completes the security provision. Especially in the first phases of IoT operation starting with setting up the connection between device and network via the point of attachment, the risks and countermeasures must be strong enough, since no association might have been built up before. The process of bootstrapping and mutual authentication between device and access point (AP) is critical and shall not prevent usage by complexity.

2.2 Standardization Activities Towards IoT Security

ITU-T. Study Group 20 (SG20) on "Internet of Things and Smart Cities and Communities" focusses on deployment of smart city platforms through global standardization activities. This includes a reference framework of converged service for identification and authentication for IoT devices in a decentralized environment. Most recently, SG20 has been working on topics including AI, blockchain, machine-to-machine communication and Big Data aspects of IoT as e.g., in terms of Focus Group on *Artificial Intelligence (AI) and Internet of Things (IoT) for Digital Agriculture* (FG-AI4A). Examination of potential emerging technologies for supporting data collation, improving agriculture systems modelling, and fostering effective communication for optimizing farming processes is done in collaboration with UNs Food and Agriculture Organization (FAO) to underscore existing gaps in current standardization on digital agriculture.

ITU has also recently developed standards ensuring the security of networks in urban areas and enabling smart sustainable cities by e.g., smart grids supporting controllable and efficient energy systems.[10]

Recommendation ITU-T Y.4811[11] is intended to develop a converged identification and authentication service to overcome relevant challenges in decentralized IoT identification and authentication management systems, to ensure efficient communication among IoT devices and services in decentralized environments. The challenges in decentralized environments are to support effective and efficient interactions e.g., secured interoperability, scalability, low latency, etc. arises from heterogeneity in IoT devices, services, and corresponding systems for identification and authentication. The introduced Converged Service for Identification and Authentication for IoT devices in Decentralized Environment (CSIADE) shall facilitate IoT devices and IoT services to identify and authenticate each other in such environments. 3GPP security features in the 5G System include:

- *Authentication* of the user equipment (UE) by the network and vice versa for mutual authentication between UE and network,
- *Security* context generation and distribution,
- *User Plane* data confidentiality and integrity protection,
- *Control Plane* signaling confidentiality and integrity protection,
- User *identity* confidentiality.

IoT specific cellular technologies as Narrow Band IoT and LTE-M or NR-M2M [12, 13] can securely connect up to millions of sensors and devices using cellular technology. [14] provides an overview about 5GS optimizations and functionality for support of Cellular Internet-of-Things (Cellular IoT, or CIoT) according to service requirements. The specific functionality of CIoT, in earlier 3GPP releases also referred to as MTC, is

---

[10] URL: https://www.itu.int/en/mediacentre/backgrounders/Pages/smart-sustainable-cities.aspx.
[11] URL: https://www.itu.int/rec/T-REC-Y.4811-202111-I.

described in the affected procedures and features of this specification, in TS 23.502 [15], TS 23.503 [16], and other specifications.

3GPP has performed five studies during Release 16 specification to support key enablers for IIoT in 5G systems, another ten studies related to enhance support for IIoT in Release 17, while for 3GPP Release 18 again five studies have been agreed on[12]. IoT non-terrestrial network (NTN) enhancements, Personal IoT and Residential networks, especially with application layer support for the latter in focus of future investigations.

Detailed security related network functions for 5G are described in TS 33.501 [17]. Especially when a UE is connected heterogeneously or in a hybrid manner via the 3GPP Next Generation Radio Access Network (NG-RAN) aka. New Radio (NR) and via a standalone non-3GPP access (e.g., WiFi or satellite access), the multiple N1 instances between UE and 5G Core (5GC) are secured using independent Non-Access Stratum (NAS) security contexts. These are - independent of access technology - each created based on the security context derived from the UE authentication in the corresponding SEAF (Security Anchor Functionality) (e.g., in the common AMF when the UE is served by the same AMF). Here the 5G specific feature for Access Traffic Steering, Switching and Splitting (ATSSS) [18] also mentioned in Sect. 3, contributes to an overarching integrated view on heterogeneously connected devices.

Furthermore, 3GPP has identified new business models for 5G systems to support such as those for IoT and enterprise managed networks. Drivers for the 5G KPIs include services such as Uncrewed Aerial Vehicle (UAV) control, Augmented Reality (AR), and factory automation. Network flexibility enhancements support self-contained enterprise networks, installed and maintained by network operators while being managed by the enterprise. Enhanced connection modes and evolved security facilitate support of Massive IoT (MIoT), expected to include tens of millions of UEs sending and receiving data over the 5G network.

Currently, for 5G as specified in 3GPP Rel. 17 [14], two out of five standardized Slice/Service Type (SST) values are specified to be suitable for IoT, namely MIoT/mMTC and High-Performance MTC, beside enhanced Mobile Broadband (eMBB), ultra-reliable low latency communications (URLLC), and Vehicle-to-anything (V2X) services. SSTs are referring to a Network Slices' expected behavior in terms of features (e.g., QoS, access technology, device capabilities) and services, providing a way for establishing global interoperability for correspondingly configured slices so that mobile networks can support the roaming use case more efficiently for the most commonly used SSTs.

ETSI. EN 303 645 [19] produced by ETSI Technical Committee Cyber Security (CYBER) brings together widely considered good practice in security for Internet-connected consumer devices in a set of high-level outcome-focused provisions. The objective is to support all parties involved in the development and manufacturing of consumer IoT with guidance on securing their products. The provisions are primarily outcome-focused, rather than prescriptive, giving organizations the flexibility to innovate and implement security solutions appropriate for their products.

---

[12] URL: https://www.3gpp.org/release18/.

Focus is on technical controls and organizational policies that matter most in addressing the most significant and widespread security shortcomings. Overall, a baseline level of security is considered; this is intended to protect against elementary attacks on fundamental design weaknesses (such as the use of easily guessable passwords).

The European Norm provides a set of baseline provisions applicable to all consumer IoT devices. It is intended to be complemented by other standards defining more specific provisions and fully testable and/or verifiable requirements for specific devices, which, together with the present document, will facilitate the development of assurance schemes.

IEEE wireless technologies as 802.11-based WiFi 6 and 7, as well as short-range radio based on 802.15 (e.g., LPAN as Bluetooth or LoRaWAN) are in use for in-house and on-campus IoT networks.

Current authentication models like 802.1X [20] are based on human intervention and thus do not fit well for simple IoT devices. Scalability would also be an issue in view of expected massive deployment. A 'hardware based' admission model would enable many new applications using radio sensing as a method to provide a token for authentication. Use of Wireless LAN (WLAN) as specified by IEEE 802.11 [21] for sensing is studied by 802.11bf task group (TGbf) [22]. Use cases for 802.11bf TG include room sensing, i.e., presence detection, counting the number of people in the room, localization of active people, audio with user detection, gesture recognition at different ranges, device proximity detection, home appliance control. There are also health care related use cases like breathing/heart rate detection, surveillance of persons of interest, building a 3D picture of an environment, in car sensing for driver sleepiness detection [23].

Besides ITU, 3GPP, ETSI, and IEEE, also IETF is investigating in IoT networking and secure authentication from different points of view. Sensing projects how to discover, negotiate, measure and exchange sensing capabilities and results.

IETF. RFC (Request for Comments) 9140 [25] describes a method for registration, authentication, and key derivation for network-connected smart devices, such as consumer and enterprise appliances that are part of the Internet of Things. These devices may be off-the-shelf hardware that is sold and distributed without any prior registration or credential-provisioning process, or they may be recycled devices after a hard reset. Thus, the device registration in a server database, ownership of the device, and the authentication credentials for both network access and application-level security must all be established at the time of the device deployment. Furthermore, many such devices have only limited user interfaces that could be used for their configuration. Often, the user interfaces are limited to either only input (e.g., camera) or output (e.g., display screen). The device configuration is made more challenging by the fact that the devices may exist in large numbers and may have to be deployed or re-configured nimbly based on user needs. [24] investigated practically into standard Extensible Authentication Protocol (EAP) framework for use in secure bootstrapping of resource-constrained devices and [25] could demonstrate secure bootstrapping of off-the shelf household devices with Visible Light Communication (VLC) via lightweight EAP-NOOB (Nimble out-of-band) authentication.

Bootstrapping using manufacturer-installed X.509 certificates combined with a manufacturer's authorizing service, both online and offline, i.e., a Secure Key Infrastructure

(SKI), is denoted as Bootstrapping Remote SKI (BRSKI) protocol [26]. The specification of automated bootstrapping in terms of authentication of devices, including sending authorizations to the device as to what network they should join, and how to authenticate that network, allows even deployment under weak security requirements. Bootstrapping is accomplished when either the cryptographic identity of the new SKI or a locally issued certificate has been deployed to the device via the established secure connection.

[27] describes and defines several operational modes for a BRSKI Manufacturer Authorized Signing Authority (MASA) specifying an IDevID (Initial Device Identifier) and other related trust anchors for device authentication while [28] provides a taxonomy of operational security of manufacturer installed keys and anchors. The question is how the Public Key Infrastructure (PKI) used for above can be evaluated and how an operator builds and manages the infrastructure to authenticate devices. The latter is discussed in [29] in terms of operational considerations for a BRSKI registrar.

[30] gives an overview on IoT device bootstrapping and related secure mechanisms for smart objects as part of an IoT network addressing different options as a function of use case specific security requirements and available user interfaces.

Recently submitted IETF draft [31] attempts to establish the general need for new authentication methods in the IoT as a future networking area beyond 5G going into 6G for standardization. Several scenarios are described where the current authentication protocols do not work or are insufficient. In addition, few new approaches are discussed such as WLAN/6G sensing and visible light, e.g., Light Emitting Diode (LED) based, which shall be further explored.

3   State of the Art in IoT Security

As pointed out in [32] for risk minimization the understanding of the features of the ICT system, a precise definition of the roles of the relevant parts and stakeholders, and the availability of control measures with defined properties concerning risk and attack potential is required. Applied to the IoT sector which may have to deal with cost pressures and attackers with an elevated potential at the same time, this methodology would recommend coordinating deployment of controls definitely between all stakeholders. A basic-level control in an IoT device and a medium-level control in the sectoral back-office may be concatenated and synchronized such that an overall high security level is achieved protecting also against elevated attack potentials.

Reliable device to device connectivity in sensor cloud systems by secure access control is not easily achieved as, e.g., pointed out in [33] claiming and resolving security flaws in terms of both device impersonation and man in middle attacks.

[34] describes research areas related to IoT and Wireless Sensor Networks (WSN), in smart city applications, towards sustainable communities in terms of, e.g., disaster management, healthcare, energy, water, surveillance, structural health monitoring, and environmental monitoring. Suitable examples are:

- Design and deployment of an IoT system for early warning purposes,
- Design and optimization of heterogeneous wireless communication for enabling real-time management of interoperable heterogeneous devices,

- Data services in serving networks (e.g., electricity, water, gas),
- Development of (low-cost) IoT sensors for monitoring of e.g., air quality, local weather conditions, or vulnerable people as patients or pedestrian road users, or
- A connected system for road, air, or water traffic and transport vehicles, i.e., autonomous or assisted driving as well as Connected, Autonomous, and Electric Vehicles (CAEV) and Uncrewed Arial Vehicles (UAV).

ETSI TS 103 701 [11] provides guidance on how to assess and assure IoT products by defining test cases and assessment criteria for each provision. Since many consumers' IoT devices and their associated services process and store personal data, the European Norm can help in ensuring that these are compliant with the General Data Protection Regulation (GDPR) [35]. Security by design is an important principle that is or should be endorsed by most of the current approaches.

As analyzed and pointed out in [36] a holistic treatment of existing IoT device standards during system design and deployment is required to provide IoT security:

- Authentication and authorization schemes which should be unique per device, shall be designed based on overall system-level threat models and frameworks as e.g., in terms of the security countermeasures defined in ETSI TS 102 165-2 [37].
- Authentication credentials shall be salted (by adding random data), hashed (i.e., by mapping the data to a fixed size bit array, or encrypted by other means.
- All applicable security aspects, i.e., confidentiality (privacy), integrity, availability, and authenticity of the information shall be guaranteed on all levels and domains – during transmission in networks or storage in the IoT application or the cloud.
- A "zero trust security model" (ZTSM) demands not to trust any data received and always verify the current state. Especially, IoT devices after discovery and identification have to be verified/authenticated towards the network before a trusted secure connection can be established – and vice versa.
- Authentication mechanisms must use strong passwords or personal identification numbers (PINs) and should consider using two-factor authentication (2FA) or multi-factor authentication (MFA) like smartphones, biometrics, etc., on top of certificates

  - In MFA compared to 2FA the authentication method granting access to a network resource requires successful presentation of more than one piece of evidence (or factor) to the authenticator. Factors may be classified as

    - knowledge (something only the user knows),
    - possession (something only the user has), or
    - inherence (something only the user is).

  - In general, MFA protects user data – which may include personal identification or financial assets – from being accessed by an unauthorized third party that may have been able to discover, for example, a single password.

The presentation of the multiple pieces as pointed out in the last item ideally is realized independently of each other via disjunctive methods, e.g., via multiple paths and technologies, media, etc. A solution is provided with 3GPP 5G in terms of ATSSS allowing a UE or IoT device to attach to the network via multiple paths concurrently (split traffic) or alternatively (via traffic steering or switching). This feature both enhances reliability and data protection since, e.g., a potential eavesdropper has to have access to all paths to detect the exchanged information. ATSSS here makes use of IETF multi-path (MP) transport protocols as MP-TCP (Transmission Control Protocol), while alternative solutions based on MP variants of Quick UDP Internet Connections (QUIC) and Datagram Congestion Control Protocol (DCCP) for non-TCP traffic are under investigation [38]. Such a solution would rather be applicable to high-end IIoT devices in e.g., company campus networks, while probably being inept for most low-cost consumer equipment and community network, so that a simplified approach should be followed.

3.1 Low-Cost IoT Authentication Approach

To lay ground for the need for new authentication models in the framework of devices (e.g., machines in IoT communication) within a (wireless or wireline-based) network the problem analysis is as follows: While the current model (such as e.g., 802.1X certificate model) is based on a human being using the machine and providing credentials (e.g., username/password or a permitted digital certificate) to the authenticator. Similarly, for UE to access a cellular network the device has to be equipped with a USIM (Universal Subscriber Identity Module) and the user has to provide a secret key, i.e., PIN. With the 5G use case of MIoT and expecting an increasing amount of devices within a household (smart home) and/or in the ownership of a customer (smart watch etc.) the need for an ease-of-use hardware based admission model arises. Focusing on corresponding procedures starting with detection (sensing) of a new device and subsequent mutual authenticating of the device by and to the network a set of potential technologies are identified and described to allow for analysis in terms of criteria as reliable operation (working), scalability, ease of use and convenience, security, and many more. Furthermore, the method should be applicable to future generations of networks and users, upcoming new applications and devices, assuming that todays established standard procedures do not fulfill the requirements sufficiently.

A potential framework may address the facts that

- User and device are separated and not physically connected.
- A unique identity for the user applying to all own/personalized devices is given.
- The authentication has to work mutually.

The simple devices may have the following characteristics:

- No pre-established relation with the intended server or user,
- No pre-provisioned device identifier or authentication credentials,
- Input or output interface that may be capable of only one-directional out-of-band communication.

All existing kinds of established certificates may be applicable as e.g., 128-bit Advanced Encryption Standard (AES) [39], ITU-T X.509[13] or ISO/IEC 9594-8[14], etc.

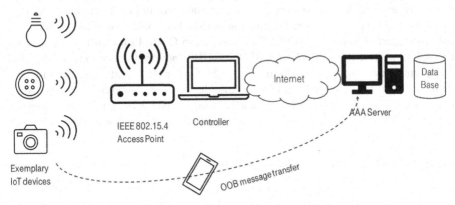

Fig. 4. Exemplary EAP-NOOB authentication deployment

Recently proposed use of WiFi sensing (as in focus of IEEE TG 802.11bf[15]) to assist authentication may provide ease of use compared to existing methods as, e.g., 802.15 Bluetooth [40] relying on IEEE 802.15.4 [41] security protocol widely used for short-range communication in the IoT environment. Secured information transmission at physical and MAC layers provide link-layer security in, e.g., IP based communication as IPv6 over Low-Power Wireless Personal Area Networks (6LoWPAN) [42]. Secure hop-by-hop communication between all network nodes is achieved by different specified security features included in encryption and/or authentication. Protection based on pre-shared keys only works in case no attacker can gain access to a key and thus compromise the whole network. Limitations of IEEE 802.15.4 are the incapability of safeguarding privacy and confidentiality of acknowledgement messages (ACK) [41]. However, as pointed out in RFC 9006 [43], additional measures are available for, e.g., TCP and on the other hand IEEE 802.15.4, e.g., provides capabilities to protect frames and restrict them to a point-to-point link or a group of devices as highlighted in [44].

As depicted in Fig. 4, an exemplary implementation setup for bootstrapping, i.e., authentication of an IoT device (e.g., camera, smoke detector or light bulb, serving as EAP-NOOB peer/client) towards the corresponding AAA (EAP-NOOB) server via optical detection by a smart phone user (OOB message transfer) is required. Next, communication between devices in the local network and towards the controller is feasible. Unfortunately, the EAP-NOOB approach may not be suitable for, e.g., sensor devices without any second user interface beside the network access technology nor in case of complete inaccessibility to any user, such as during autonomous deployment of, e.g., sensors for environmental monitoring purposes in the wild.

---

[13] ITU-T X.509. URL: https://www.itu.int/ITU-T/recommendations/rec.aspx?id=14033.

[14] ISO/IEC 9594-8. URL: https://www.iso.org/standard/80325.html.

[15] IEEE P802.11 – Task Group BF. URL: https://www.ieee802.org/11/Reports/tgbf_update.htm.

3.2 IoT Sensing for Authentication Research

Using sensor data and WiFi sensing for securing and authentication a user and a device is investigated widely, and a range of approaches have been proposed and analyzed so far: The integrity of IIoT systems is discussed in [45] highlighting the existing security approaches for the most significant industrial applications. Classifying attacks and possible security solutions regarding IoT layers architecture, attacks are usually connected to one or more layers of the architecture and corresponding IoT security countermeasures can safeguard those attacks. [46] has studied security problems in IoT and classified possible cyberattacks on each layer of IoT architecture. Multiple authentication mechanisms (e.g., OAuth 2.0, certificates, cryptography) and access control techniques (e.g., user managed, group based, service level) are compared in terms of the application environment (smart home, multi-agent IoT) and used security protocols as Transport Layer Security (TLS), AES, and PKI.

[47] presents a comprehensive survey of recent advances in the so-called 'device-free' WiFi sensing mechanism based on Channel State Information (CSI) providing both advantages compared to Received Signal Strength Indicator (RSSI) as drawbacks. [48] provides a holistic overview on the evolution of WiFi technology and on investigations in opportunistic applications of WiFi signals for gesture and motion detection as well as authentication and security. Changing pattern of CSI influenced by intense human motion and extracted features in the pattern have been studied in [49] in numerous experiments. By distinguishing between Line-of-Sight (LOS) and Non-Line-of-Sight (NLOS) conditions in case of obstacles appearing between transmitter and receiver an improved overall performance could be achieved.

[50] has proposed Human Activity Recognition (HuAc) as a combination of WiFi-based and Kinect-based activity recognition system, to sense human activity in an indoor environment. Comparing HuAc using commercial WiFi devices and evaluating it in three kinds of scenarios with WiFi-based Activity Recognition (WiAR) as benchmark shows on the average a better accuracy.

Mechanisms for wireless sensing and radio environment awareness as analyzed in [51] show vulnerabilities such as dependency of sensing modes on external signals. Potential solutions for mitigating, e.g., different threats to Radio Environment Mapping (REM) are provided in the context of a vehicular communication scenario. [51] recommends developing sensing-centric security mechanisms for next-generation wireless networks. Vehicular applications are also in focus of [52] proposing a cipher utilizing the fingerprint concept to create a unique and dynamic keystream. A vehicle's fingerprint is a nonlinear time-dynamic function and can be shared only between the car and edge Anchor Nodes (ANs). A simple fingerprint would be a vehicle's historical connections to APs, which is unique to each vehicle and aware by ANs. This fingerprint-based cipher can enable security services in terms of authentication: Without requiring real-time authentication, the dynamic cipher can seamlessly integrate with the latest authentication schemes. After authentication, ANs will send a key to start the cipher.

[53] has anticipated enhanced security of industrial WSNs (IWSNs) by algorithms for sensor nodes' authentication based on neural networks and implementations in IWSNs have shown that an improved convolution preprocessing neural network (CPNN)-based

algorithm requires few computing resources and has extremely low latency, thus enabling a lightweight multi-node PHY-layer authentication.

A data augmented multiuser PHY-layer authentication scheme is recommended in [54] to improve the security of mobile-edge computing system applied to IoT. Three data augmentation algorithms are proposed to speed up the establishment of the authentication model and improve the authentication success rate. By combining the deep neural network with data augmentation methods, the performance of the proposed multiuser PHY-layer authentication scheme is improved and the training speed is accelerated, even with fewer training samples.

An overview on Physical Layer Authentication (PLA) in wireless communication networks is provided by [55]. Both, key-based and key-less PLA systems are described and three typical architectures to provide authentication based on:

1. channel information,
2. radio frequency (RF) features of devices (RF fingerprint), and
3. identity watermarks (inspired by conventional cryptography-based authentication).

Further research on PLA may address future multiuser communication networks such as cognitive radio and address IoT issues. [56] applies the RF fingerprint of a communication signal to establish a communication device authentication supported by neighborhood component analysis (NCA) method and the support vector data description (SVDD) algorithm. Simulations result in an authentic devices authentication success rate (ASR) and rogue devices detection success rate (RSR) of both 90% for a signal-to-noise ratio (SNR) of 15 dB.

[57] proposes a non-intrusive gait recognition-based mechanism to enhance the security of smartphones by rapid user identification with a high degree of confidence and securing sensitive data in case of an attack. Motion sensors on a user device provide data to create a statistical model of a user's gait, which is later used for identification. The attack-resistant user authentication mechanism for smartphones proposed in [58] is based on hand gesture detected by touch, accelerometer, and gyro sensors wherefrom a signature is created.

A current drawback for usage of WiFi sensing for device authentication might be that the accuracy of, e.g., high-resolution gesture detection is not sufficiently high in the typical radio frequency ranges used for communication below 6 GHz[16]. Additional research on supporting technology as AI may improve those figures in the future.

3.3 Architectures and Procedures for Future IP-Based IoT-Authentication

On IP or network layer for IPv6 IPsec protocol suite is mandatory and provides E2E security for authentication procedures, ensuring confidentiality and integrity of the transmitted data.

Authentication for IoT may rely on a protocol as 6LowPAN (Low-power Wireless Personal Area Network) which is defined for optimizing the efficient routing of IPv6 packets for resource constrained MTC applications.

---

[16] URL: https://www.ieee802.org/11/IEEE%20802-11-Overview-and-Amendments-Under-Dev elopment.pptx.

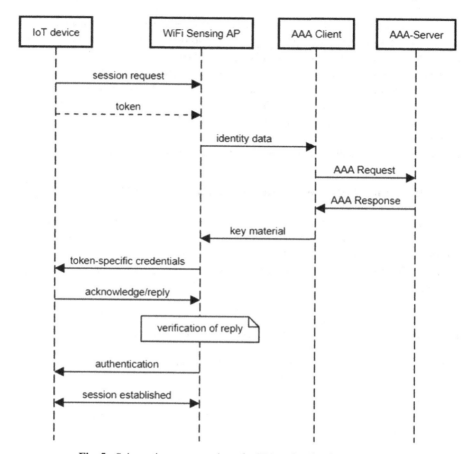

Fig. 5. Schematic representation of a 2FA authentication procedure

Any exchange of authentication messages between a device attaching to a network via, e.g., a WiFi AP and the responsible backend server for Authentication, Authorization, and Accounting (AAA) may be depicted as shown in Fig. 5. The generalized message sequence diagram shows an exemplary 2FA towards a WiFi sensing enabled AP via two disjunct paths – the radio communication path (straight line arrow) and the radio sensing signal detection (dashed line arrow) in terms of a so-called token. The exemplary WiFi sensing appliance at the AP proceeds with the received session request by creating from the device identification and the token in terms of a detected radio sensing pattern, i.e., the identity data. The AAA client at, e.g., the local or edge IoT gateway together with the (central) AAA server performs AAA procedures resulting in creation of key material, which is sent to the AP. The device has to reply on the presented credentials with the correct acknowledgement upon which the AP authenticates the device and access and session are established.

When compared to a fully certificate-based authentication, however, a hardware-based AAA mechanism relying, e.g., on WiFi sensing gesture detection does not require the user to know any key, identifier, or password for the device to be authenticated. A pre-defined type of access to the device (e.g., physical, photographic, or video representation, unique description in terms of parameters, etc.) shall be sufficient for authentication.

Like the EAP approach providing an authentication framework supporting multiple authentication methods, we try to generalize an AAA mechanism operating over any layer or medium not requiring pre-authentication.

The AAA method is intended for authenticating all kind of IoT devices without any pre-configured authentication credentials by making use of a general token created in a mutual agreed method making use of a user-assisted or -unassisted detection process.

4   Community Approach: Automatic Packet Reporting System

Automatic Packet Reporting System (APRS) is a worldwide network of radio ama-teurs, which has been designed to rapport localization information for track and trace of portable and mobile radio stations. Its first definition has been published in 1994[17], based upon the AX.25 protocol [59]. Over the years, the possible payload has been extended to telemetry data, which mainly covers sensor data. Data types are:

- Spatial data: location (LL), altitude (h), speed (v), and course ($°$)
- Weather data: temperature (T), humidity (rH), air pressure (p) or air quality,
- Operational data: voltage (U),
- Radio transmission data: field strength (RSSI) or SNR.

In addition, short message bulletins like technical equipment information or ad-hoc user generated messages are possible contents. The APRS specification is an ongoing community development, by collecting new proposals [60].

4.1   APRS Network Architecture

The access basic architecture consists of portable end devices (nodes) and fixed entry points (iGates), which are connected to the public Internet or radio amateur operated Hamnet as depicted in Fig. 6. A two-tier core server network handles all incoming data world-wide in five regions and eliminates duplicated packets, which might result out of multiple iGates, receiving the same packet.

4.2   APRS Access Air Interface

While traditionally Amplitude Frequency Shift Keying (AFSK) on 144-MHz-amateur-radio-band is applied for data transfer, nowadays more and more LoRaWAN-APRS technology is emerging on 433-MHz-band, either simplex or semi-duplex. Due to their license radio amateurs can exceed the power limitations of Industrial, Science and Med-ical (ISM) applications. With a power of 100 mW (+20 dBm), transmission distances of more than 100 km can be bridged, provided Line of Sight (LoS) using the following modulation parameters:

---

[17] APRS spec version 1.01. URL: http://aprs.org/APRSdocs/protocol.txt

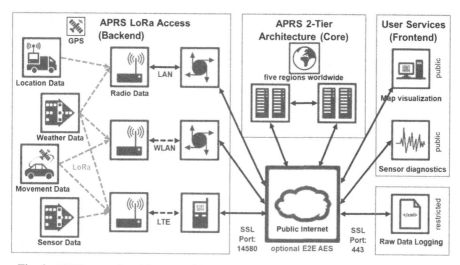

Fig. 6. APRS network architecture with access frontend, core network and service backend

- RF bandwidth: 125 kHz (with low influence of other radio services)
- Spreading factor: 12 (coding of $2^{12} = 4096$ possible different values in one chirp)
- Forward error correction C/R: 4/5 (as no handshake is applied)

4.3 APRS User Authentication

Amateur radio is always based on open, non-encrypted communication. Every radio amateur is assigned a unique call-sign by its national telecommunication authority. Its prefix is compliant with the International country allocation. To identify different device application types, owned and operated by the same radio amateur, an SSID extension is used e.g., DL1DSR-10 identifies a licensed German radio amateur (DL) and an iGate (ID 10) as device. In addition, a station-related map symbol is defined.

To unify the communication within the Internet, a unique numeric hash is applied, which is generated out of the call-sign without SSID and stored in a database of valid codes. Misuse of call-signs is supervised by both, the open ham community of radio amateurs and if required, by public telecommunication authorities. One might be surprised that such a community approach works successfully for many decades. For efficiency at the shared air interface, data compression for location, speed and course with an open algorithm can be applied.

4.4 APRS Data Visualization

Open data can be used for multiple services. The access to raw packet data is limited to registered radio amateurs only. Most popular is a map-based visualization of nodes and iGates with many filter options[18]. Figure 7 shows a trace of a car over 400 km movement and the LoRa iGates <L>, which were involved of collecting transferred

---

[18] APRS map visualization. URL: https://aprs.fi/.

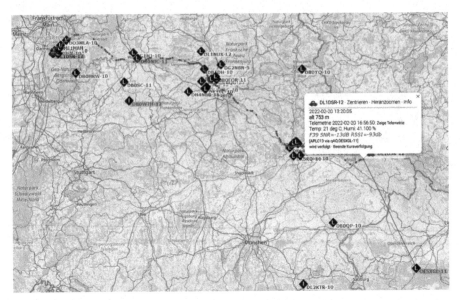

Fig. 7. Overlay of a trace of mobile station DL1DSR-12, February 20, 2022 on openstreetmap

data and reporting them to the core APRS network. Transmission conditions: +28 dBm on a vertical-stocked car antenna. Each red point indicated a successfully received single packet. By clicking, additional information is provided.

Nowadays, so-called smart beaconing becomes popular, which let the node decide on its own, when to send the next packet, based on several threshold parameters like time, speed or change of direction. It helps to omit a channel overload as all reporting stations share the same frequency for packet transmission. As there is no coordinated planning, the regional coverage is very different, but increasing month by month in Austria and Germany.

5 Conclusion and Outlook

The *COREnect* project within 5GPPP [61] sees 6G era as successor network concept built on 5G. It enables Industry 4.0 and IoT systems, whereas the 6G connectivity shall be an archetype of Internet of Anything (IoX). This is driving further overall digitalization by allowing real-time connectivity among physical, digital, and biological worlds while relying on their digital twin representation or virtual world in the sense of Extended Reality (XR) to follow Augmented/Virtual Reality (AR/VR) as in focus of today's challenging applications.

After assessment of various exemplary use cases and application scenarios for IoT/M2M/MTC as summarized above, a classification of functional and operational demands for IoT result in technical requirements grouped in a handful of major aspects as shown in Fig. 8. Here key current mainly technical challenges in IoT, which may help in designing the best architecture and technology are depicted.

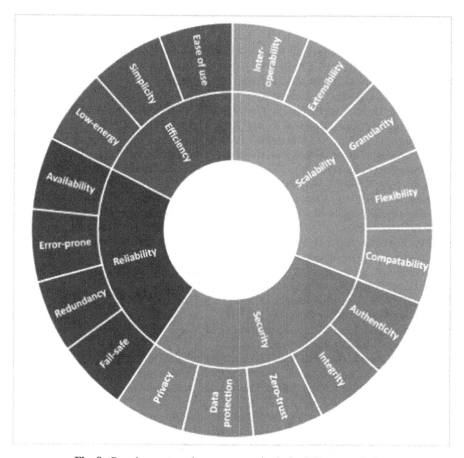

Fig. 8. Requirements and assessment criteria for IoT system design

With respect to such visions, the need for sustainable and reliable solutions to secure the upcoming IoT world is a crucial issue. This paper has addressed challenges of next generation IoT systems from a technical point of view and discussed the new approach of a hardware based two factor authentication method using radio sensing for identification and authorization of IoT devices. In future 'beyond 5G' heterogeneous IoT networks such new universal authentication concepts for simple smart "things" will be essential to enable an expected "Internet of Everything" (IoE) or IoX. The status of active research and development work is reviewed and aspects for future investigations have been outlined.

Planned new work in IETF may focus on applicability of existing approaches for multi-factor and multi-path authentication for wireless connection of simple and low-cost 'off-the-shelf' IoT devices. Instead of creating new security concerns, aim of the envisaged investigation is to identify means to increase security in future IoT networks in terms of robust but easily manageable authentication mechanisms.

References

1. Ono, T., Iida, K., Yamazaki, S.: Achieving sustainable development goals (SDGs) through ICT Services. FUJITSU Sci. Tech. J. **53**, 6 (2017)
2. Federal Ministry of the Interior, Building and Community, Cyber Security Strategy for Germany 2021, Berlin, Germany (2021)
3. Mortier, R., Haddadi, H., Henderson, T., McAuley, D., Crowcroft, J.: Human-data interaction: the human face of the data-driven society (2014). https://doi.org/10.2139/ssrn.2508051
4. von Hugo, D., Eichler, G., Rosowski, T.: A holistic communication network for efficient transport and enhanced driving via connected cars. In: Lüke, K.-H., Eichler, G., Erfurth, C., Fahrnberger, G. (eds.) I4CS 2019. CCIS, vol. 1041, pp. 11–24. Springer, Cham (2019). https://doi.org/10.1007/978-3-030-22482-0_2
5. Zhang, Y., Love, D.J., Krogmeier, J.V., Anderson, C.R., Heath, R.W., Buckmaster, D.R.: Challenges and opportunities of future rural wireless communications. IEEE Commun. Mag. **59**(12), 16–22 (2021)
6. Lüke, K.-H., von Hugo, D., Eichler, G.: 5G network quality of service supporting adequate quality of experience for industrial demands in process automation. In: Krieger, U.R., Eichler, G., Erfurth, C., Fahrnberger, G. (eds.) I4CS 2021. CCIS, vol. 1404, pp. 201–222. Springer, Cham (2021). https://doi.org/10.1007/978-3-030-75004-6_14
7. NGIOT (Next Generation Internet of Things): IoT research, innovation and deployment priorities in the EU White Paper, D3.3 (2021)
8. Kolovou, L.: Building a Roadmap for Next Generation Internet of Things, Scoping Paper, NGIOT workshop October 2019 (2019)
9. Ylonen, T., Lonvick, C.: SSH Authentication Protocol, RFC 4252 (2006)
10. Kent, S., Seo, K.: Security Architecture for the Internet Protocol, RFC 4301 (2005)
11. ETSI TS 103 701 (V1.1.1): CYBER; Cybersecurity assessment for consumer IoT products (2021)
12. 3GPP TS 33.187: Security aspects of Machine-Type Communications (MTC) and other mobile data applications communications enhancements
13. 3GPP TR 33.861: Study on evolution of Cellular Internet of Things (CIoT) security for the 5G System
14. 3GPP TS 23.501: System architecture for the 5G System (5GS); Stage 2 (Release 17)
15. 3GPP TS 23.502: Procedures for the 5G system, Stage 2 (Release 17)
16. 3GPP TS 23.503: Policy and Charging Control Framework for the 5G System (Release 17)
17. 3GPP TS 33.501: Security architecture and procedures for 5G system
18. 3GPP TS 24.193: 5G System; Access Traffic Steering, Switching and Splitting (ATSSS); Stage 3
19. ETSI EN 303 645 (V2.1.1): CYBER; Cyber Security for Consumer Internet of Things: Baseline Requirements (2020)
20. IEEE, 802.1X-2020: Port Based Network Access Control. https://standards.ieee.org/ieee/802.1X/7345/ (2020)
21. IEEE, Std. 802.11-2016. https://standards.ieee.org/findstds/standard/802.11-2016.html (2016)
22. IEEE, P802.11 - Task Group BF (WLAN Sensing) 11-21/0504r2: Specification Framework for TGbf (2021)
23. IEEE, P802.11 - Task Group BF (WLAN Sensing) 11-20/1712r2: WiFi Sensing Use Cases (2021)
24. Peltonen, A., et al.: Enterprise security for the internet of things (IoT): lightweight bootstrapping with EAP-NOOB. Sensors **20**, 6101 (2020). https://doi.org/10.3390/s20216101

25. Aura, T., Sethi, M., Peltonen, A.: Nimble Out-of-Band Authentication for EAP (EAP-NOOB), RFC 9140 (2021)
26. Pritikin, M., Richardson, M., Eckert, T., Behringer, M., Watsen, K.: Bootstrapping Remote Secure Key Infrastructure, RFC 8995 (2021)
27. Richardson, M., Pan, W.: Operational Considerations for Voucher infrastructure for BRSKI MASA, draft-Richardson-anima-masa-considerations, work in progress (2021)
28. Richardson, M.: A taxonomy of operational security of manufacturer installed keys and trust anchors, draft-richardson-t2trg-idevid-considerations, work in progress (2022)
29. Richardson, M., Yang, J.: Operational considerations for BRSKI registrar, draft-richardson-anima-registrar-considerations-04, work in progress (2020)
30. Sethi, M., Sarikaya, B., Garcia-Carrillo, D.: Terminology and processes for initial security setup of IoT devices, draft-irtf-t2trg-secure-bootstrapping-01, work in progress (2021)
31. Sarikaya, B., von Hugo, D.: The need for new authentication methods for internet of things, draft-hsothers-iotsens-ps-01.txt, work in progress (2022)
32. ENISA, Methodology for Sectoral Cybersecurity Assessments - EU Cybersecurity Certification Framework (2021)
33. Chaudhry, S.A., Yahya, K., Al-Turjman, F., Yang, M.-H.: A secure and reliable device access control scheme for IoT based sensor cloud systems. IEEE Access **8** (2020). https://doi.org/10.1109/ACCESS.2020.3012121
34. Ramesh, M.V., et al.: Achieving sustainability through smart city applications: protocols, systems and solutions using IoT and wireless sensor network. CSI Trans. ICT **8**(2), 213–230 (2020). https://doi.org/10.1007/s40012-020-00285-5
35. Regulation (EU) 2016/679 of the European Parliament and of the Council of 27 April 2016 on the protection of natural persons with regard to the processing of personal data and on the free movement of such data, and repealing Directive 95/46/EC (General Data Protection Regulation) (2016)
36. European Union Agency for Cybersecurity (ENISA): IoT Security Standards Gap Analysis - Mapping of existing standards against requirements on security and privacy in the area of IoT, V1.0 (2018), available at https://www.enisa.europa.eu/publications/iot-security-standards-gap-analysis. Accessed 09 March 2022
37. ETSI TS 102 165-2 (V4.1.1) Telecommunications and Internet Protocol Harmonization Over Networks (TIPHON) Release 4; Protocol Framework Definition; Methods and Protocols for Security; Part 2: Counter Measures (2003)
38. 3GPP TR 23.700-53: Study on access traffic steering, switching and splitting support in the 5G system architecture; Phase 3 (Release 18), work in progress
39. NIST, Advanced Encryption Standard (AES). https://www.nist.gov/publications/advanced-encryption-standard-aes (2001)
40. IEEE 802.15 WPAN TG1 website. https://www.ieee802.org/15/pub/TG1.html. Accessed 09 March 2022
41. IEEE: IEEE Standard for Low-Rate Wireless Networks. IEEE Standard 802.15.4-2015 (2016). https://doi.org/10.1109/IEEESTD.2016.7460875
42. Montenegro, G., Kushalnagar, N., Hui, J., Culler, D.: IPv6 over IEEE 802.15.4, RFC 4944 (2007)
43. Gomez, C., Crowcroft, J., Scharf, M.: TCP Usage Guidance in the Internet of Things (IoT), RFC 9006 (2021)
44. Gündoğan, C., Schmidt, T., Wählisch, M., Scherb, C., Marxer, C., Tschudin, C.: Information-Centric Networking (ICN) Adaptation to Low-Power Wireless Personal Area Networks (LoWPANs), RFC 9139 (2021)
45. Abosata, N., Al-Rubaye, S., Inalhan, G., Emmanouilidis, C.: Internet of things for system integrity: a comprehensive survey on security, attacks and countermeasures for industrial applications. Sensors **21**, 3654 (2021). https://doi.org/10.3390/s21113654

46. Ali, I., Sabir, S., Ullah, Z.: Internet of things security, device authentication and access control: a review. Int. J. Comput. Sci. Inf. Technol. Secur. (IJCSIS) **14**(8) (2016)
47. Al-Qaness, M.A.A., et al.: Channel state information (CSI) from pure communication to sense and track human motion: a survey. Sensors **19**(15) (2019). https://doi.org/10.3390/s19 153329, PMID: 31362425 PMCID; PMC6696212
48. Pahlavan, K., Krishnamurthy, P.: Evolution and impact of Wi-Fi technology and applications: a historical perspective. Int. J. Wireless Inf. Netw. **28**(1), 3–19 (2020). https://doi.org/10.1007/s10776-020-00501-8
49. Liu, J., Wang, L., Fang, J., Guo, L., Lu, B., Shu, L.: Multi-target intense human motion analysis and detection using channel state information. Sensors **18**(10), 3379 (2018). https://doi.org/10.3390/s18103379
50. Guo, L., Wang, L., Liu, J., Zhou, W., Lu, B.: HuAc: human activity recognition using crowd-sourced WiFi signals and skeleton data. Hindawi Wirel. Commun. Mob. Comput. **2018** (2018). https://doi.org/10.1155/2018/6163475
51. Furqan, M., Solaija, M.S.J., Türkmen, H., Arslan, H.: Wireless communication, sensing, and REM: a security perspective. IEEE Open J. Commun. Soc. **2**, 287–321 (2021). https://doi.org/10.1109/OJCOMS.2021.3054066
52. Lin, S.-C., Chen, K.-C., Karimoddini, A.: SDVEC: software-defined vehicular edge computing with ultra-low latency. IEEE Commun. Mag. (2021). https://doi.org/10.1109/MCOM.004.2001124
53. Liao, R.-F., et al.: Deep-learning-based physical layer authentication for industrial wireless sensor networks. Sensors **19**(11), 2440 (2019). https://doi.org/10.3390/s19112440
54. Liao, R., et al.: Multiuser physical layer authentication in internet of things with data augmentation. IEEE Internet Things J. **7**(3), 2077–2088 (2020). https://doi.org/10.1109/JIOT.2019.2960099
55. Bai, L., Zhu, L., Liu, J., Choi, J., Zhang, W.: Physical layer authentication in wireless communication networks: a survey. J. Commun. Inform. Netw. **5**(3), 237–264 (2020)
56. Tian, Q., Lin, Y., Guo, X., Wang, J., AlFarraj, O., Tolba, A.: An identity authentication method of a MIoT device based on radio frequency (RF) fingerprint technology. Sensors **20**(4), 1213 (2020). https://doi.org/10.3390/s20041213
57. Axente, M.-S., Dobre, C., Ciobanu, R.-I., Purnichescu-Purtan, R.: Gait recognition as an authentication method for mobile devices. Sensors **20**, 4110 (2020). https://doi.org/10.3390/s20154110
58. Wang, H., Lymberopoulos, D., Liu, J.: Sensor-based user authentication. In: Abdelzaher, T., Pereira, N., Tovar, E. (eds.) EWSN 2015. LNCS, vol. 8965, pp. 168–185. Springer, Cham (2015). https://doi.org/10.1007/978-3-319-15582-1_11
59. Beech, W.A., Nielsen, D.A., Taylor, J.: AX.25 Link Access Protocol for Amateur Packet Radio: https://www.tapr.org/pdf/AX25.2.2.pdf. Accessed 28 Feb 2022
60. APRS SPEC Addendum 1.2 Proposals. http://aprs.org/aprs12.html. Accessed 28 Feb 2022
61. COREnect project D 2.1: Initial vision and requirement report, December 2020 (2020)

Applied Machine Learning

Towards Simulating a Global Robust Model for Early Asthma Detection

Bhabesh Mali and Pranav Kumar Singh[(✉)]

Central Institute of Technology Kokrajhar, BTR, Kokrajhar 783370, Assam, India
p.singh@cit.ac.in

Abstract. Asthma is a chronic non-communicable disease that affects the lungs and can cause breathlessness leading to fatal exacerbation. This disease mainly starts developing in childhood and can affect the lungs and lifestyle throughout life. Ignoring asthma at any age can be fatal. Therefore, this disease should be detected as early as possible. So, in this regard, we propose a machine learning model to predict early asthma in children. We simulated the federated learning process to build the model and created four virtual hospitals. We have simulated federated learning to build a global robust model where multiple datasets from the different institutions can take part in the training process, which can be used in various regions of the world for predicting early asthma. We have trained the models using both IID (Independent and Identically Distributed) and non-IID approaches of splitting the dataset. We also checked the performance of the models by measuring the predictive accuracy and AUC (Area Under the Receiver Operating Characteristic Curve) score for test data. We got a predictive accuracy of 91.57% and 93.68% for the IID and non-IID approaches. At the same time, we got the AUC score of 0.895 and 0.918 for the IID approach and non-IID approaches.

Keywords: Federated learning · Asthma prediction · User privacy · Federated averaging

1 Introduction

Asthma is a serious non-communicable disease that is affecting a huge population around the world. It is a common lung condition that causes irregular difficulties in breathing, further leading to exacerbation. Though it often starts in childhood, it can also develop in adults and can affect people of all ages [3]. Around 1% to 18% population of the world is affected by this disease [1]. The symptoms of asthma include wheezing, breathlessness, coughing, etc. The frequency and severity of the symptoms vary from person to person and may become worse during physical exercise [3].

Diagnosis of asthma in children is very important to avoid fatal exacerbation. Initially, the diagnosis begins with asking some of the symptomatic questions either to the child itself or to the child's parent. Question regarding the parental asthma history was also asked as asthma may be hereditary. It is often seen that three-fifths of all asthma cases are hereditary [2].

© The Author(s), under exclusive license to Springer Nature Switzerland AG 2022
F. Phillipson et al. (Eds.): I4CS 2022, CCIS 1585, pp. 257–266, 2022.
https://doi.org/10.1007/978-3-031-06668-9_18

Asthma prediction is a popular topic in the field of biomedical engineering. There are many models present to predict asthma disease based on various features, which may include both medical tests and symptomatic features. Almost all the current models are trained using the traditional machine learning process where a single dataset is kept in a central server, and the model is trained using these data. This centralized approach of training may give a good accuracy, but the models may not be robust. A single dataset may be region-specific, because of which the values for the same attribute in different regions may vary, and so, the models are not very eligible to be used in different regions, as we have seen in the case of asthma in [4]. Therefore, we decided to simulate federated learning to show that a global robust model can be built, where datasets from different institutes and from different locations can be used together to predict early disease in various regions of the world. Moreover, in federated learning, the data from the local institutions/clients never gets shared to each other or to a central server. They always remain private to themselves. Rather only the model weights and biases are shared to a central server, which is used to form a global robust model.

In our work, we created four virtual hospitals using specific packages to simulate the federated learning process. A hospital is an institution where patients are diagnosed with the disease(s) and treated accordingly. We initiated the training process both centrally and locally for multiple epochs. We trained the models using both IID (Independent and Identically Distributed) and non-IID approaches of splitting the dataset. We checked the accuracies using test data and got an accuracy of 91.57% for the IID approach and 93.68% for the non-IID approach. Further, we also measured the AUC (Area Under the Receiver Operating Characteristic Curve) Score and got a score of 0.895 and 0.918 for the IID approach and non-IID approaches.

The rest of the document is as follows. Section 2 discusses the related works. Section 3 presents the proposed methodology. Section 4 presents the experimental evaluation, dataset collection, dataset pre-processing, and federated training of the model. Section 5 shows the results for both the IID and non-IID approaches. Finally, the paper concludes in Sect. 6.

2   Related Works

Akhil et al. [15] have built a COVID-19 mortality prediction model using the federated learning approach. They have collected their dataset from five different hospitals within the Mount Sinai Health System (MSHS). They have tried two different federated learning base models, i.e., they have checked both the local and global accuracy for the models: Logistic Regression with L1 regularization (LASSO) and Multilayer Perceptron (MLP). They found that both the models outperformed well globally than the local model counterparts,i.e, the individual institutions.

IItai et al. [8] have built a model that predicts the future oxygen requirements of COVID-19 patients with symptoms. They have used a federated learning approach and used datasets from 20 different institutes across the globe. Their datasets have a total of 20 input features, and the number of instances in total is 16,148 cases. They have achieved a very good accuracy for predicting outcomes at 24 and 72 h from the time of initial presentation to the emergency rooms. They have also achieved a good accuracy for predicting mechanical ventilation treatment or death at 24 h with a specificity of 0.882 and a sensitivity of 0.950.

Bhabesh et al. [11] have built a machine learning model to predict early asthma in children. They have used their dataset downloaded from the ISAAC (International Study of Asthma and Allergies in Children) website. They have trained and tested their dataset with different models and compared the accuracies. They have found that the artificial neural network (ANN) model gave the highest predictive accuracy of 91.6% for the test data. They have also achieved an AUC score of 0.905 for the ANN model.

Wasif A. et al. [6] have proposed a model to classify the severity of Asthma based on medical records of patients. They have collected their dataset from various hospitals in Pakistan. The features of this dataset include shortness of breathing, fev1 (Forced Expiratory Volume in 1 second) predicted, fev1 and fvc (Forced Vital Capacity) ratio, etc. They have used four different models to compare the accuracies. The models were Naïve Bayes, J48, Random Forest, and Random tree. They concluded that the Naive Bayes Classifier is the best model to predict the severity of Asthma. The authors have divided the severity of Asthma into intermittent, mild, moderate, and severe. They obtained a predictive accuracy of 98.75% with Naive Bayes Classifier.

Dilini et al. [10] have built a machine learning model for predicting asthma development in children in the early life at school age (age 10) and preschool age. They have used the IOWBC (Isle of Wight Birth Cohort) [7] dataset, which contains a total of 1456 instances. The authors have used the RFE method, i.e., Recursive Feature Elimination method with a random forest algorithm and 5-fold CV (cross-validation) to select the features. The authors have trained and tested the models with seven different machine learning classifiers to select the best one and found that SVM (Support Vector Machine) gives the highest performance for prediction on their dataset, with an AUC score of 0.71 for the CAPE (Childhood Asthma Prediction in Early Life) model and 0.82 for the CAPP (Childhood asthma Prediction at Preschool age) model.

We have observed various others works related to predicting asthma in children using machine learning classifiers. Many of them have acquired good accuracies with their models. But, almost all of them have trained their models keeping the data centrally at a central server. Also, while training up the models, they have used only a single dataset placed at a single location. This may have given very good accuracies for the testing data; however, the models may not be robust to predict asthma in different regions. It means that the symptoms might be slightly different from region to region, continent to continent. Therefore, using only a single dataset of a specific region may not give us a robust model to predict the disease.

The work which we have done to predict early asthma in children is very difficult to compare with other works. This is because, as per our observation, we have not previously seen any other asthma model built using a federated learning process and getting such good accuracies. We demonstrated both the IID and non-IID approaches of training the model and also checked the performance of the models with test data accuracy and AUC (Area Under the Receiver Operating Characteristic Curve). Both the IID and non-IID models outperformed well in the federated training and testing process.

3   Proposed Methodology

This section shows how the work has been taken to simulate federated learning to create a robust global model.

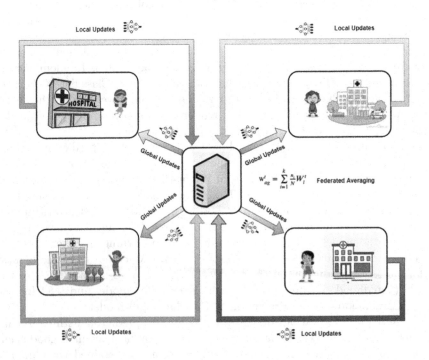

Fig. 1. Proposed global robust model training architecture

3.1   System Architecture for Training the Model

We build our global robust model initially by collecting the appropriate datasets. After collecting the dataset, we divided it into four different sub-datasets using both the IID and non-IID approaches. We then started the main simulation process by creating four virtual workers where each of the workers represents a hospital present in a different location. We then forwarded each of the four sub-datasets to these four virtual hospitals. In the case of the IID approach, all four hospitals have an equal amount of data present. While in the case of the non-IID approach, all four hospitals have a random amount of data.

The basic architecture for training the model also includes a central server that acts as the brain of the federated learning process. In the central server, mainly the aggregation of the local weights and biases, forwarded from the virtual hospitals, takes place. The central server creates a new model after aggregating the local model weights, and then again, this new model is sent to these virtual hospitals. In virtual hospitals, local training takes place with the local data for multiple epochs. After finishing the local training process, the model, along with weights and biases are again sent to the central server for global aggregation. This process takes place multiple times, both centrally and locally, until and unless we get our required convergence. The basic system approach to train the model is illustrated in Fig. 1.

Mainly for the aggregation process, we use a special algorithm known as the federated averaging algorithm (FedAvg), which was first introduced by McMahan [12] in 2017. The main concept of this algorithm is to aggregate the weights and biases each time during the central epoch, which takes place in the central server. Mathematically, the FedAvg algorithm is written as:

$$W_{ag}^t = \sum_{i=1}^{k} \frac{n_i}{N} W_i^t \tag{1}$$

where n_i is the number of admissions in the ith data source, W_{ag} is the combined parameter, k is the number of data sources, W_i is the parameters learned locally from the ith data source and N is the total number of admissions. t is the global cycle number in the range of [1,T].

3.2   FL Base Model

The base model that we have used for the federated learning process is the artificial neural network model (ANN). ANN is a very popular machine learning used mostly for prediction and classification processes. To prepare our base model, we have taken three hidden layers where the first, the second, and third hidden layer contains 12, 7, and 3 neurons. The input layer contains a total of 17 input features, while the output layer contains 1 neuron. The optimizer we have used is 'Adam' [9], while the activation function we have used is 'ReLU' [5] and 'Sigmoid' [13]. Our proposed architecture is shown in Fig. 2.

3.3   PySyft and PyTorch

PyTorch is a machine learning (ML) framework that facilitates developing deep learning (DL) projects. It allows DL models to be presented in idiomatic Python

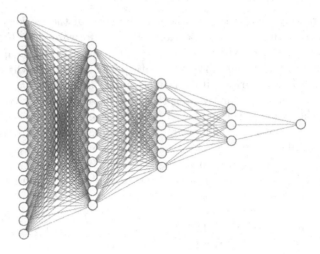

Fig. 2. ANN architecture

and also emphasises flexibility. PyTorch is naturally used with libraries like SciPy/Numpy/ Scikit-learn etc., but with good GPU acceleration. It allows bidirectional data exchange with external libraries [14].

PySyft is an open-source framework with a multi-language facility enabling private and secure machine learning (ML) by extending popular deep learning (DL) frameworks such as PyTorch in a lightweight, transparent and user-friendly manner. The basic aim of PySyft is to popularize privacy-preserving techniques in ML by making it accessible through Python bindings and common extensions that are familiar to data scientists and researchers, as well as to make new Federated Learning (FL), Differential Privacy methods, or Multi-Party Computation more flexible and simple to use [16].

4   Experimental Evaluation

4.1   Dataset Collection

The dataset that we have used to build the asthma model and to simulate the federated learning model was collected from the International Study of Asthma and Allergies in Children (ISAAC) website. The data was initially in SPSS (Statistical Package for the Social Sciences) format and was later converted to CSV (Comma Separated Value) format for our use. We extracted the most important attributes [4] from the dataset to predict early asthma in children and created a new dataset from these extracted attributes. We had taken a total of 17 input features which are completely symptomatic features. At the same time, the output predicts whether a child has asthma or not. The input features are shown in the Table 1. The dataset initially contained 58473 instances. We removed the rows from the dataset where at least one attribute value is null. The final dataset contains 4257 instances after removing all the null values.

4.2 Dataset Preprocessing

After collecting and removing the null values from the dataset, we did a standardization process. Standardization is a process to limit the range of the attributes to a certain range, which makes the data suitable for the training process. We have used the framework Pytorch to train the federated learning model and therefore converted the input features to tensors from NumPy arrays. Then we created the four virtual hospitals with the help of Pytorch and PySyft to simulate federated learning. We then divided the dataset into train and test data with a ratio of 8:2. Further, the training data is divided into four sub-datasets with both IID and non-IID approaches. In the case of the IID approach, we divided the dataset into four equal parts, where each part contains 958 instances. While in the case of the non-IID approach, the first, second, third, and fourth sub-dataset contain 672, 1180, 232, and 1750 instances. Then the sub-datasets were sent to these four hospitals, each time separately for both IID and non-IID approaches as both the IID and non-IID training processes were done separately.

4.3 Federated Training

The training process to simulate federate learning was carried out completely in Google Colab with the support of a free GPU. Initially, a model was created in the central server with random weights. The initial model was then sent to these four virtual hospitals for the training process. These virtual hospitals are the main actors of the federated learning process as the most important data is present in them. Then, along with local hospital data, the local training begins for each of the hospitals. The number of local training epochs, each time a model is sent from the central server to train locally, is 10. After completing the local training, the model with weights and biases from each of the four hospitals is sent to the central server. In the central server, with the help of the FedAvg algorithm, the weights and biases of all the local models get aggregated, and a new model is created. This new model is again sent to these virtual hospitals for local training. This process took place for multiple iterations, i.e., we did 500 epochs of central server training and aggregation process. After the 500th epoch, the global model, i.e., the central server aggregated model, is taken as the final model to predict early asthma in children.

5 Results and Discussion

The training process was taken for a total of 500 central epochs, and for each central epoch, the local training took place for 10 epochs. Therefore, the total iteration to train each model is 5000. The training accuracy and loss for all the four virtual hospitals in the case of the IID approach are shown in Fig. 3a and Fig. 3b, respectively.

While in the case of the non-IID approach, the training accuracy and loss for all the four virtual hospitals are shown in Fig. 4a and Fig. 4b, respectively.

Table 1. Input features of the dataset

Input Features	Values
Age of the child	8–12 years
Sex of the child	Male, Female
Whistling or wheezing in the chest in the past at any time	Yes, No
Whistling or wheezing in the chest in last twelve months	Yes, No
Wheezing attack in the child in the last twelve months	None, 1 to 3, 4 to 12, More than 12
Average sleep disturbance of the child in last twelve months due to wheezing	Never woken with wheezing, Less than one night per week, One or more nights per week
Severe wheezing in last twelve months limiting the speech of the child to only one or two words at a time between breaths	Yes, No
Wheezy chest sound of the child during or after exercise in last twelve months	Yes, No
Apart from having a cough associated with chest infection or cold, child having a dry cough at night in the last twelve months	Yes, No
Wheezy chest sound of the child when she or he had not taken exercise in last twelve months	Yes, No
Whistling or wheezing in the chest when the child had 'flu' or a cold in last twelve months	Yes, No
Whistling or wheezing in the chest when the child didn't had 'flu' or a cold in last twelve months	Yes, No
Child woken up with shortness of breath at any time in his or her life	Yes, No
Child woken up with tightness of the chest at any time in his or her life	Yes, No
Child's father ever had asthma	Yes, No
Child's mother ever had asthma	Yes, No
Child ever had hay fever	Yes, No

After training both models, we checked the testing accuracy with the test data. We got an accuracy of 91.57% for the IID approach and 93.68% for the non-IID approach. We also checked the AUC (Area Under the Receiver Operating Characteristic Curve) score and got a score of 0.895 for the IID approach and 0.918 for the non-IID approach.

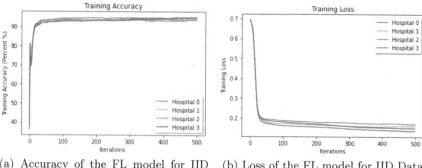

(a) Accuracy of the FL model for IID Data

(b) Loss of the FL model for IID Data

Fig. 3. Accuracy and loss of the FL model for IID data

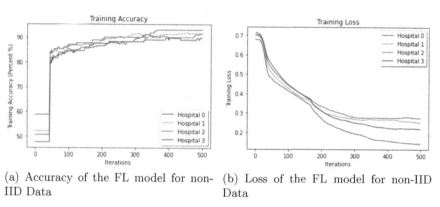

(a) Accuracy of the FL model for non-IID Data

(b) Loss of the FL model for non-IID Data

Fig. 4. Accuracy and loss of the FL model for non-IID data

6 Conclusion

In this work, we have developed a model to predict early asthma in children. As we know that medical data is very case sensitive as it contains the most crucial health information of patients, and so, it is not shareable. But these datasets are highly important to make a robust machine learning model, which could predict the disease tremendously accurate.

Therefore, to solve these problems of data sharing and building robust machine learning models, a new technique of learning is introduced firstly by [12]. This new technique is called federated learning (FL). So, in our case, to develop the early asthma prediction model, we proposed to use federated learning to build a robust model along with maintaining the privacy of data. We have created four virtual hospitals for this process and trained the models for both the IID and non-IID approaches of dividing the dataset. Further, we checked the test data accuracies for both these approaches and got a predictive accuracy of 91.57% for the IID approach and 93.68% for the non-IID approach. In the future, we will try to make the performance better for the prediction purpose.

References

1. Asthma: Available at: https://www.who.int/news-room/fact-sheets/detail/asthma. Accessed 2022
2. Asthma Risk Factors: Available at: https://www.webmd.com/asthma/asthma-risk-factors. Accessed 2022
3. Chronic respiratory diseases: asthma: Available at: https://www.who.int/news-room/questions-and-answers/item/chronic-respiratory-diseases-asthma. Accessed 2022
4. ISAAC-The International Study of Asthma and Allergies in Childhood: Available at: http://isaac.auckland.ac.nz/index.html. Accessed 2022
5. Agarap, A.F.: Deep learning using rectified linear units (ReLU). arXiv preprint arXiv:1803.08375 (2018)
6. Akbar, W., Wu, W.P., Faheem, M., Saleem, M.A., Golilarz, N.A., Haq, A.U.: Machine learning classifiers for asthma disease prediction: a practical illustration. In: 2019 16th International Computer Conference on Wavelet Active Media Technology and Information Processing, pp. 143–148. IEEE (2019)
7. Arshad, S.H., et al.: Cohort profile: the Isle of Wight whole population birth cohort (IOWBC). Int. J. Epidemiol. 47(4), 1043–1044i (2018)
8. Dayan, I., et al.: Federated learning for predicting clinical outcomes in patients with COVID-19. Nat. Med. 27(10), 1735–1743 (2021)
9. Kingma, D.P., Ba, J.: Adam: a method for stochastic optimization. arXiv preprint arXiv:1412.6980 (2014)
10. Kothalawala, D.M., et al.: Development of childhood asthma prediction models using machine learning approaches. medRxiv (2021). https://doi.org/10.1101/2021.03.31.21254678
11. Mali, B., Dhal, S., Das, A.K.: Diagnosis of asthma in children based on symptoms: a machine learning approach. In: TENCON 2021 IEEE Region 10 Conference (TENCON), pp. 782–787. IEEE (2021)
12. McMahan, B., Moore, E., Ramage, D., Hampson, S., y Arcas, B.A.: Communication-efficient learning of deep networks from decentralized data. In: Artificial Intelligence and Statistics, pp. 1273–1282. PMLR (2017)
13. Nwankpa, C., Ijomah, W., Gachagan, A., Marshall, S.: Activation functions: comparison of trends in practice and research for deep learning. arXiv preprint arXiv:1811.03378 (2018)
14. Paszke, A., et al.: PyTorch: an imperative style, high-performance deep learning library. Adv. Neural Inf. Process. Syst. 32 (2019)
15. Vaid, A., et al.: Federated learning of electronic health records improves mortality prediction in patients hospitalized with COVID-19. medRxiv (2020)
16. Ziller, A., et al.: PySyft: a library for easy federated learning. In: Rehman, M.H.u., Gaber, M.M. (eds.) Federated Learning Systems. SCI, vol. 965, pp. 111–139. Springer, Cham (2021). https://doi.org/10.1007/978-3-030-70604-3_5

Practical Method for Multidimensional Data Ranking
Application for Virtual Machine Migration

Chérifa Boucetta[✉], Laurent Hussenet, and Michel Herbin

University of Reims Champagne-Ardenne, CReSTIC EA 3804, 51097 Reims, France
{cherifa.boucetta,laurent.hussenet}@univ-reims.fr
michel.herbin51@laposte.net

Abstract. This paper proposes a practical and generic approach for multidimensional data ranking in order to facilitate the exploration of data in an orderly manner. We examine each dimension and we calculate the rank per variable. Then, we transform the number of possibly correlated variables into a smaller number of variables called principal components in order to extract the important information from the data set. We validate this method using open datasets. To assess the proposed method, we consider as a criterion the number of the class changes when scanning multidimensional data set. Finally, we apply this method to rank the virtual machines of the IT department in Networking & Telecommunication of our institute according to their resource consumption in order to identify those that consume many resources.

Keywords: Ranking · Data analysis · Multidimensional data · Virtual machine migration

1 Introduction

Lots of applications use a method of ranking: applications to popular sports [10], problems of multi-criteria decision [9], political studies [16], health system performance and sustainability [17]... Generally, the objects to be ranked are characterized by several variables which assess performances, costs, risks, quality,... Thus, the objects are often considered as multidimensional numeric data where each column presents a dimension and each row is a data item. Dealing with multidimensional data sets is challenging because it is difficult to comprehend the pattern in more than three dimensions. In several fields such as data mining and pattern recognition, many researches have been conducted to address this problem and most of them focus on the most suitable dimension for their application to build a better classifier or to detect a specific pattern.

The goal of this paper is to propose a simple practical method for ranking multidimensional data. The ranking of one-dimensional data is trivial. One-dimensional data is characterized by a single variable. Hence, the ranking is easily obtained by sorting numerical values of this variable. When data is multidimensional, each variable gives its own ranking. In essence, these rankings should be aggregated to obtain a final ranking of the objects. Trade off between the variable rankings could be tedious, especially when there are many variables. In this work, we investigate a new ranking method based on the principal component analysis (PCA). Instead of sorting the principal components based on data, we consider the ranks. Then, we propose the idea of using the first principal component which is selected as the one that gives the most information in the statistical meaning of Fisher. The method is not restricted to any particular probability distribution.

Evaluation experiments are conducted under multidimensional open datasets. We compare the proposed method with the Borda approach [4]. Because, there is no standard of multidimensional data ranking however a lot of multidimensional data sets have classes, we consider these classes to evaluate the ranking proposed method. In fact, we calculate the number of class changes in each dataset. The ranking method is optimal if the number of the class changes is small. Results show that the proposed method outperforms generally the simple Borda method. In addition, these results are more satisfactory when the number of classes increases. Finally, we apply our method to rank Virtual machines (VMs) of the data center of our department considering realistic workload traces. Migrating VMs is a useful tool for managing computing resources, load balancing, reducing energy consumption and facilitating fault management in cloud computing. A VM migration [5] involves transferring the VM's information such as running state of the VM (CPU state, memory state), VM storage, VM virtual disks and client's information. Applying the ranking method allows us to better manage the data center resources and ensure load balancing when receiving alerts.

The requirements to an optimal ranking should be explained.

The remainder of the paper is organized as follows. Section 2 enumerates pertinent references related to multidimensional data ranking. Section 3 describes the proposed ranking approach. Section 4 presents the simulated data sets and discusses performance analysis and obtained results when testing the proposed method under open multidimensional datasets. Finally, Sect. 5 concludes the paper.

2   Related Work

There are mainly two families of methods to obtain a ranking of multidimensional data. The first family is based on the Condorcet's approach [6]. Such methods are well-known in the framework of social choice theory. They consist in searching an optimal ranking through pairwise comparisons of data. When using this approach, an optimal ranking could be obtained by Kemeny's method [14]. Unfortunately the computation of Kemeny's ranking is NP-hard. Thus, the methods based on the Condorcet's approach generally have a high computational cost. In [8], the authors proposed a Condorcet clustering method with a fixed number of groups based on similarity and dissimilarity measures. The Condorcet criterion was considered in [2] by Ando et al. for the ordering linear problem which allows to have more pairs of indices whose relative orders are fixed for all optimal solutions.

The second family of methods is based on Borda's approach [4]. These methods are arguably simpler than the first ones [15]. They consists in computing an individual score for each piece of data. So each variable contributes to the individual data scores. The final ranking is obtained by sorting the data scores. Many extension of Borda are proposed in the literature. For example, in [19], the authors extend and generalize Borda Count to quantile-based Borda Count. They present case studies on real data sets to demonstrate the effectiveness of the generalized Borda Count ranking. Another approach in [12] combines Borda and Condorcet in order to transform a collection of rankings, defined over a set of alternatives, into a complete, transitive, and cardinal assessment by computing the support that each alternative receives on average when confronted with any other. In [7], Effrosynidiset al. presented an experimental study of 12 individual using Borda Count and Condorcet for classification tasks on environmental data more specifically on the species distribution modeling domain. Guo et al. [11] proposed a feature selection method to select a subset of variables in principal component analysis (PCA) that preserves as much information present in the complete data as possible.

Unlike the methods based on Condorcet's approach, methods based on Borda's approach are generally simple. Hence, this study proposes a practical method of ranking using Borda's approach based on a score. Furthermore, usual existing solutions are not generic and demand expert knowledge on the specification of the weight of each component. Unlike Condorcet's approach, there is no optimal ranking corresponding to the Borda's approach. Generally, the score is adapted to the intended application. However, the adaptation is not always obvious. Without assumption on a possible adapted score, Borda's count gives the reference score which is generally used. For theses reasons, this paper proposes a practical method of ranking using the principal component analysis that we compare with the ranking obtained by the classical Borda's count. We consider many open datasets and then we apply this method to rank virtual machines for an effective placement in a cluster of physical machines.

3 Ranking Method

Let Ω be a set of n multidimensional data with $\Omega = \{X_1, X_2, X_3, ...X_n\}$. Data is defined through p variables. Thus, data is defined through tuples. We note $X_i = (x_{i1}, x_{i2}, ...x_{ip})$ where x_{ij} is the value of X_i obtained with the variable x_j. Then, we have $x_{ij} = x_j(X_i)$.

Each variable allows to rank the data. Thus, we obtain one ranking per variable.

Our goal is to aggregate these rankings.

Let r_{ij} be the rank of the data X_i for the jth variable. So the rank r_{ij} lies between 1 and n. But the ranking with each variable has two directions that are obtained either by increasing values or by decreasing values. In this paper, the ranking with the first variable is obtained by increasing values. And the rankings with the other variables should have the same direction as the first one. In fact, we select the direction that gives a positive correlation with the first ranking. For this we use the classical Spearman's correlation [18] to assess the correlation of ranks. So we obtain the rankings r_{ij} with $2 \leq j \leq p$ that each has the same direction as r_{i1}.

Then each data X_i could be located with a rank vector $(r_{i1}, r_{i2}, ...r_{ip})$ within the rank space. Using Borda's count approach, the usual way for aggregating the ranks consists in computing a score based on these ranks. The score values are themselves sorted defining the final ranking. The rank aggregation is based on the score function we use. The following presents two methods respectively based on the Borda's count and the principal rank we propose.

3.1   Borda's Method

The most classical score is the sum of ranks which is call Borda's Count (BC). Thus, we have

$$BC_i = \sum_{j=1}^{p} r_{ij} \tag{1}$$

where BC_i be the score of data X_i. So r_{ij} is the contribution of j-th variable to the score of X_i. In other words, r_{ij} is a preference given by variable x_j to data X_i. The sum is the aggregation of these preferences. Lower the score of X_i, lower the final rank of X_i.

3.2   Principal Rank Method

For the second method, let us consider the principal component analysis (PCA) of data ranks (r_{ij}). This method consists on transforming a number of possibly correlated variables into a smaller number of variables called principal components [1]. In essence, its goal is to extract the important information from the data table, to represent it as a set of new orthogonal variables (principal components), and to display the pattern of similarity of the observations and of the variables as points in maps. For our knowledge, PCA is probably the most popular multivariate statistical technique and it is used by almost all scientific disciplines. It is also likely to be the oldest multivariate technique.

Unlike the PCA method, we use the ranks (r_{ij}) instead of data (x_{ij}). The first principal component is the one that gives the most information in the statistical meaning of Fisher [13]. So the proposed score is the first principal component. This score is called Principal Rank that we note PR. Then, the final ranking of multidimensional data is obtained using PR_i values. Algorithm 1 illustrates the steps of the proposed ranking method where the input is a multidimensional data and the output is the ranking based on the principal rank. We use the correlation to arrange the other variables in the same direction as the first one.

Algorithm 1. Ranking of multidimensional data with the Principal Rank

---

Require: (x_{ij}) is a multidimensional data set with
$\qquad$ n data $(1 \leq i \leq n)$ and p variables $(1 \leq j \leq p)$
Ensure: Ranking (x_{ij})
$\quad$ $r_{i1} \leftarrow rank(x_{i1})$
$\quad$ **for** $j \leftarrow 2$ to p **do**
$\qquad$ $r_{ij} \leftarrow rank(x_{ij})$
$\qquad$ **if** $correlation(r_{i1}, r_{ij}) < 0$ **then**
$\qquad\quad$ $r_{ij} \leftarrow n - r_{ij} + 1$
$\qquad$ **end if**
$\quad$ **end for**
$\quad$ $pca1_i \leftarrow first\_principal\_component(r_{ij}))$
$\quad$ $PR_i \leftarrow rank(pca1_i)$
$\quad$ **if** $correlation(r_{i1}, PR_i) < 0$ **then**
$\qquad$ $PR_i \leftarrow n - PR_i + 1$
$\quad$ **end if**
$\quad$ **return** PR_i

3.3   Assessment of Ranking

This section proposes to compare the ranking methods. One method is better than another one when the results of the first one are closer to a standard than the results of the second one. Unfortunately, we have no standard of multidimensional data ranking. But a lot of multidimensional data sets have classes. Thus, we consider that these classes make sense with respect to the ranking of data. The ranking gives a scanning of a multidimensional data set. We assume that two successive data should often belong to the same class. Therefore, the better the scanning, the lower the number of class changes. We suppose that the criterion to assess a ranking is the number of the class changes when scanning. The validation of the principal ranking method will be presented in the next section. First, we will consider known multidimensional data sets with classes to validate the proposed principal ranking method. Then, we apply it to rank the virtual machines of the IT department in Networking & Telecommunication of our institute according to their resource consumption in order to identify those that consume many resources.

4   Results

In this section we compare first the method based on Borda's count with the proposed approach based on principal rank. The assessment criterion needs for multidimensional data sets with classes.

4.1   Simulated Data Sets

First, let us describe the methodology to simulate the multidimensional data with classes. We consider a data set with n data. Each data is defined through p

independent variables. Therefore, the dimension of data space is equal to p. We simulate k classes within data set using k Gaussian distributions.

In the following an example of such simulated data set. We simulate a data set with 100 data, 5 variables and 3 classes ($n = 100$, $p = 5$ and $k = 3$). Hence, the dimension of the data space is equal to 5. The class sizes are equal to 9, 65 and 26.

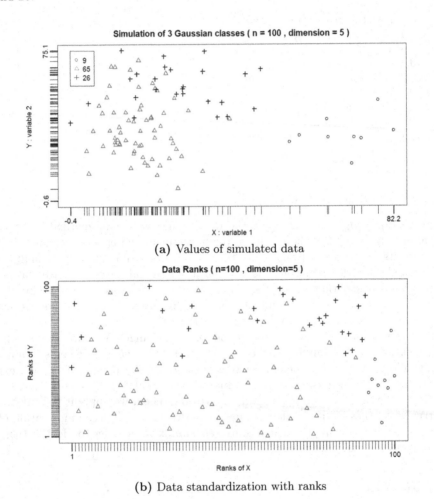

(a) Values of simulated data

(b) Data standardization with ranks

Fig. 1. Data values and ranks

Figure 1a shows the projection of the simulated data set using first and second coordinates of data. Using low dimensional projections is commonly used to handle multidimensionality because human eyes and minds are effective in understanding at most three-dimensional (3D) objects. The first coordinate varies between −0.4 and 82.2 and the second one between −0.6 and 75.1. The three classes 9, 65 and 26 are represented by the red, green and blue colors respectively.

Figure 1b displays the ranks of data for the first and second coordinates. It is clear that the data are standardized between 0 and n ($n = 100$) using the ranks. We note that the projection of the classes is different comparing with the first figure.

Figure 2a and Fig. 2b display the scanning of the multidimensional data with respectively the classical Borda's Count (BC) and the proposed principal rank (PR) method.

We compare the number of class changes obtained for both methods. This evaluation score is calculated based on the ranking inside the classes. It is presented by black lines. In the first figure, it is equal to 28 and the second one is equal to 18.

Thus, our method of ranking based on PR gives better results than the method based on classical BC.

In the last step of validation, we change the parameters of the simulation. Table 1 gives the obtained results with 12 different simulations. We vary the number of independent variables p (by considering two values 5 and 10) and the number of classes k (3, 5 and 10). Then, we test several combinations. We depict that we have in only one case (line in bold in the table), scanning by Borda's method seems better than the proposed method.

Table 1. Number of class changes obtained with Borda's count (BC) method and principal rank (PR) method: n is the number of data, p is the number of variables, k is the number of classes.

n	p	k	BC	PR
100	5	3	28	18
100	5	5	**27**	**31**
100	5	10	53	42
100	10	3	8	6
100	10	5	31	27
1000	5	3	310	142
1000	10	3	198	142
1000	10	5	329	225
1000	10	10	519	419

The reader can simulate different data sets and assesses the scanning with the online demonstrator. This interactive web application is coded with R and *Shiny*.

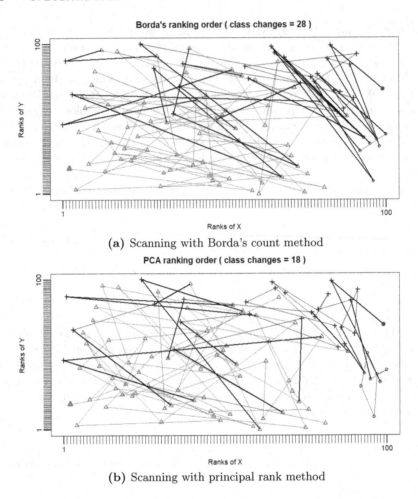

(a) Scanning with Borda's count method

(b) Scanning with principal rank method

Fig. 2. Data values and ranks

4.2   Real Datasets

In this part, we study our method in real data sets. We use classical data sets that the readers find on UCI Machine Learning Repository or Kaggle.

We consider known data sets in the literature such as iris, wine, ecoli, banknote, wifi localization... All these datasets present at least two classes. The size of the data sets n varies between 150 for the iris data set and 153000 for the accelerometer dataset. Hence, we validate the method under small and large datasets. Furthermore, the number of variables p is different form one dataset to another and can reach 13 for the wine dataset.

Table 2 shows that the proposed PR method outperforms the Borda's count approach in general. In only one case (banknote data set), scanning by Borda's method gives better results than the proposed method and we note that the

Table 2. Number of class changes obtained with Borda's count (BC) method and principal rank (PR) method: n is the number of data, p is the number of variables and k is the number of classes of the data set.

Data set	n	p	k	BC	PR
Iris	150	4	3	20	14
Wine	178	13	3	58	38
Ecoli	336	7	8	134	119
Glass	214	9	6	134	124
Seeds	210	7	3	52	46
Social network ads	400	2	2	105	99
Banknote	1372	4	2	**473**	**475**
Wifi localization	2000	7	4	918	722
Accelerometer	153000	4	3	98587	98151

number of changes is close for both methods. This is because the number of classes and variables are equal to 2.

We conclude that the proposed ranking method is efficient and gives better results than Borda's count approach. The validation is based on the number of class changes. It is generic and can be applied to the majority of datasets. In the next section, we consider a classless dataset.

4.3 Virtual Machine Ranking

Migrating Virtual Machines (VM) is a useful tool for managing computing resources, load balancing and reducing energy consumption. Nowadays, renewable energy is used by cloud providers to be used as a supplement of traditional brown energy. In essence, it is preferable to maximize energy consumption on data centers which have more availability of green energy.

We consider the architecture of the pedagogic data center of our IT department. It is composed of two separated clusters dedicated to administrative and pedagogic uses. The first one is used for hosting administrative virtual machines, which are globally stable in time. The second one hosts virtual machines for students. It is composed of three servers (three hypervisors) and consumes more resources than the first one. The number of deployed VMs is very variable and depends on the training course during the academic year. In essence, we need to migrate VMs from one server to another in order to ensure the load balancing, minimise the energy consumption and the optimization in the resource utilization.

For security and redundancy reasons, we avoid concentrating all VMs on one or two servers. We apply the proposed PR ranking method to identify VMs that consume a lot of resources and energy and are more suitable to be migrated. The selection of VMs to be migrated is important because it impacts the stability of the cluster.

Resource consumption consisting of CPU, RAM, network usage, disk usage, of each VM are collected and used as an input for the ranking approach. We consider a dataset containing 165 VMs. the number of variable p is equal to 4: cpu usage (Mhz), memory usage (MB), disk usage (kBps) and network usage (MBps). We tested the Borda's Count method and the proposed PR approach to rank VMs. In this case, there are no classes in the dataset. Hence, in the future work we will validate the efficiency of the ranking method when moving VMs by evaluating the resource consumption of the pedagogic cluster before and after migration.

5 Conclusion

In this paper, we proposed a generic ranking method based on the first principal component for multidimensional data. First, we compute the data ranks for each variable. Then, we compute principal components over the ranks. Finally, the first principal component defines the score to compute Principal Rank (PR). It is evaluated under many open datasets and we calculate the number of class changes. The proposed method gives generally better results than the simple Borda method. Furthermore, the results seem more satisfactory when the number of classes increases. Our method does not claim to be the best. Note that no ranking method, even Kemeny's method based on Condorcet's approach, is entirely satisfactory in the sense of social choice theory (see Arrow's impossibility theorem [3]). Facing our data center load balancing problem, we apply the PR method to rank the VMs in order to select the VMs to migrate. In the future work, we will test the ranking method with optimization models for VM migration in geo-distributed cloud systems taking into account the migration energy cost to better manage the energy in cloud computing.

References

1. Abdi, H., Williams, L.J.: Principal component analysis. Wiley Interdiscip. Rev. Comput. Stat. **2**(4), 433–459 (2010)
2. Ando, K., Sukegawa, N., Takagi, S.: Strong condorcet criterion for the linear ordering problem. J. Oper. Res. Soc. Jpn. **65**(2), 67–75 (2022)
3. Arrow, K.: Social Choice and Individual Values, 2nd edn. Wiley, New York (1963)
4. Borda, J.C.: Mémoire sur les élections au scrutin. Histoire de l'Académie royale des sciences. Paris (1781)
5. Boutaba, R., Zhang, Q., Zhani, M.F.: Virtual machine migration in cloud computing environments: benefits, challenges, and approaches, pp. 383–408 (2013)
6. Condorcet, J.-A.-N.: Essai sur l'application de l'analyse á la probabilité des décisions rendues á la pluralité des voix. Imprimerie Royale, Paris (1785)
7. Effrosynidis, D., Arampatzis, A.: An evaluation of feature selection methods for environmental data. Eco. Inform. **61**, 101224 (2021)
8. Faouzi, T., Firinguetti-Limone, L., Avilez-Bozo, J.M., Carvajal-Schiaffino, R.: The α-groups under condorcet clustering. Mathematics **10**(5), 718 (2022)

9. Gogodze, J.: Ranking-theory methods for solving multicriteria decision-making problems. Adv. Oper. Res. (2019)
10. Govan, A.Y.: Ranking theory with application to popular sports. PhD thesis, North Carolina State University (2008)
11. Guo, Q., Wu, W., Massart, D.L., Boucon, C., De Jong, S.: Feature selection in principal component analysis of analytical data. Chemom. Intell. Lab. Syst. **61**(1), 123–132 (2002)
12. Herrero, C., Villar, A.: Group decisions from individual rankings: the Borda–Condorcet rule. Eur. J. Oper. Res. **291**, 10 (2020)
13. Jolliffe, I.T., Cadima, J.: Principal component analysis: a review and recent developments. Philos. Trans. A: Math. Phys. Eng. Sci. **374**, 20150202 (2016)
14. Kemeny, J.G.: Mathematics without numbers. Daedalus **88**(4), 577–591 (1959)
15. Lansdowne, Z.F., Woodward, B.S.: Applying the Borda ranking method. Air Force J. Logist. **20**(2), 27–29 (1996)
16. Lee, P.H., Yu, P.L.H.: Mixtures of weighted distance-based models for ranking data with applications in political studies. Comput. Stat. Data Anal. **56**(8), 2486–2500 (2012)
17. Müller, L., Oakley, R., Saad, M., Mokdad, A., Etolhi, G., Flahault, A.: A multi-dimensional framework for rating health system performance and sustainability: a nine plus one ranking system. J. Glob. Health **11**, 05 (2021)
18. Xiao, C., Ye, J., Esteves, R.M., Rong, C.: Using Spearman's correlation coefficients for exploratory data analysis on big dataset. Concurr. Comput. Pract. Exp. **28**(14), 3866–3878 (2016)
19. Zhang, Y., Zhang, W., Pei, J., Lin, X., Lin, Q., Li, A.: Consensus-based ranking of multivalued objects: a generalized Borda count approach. IEEE Trans. Knowl. Data Eng. **26**, 83–96 (2014)

Quantum Computing

Distributed Quantum Machine Learning

Niels M. P. Neumann$^{(\boxtimes)}$ and Robert S. Wezeman

The Netherlands Organisation for Applied Scientific Research,
Anna van Buerenplein 1, 2595DA The Hague, The Netherlands
{niels.neumann,robert.wezeman}@tno.nl

Abstract. Quantum computers can solve specific complex tasks for which no reasonable-time classical algorithm is known. Quantum computers do however also offer inherent security of data, as measurements destroy quantum states. Using shared entangled states, multiple parties can collaborate and securely compute quantum algorithms. In this paper we propose an approach for distributed quantum machine learning, which allows multiple parties to securely perform computations, without having to reveal their data. We will consider a distributed adder and a distributed distance-based classifier.

Keywords: Distributed quantum computing · Quantum multi-party computation · Quantum machine learning · Quantum arithmetic

1 Introduction

Quantum computers are in rapid development and the first classically intractable problems are already solved using quantum computers [1]. Even though these problems are artificial, specifically designed to show the power of quantum computers, it is expected that in the next few years, similar results will be achieved for practical problems.

Apart from quantum computers, also in quantum internet there are rapid developments and the first small-scale networks are already realized [2]. A quantum network allows for many new applications, including new forms of encryption [3] and enhanced clock synchronization [4,5].

Quantum networks also allow for another application: distributed quantum computing, where different quantum computers are linked via a quantum network. We typically identify two types of distributed quantum computing. In the first, a single algorithm which is too large to be run on a quantum device, is subdivided in smaller parts, each of which can be run on a quantum device. In the second, multiple parties have access to local quantum computers which are linked via a quantum network. The parties can collaboratively perform quantum computations on their inputs without having to explicitly share it.

The first type is a resource-problem. As hardware develops, larger problems can be run and the need to distribute the algorithms vanishes. The second type is the more interesting one as it opens up the way to completely new applications.

© The Author(s), under exclusive license to Springer Nature Switzerland AG 2022
F. Phillipson et al. (Eds.): I4CS 2022, CCIS 1585, pp. 281–293, 2022.
https://doi.org/10.1007/978-3-031-06668-9_20

In this work we will therefore focus on the second type of distributed quantum computing.

Distributed quantum computing naturally extends classical multi-party computation, which allows multiple parties to collaborate securely [6]. We consider two applications of distributed quantum computing. The first being distributed arithmetic, the second being distributed distance-based classification. We show how both approaches work in a distributed setting and argue why information remains secure during the protocol execution. For both applications, multiple parties provide input and together perform the algorithm in such a way that the output is only revealed to one specific party without leaking information on individual parties input.

In the next section, we give a brief introduction to quantum computing and some basic concepts of distributed quantum computing. In Sect. 3 and Sect. 4 we discuss a distributed quantum adder and a distributed distance-based classifier, respectively. In Sect. 5 we provide a resource count of the distributed approaches. We conclude with some conclusions and an outlook.

2   Methods

2.1   Brief Introduction to Quantum Computing

Classical computers and quantum computers work similarly: Both operate on elementary units of computation and by performing the correct operations in the right order, problems can be solved. Classical computers operate on bits, zeros and ones, using classical gates, such as AND, OR and NOT gates. Quantum computers operate on qubits, superpositions of zeros and ones, using quantum operations, such as single qubit rotations and controlled-NOT (CNOT) gates. The CNOT gate is a two-qubit gate that flips the state of the second qubit, if the first qubit is in the one state.

A key difference between classical and quantum computers is that qubits do not have to be in one definite computational basis state $|0\rangle$ or $|1\rangle$. A qubit $|\psi\rangle$ can be in a superposition, a complex linear combination, of these basis states, which we can write as $|\psi\rangle = \alpha |0\rangle + \beta |1\rangle$ for $\alpha, \beta \in \mathbb{C}$ with $|\alpha|^2 + |\beta|^2 = 1$. The computational basis states for multi-qubit states are given by $|x\rangle = |x_{n-1}\rangle \otimes ... \otimes |x_0\rangle$ for $x_i \in \{0, 1\}$. Upon observing a quantum state, only one of the definite states is found. The probability to observe a given state equals the sum of the squared of the corresponding amplitudes.

Another aspect in which quantum computers differ from classical ones is entanglement. Two or more quantum states can be correlated beyond what is possible classically. One of the most well-known entangled states is the GHZ-state given by

$$\frac{1}{\sqrt{2}}(|00\rangle + |11\rangle), \tag{1}$$

which is obtained by bringing the first qubit in a uniform superposition and then applying a CNOT gate. Upon measuring one qubit, the state of the other

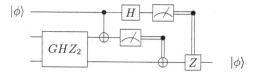

Fig. 1. A quantum circuit that teleports a state $|\phi\rangle$ to a third qubit. Double lines indicate classical information.

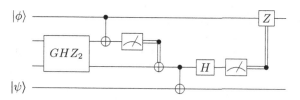

Fig. 2. A quantum circuit for the non-local CNOT-gate between $|\phi\rangle$ and $|\psi\rangle$. The top and bottom qubit might belong to different quantum devices that share a GHZ-state. Double lines represent classical information.

is instantaneously known, even if the entangled qubits are physically far apart. The GHZ-state naturally extends to more than two qubits and it has many applications. We will make use of GHZ-states to distribute gate operations to different quantum computers.

We refer to [7] for a more elaborate introduction to quantum computing.

2.2 Distributed Quantum Computing

To distributed quantum operations over multiple devices, it might seem natural to physically transport the qubits. However, as quantum states are fragile, this is likely to introduce errors. Instead, we propose to use shared entangled states. Two notable examples are quantum teleportation [8] and non-local CNOT gates [9,10]. The quantum circuits for both approaches are similar and both use shared entangled states, for simplicity often assumed to be GHZ-states.

The shared entangled states can also introduce noise in the computations. However, as they do not hold any information themselves, we can use techniques such as entanglement purification to minimize the effect of imperfect shared entanglement [11–13]. These protocols focus the entanglement of multiple partially entangled states in fewer entangled states of higher quality using only local operations. We can generate these entangled states of high quality before we start a distributed algorithm, and hence the effect of noise is limited.

The quantum circuits for quantum teleportation and the non-local CNOT gate are shown in Fig. 1 and Fig. 2, respectively. Both circuits extend naturally to more parties. The two circuits show similarities, however their effect is different. The first circuit teleports a quantum state from one qubit to another. These qubits can be hosted on different devices. The first qubit is measured and hence destroyed. Distributed computations can be performed by teleporting the quantum state from one device to another and then perform all operations locally on the second device. The second circuit applies a two-qubit CNOT operation between one qubit and another that can, again, be hosted on another device. Both qubits remain coherent and further operatoins can be applied to them.

It is known that single qubit rotations and a multi-qubit gate, such as the CNOT gate are universal for quantum computing [14]. This means that any quantum operation can be broken down in a sequence of single qubit gates and two-qubit gates. We can hence distribute quantum algorithms once we can distribute the two-qubit operations. In this work, we used non-local CNOT gates to implement distributed algorithms. This way, the qubit remains intact on the first device and we do not require a second step of teleportation to get the qubit back to the first device again.

Note that a non-local CNOT gate does not create an independent copy of a state. Instead, it creates an entangled state, i.e., given a state $|\phi\rangle = \alpha |0\rangle + \beta |1\rangle$ the non-local CNOT gate implements the map

$$|\phi\rangle |0\rangle \mapsto \alpha |00\rangle + \beta |11\rangle. \tag{2}$$

A property that we will use later is that phases applied to any qubit of a GHZ-state have a global effect: A phase applied to the first qubit of a GHZ-state results in the same state as when that phase was applied to any of the other qubits of the GHZ-state. This is independent of the physical location of the qubits: The qubits might even be hosted on different devices.

We will use this property together with the non-local CNOT-gate to distribute operations among various parties. in the next two sections, we will show how to do this for two quantum machine learning applications.

3 Distributed Adder

We first consider how to perform arithmetics with multiple parties. This simple yet relevant topic provides a first insight in the value of distributed quantum computing. It is also a relevant topic, as arithmetics form an important pillar in many algorithms, for instance to compute the mean of a set of number [15].

In this section we will solely focus on adding numbers. More complex arithmetics such as multiplication follow naturally by repeated addition. Given two basis states $|a\rangle$ and $|b\rangle$, a quantum adder implements $|a\rangle |b\rangle \mapsto |a\rangle |a+b\rangle$. The addition is modulo 2^N by definition, with N the number of qubits per register. By linearity of quantum computing, a quantum adder also works on arbitrary superpositions.

We can implement a quantum adder in multiple ways. Most approaches do however require gates that are not directly supported by underlying hardware. Draper [16] presented an approach that only uses single qubit gates and controlled-phase gates. Later this work was extended to multiplication and modular arithmetic [16–18]. This method applies a quantum Fourier transform on a quantum state $|b\rangle$ to obtain $|\phi(b)\rangle$. On this transformed state, we can now apply controlled phase-gates with predetermined phases, targets and controls, to add integers. An inverse quantum Fourier transform then gives the desired quantum state.

The quantum circuit for addition is shown in Fig. 3. The blocks represent R_Z-gates, with the argument shown inside the block. The matrix representation of these gates is

$$R_Z(\theta) = \begin{pmatrix} 1 & 0 \\ 0 & e^{i\theta} \end{pmatrix}. \tag{3}$$

As we use controlled operations, they are only applied if the controlling qubit is in the $|1\rangle$ state. The state $|\phi(b)_j\rangle$ represents the j-th qubit of the quantum Fourier transformed state $|\phi(b)\rangle$, given by $|\phi(b)_j\rangle = \frac{1}{\sqrt{2}}\left(|0\rangle + \exp(2\pi i \cdot b/2^j)|1\rangle\right)$. Note that for the j-th qubit of the quantum Fourier transformed state, only the first j bits of a and b are relevant. All other bits will contribute an integer value to the fraction $b/2^j$ and hence will have no physical effect. After the phase-gates are applied, the state of the j-th qubit is given by

$$\frac{1}{\sqrt{2}}\left(|0\rangle + e^{2\pi i \cdot (b+a)/2^j}|1\rangle\right) = |\phi(b+a)_j\rangle. \tag{4}$$

An inverse quantum Fourier transform indeed gives the j-th bit of the sum $b+a$.

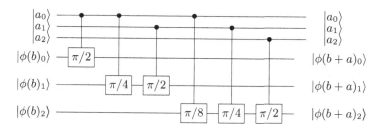

Fig. 3. The addition part of a quantum Fourier transform-based adder. $|\phi(b)_j\rangle$ represents the j-th bit of the Fourier transform of b. The gates represent controlled-R_Z gates, where the argument shown is the argument of the R_Z-gate. An inverse quantum Fourier transform is needed to retrieve the quantum state $|a\rangle|b+a\rangle$.

Even though the shown circuit only concerns computational basis states, it works equally well for superpositions as input. For our application, computational basis states are sufficient and this also allows us to apply the phase-gates controlled by classical bits instead of by qubits. This method extends naturally to adding multiple numbers in parallel by using larger GHZ-states and distributing the quantum state to more parties.

Suppose we have K parties, each with N qubits. Additionally, we have one server party that prepares and distributes the initial quantum state using GHZ-states and non-local CNOT gates. After distribution, each party applies the phases to their part of the shared entangled state. The server party then again uses GHZ-states and non-local CNOT gates to assure that an inverse quantum Fourier transform indeed gives the correct sum. The distributing operation of the server party thus implements the following map for each of the N bits:

$$|\phi(b)_j\rangle |0\rangle^{\otimes K} \mapsto \frac{1}{\sqrt{2}} \left(|0\rangle^{\otimes K+1} + e^{2\pi i \cdot b/2^j} |1\rangle^{\otimes K+1} \right). \tag{5}$$

After each party has locally applied the phase gates corresponding to their input, we are left with the quantum state

$$\frac{1}{\sqrt{2}} \left(|0\rangle^{\otimes K+1} + e^{2\pi i \cdot (b + \sum_k x^k)/2^j} |1\rangle^{\otimes K+1} \right), \tag{6}$$

where x^k is the input of party k. The server party uses GHZ-states and non-local CNOT gates to obtain

$$\frac{1}{\sqrt{2}} \left(|0\rangle + e^{2\pi i \cdot (b + \sum_k x^k)/2^j} |1\rangle \right) |0\rangle^{\otimes K}. \tag{7}$$

An inverse quantum Fourier transform now indeed gives the sum $b + \sum_k x^k$, as desired.

If we would omit this operation, the remaining entanglement would stop states from cancelling out under the inverse quantum Fourier transform and we would be left with the wrong final state.

The server can follow two approaches to distribute the operations and allow multiple parties to add their input. In the first approach, shown in Fig. 4, non-local CNOT gates with more targets are used. In the second approach, shown in Fig. 5, more non-local CNOT gates with only one target are used.

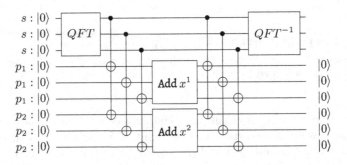

Fig. 4. Addition of integers by two parties, using one server party. We use CNOT gates with multiple targets. The blocks Add x^k stand for the phase-gates needed to add integer x^k, similar to Fig. 3. The final quantum state in the first register is $|x^1 + x^2\rangle$.

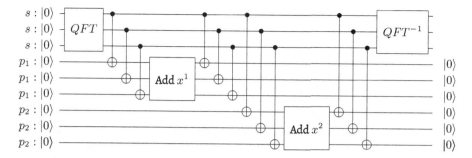

Fig. 5. Addition of integers by two parties, using one server party. We use CNOT gates with a single target and as such require the parties to add their input sequentially. The blocks Add x^k stand for the phase-gates needed to add integer x^k, similar to Fig. 3. The final quantum state in the first register is $|x^1 + x^2\rangle$.

The difference between both approaches becomes clear when we replace the CNOT-gates by non-local variants. In the first approach shown in Fig. 4, we require larger GHZ-states, but less in total. In the second approach shown in Fig. 5, we require smaller GHZ-states, which are easier to create, however, we require more of them.

Note that in the shown circuits we used a single designated server party to create and distribute the initial state. It is also this server party that learns the sum of the inputs, whereas the other players will measure only the zero-state. We can allow the server party to also provide input for the summation, which, in some use-cases, might be practical. The analysis remains the same.

None of the parties can learn the input of other parties, including the server party. This follows as the information is encoded in the phases of the quantum states. Only after we have the state of (7) and apply an inverse quantum Fourier transformation on it, can we access the sum of the inputs. Otherwise, measurements will return no useful information.

Finally, note that only the server can have a non-zero measurement outcome if the procedure is performed correctly. The server party learns only the sum of all inputs, but learns no information on the input of individual parties.

4 Distributed Distance-Based Classifier

The second distributed machine learning approach is a distributed classifier. We consider a distance-based classifier [19]. Given N normalised data points $\boldsymbol{x}_i$, each having M features, and labels $y_i \in \{-1, 1\}$, this classifier computes a label $\tilde{y}$ for a new data point $\tilde{\boldsymbol{x}}$ by evaluating the function

$$\tilde{y} = \mathrm{sgn}\left(\sum_i y_i \left[1 - \frac{1}{4N}|\tilde{\boldsymbol{x}} - \boldsymbol{x}_i|^2\right]\right). \tag{8}$$

We can evaluate this function and determine the new label by manipulating the initial quantum state

$$|\psi\rangle = \frac{1}{\sqrt{2N}} \sum_{n=0}^{N-1} |n\rangle \left(|0\rangle |\psi_{\tilde{x}}\rangle + |1\rangle |\psi_{x_n}\rangle \right) |y_n\rangle. \tag{9}$$

Here $|\psi_x\rangle$ is the amplitude encoding of a normalised data point x: $|\psi_x\rangle = \sum_i x_i |i\rangle$. This state requires $n = \lceil \log_2 N \rceil$ qubits for the data point counter and $m = \lceil \log_2 M \rceil$ qubits for the representation of a data point. In total $n + m + 2$ qubits are required. To evaluate the kernel function, we first apply a Hadamard gate on the second register and then measure the second and fourth register. If the measurement of the second register equals zero, the probability distribution of the measurement of the last register corresponds precisely to the sum of the magnitude of the positive and negative terms of (8).

The power of this algorithm is especially clear if the initial quantum state is given as starting point. Otherwise we have to explicitly prepare it. Multiple extensions of this distance-based classifier have since been proposed [20,21] extending the number of data points, the number of features and removing the need for a label qubit. An example how the state can be prepared is shown in Fig. 6 for the case of four data points each having four features.

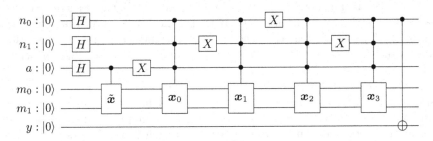

Fig. 6. Initial state preparation for the distance-based classifier for four data points, each having four features. Each (multi-)controlled block represents amplitude encoding of a normalised data point x.

An important aspect of creating this initial state is the amplitude encoding of data points. Amplitude encoding of arbitrary data points can be obtained using only R_Y- and controlled R_Y-gates, as was shown by [22]. An example of such a circuit for a data point with four features is shown in Fig. 7.

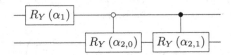

Fig. 7. Generic circuit for amplitude encoding of a normalised data point x with four features. Using trigonometry the angles α can be calculated [22].

We now consider the case where multiple parties wish to evaluate this distance-based classifier using their input data. The input data from these parties can either be horizontally or vertically separated. Horizontally separated data means that each party has some of the different data points, while for those data points having access to all features. Vertically separated data means that parties have information for the same data points but each party now has access to different features of the data. We only consider the case of horizontally separated data, however, extensions to vertically separated data are possible.

Consider the following setting: One computing server party wishes to classify a data point $\tilde{x}$ based on input data that is provided by K different parties. We assume that each of these K parties provides N data points each having M features. Their goal remains to create the state of (9) on the device of the server party, where the only difference is that now the data encoding is performed in a distributed manner. From the amplitude encoding circuit we can see that this can be done if it is possible to perform controlled-R_Y operations in a distributed manner. To do so, we use that rotations around the Y-axis can be replaced by rotations around the Z-axis given a suitable basis transformation: $R_Y(\theta) = R_X(-\frac{1}{2}\pi)R_Z(\theta)R_X(\frac{1}{2}\pi)$. A circuit for controlled R_Y-operation using R_Z gates is shown in Fig. 8.

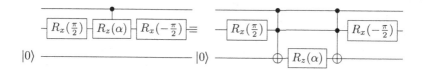

Fig. 8. Circuit identity for a controlled-R_Y rotation

Suppose that the first two qubits belong to the device of the server party and the third qubit belongs to a device of one of the K parties. We can distribute a controlled R_Y-operation using the shown circuit and by then replacing the controlled-gates by distributed controlled-gates, as introduced in Subsect. 2.2. It is then straightforward to use this circuit as a building block to implement amplitude encoding in a distributed manner. Note that each party requires only their share of a GHZ-state and one additional qubit, independent of the number of features.

An example of the final circuit used to obtain the initial state from two data providing parties is shown in Fig. 9. In this figure we have not explicitly drawn the GHZ qubits needed to perform the distributed data encoding. Only the qubits that are numbered in the multi-qubit gates are involved in the encoding operation.

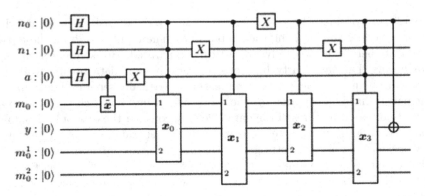

Fig. 9. Initial state preparation for distributed distance-based classifier. Each party provides two data points each with two features. The first five qubits are hosted on the server, qubit six and seven are controlled by party one and party two respectively.

5   Results

To show the potential of the distributed quantum adder from Sect. 3 and the distributed distance-based classifier from Sect. 4, we implemented them and compared the results to those of a simulation with all computations performed on a single device. For the final result is should not matter whether computations are performed distributed or whether they are run on a single larger quantum computer. We simulated both distributed machine learning algorithms using Qiskit [23] and found that the final quantum states and the measurements thereof were identical for both the distributed versions and the local versions.

We considered multiple ways to distribute operations, for instance using bigger GHZ-states and applying a non-local CNOT gate with multiple targets at once, or using multiple 2-party GHZ-states and apply multiple smaller non-local CNOT gates sequentially. Below we consider the resource requirements for both approaches.

5.1   Distributed Adder

For the distributed quantum adder, we consider the case with a server party and K different parties, each inputting an integer. Let N be the maximum bit size of integers. The total number of qubits that are needed to represent the output and input from the K parties is $N \cdot (K + 1)$ qubits. The circuit contains $2N \cdot K$ CNOT operations. We consider four different methods to implement the distributed circuit:

1. Use local CNOT gates. This is not a distributed implementation and is used as benchmark case;
2. Use 2-party GHZ-states and apply multiple sequential non-local CNOT gates with a single target. This method increases the total number of qubits by $4N \cdot K$;

3. Use $K+1$-party GHZ-states and apply non-local CNOT gates with K targets, one for each party. This method increases the total number of qubits by $2N \cdot (K+1)$;
4. Use $K+1$-party GHZ-states and apply non-local CNOT gates with K targets. Qubits used for the GHZ-states are reused. This method increases the total number of qubits by $K+1$.

The last method is especially useful for simulation purposes. In practice it might be challenging to reuse qubits. The resource requirements for these different methods are summarized in Table 1.

Table 1. Required number of qubits and GHZ-states to implement the (distributed) quantum adder using different methods to distribute operations

Method	Total number of qubits	Number of GHZ states
1	$N \cdot (K+1)$	0
2	$N \cdot (5K+1)$	$2N \cdot K$ GHZ$_2$
3	$N \cdot (3K+3)$	$2N \cdot N$ GHZ$_{K+1}$
4	$(N+1) \cdot (K+1)$	$2N \cdot N$ GHZ$_{K+1}$

5.2 Distributed Distance-Based Classifier

For the distributed distance-based classifier, we consider the case where the initial state (9) has to be prepared explicitly on a server parties quantum device. We consider K parties with each N horizontally separated data points having M features each. The server needs $\lceil \log_2(K \cdot N) \rceil + 1 + \lceil \log_2(M) \rceil + 1$ qubits. The K different parties only need one qubit each and the additional qubits for the GHZ states. The total number of (distributed) CNOT operations that are needed can be calculated by the number of data point that need to be encoded, $K \cdot N$, and multiply it by twice the number of R_Y gates that are needed to encode a data point with M features: $M-1$.

Similar to the distributed adder, we consider two methods of implementing CNOT operations

1. Use local CNOT gates. This is not a distributed implementation and is used as benchmark case;
2. Use 2-party GHZ-states and apply multiple non-local CNOT gates with a single target. This method increases the total number of qubits with $2N \cdot K \cdot (M-1)$;
3. Use 2-party GHZ-states and apply multiple non-local CNOT gates with a single target. Qubits used for the GHZ-states are reused. This method increases the total number of qubits by 2.

The results for these different methods are summarized in Table 2.

Table 2. Required number of qubits and GHZ-states to implement the (distributed) distance-based-classifier using different methods to distribute operations

Method	Total number of qubits	Number of GHZ states
1	$\log_2(K \cdot N) + \log_2(M) + 2$	0
2	$\log_2(K \cdot N) + \log_2(M) + 2 + 2N \cdot K \cdot (M-1)$	$N \cdot K \cdot (M-1)$ GHZ$_2$
3	$\log_2(K \cdot N) + \log_2(M) + 4$	$N \cdot K \cdot (M-1)$ GHZ$_2$

6   Conclusion

In this work we considered two applications of distributed quantum computing: distributed arithmetics and distributed distance-based classifiers. We showed how GHZ-states can allow multiple parties to simultaneously perform computations without having to directly share their data. Instead of physically having to share (encrypted) data, parties can apply local phase-gates and in that way share their data. These individual phases are immeasurable and only after all parties inputted their data and a suitable transformation is applied, will we learn the outcome.

Our simulations showed that the distributed approaches indeed give the same answer as when the computations would be run locally. More research on the practical implementation of these methods is however needed, as then other aspects, including decoherence will play a more prominent role.

A final important aspect of great importance is the security of the data encoded by the different parties. Each party adds a phase to their part of the entangled state. These phases are however immeasurable in its current form. Only after a suitable operation can we learn this information. Intermediate adverserial measurements destroy the quantum state and information encoded in the phases is lost.

Our work showed the potential of distributed quantum machine learning. More interesting application exist, such as federated quantum machine learning. Another future research direction is incorporating physical effects in the simulations. We already briefly discussed this topic in Sect. 2 on why shared entangled states are better than actually transporting data qubits. It is important to know the cost of creating shared entangled states of sufficient quality and their effect on the quality of the algorithm.

References

1. Arute, F., et al.: Quantum supremacy using a programmable superconducting processor. Nature **574**(7779), 505–510 (2019)
2. Pompili, M., et al.: Realization of a multinode quantum network of remote solid-state qubits. Science **372**(6539), 259–264 (2021)
3. Chandran, N., Goyal, V., Moriarty, R., Ostrovsky, R.: Position based cryptography. In: Halevi, S. (ed.) CRYPTO 2009. LNCS, vol. 5677, pp. 391–407. Springer, Heidelberg (2009). https://doi.org/10.1007/978-3-642-03356-8_23

4. Jozsa, R., Abrams, D.S., Dowling, J.P., Williams, C.P.: Quantum clock synchronization based on shared prior entanglement. Phys. Rev. Lett. **85**, 2010–2013 (2000)

5. Chuang, I.L.: Quantum algorithm for distributed clock synchronization. Phys. Rev. Lett. **85**(9), 2006–2009 (2000)

6. Yao, A.C.: Protocols for secure computations. In: 23rd Annual Symposium on Foundations of Computer Science (sfcs 1982), pp. 160–164 (1982)

7. Nielsen, M.A., Chuang, I.L.: Quantum Computation and Quantum Information. Cambridge University Press, Cambridge (2010)

8. Bennett, C.H., Brassard, G., Crépeau, C., Jozsa, R., Peres, A., Wootters, W.K.: Teleporting an unknown quantum state via dual classical and Einstein- Podolsky-Rosen channels. Phys. Rev. Lett. **70**, 1895–1899 (1993)

9. Eisert, J., Jacobs, K., Papadopoulos, P., Plenio, M.B.: Optimal local implementation of nonlocal quantum gates. Phys. Rev. A **62**, 052317 (2000)

10. Yimsiriwattana , A., Lomonaco, J.: Generalized GHZ states and distributed quantum computing. In: Coding Theory and Quantum Computing, vol. 381 (2004)

11. Bennett, C.H., Brassard, G., Popescu, S., Schumacher, B., Smolin, J.A., Wootters, W.K.: Purification of noisy entanglement and faithful teleportation via noisy channels. Phys. Rev. Lett. **76**, 722–725 (1996)

12. Bennett, C.H., Bernstein, H.J., Popescu, S., Schumacher, B.: Concentrating partial entanglement by local operations. Phys. Rev. A **53**, 2046–2052 (1996)

13. Bennett, C.H., DiVincenzo, D.P., Smolin, J.A., Wootters, W.K.: Mixed-state entanglement and quantum error correction. Phys. Rev. A **54**, 3824–3851 (1996)

14. Barenco, A., et al.: Elementary gates for quantum computation. Phys. Rev. A **52**, 3457–3467 (1995)

15. Kiltz, E., Leander, G., Malone-Lee, J.: Secure computation of the mean and related statistics. In: Kilian, J. (ed.) TCC 2005. LNCS, vol. 3378, pp. 283–302. Springer, Heidelberg (2005). https://doi.org/10.1007/978-3-540-30576-7_16

16. Draper, T.G.: Addition on a Quantum Computer (2000). eprint: arXiv:quant-ph/0008033v1

17. Beauregard, S.: Circuit for Shor's algorithm using 2n+3 qubits. Quantum Info. Comput. **3**(2), 175–185 (2003)

18. Ruiz-Perez, L., Garcia-Escartin, J.C.: Quantum arithmetic with the quantum Fourier transform. Quantum Inf. Process. **16**(6), 1–14 (2017). https://doi.org/10.1007/s11128-017-1603-1

19. Schuld, M., Fingerhuth, M., Petruccione, F.: Implementing a distance-based classifier with a quantum interference circuit. EPL (Europhys. Lett.) **119**(6), 60002 (2017)

20. Wezeman, R., Neumann, N., Phillipson, F.: Distance-based classifier on the quantum inspire. Digitale Welt **4**(1), 85–91 (2019)

21. Blank, C., da Silva, A.J., de Albuquerque, L.P., Petruccione, F., Park, D.K.: Compact quantum distance-based binary classifier (2022). eprint: arXiv:2202.02151

22. Long, G.L., Sun, Y.: Efficient scheme for initializing a quantum register with an arbitrary superposed state. Phys. Rev. A **64**(1), 014303 (2001)

23. Anis, M.S., et al.: Qiskit: an open-source framework for quantum computing (2021)

A Quantum Annealing Approach for Solving Hard Variants of the Stable Marriage Problem

Christoph Roch[1]([✉]), David Winderl[1], Claudia Linnhoff-Popien[1], and Sebastian Feld[2]

[1] Ludwig-Maximilians-Universität in Munich, Munich, Germany
christoph.roch@ifi.lmu.de
[2] Department of Quantum and Computer Engineering and QuTech,
Delft University of Technology, Delft, The Netherlands

Abstract. The Stable Marriage Problem (SMP) describes the problem, of finding a stable matching between two equally sized sets of elements (e.g., males and females) given an ordering of preferences for each element. A matching is stable, when there does not exist any match of a male and female which both prefer each other to their current partner under the matching. Finding such a matching of maximum cardinality, when ties and incomplete preference lists are allowed, is called MAX-SMTI and is an NP-hard variation of the SMP.

In this work a Quadratic Unconstrained Binary Optimization (QUBO) formulation for MAX-SMTI is introduced and solved both with D-Wave Systems quantum annealing hardware and by their classical meta-heuristic QBSolv. Both approaches are reviewed against existing state-of-the-art approximation algorithms for MAX-SMTI. Additionally, the proposed QUBO problem can also be used to count stable matchings in SMP instances, which is proven to be a #P-complete problem. The results show, that the proposed (quantum) methods can compete with the classical ones regarding the solution quality and might be a relevant alternative, when quantum hardware scales with respect to the number of qubits and their connectivity.

Keywords: Quantum annealing · Stable marriage problem · Optimization · D-wave systems · Heuristic · MAX-SMTI

1 Introduction

The Stable Marriage Problem (SMP) was first defined by Gale and Shapley in 1962 [6]. The problem consists of two sets with n males and n females, which rank the opposite gender in strictly ordered and complete preference lists. The goal is then to find stable matchings for those males m and females w. Stable means, that there is no pair (m_i, w_j) such that both would prefer each other to their current match.

F. Phillipson et al. (Eds.): I4CS 2022, CCIS 1585, pp. 294–307, 2022.
https://doi.org/10.1007/978-3-031-06668-9_21

SMP and its generalized variants have large applications in industry and science. For instance, Maggs et al. used the Stable Marriage Problem in order to explain a content delivery network (CDN) in which clients are mapped to server clusters of the CDN [17]. Other well known applications are the assignment of graduating medicine students to their first hospital appointments [22] or the design of the clearinghouse adopted by the National Residency Matching Program [23].

Since SMP has a large field of applications a lot of research has been made over the years. A survey, regarding SMP and its variants is given in [12]. In our work an NP-hard variation of the SMP, where the goal is to find the maximum cardinality with ties and incomplete preference lists, the MAX-SMTI, will be investigated. Podhradsky et al. compared the state-of-the-art approximation algorithms for MAX-SMTI [21], while Delorme et al. reviewed the mathematical models for MAX-SMTI [5].

With Quantum Computing (QC) technology emerging, there is now the possibility to solve such kind of problems in a completely different way. One field of QC is Quantum Annealing (QA), a meta-heuristic, which is implemented in hardware by D-Wave Systems. In order to perform quantum computations on such a machine, it is necessary to cast the problem into a certain mathematical form, the Quadratic Unconstrained Binary Optimization (QUBO) or the equivalent Ising formulation. In [8] and [16], many QUBO and Ising formulations for well known NP-hard problems are introduced.

In the following, SMP and the more complex variation MAX-SMTI are defined in Sect. 2. After giving some fundamentals of Quantum Annealing, our QUBO formulation for MAX-SMTI is presented in Sect. 3. In Sect. 4 the experimental setup is given and the results of the MAX-SMTI QUBO formulation by using D-Wave Systems 2000Q Quantum Annealer and the classical software tool QBSolv are compared against two state-of-the-art approximation algorithms, SHIFTBRK and Kiraly2 [21]. The optimal solutions (ground truth) of the small test instances are determined by a linear programming solver [24]. The algorithms are compared regarding their solution quality and a theoretical outlook w.r.t the computational time is given.

2 Background

2.1 Stable Marriage Problem

The Stable Marriage Problem describes the problem of finding a stable matching between two sets, males $\mathcal{M} = \{m_1, m_2, ..., m_n\}$ and females $\mathcal{W} = \{w_1, w_2, ..., w_n\}$. Elements of both, $\mathcal{M}$ and $\mathcal{W}$, rank the other sex in strictly ordered and complete preference lists. Therefore every preference list has the length of n.

Let $M(m|w)$ describe the notation for $m|w$'s matching partner and let $w_2 \succ_{m_2} w_3$, describe the notation that m_2 (strictly) prefers w_2 over w_3. A pair $p = (m, w)$ is considered as blocking towards M, if $w \succ_m M(m)$ and $m \succ_w M(w)$.

A matching $M = \{(m_i, w_j), ...\}$ of size n is considered as stable, if there exists no blocking pair p.

Note, that this doesn't mean everybody is "happy" in terms of being matched to the most desired possibility available. Furthermore this can be expressed, that everybody is matched in a way he or she cannot complain.

It is known, that SMP can be solved in $O(n^2)$ by the Gale-Shapley (GS) algorithm [18]. The basic GS algorithm only works for complete and strict preference lists, nevertheless this often does not suit reality well. Therefore, mainly three variants of the SMP were developed. The Stable Marriage Problem with ties in its preference lists (SMT), the Stable Marriage Problem with incomplete preference lists (SMI), and the combination of both, the Stable Marriage Problem with ties and incomplete preference lists (SMTI).

SMT - Stable Marriage Problem with Ties. In the basic SMP, the preference lists must be ordered in a strict way. Relaxing this rule, so that indifferences are allowed in preference lists, results in two different ways of describing preferences and in three definitions of stability.

- **Strict Preference:** This is true for (m_1, w_2, w_3), if m_1 prefers w_2 over w_3 and does not tie w_2 and w_3. It is denoted as $w_2 \succ_{m_1} w_3$.
- **(Weak) Preference:** This is true for (m_1, w_2, w_3), if m_1 prefers w_2 over w_3 and both are tied on m_2's preference list. The notation here is $w_2 \succeq_{m_1} w_3$.

Consequently, three definitions for stability of a matching can be made [18]:

- **Weakly Stable:** There is no pair that would strictly prefer each other over their partner in M.
- **Strongly Stable:** There is no pair (m, w), so that $w \succ_m M(m)$ and $m \succeq_w M(w)$.
- **Super Stable:** There is no pair that would (weakly) prefer each other over their current match.

Such a pair (described in the manner of weakly, strongly and super stability), like in SMP, is a blocking pair if it exists.

SMI - Stable Marriage Problem with Incomplete Preference Lists. Incomplete preference lists do refer to the term that not every person of the opposite sex needs to be listed on a persons preference list. This results in the fact that not every male can be matched to every female.[1] Therefore an acceptable pair can be defined as followed.

Acceptable Pair: A pair (m, w) is acceptable if m has listed w on his preference list and w has listed m. In SMI, a matching is stable, if it is stable in terms of SMP and no unacceptable pair was matched.

---

[1] Consider the situation, in which m has w on his preference list, but w does not mention m. A match (m, w) is therefore impossible.

SMTI - Stable Marriage Problem with Ties and Incomplete Preference Lists. Combining both generalizations from before, we obtain the Stable Marriage Problem with ties and incomplete preference lists (SMTI). Finding a weakly stable match for a given SMTI problem, by breaking down ties arbitrarily (like in SMP), will affect the size of the resulting match, as explained in Example 1. This effect will be interesting for MAX-SMTI and therefore, in the scope of this work, weakly stable SMTI will be reviewed as SMTI. So a pair (m, w) is considered as blocking towards a matching M, when the following takes account:

$$(free(m) \vee w \succ_m M(m)) \wedge (free(w) \vee m \succ_w M(w)) \tag{1}$$

where $free(m|w)$ denotes if $m|w$ are matched to anyone in M. Note, that either $w \succ_m M(m))$ or $free(m)$ is sufficient to create an unblocking pair towards the matching M.

Example 1. Consider the example from Table 1, with $n = |\mathcal{M}| = |\mathcal{W}|$. It is easy to review that $M_1 = \{(m_2, w_3), (m_3, w_1)\}$ is weakly stable (has no blocking pairs). Also $M_2 = \{(m_2, w_2), (m_3, w_1), (m_1, w_3)\}$ can be reviewed as weakly stable. Note that the cardinality of the two stable matchings differ in size. This effect of possible indifference in the cardinality of the matchings does only occur in the weakly stability criteria.

Table 1. Arbitrary SMTI instance: the persons in the brackets are tied.

Males				Females			
m_1:	w_1	w_3		w_1:	$(m_2$	$m_3)$	
m_2:	$(w_2$	$w_3)$	w_1	w_2:	$(m_1$	m_2	$m_3)$
m_3:	w_1	w_3	w_2	w_3:	$(m_3$	$m_2)$	m_1

MAX-SMTI. In the previous section it was discussed, that breaking ties arbitrarily in SMTI will affect the size of the resulting match. Trying to find the matching with the largest cardinality is an NP-hard optimization problem, referenced in the following by MAX-SMTI [11].

2.2 Quantum Annealing

Quantum Annealing is a meta-heuristic, which was formulated in its general and present form by T. Kadowaki and H. Nishimori in 1998 [14] and is commonly used to solve problems with a discrete search space with many local minima. D-Wave Systems implemented the meta-heuristic in their hardware, in order to find low energy states of a spin glass system, described by an Ising Hamiltonian,

$$\mathcal{H}(s) = \sum_i h_i x_i + \sum_{i<j} J_{ij} x_i x_j \tag{2}$$

where h_i is the energy, which directly affects qubit i. J_{ij} represent the energies interacting between the two qubits i and j and x_i is the spin $(-1, +1)$ of the i-th qubit. Many optimization problems can be formulated as an Ising Hamiltonian and therefore be executed on D-Wave's quantum annealing hardware [16], in attempt to find good or acceptable solutions.

Within the quantum annealing process an initial Hamiltonian H_I with an easy to prepare minimal energy configuration (or ground state) is physically interpolated to a problem Hamiltonian H_P, whose minimal energy configuration is sought and corresponds to the best solution of the defined problem, see (3). This transition is described by an adiabatic evolution path which is mathematically represented as function $s(t)$ and decreases from 1 to 0 [19].

$$H(t) = s(t)H_I + (1 - s(t))H_P \qquad (3)$$

If this transition is executed sufficiently slow, the probability to find the ground state of the problem Hamiltonian is close to 1 [1]. Thus, by mapping the MAX-SMTI problem onto a spin glass system, quantum annealing in theory is able to find the solution of it.

For completeness, we map our optimization problem to a QUBO problem, which is an alternative formulation of the Ising spin glass system. It is mathematically equivalent and uses 0 and 1 for the spin variables [2,25]. The quantum annealer is also capable of minimizing the functional form of the QUBO problem,

$$\min x^t Q x \qquad \text{with } x \in \{0,1\}^n \qquad (4)$$

with x being a binary vector of size n, and Q being an $n \times n$ real-valued matrix describing the relationship between the variables. Given matrix $Q : n \times n$, the annealing process tries to find binary variable assignments $x \in \{0,1\}^n$ to minimize the objective function in (4).

3   QUBO Formulation for MAX-SMTI

In the following section, the QUBO formulation for MAX-SMTI gets introduced.

3.1   Encoding

When reformulating MAX-SMTI towards a QUBO problem, every bit variable of the bit-vector x corresponds to an acceptable pair in the SMTI problem instance. Therefore, the size of the bit-vector and the QUBO matrix is determined by the number of acceptable pairs in the SMTI instance. The index of a bit-variable x_i is therefore a unique identifier for one possible match in SMTI. Hence, the notation x_{m_i,w_j} references the unique index for the acceptable pair (m_i, w_j).[2] The reversed encoding (deduce the male/female from the current index of x_i) is written as m_{x_i} or w_{x_i}. In case of $x_i = 1$, it can be concluded that (m_{x_i}, w_{x_i}) are matched.

---

[2] This kind of notation implies, that the referenced pair is always acceptable.

3.2   Objective Function and Constraints

In MAX-SMTI it must be ensured that no one is matched twice and that the matching is stable. Additionally, the matching with the maximum cardinality is searched. In the following sections, those two constraints and the objective function will be explained in detail.

Constraint - No One is Matched Twice. Since QUBO is unconstrained, the quantum annealer could try to match a person twice, in order to gain a smaller final solution energy.

This would not result in a stable matching nor any valid response. So, the constraint needs to be enforced by (5).

$$p_3 \cdot \sum_{i,j} x_i x_j \cdot [i \neq j]([m_{x_i} == m_{x_j}] + [w_{x_i} == w_{x_j}]) \tag{5}$$

Note, that the square brackets indicate boolean formulations, which values are cast to their integer counterparts 0 and 1 for false and true, respectively. So, if either one of the males or females in that formula equals each other, both bit variables are 1 and they are matched twice. Therefore, the penalty p_3 is added to the solution energy and states it as invalid.

Constraint - The Matching is Stable. In order to assure the stability of the match, (1) was reformulated into the following constraint:

$$p_2 \cdot (\sum_{i,j}^{n} x_{m,w_j} x_{m_i,w} \cdot [\neg w \succ_m w_j \wedge \neg m \succ_w m_i]$$
$$- \sum_{i}^{n} x_{m_i,w} [\neg m \succ_w m_i] - \sum_{i}^{n} x_{m,w_i} [\neg w \succ_m w_i] + 1) \tag{6}$$

Note that (6) must hold for all $(m, w) \in A$, with A being the set of acceptable pairs.

The first term ensures, that two matched pairs that would create a blocking pair are less energy effective. The second and third terms enforce a couple (w, m_i), where $\neg m \succ_w m_i$, regardless of whether (w, m_i) gets matched or not. So while the first part adds up a penalty in case a pair tends to be blocking, the second part promotes pairs, which are more likely to be stable by adding negative values on the diagonal of the QUBO matrix.

Objective Function - The Maximum Cardinality is Found. To enforce the stable matching with the maximum cardinality, $-p_1$ needs to be assigned onto every element of the diagonal. This has the effect, that solutions with more matched pairs have a lower energy than solutions with less matched pairs.

$$-p_1 \sum_{i} x_i \quad \forall i \in |A| \tag{7}$$

3.3 Penalty Assignment

By giving the constraints in the sections above, three penalties (p_1, p_2 and p_3) were introduced. p_1 was set to 1 by default, since it is just used for the objective function to define, respectively count, the maximum cardinality. However, it is more important to ensure that a match is stable than finding a match of maximum cardinality. Therefore, p_2 was set to n, with n being the size of the sets of males/females. The last penalty is $p_3 = n \cdot p_2 + p_1$. Since p_3 references the hard constraint that no one is matched twice, it needs to be larger than every value assigned to the diagonal of the QUBO matrix. The minimum value, that can be assigned onto the diagonal is, $n \cdot p_2 + p_1$.

3.4 Resulting Energy

For a simple verification of the solution, the resulting energy e can be used. Considering (6), it can be seen, that per acceptable pair, the equation equals $-p_2$. Since this constraint needs to hold for all acceptable pairs, the energy for a stable solution has to be $e \leq -p_2 \cdot |A|$. In (7), $-p_1$ is assigned to every element of the diagonal and added up per couple in the resulting match. Combining the two observations, the resulting energy of a stable solution is defined in (8). Here n_r is the size of the resulting match with $n_r > 0$.

$$e = -(p_2 \cdot |A| + p_1 \cdot n_r) \qquad (8)$$

So in general, with having the energy to a solution, the stability criteria can be verified easily. However, without knowing the maximum cardinality, it is not possible to determine the energy of the optimal solution for MAX-SMTI.

4 Experimental Setup

4.1 Datasets

For the computational experiments, two kinds of datasets were created. One consists of random SMTI-Instances, while the other one consists of random SMP-Instances, further called SMTI-Dataset and SMP-Dataset, respectively.

SMTI-Dataset. For the SMTI-Dataset, 50 instances per size in the range of [3; 30] were created by an algorithm proposed by Gent et al. [7]. This algorithm takes two parameters g_1 and g_2. g_1 describes the probability of one element being added to a preference list and g_2 describes the probability of the occurrence of a tie in a preference list. For each sample, both parameters were randomly drawn to promote uniformly distributed ties and preference lists over all samples per size.

SMP-Dataset. For the creation of the SMP-Dataset, the same approach as for the SMTI-Dataset has been used just with 20 samples per size. For the generation of SMP instances it is sufficient to shuffle each preference list to create a new SMP instance.

4.2   Methods

Linear Programming Solver. Regarding MAX-SMTI, the optimal solution can be found by computing every matching for every possible arrangement of tie breaks and return the matching with the maximum cardinality. Since this brute force approach is quite inefficient, another approach to find the optimal solution was developed by Roth et al. using integer linear programming (LP) [24]. For our experiments, we used COIN-OR's branch and cut method to solve the LP model of Roth et al. [13]. In this work this LP approach will be reviewed as MAX-SMTI-LP.

Kiraly2. Kiraly et al. introduced two simple linear approximation algorithms for MAX-SMTI [15]. The first, a linear 3/2-approximation algorithm, works for SMTI instances with men strict preference lists. This was followed by a second algorithm for general SMTI problems with an approximation ratio of 5/3, based on the former mentioned algorithm. See [21] for a detailed description and implementation.

SHIFTBRK. Halldòrsson et al. introduced SHIFTBRK, an approximation algorithm with a ratio of $2/(1 + L^2)$, where L is the length of the longest tie among all ties in the preference lists [9]. So the approximation ratio decreases within the increase of the length of the longest tie. The algorithm is based on iteratively breaking and shifting ties and can solve the resulting SMI instances via the well known GS algorithm [6].

D-Wave Systems Quantum Annealing. As already mentioned in Sec. 2.2, D-Wave Systems Quantum Annealer takes a QUBO problem as input and takes care of the annealing process. However, since the hardware is still quite restricted in its resources, w.r.t. the number of qubits and their connectivity, we could only use it for relatively small problem instances up to a size of $n = 7$. In this work this approach is reviewed as QUBO-MAX-SMTI (QA).

QBSolv. QBSolv is a software tool, which splits a QUBO problem into smaller components (subQUBOs) of a predefined subproblem size, which are then solved independently of each other. This process is executed iteratively as long as there is an improvement and it can be defined using the QBSolv parameter "num_repeats". This parameter determines the number of times to repeat the splitting of the QUBO problem matrix after finding a better sample. With doing so, the QUBO matrix is split into different components using a classical tabu search heuristic in each iteration. QBSolv can be used in a completely classical way to solve the subQUBOs or as a quantum-classic hybrid method by solving the single subQUBOs on the quantum annealer.

Besides embedding and splitting the QUBO into subQUBOs, QBSolv also takes care of unembedding and merging of the subproblems' solutions. See [20] for more details on QBSolv. In this work this approach is reviewed as QUBO-MAX-SMTI (QBSolv).

5   Results and Discussion

5.1   Solution Quality

In Fig. 1 we evaluated the solution quality of our QUBO-MAX-SMTI (QA/QBSolv) methods against two state-of-the-art approximation algorithms for MAX-SMTI, Kiraly2 and SHIFTBRK. The ground truth was calculated using the MAX-SMTI-LP solver. For problem sizes ranging from 3 to 30, 50 randomly sampled instances per size were used. The approximation ratio was calculated by the number of optimal solutions found divided by the number of samples per size.

One can see, that the QUBO-MAX-SMTI (QBSolv) could find every optimal stable matching of the problem instances till the size of $n = 13$ and even outperforms the other approximation methods in some cases ($n = 10, 11, 12, 15$). Regarding the larger problem instances, QUBO-MAX-SMTI (QBSolv) decreases in solution quality to a minimum of 35% in problem size $n = 30$, while SHIFT-BRK, for example, stays in the approximation ratio of around 90%.

QUBO-MAX-SMTI (QA) was run on the D-Wave 2000Q quantum chip for only the relatively small problem instances, due to the reasons mentioned in Sect. 4.2. The number of measurements per problem was set to 100. The results show, that the proposed approach can keep up with QUBO-MAX-SMTI (QBSolv) and SHIFTBRK and even outperforms Kiraly2 till the problem size of $n = 5$. However, afterwards the approximation ratio decreases to around 60%. This might be due to large physical qubit chains, which occur, when the logical qubits of the QUBO problem don't fit directly to the physical qubits and their connectivity of the quantum architecture. However, one could improve performance by adjusting the hyperparameter *chain_strength* of those qubit chains [4]. Additionally, we ran the two proposed methods against an exact solver, the MAX-SMTI-LP, for the same problem instances as above. In Fig. 2 the solution energies of QUBO-MAX-SMTI (QA/QBSolv) are compared against the energy of the global optimum found by the MAX-SMTI-LP and the solution energies describing a stable matching, which can be determined as described in Sect. 3.4. The energy of the global optimum can be calculated by encoding the exact MAX-SMTI-LP solution on the binary vector x of the QUBO formulation and computing the matrix multiplication $x^t Q x$.

In Fig. 2a the QUBO-MAX-SMTI (QA) method found for the two smallest problem sizes ($n \leq 4$) the optimal solution (determined by the resulting energy) in every problem instance. For the larger problem sizes ($5 \leq n$), the percentage

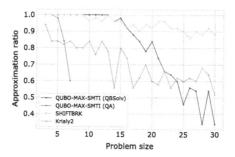

Fig. 1. Solution qualities of the approximation algorithms for different sized MAX-SMTI problem instances. For each problem size, 50 random sampled instances were used. The approximation ratio was calculated by the number of optimal solutions found, divided by the number of samples per size.

of optimal solved instances decreases to a minimum of 60%. Additionally one can see, that for problem size $n = 6$ and $n = 7$, the MAX-SMTI-LP found a better solution, i.e. it has a lower solution energy, for 5% respectively 8% of the instances. In some cases, the QUBO-MAX-SMTI (QA) method could not find stable matches, as shown in light blue.

The QUBO-MAX-SMTI (QBSolv) method found for a problem size of $n \leq 13$ every optimal solution of the used problem instances, except for $n = 11$, as shown in Fig. 2b. From then on, the percentage of optimal solved instances decreases to a minimum of 35% in problem size 30. Moreover, it can be seen, that for the largest problem size ($n = 30$), the percentage of optimal solved instances roughly equals the percentage of non optimal solved instances and invalid, i.e. unstable solutions. Besides that, another finding is, that QUBO-MAX-SMTI (QA/QBSolv) can be used to find and count the number of stable solutions for SMP instances, which in general is #P-complete [10]. In Fig. 3 the percentage of all stable matchings per problem size found by the proposed methods, are shown. For each problem size, 20 instances were used. The baseline was delivered by the backtracking algorithm proposed in [26] and was run as long as QBSolv. The results show, that QUBO-MAX-SMTI (QBSolv) found every stable matching till the size of $n \leq 11$ for every problem instance. From then on, the percentage of finding all stable matchings decreases to a minimum of 9% in problem size 18. However, for larger problem instances ($n \geq 15$), QUBO-MAX-SMTI (QBSolv) found more stable matches in the same amount of time as the backtracking algorithm. The QA approach was only able to find every stable matching for $n \leq 4$. With $n = 5$ only 30% of the stable matchings were found, while for $n \geq 6$ QUBO-MAX-SMTI (QA) was not able to find any stable machting for those SMP instances. The reason why this QA method finds stable solutions for the SMTI instances for the same problem size lies in the size of the actual QUBO matrix, which is proportional to the number of acceptable pairs. For SMTI, the number of acceptable pairs is less or equal to n^2, due to the incomplete preference

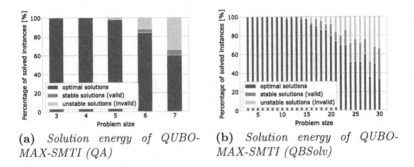

(a) *Solution energy of QUBO-MAX-SMTI (QA)*

(b) *Solution energy of QUBO-MAX-SMTI (QBSolv)*

Fig. 2. The percentage of optimal (dark blue), stable but not optimal (medium blue) and unstable (light blue), i.e. invalid, solutions of the problem instances. The problem size varies from 3 to 30. For each problem size 50 problem instances were used. (Color figure online)

lists, while the number of acceptable pairs for SMP is equal to n^2. As a result, the size of the QUBO matrix for SMP instances increases much faster than for the SMTI instances and therefore the corresponding solution space.

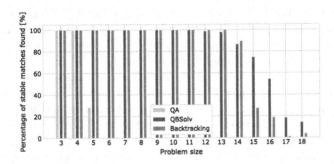

Fig. 3. The percentage of all stable matchings per problem size found by the proposed methods. For each problem size 20 instances were used. The baseline was delivered by the backtracking algorithm proposed in [26]. The backtracking algorithm was run as long as QBSolv and then stopped.

5.2 Computational Results

Regarding the computational results, it is hard to draw a fair practical comparison between the state-of-the-art classical methods for MAX-SMTI and the quantum annealing approach presented in this paper. Since the interaction of classical and quantum hardware in our approach leads to additional overhead (cloud access time and job queuing time at D-Wave Systems) we didn't do a time to solution comparison but rather give a theoretical outlook of the computation times.

The preprocessing time of MAX-SMTI-QUBO (QA/QBSolv) is in $O(n^4)$ and contains the computation of acceptable pairs and the creation of the QUBO matrix. MAX-SMTI-LP has a slightly better preprocessing time of $O(n^3)$, when setting up the integer linear program. However, when it comes to solving the models (QUBO and ILP) we expect the former being computational superior. The QA algorithm implemented in D-Wave Systems QPU basically runs in constant time $O(1)$, while the runtime of the mixed-integer-programming solver (COIN-OR's branch and cut) is definitely larger than $O(1)$ and since it is a heuristic its runtime complexity is hard to determine exactly. We expect, that with quantum annealing hardware getting larger in the number of qubits and their connectivity, it could outperform the state-of-the-art methods w.r.t. bigger problem size instances $(n > 7)$.

6 Conclusion

We introduced QUBO-MAX-SMTI (QA/QBSolv), the first QUBO formulation for solving MAX-SMTI instances with classical and also quantum annealing hardware. The QUBO formulation for MAX-SMTI requries maximal n^2 variables with n being the number of acceptable pairs and therefore does not need any additional slack variables. Our experiments show the current state of applicability and provide a comparison to some state-of-the-art classical algorithms.

Regarding the solution quality, the approach of using the QUBO formulation with QA and QBSolv can keep up with the state-of-the-art algorithms and even outperform them in some cases. Additionally, the QUBO formulation can be used to find and count multiple stable solutions, which is a #P-complete task. However, since the quantum hardware is still in its infancy the QA method was only applicable for $n \leq 7$ and is therefore at the moment not competitive with the classical methods for the relevant problem sizes. Nevertheless, the experiments give hope, that the quantum approach gains in importance when the corresponding hardware increases w.r.t the number of qubits and their connectivity.

The addressed problem of the immaturity of the quantum hardware makes it likewise hard to draw a final conclusion regarding the hoped computational quantum advantage. Since at the moment the classical methods outclass the quantum method from a practical point of view (time to solution), the theoretical outlook predicts, that using quantum annealing hardware for solving QUBO fomulation might be comparatively more efficient.

Regarding future work it would be interesting to see, if the computational times and the solution quality improve when using D-Wave Systems new annealer called Advantage [3]. The new hardware chip has up to 5000 qubits and a better connectivity. This enables to solve larger fully connected QUBO problems and a shorter total computation time might be achieved.

Concluding, the proposed QUBO approach might be a relevant alternative to the classical methods, when quantum hardware scales.

Acknowledgment. This work was partially funded by the BMWK project PlanQK.

References

1. Albash, T., Lidar, D.A.: Adiabatic quantum computation. Rev. Mod. Phys. **90**(1), 015002 (2018)
2. Boros, E., Hammer, P.L., Tavares, G.: Local search heuristics for quadratic unconstrained binary optimization (QUBO). J. Heurist. **13**(2), 99–132 (2007)
3. D-Wave Systems: D-wave announces general availability of first quantum computer built for business, September 2020. https://www.dwavesys.com/press-releases/d-wave-announces-general-availability-first-quantum-computer-built-business
4. D-Wave Systems Inc.: White paper: Programming the d-wave QPU: Setting the chain strength. Technical report MSU-CSE-06-2, D-Wave Systems Inc., April 2020. https://www.dwavesys.com/sites/default/files/14-1041A-A_Setting_The_Chain_Strength.pdf
5. Delorme, M., García, S., Gondzio, J., Kalcsics, J., Manlove, D., Pettersson, W.: Mathematical models for stable matching problems with ties and incomplete lists. Eur. J. Oper. Res. **277**(2), 426–441 (2019). https://doi.org/10.1016/j.ejor.2019.03.017, http://arxiv.org/abs/1810.02711
6. Gale, D., Shapley, L.S.: College admissions and the stability of marriage. Am. Math. Mon. **69**(1), 9–15 (1962)
7. Gent, I.P., Prosser, P.: An empirical study of the stable marriage problem with ties and incomplete lists. In: Proceedings of the 15th European Conference on Artificial Intelligence, ECAI 2002, pp. 141–145. IOS Press, NLD (2002)
8. Glover, F., Kochenberger, G.: A tutorial on formulating and using QUBO models, November 2018. http://arxiv.org/abs/1811.11538
9. Halldórsson, M.M., Iwama, K., Miyazaki, S., Yanagisawa, H.: Improved approximation of the stable marriage problem. In: Di Battista, G., Zwick, U. (eds.) ESA 2003. LNCS, vol. 2832, pp. 266–277. Springer, Heidelberg (2003). https://doi.org/10.1007/978-3-540-39658-1_26
10. Irving, R.W., Leather, P.: The complexity of counting stable marriages. SIAM J. Comput. **15**(3), 655–667 (1986)
11. Irving, R.W., Manlove, D.F., Scott, S.: The stable marriage problem with master preference lists. Discrete Appl. Math. **156**(15), 2959–2977 (2008). https://doi.org/10.1016/J.DAM.2008.01.002, https://www.sciencedirect.com/science/article/pii/S0166218X0800022X
12. Iwama, K., Miyazaki, S.: A survey of the stable marriage problem and its variants. In: International Conference on Informatics Education and Research for Knowledge-Circulating Society (ICKS 2008), pp. 131–136. IEEE (2008)
13. Forrest, J.J., et al.: Coin-or/Cbc: version 2.10.5, March 2020. https://doi.org/10.5281/zenodo.3700700
14. Kadowaki, T., Nishimori, H.: Quantum annealing in the transverse Ising model, April 1998. https://doi.org/10.1103/PhysRevE.58.5355, http://arxiv.org/abs/cond-mat/9804280, https://dx.doi.org/10.1103/PhysRevE.58.5355
15. Király, Z.: Better and simpler approximation algorithms for the stable marriage problem. In: Halperin, D., Mehlhorn, K. (eds.) ESA 2008. LNCS, vol. 5193, pp. 623–634. Springer, Heidelberg (2008). https://doi.org/10.1007/978-3-540-87744-8_52
16. Lucas, A.: Ising formulations of many np problems. Front. Phys. **2**, 5 (2014)
17. Maggs, B.M., Sitaraman, R.K.: Algorithmic nuggets in content delivery. ACM SIGCOMM Comput. Commun. Rev. **45**, 52–66 (2015). https://doi.org/10.1145/2805789.2805800

18. Manlove, D.F., Irving, R.W., Iwama, K., Miyazaki, S., Morita, Y.: Hard variants of stable marriage. Theor. Comput. Sci. **276**(1–2), 261–279 (2002). https://doi.org/10.1016/s0304-3975(01)00206-7, https://www.sciencedirect.com/science/article/pii/S0304397501002067
19. McGeoch, C.C.: Adiabatic quantum computation and quantum annealing: theory and practice. Synthesis Lect. Quantum Comput. **5**(2), 1–93 (2014). https://doi.org/10.2200/S00585ED1V01Y201407QMC008
20. Michael Booth, S.P.R., Roy, A.: Partitioning optimization problems for hybrid classical/quantum execution. Technical report, D-Wave System Inc., January 2017. https://www.dwavesys.com/sites/default/files/partitioning_QUBOs_for_quantum_acceleration-2.pdf
21. Podhradský, A.: Aproximativní algoritmy pro problém stabilního párování (2011). https://is.muni.cz/th/172646/fi_m
22. Roth, A.E.: The evolution of the labor market for medical interns and residents: a case study in game theory. J. Polit. Econ. **92**(6), 991–1016 (1984)
23. Roth, A.E., Peranson, E.: The redesign of the matching market for American physicians: Some engineering aspects of economic design. Am. Econ. Rev. **89**(4), 748–780 (1999)
24. Roth, A.E., Rothblum, U.G., Vate, J.H.V.: Stable matchings, optimal assignments, and linear programming. Math. Oper. Res. **18**(4), 803–828 (1993). http://www.jstor.org/stable/3690124
25. Su, J., Tu, T., He, L.: A quantum annealing approach for boolean satisfiability problem. In: Proceedings of the 53rd Annual Design Automation Conference, p. 148. ACM (2016)
26. Wirth, N.: Algorithms + Data Structures = Programs. Prentice Hall PTR, USA (1978)

Learning Based Hardware-Centric Quantum Circuit Generation

Merel A. Schalkers$^{(\boxtimes)}$ and Matthias Möller

Delft Institute of Applied Mathematics, Delft University of Technology,
Delft, The Netherlands
m.a.schalkers@tudelft.nl

Abstract. In this paper we present an approach to find quantum circuits suitable to mimic probabilistic and search operations on a physical NISQ device. We present both a gradient based and a non-gradient based machine learning approach to optimize the created quantum circuits. In our optimization procedure we make use of a cost function that differentiates between the vector representing the probabilities of measurement of each basis state after applying our learned circuit and the desired probability vector. As such our quantum circuit generation (QCG) approach leads to thinner quantum circuits which behave better when executed on physical quantum computers. Our approach moreover ensures that the created quantum circuit obeys the restrictions of the chosen hardware. By catering to specific quantum hardware we can avoid unforeseen and potentially unnecessary circuit depth, and we return circuits that need no further transpilation. We present the results of running the created circuits on quantum computers by IBM, Rigetti and Quantum Inspire.

Keywords: Quantum computing · NISQ · Quantum machine learning · Quantum compiling · Hybrid quantum computing

1 Introduction

Quantum computers are the quantum equivalent of classical computers, which have quantum specific properties, such as qubit entanglement and superposition of states. When properly exploited these properties can provide a speed-up over classical computers for some computational problems [15].

We are currently at the stage of Noisy Intermediate Scale Quantum (NISQ) devices. NISQ devices have approximately 50 to 100 noisy qubits at their disposal [16]. The noisiness of the qubits imply that we can only perform a set amount of operations on each qubit before the influence of noise on the system becomes too large, and the outcome of the computation meaningless. Since NISQ devices only have a limited amount of noisy qubits available, we are furthermore restricted in the quantum algorithms we can execute on today's and near-future quantum computers. In this paper we focus on finding quantum circuits, which are designed to take into account the physical constraints of a specific NISQ device and as such can be reliably used in the near term.

© The Author(s), under exclusive license to Springer Nature Switzerland AG 2022
F. Phillipson et al. (Eds.): I4CS 2022, CCIS 1585, pp. 308–322, 2022.
https://doi.org/10.1007/978-3-031-06668-9_22

Aside from noise, other physical limitations of typical NISQ hardware entail that not all qubits are physically connected and only a few gates can be natively applied to the qubits. The first property implies that when a quantum circuit, which uses a two-qubit gate between non-connected qubits, gets compiled, it needs to be decomposed using multiple additional swap operations. Due to the second property many quantum gates used in a theoretical description of a quantum algorithm need to be decomposed into a sequence of native gates when run on the physical qubits. Both the first and second property described add extra depth to the quantum circuit. Since NISQ devices are rather noisy, extra depth of the circuit means less reliable results upon measurement. The aforementioned limitations of current quantum computers imply that the algorithms that can be reliably run on current quantum devices are limited.

1.1 Paper Outline

In this paper we introduce an approach that can be used to create a quantum circuit to mimic a probabilistic operation or a search operation. In Sect. 2 we give an outline of the problem and in Subsects. 2.1 and 2.2 we further elaborate on these types of operations. Furthermore the circuits found are such that they are specifically catered to a chosen quantum hardware. The circuits take into account the limitations of the hardware by restricting the potential ansatzes[1] to only use gates native to the chosen hardware. Our approach can be directly used on a physical quantum computer, which allows us to take device specific noise into account and find noise resilient circuits. Since we let our ansatz design depend on the properties of the hardware, ours is a so-called hardware-centric approach. The properties of the hardware considered in this paper and the noise-resilience of the approach are further discussed in Subsect. 2.3.

In order to be able to optimize the circuits we need to define a cost function to quantify the goodness of fit of a considered quantum circuit. Our cost function, which we introduce in Sect. 3, is such that it only distinguishes between the probability of finding each basis state upon measurement after running the found quantum circuit. We are, to our knowledge, the first to choose such a cost function for finding quantum circuits geared at mimicking probabilistic operations and search operations for learning quantum circuits. A similar cost function was used in [7], where they use this cost function to optimize a reference circuit.

Section 4 gives an overview of the method currently used to determine the ansatzes of which we optimize the continuous parameters.

We make use of both a gradient-based and a non-gradient based machine learning approach as an optimization procedure to optimize the parameters of the quantum circuit ansatzes. The non-gradient based machine learning technique we use is Particle Swarm Optimization (PSO), which we implement using PySwarms [6], and is further described in Subsect. 5.1. The gradient-based machine learning technique is implemented using PyTorch [4], in combination with Pennylane [5], and is further described in Subsect. 5.2.

---

[1] Here the term ansatz refers to the initial layout of the quantum circuit in terms of which gate is applied to which qubit in each layer.

We evaluated the performance of our approach by finding hardware-centric quantum circuits that mimic a thin predetermined circuit and the amplitude amplification step of Grover's search operation, respectively, using the native gate sets of physical quantum computers from Rigetti [17,18], IBM [1] and Quantum Inspire [3]. We present the resulting quantum circuits in Sect. 6.

1.2 State of the Art

There have been several other techniques which make use of a hardware-centric approach to find quantum circuits, with the aim to make optimal use of the properties of NISQ devices [8–14]. In this subsection we give a short overview of those approaches and explain how they differ from ours.

In [8] the Hilbert-Schmidt test is used to determine the cost of a chosen ansatz, which distinguishes between the desired and the created unitary and not between the resulting measurement probabilities of the basis states. Furthermore the authors evaluate their cost function by running the desired unitary and the learned quantum circuit in parallel on maximally entangled qubits. As a result their method requires $2n$ qubits and a functioning implementation of the desired unitary must be known and at the users disposal, which we do not require.

In [9] the authors also make use of a cost function that distinguishes between the quantum states, not probability vectors upon measurement. Therefore their choice of cost function is also not suitable for our use cases.

Paper [10] again distinguishes between the unitary created by the ansatz and the desired unitary, not the associated probability vectors. This requires to find the exponentially large matrix expressions for the desired and created unitaries and calculate the distance between the two.

Papers [11–13] only learn quantum circuits that create one specific probability distribution given a specific input vector. The proposed approaches do not learn circuits that can be used on a more general input.

In Paper [14] the authors also make use of a cost function distinguishing between the fidelity of the resulting and desired quantum states, not the probability of finding each basis state upon measurement. Next to that they do not built up the learned circuits using quantum gates native to a chosen quantum computer, meaning that their resulting circuits would still need to be decomposed into native gates before they can be run on a physical quantum device.

2 Problem Description

Given a function $f(x) : \mathbb{C}^{2^n} \to \mathbb{R}_+^{2^n}$, where we assume $\|x\|_2 = 1$ and $\|f(x)\|_1 = 1$, we want to find a quantum circuit $U(\Theta)$, such that $|\langle i| U(\Theta) |x\rangle|^2 \approx f(x)_i$ for all $i \in \{0, 1, \dots, 2^n - 1\}$. Here, $|i\rangle$ represents a computational basis state for the space $\mathbb{C}^{2^n}$. Our method works equally well with any orthonormal choice of basis, we have chosen the computational basis for readability. In this paper we describe our method to learn such a quantum circuit $U(\Theta)$, which can be used to mimic probabilistic operations and search operations.

2.1 Probabilistic Operations

Definition 1. *Let $g : \mathbb{C}^N \to S$ be a probabilistic operation, where $S := \{0, 1, \ldots, N-1\}$ and we restrict the input vectors to $x \in \mathbb{C}^N$ such that $\|x\|_2 = 1$. The probabilistic operation g takes input $x \in \mathbb{C}^N$ and returns i with probability p_i.*

Notice that a probabilistic operation is not a function, as the same input can give different outputs. We can use g to create a function f, for which $f(x)_i = p_i$. We can then use our approach to find the quantum circuit $U(\Theta)$, that acts on $n = \lceil \log_2(N) \rceil$ qubits, for which $|\langle i| U(\Theta) |x\rangle|^2 \approx f(x)_i$ holds. Let $|i\rangle$ represent $i \in S$, then applying such a circuit $U(\Theta)$, followed by a measurement in the computational basis, acts precisely like g on an input state in the space $\mathbb{C}^{2^n}$.

An example of a probabilistic operation is the application of a quantum circuit V on a quantum state $|\phi\rangle$, followed by a measurement in a predetermined basis. This implies that our approach can be used to find a circuit $U(\Theta)$, that simulates the behaviour of any chosen quantum circuit V followed by a measurement. Since we limit our approach to learn the correct circuit up to measurement in a predetermined basis, we can find thinner circuits than theoretically possible[2] when finding a decomposition for a quantum circuit into native gates.

Seeing a quantum circuit as a probabilistic operation can be particularly useful for hybrid quantum computing, where a subroutine is run on a quantum computer and its resulting measurement used in the remainder of the routine.

2.2 Search Operations

Definition 2. *A search operation $h(x) : \mathbb{C}^N \to S$, with $S := \{0, 1, \ldots, N-1\}$, is such that it returns a result $i \in \mathcal{M}_x$, where $\mathcal{M}_x \subseteq S$ is the set of solution states for the given input x. When two solution states k and l are in the same set of possible outcomes $\mathcal{M}_x$, we say they are equivalent under x. For the search operation the probabilities of returning each specific state is irrelevant as long as the state returned is in the set $\mathcal{M}_x$.*

Notice that a search operation is also not a function as it can return different states for the same input, as long as they are equivalent under the input. We can then use h to create a function f, such that

$$f(x)_i = \begin{cases} \frac{1}{|\mathcal{M}_x|} & \text{for } i \text{ in } \mathcal{M}_x \\ 0 & \text{otherwise.} \end{cases}$$

Subsequently we employ our approach to find a quantum circuit $U(\Theta)$, such that $|\langle i| U(\Theta) |x\rangle|^2 \approx f(x)_i$. Note that we could choose any other function $\tilde{f}$

---

[2] An example of this is the Hadamard gate H. There are multiple textbook decompositions into rotation operations, all requiring 3 rotations, an example is $H = e^{\frac{i\pi}{2}} R_Z\left(\frac{\pi}{2}\right) R_X\left(\frac{\pi}{2}\right) R_Z\left(\frac{\pi}{2}\right)$. When the application of H is followed by a measurement in the computational basis, however, it suffices to apply $\tilde{H} = R_Z\left(\frac{\pi}{2}\right) R_X\left(\frac{\pi}{2}\right)$ to the qubits instead.

to describe our search operation h, as long as $\tilde{f}(x)_i$ exclusively returns nonzero values for $i \in \mathcal{M}_x$

An example of a search operation is Grover's search algorithm [23]. Here the goal is to identify a non-zero index i of a given binary vector y. In the problem the size N and Hamming weight[3] t of the vector y are assumed to be known. Furthermore access to an oracle function $\mathcal{O}_y$ is assumed. One can translate this to a search operation by translating the binary vectors y to an input state $s \in \mathbb{C}^N$ and subsequently returning a basis state representing an index i for which $x_i = 1$. In Subsect. 6.2 we go into further detail of Grover's search operation and explain how to uniquely translate a binary vector y to a corresponding input state s.

2.3 Properties of Quantum Computers Considered

We restrict possible ansatzes to have a predetermined depth and to be built up from gates native to the chosen quantum computer between physically connected qubits. These restrictions are implemented to ensure that the found circuits $U(\Theta)$ will be directly executable on near term quantum devices. We implemented a Python program to randomly create such ansatzes with a predetermined number of qubits n and circuit depth D, for a chosen quantum hardware.

An example of such a native gate set used in our study is $\{R_X(\pm\frac{\pi}{2}), R_Z(\theta),$ CZ, XY$(\theta)\}$, which is the set of native gates used by Rigetti [17, 18]. We also consider the IBM [1] and Quantum Inspire [3] native gate sets which are $\{R_X(\frac{\pi}{2}),$ $R_X(\pi), R_Z(\theta),$ CNOT$\}$ and $\{R_X(\theta), R_Y(\theta), R_Z(\theta),$ CZ$\}$, respectively.

Some native gates on a quantum computer are parameterized, meaning that the created ansatz $U(\Theta)$ has continuous variables Θ to optimize. The vector $\Theta \in [0, 2\pi)^{|\Theta|}$ consists of the parameters θ of the parameterized quantum gates in the ansatz. In this paper we optimize over the quantum gate parameters. In future work we plan to extend our method to include optimization approaches for the discrete problem of determining which gates to apply to the qubits.

Note that when we use our quantum circuit generation approach in combination with a physical quantum computer or noisy simulator, we automatically take noise into account. This implies that we might find quantum circuits which have a slight offset on paper but perform better in practice when run on real hardware. In this way our approach is particularly well suited for the NISQ era.

3 Cost Function

In order to distinguish the goodness of fit of a certain quantum circuit $U(\Theta)$, we use the following cost function:

$$C(U(\Theta), \mathcal{S}) = \frac{1}{|\mathcal{S}|} \sum_{|\phi\rangle \in \mathcal{S}} \|f(|\phi\rangle) - f_{U(\Theta)}(|\phi\rangle)\|_2. \tag{1}$$

---

[3] The Hamming weight of a binary vector equals the amount of nonzero indices.

Here, $\mathcal{S} = \{|\phi_0\rangle, \ldots, |\phi_{l-1}\rangle\}$ is the batch of input states considered for the training. The function f expresses the desired behaviour as described in Sect. 2 and $f_{U(\Theta)}$ is defined as in [7]:

$$f_{U(\Theta)}(|\phi\rangle) = \left(|\langle i|U(\Theta)|\phi\rangle|^2 \right)_{i=0,\ldots,2^n-1}, \tag{2}$$

where $U(\Theta)$ is the quantum circuit to be created. Notice that our cost function is defined over the probabilities of finding each basis state after applying the circuit $U(\Theta)$ to the quantum states $|\phi\rangle \in \mathcal{S}$. We stress that our cost function does not distinguish between two quantum states which are distinct, but will lead to the same measurement outcomes in the chosen basis.

Since we define our cost function over the resulting probability vectors of applying our learned circuit to the quantum states in the batch $\mathcal{S}$ and subsequently performing a measurement, we do not need expressions for the resulting quantum states $U(\Theta)|\phi\rangle$ or the created circuit $U(\Theta)$. Only the vectors $f_{U(\Theta)}(|\phi\rangle)$ are required, and these can be estimated by performing measurements in the chosen basis after performing the circuit $U(\Theta)$ to the input states $|\phi\rangle$.

As we learn over a batch of possible input quantum states and their associated measurement results, it is also not necessary to have a known expression or quantum circuit for the "perfect" quantum operation V. In fact, a quantum operation which perfectly performs our chosen probabilistic or search operation need not even exist for our method to work. This feature makes our approach widely applicable as we are not limited to learning quantum circuits we can already (theoretically) perform. This is one of the outstanding features of our approach we wish to highlight.

A common choice of function to evaluate the distance between two probability vectors is the Kullback-Leibler divergence [15]:

$$D_{\mathrm{KL}}(f|f_{U(\Theta)}) = \sum_{i=1}^{2^n-1} f(|\phi\rangle)_i \log \frac{f(|\phi\rangle)_i}{f_{U(\Theta)}(|\phi\rangle)_i}. \tag{3}$$

Note that our cost function (1) is relatively cheap compared to the Kullback-Leibler divergence. Taking the logarithm is an expensive operation, and since in our use cases many indices $f(|\phi\rangle)_i$ will have value 0 we will need to replace those with a small value ϵ to avoid NaNs. These properties make our cost function more suited for the chosen application than the Kullback-Leibler divergence.

Our cost function takes the 2-norm between the found probability distribution and the sought after probability distribution. Therefore the outcome of our cost function is not directly informative, as its value is influenced by the number of qubits n and the chosen batch $\mathcal{S}$ to learn over. This implies that we cannot use its value as a measure for the goodness of fit of the quantum circuit $U(\Theta)$. However, our cost function is suited to distinguish between good and bad ansatzes and parameter values Θ, and is therefore a good choice for practical use.

4 Determining Ansatzes

As described in Sect. 2, we only consider ansatzes composed of hardware native gates and respecting the sparse connectivity of qubits.

In the current approach we create a random ansatz $U(\Theta)$ of predetermined depth D and number of qubits n for a chosen quantum hardware, with the ansatz restricted to the native gate set and hardware topology. We subsequently optimize the parameters Θ to determine the value of the cost function $C(U(\Theta),\mathcal{S})$ as given in (1) for a batch of input states $\mathcal{S}$ of predetermined size $|\mathcal{S}|$. Figure 1 illustrates such a random ansatz $U(\Theta)$ and a zoom in of a single layer. We create a large amount of random ansatzes and optimize their continuous parameters Θ as described in Sect. 5, from which we determine the best one afterwards.

In this paper we focus on the optimization of the continuous parameters Θ for a fixed U. As subject of ongoing research we are currently working on adding layers of discrete optimization to our method. In the current method, using the computational basis, we have made use of certain rules such as that any R_Z or CZ gate appearing right before measurement falls away.

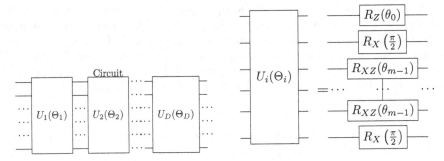

(a) Quantum circuit representing the found valid ansatz of which the unitary operations are built up using only natively implemented quantum gates

(b) An example of a valid layer U_i for an IBM quantum computer, where all the gates used are natively implemented on the specified hardware

Fig. 1. Representation of a random quantum ansatz $U(\Theta)$

5 Optimization of Continuous Parameters

Once we have created a hardware-centric ansatz for our quantum circuit $U(\Theta)$, we need to optimize the continuous parameters Θ. In this work we consider two different optimization approaches to find the optimal value of Θ, one non-gradient based approach called Particle Swarm Optimization (PSO) and one gradient-based optimization approach.

5.1 Particle Swarm Optimization

Particle Swarm Optimization (PSO) is an evolutionary meta-heuristic which mimics swarm intelligence to find a point of minimal cost in a large scale space. In this paper the particles Θ represent an instance of the parameter vector, therefore our particles live in a $|\Theta|$ dimensional hypercube $\Theta \in [0, 2\pi)^{|\Theta|}$. In each iteration i of the scheme the particles Θ move through the parameter space and their velocity v_j is subsequently updated:

$$v_j^{i+1} = \omega v_j^i + c_1 (p_j - \Theta_j) + c_2 (\Theta_{\text{opt}} - \Theta_j). \tag{4}$$

Here Θ_{opt}, p_j and Θ_j are parameters which are updated in each iteration, whereas ω, c_1 and c_2 are hyperparameters determined beforehand. The parameter Θ_{opt} represents the best position in space found by any particle so far and the parameter p_j represents the best position found by the particle j. The hyperparameter ω represents the inertia coefficient, i.e. the particles unwillingness to change direction. The hyperparameter c_1 is the memory coefficient which determines how heavily past success influences the direction the particle travels in. Finally, c_2 is the social coefficient which represents how heavily the best location in space found by any particle influences the velocity in the next iteration.

By iteratively running this scheme for many particles, all the Θ_j will slowly cluster together at a point in space $\tilde{\Theta}$ which represents a (global) minimum. As PSO is a meta-heuristic it cannot give any guarantees that a minimum will be found. Our results presented in Sect. 6 show that PSO performs very well for the different test cases considered in this paper. For our implementation of the non-gradient based approach we used PySwarms version 1.3.0 [6].

5.2 Gradient-Based Optimization

As an alternative to the PSO approach we utilized a gradient-based optimization method to find the optimal parameters Θ of the quantum circuit U.

In this case we optimize the circuit parameters Θ by calculating the gradient of the cost function (1), with respect to θ, where θ is the i-th index of Θ. We then update Θ in the direction of the negative gradients:

$$\Theta = \Theta - l \nabla c (\Theta). \tag{5}$$

In the above equation l is a hyperparameter which represents the learning rate. As there are $|\Theta|$ input parameters and only one output parameter, backpropagation is used to calculate the gradients in a computationally efficient way. To calculate the gradients, set $\hat{Z}_i := |i\rangle \langle i|$ to get the following equality:

$$\langle \hat{Z}_i \rangle_{U(\Theta)} = f_{U(\Theta)}(|\phi\rangle)_i. \tag{6}$$

Here $\langle \hat{Z}_i \rangle_{U(\Theta)}$ is the expectation value of the observable $\hat{Z}_i$ upon measurement of $U(\Theta) |\phi\rangle$. It follows that the cost function can be expressed as the expectation value of the observable $\hat{Z}_i$, of which the gradient can be calculated as shown in the Paper by Schuld et al. [19]. Gradients of an expectation value of an observable with respect to θ can be evaluated on a quantum computer directly. Let us define:

$$U(\Theta) = V(\Theta_0^{i-1})G(\theta_i)W(\Theta_{i+1}^{|\Theta|}) = VG(\theta_i)W. \tag{7}$$

In the above equation $G(\theta_i)$ represents the layer which only consists of the quantum gate depending on the parameter θ_i. Furthermore we set $|\phi'\rangle = W|\phi\rangle$ and $\hat{Q}_i = V^\dagger \hat{Z}_i V$, note that $\hat{Q}_i$ is still an observable.[4]

For all native gates except $XY(\theta)$ considered in this paper the partial derivative with respect to θ_i can be calculated using the following equality [19]:

$$\partial_{\theta_i} f(\Theta) = \frac{r}{2} \left\langle \phi' | G^\dagger \left(\theta_i + \frac{\pi}{4r} \right) \hat{Q}_i G \left(\theta_i + \frac{\pi}{4r} \right) | \phi' \right\rangle$$
$$- \frac{r}{2} \left\langle \phi' | G^\dagger \left(\theta_i - \frac{\pi}{4r} \right) \hat{Q}_i G \left(\theta_i - \frac{\pi}{4r} \right) | \phi' \right\rangle. \tag{8}$$

In the above equation r is a constant that depends on the operation $G(\theta)$ of which we determine the derivative. Since $XY(\theta)$ has more than two distinct eigenvalues $\pm r$, we need a different technique to calculate the gradients. This can either be accomplished by using the second method presented by Schuld et al. [19], or using the method presented by Banchi and Crooks in [20].

The partial derivative of the cost function with respect to θ_i, $\partial_{\theta_i} f(\Theta)$, can be evaluated on a classical computer in combination with backpropagation [21].

For our implementation of the gradient based optimization approach we made use of PyTorch version 1.10.0 [4] and Pennylane version 0.19.1 [5].

6   Results

In this section we demonstrate the performance of our approach in generating executable quantum circuits that mimic probabilistic operations and search operations. We first use our quantum circuit generator to mimic a probabilistic operation we have named thin circuit. We subsequently use our approach to generate a quantum circuit to mimic the amplitude amplification step of Grover's search algorithm, which is a search operation as described in Subsect. 2.2.

6.1   Thin Circuit

The first test for our machine learning approach is to learn the function f, where $f : \mathbb{C}^{2^n} \to \mathbb{R}_+^{2^n}$ and $f(|x\rangle) = |\langle i| A |x\rangle|^2$, here

$$A := \begin{cases} (X \otimes H)^{\otimes \frac{n}{2}}, & \text{for } n \text{ even} \\ (X \otimes H)^{\otimes \frac{n-1}{2}} \otimes X, & \text{for } n \text{ odd}. \end{cases} \tag{9}$$

---

[4] An observable is a Hermitian matrix, multiplying a Hermitian matrix from both sides with some unitary V results in a Hermitian matrix $Q = V^\dagger \hat{Z} V$. In this case, since $\hat{Z}_i = |i\rangle\langle i|$ we get $\hat{Q}_i = V^\dagger \hat{Z}_i V = |\xi\rangle\langle\xi|$, where $|\xi\rangle$ is some quantum state.

In the above expression, H is the Hadamard and X the NOT gate.

Using our approach we were able to find a decomposition $U(\Theta)$ using only two layers $U_i(\Theta_i)$ where $i \in \{1, 2\}$, whereas the theoretical decomposition requires three layers. This has to do with our choice of the cost function. Our generated quantum circuit creates the same size amplitudes for each possible outcome state, but with a relative phase shift between the states.

After using our approach to find a circuit for $n = 2$, we extrapolated this circuit to $n \in \{5, 8, 10, 20\}$ and optimized those instances. With PSO we were able to find optimal quantum circuits for all instances. Our gradient-based approach was able to find optimal quantum circuits for $n \in \{2, 5, 8\}$, for larger n we ran into the issue of barren plateaus. In the literature barren plateaus have been shown to occur for growing circuit depths [22], as well as when the number of qubits grows [8]. Using PSO, our approach was able to correctly optimize the created quantum circuit, with a cost function defined over a batch as small as $|\mathcal{S}| = 2$ for $n \in \{2, 5, 8, 10, 20\}$. This shows that in certain cases we are able to find the right results, while optimizing over a subspace much smaller then theoretically required to span the space. Our gradient-based approach was able to optimize the quantum circuit for batch sizes as small as $|\mathcal{S}| = 2$ for $n \in \{2, 5\}$, a batch of size $|\mathcal{S}| = 4$ was required to correctly optimize the circuit for $n = 8$.

6.2   Grover's Search

Next we use our approach to learn a circuit $U(\Theta)$ to mimic the amplitude amplification step of Grover's search algorithm [23]. Grover's search algorithm can be used to find the non-zero indices of a binary vector x of length N and Hamming weight t, assuming that access to the oracle $\mathcal{O}_x$ is provided. The oracle $\mathcal{O}_x$ is defined as follows: Let $|i\rangle$ be a computational basis state, then $\mathcal{O}_x |i\rangle = (-1)^{x_i} |i\rangle$. Furthermore it is assumed that N and t are known to the user.

In this paper we restrict ourselves to finding circuits for the amplitude amplification step of Grover's search algorithm for vectors x with $t = \frac{N}{4}$. We restrict ourselves to this case, as it is such that the amplitude amplification step of Grover's search algorithms only requires one query to the oracle.

To summarise, we try to find a quantum circuit $U(\Theta)$ that mimics:

$$f(\mathcal{O}_x |+\rangle)_i = \begin{cases} \frac{1}{t}, & \text{if } x_i = 1, \\ 0, & \text{otherwise,} \end{cases} \tag{10}$$

with $i \in \{0, 1, \dots, N-1\}$ for all possible inputs $x \in \text{bin}(N, t)$, where $\text{bin}(N, t)$ is the set of binary vectors of length N with Hamming weight t. Since we are working in a space of size N, we require $n = \log_2(N)$ qubits. In (10) the quantum state $|+\rangle$ is defined as $|+\rangle := H^{\otimes n} |0\rangle$.

Let us define the states $|\phi_x\rangle := \mathcal{O}_x |+\rangle$, which represent the quantum state reached in Grover's search algorithm after applying the oracle function. In our approach we learn over the batch $\mathcal{S}_{N,t} = \{|\phi_x\rangle\}$, for $x \in \text{bin}(N, t)$. By learning over $\mathcal{S}_{N,t}$ we find a $U(\theta)$, which can be used as the amplitude amplification step in Grover's search algorithms for problems with size N and Hamming weight t.

We first use our approach to find circuits to mimic the amplitude amplification step for the case $N = 4$ and $t = 1$. Using the IBM native gate set we were able to find a circuit of depth $D = 4$ that solves the problem with certainty, whereas the textbook circuit compiled by the IBM toolchain gives rise to a circuit of depth $D = 14$. For the Rigetti native gate our approach found a circuit of depth $D = 2$ that solves the problem with certainty. On the other hand, the textbook circuit compiled using Rigetti's toolchain [2] results in a quantum circuit of depth 10. For the Starmon 5 quantum processor available through the Quantum Inspire cloud service we were able to find a quantum circuit with depth $D = 3$ that solves the problem with certainty. As we do not have access to the compiled version of the textbook circuit, we compare our result with a theoretical decomposition which suggests it would have a depth $D = 7$.

This shows that our method can lead to a significantly thinner quantum circuits, while still finding the correct quantum state upon measurement with certainty. Figure 2 depicts the textbook circuit compiled for Rigetti and its counterpart produced by our quantum circuit generation approach. In what follows, we will use the abbreviation QCG whenever we refer to our approach.

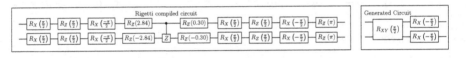

Fig. 2. Example of executable quantum circuits for the 2-qubit amplitude amplification step of Grover's search algorithm. Left: compiled textbook circuit. Right: QCG circuit

For the amplitude amplification step of Grover's search algorithm with $N = 8$ we were able to create significantly thinner circuits for both the IBM and Rigetti native gate sets. For instance, the QCG circuit has depth 8, whereas the textbook circuit compiled with the Rigetti compiler [2] consists of 63 layers. It needs to be stressed that these QCG created circuits do not return the correct result with certainty, the probabilities of returning the correct results are around 55 percent. This appears to be a result of the known barren plateau issue in quantum machine learning training landscapes [8,22]. We plan to combat this issue in future work, by adding layers of discrete optimization.

7   Experimental Results on Quantum Computers

In this section we present a representative selection of experimental results that were obtained by executing the QCG circuits on physical quantum computers. We compare the measurement outcomes with that of textbook circuits, which were turned into executable circuits with the help of the vendor toolchains.

7.1   Rigetti - Aspen 10

The Rigetti Aspen 10 quantum computer has a total of 32 qubits. We used this computer to test and compare the results of the generated and textbook version of the thin circuit operation and amplitude amplification step of Grover's search.

For the thin circuit example, Fig. 3a shows that the QCG circuit outperforms the compiled textbook circuit as the number of qubits grows, though the overall result becomes dominated by noise in both cases. Figure 3b shows that the QCG version of the amplitude amplification step of Grover's search returns the correct result with a slightly higher percentage then the compiled textbook circuit.

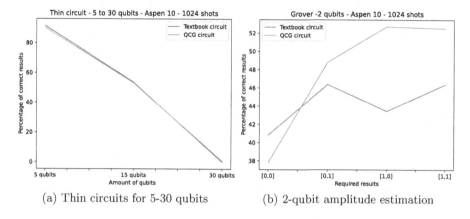

(a) Thin circuits for 5-30 qubits   (b) 2-qubit amplitude estimation

Fig. 3. Performance comparison between compiled textbook circuits and circuits created with our QCG approach for the Rigetti Aspen 10 quantum computer

7.2   IBM - Lima and Manila

The IBM Lima and Manila machines are open access quantum computers which both have 5 qubits available. We used the IBM Lima computer to compare the results of our QCG circuits with that of the compiled textbook thin circuit for 5 qubits. We used the IBM Manila computer to compare the results of our QCG amplitude amplification step of Grover's search for 2 qubits to the compiled textbook circuit. The results of these runs are shown in Fig. 4. It can be seen that in both cases the QCG circuits performs slightly better.

7.3   Quantum Inspire - Starmon 5

The Quantum Inspire Starmon 5 is an open access quantum computer with 5 qubits available. In contrast to IBM and Rigetti, Quantum Inspire does not provide a full software stack that decomposes a given quantum circuit into one that can be run on the hardware. Here the benefit of our approach is particularly apparent as any found QCG circuit can always be directly applied to the

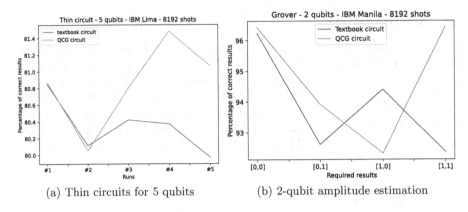

(a) Thin circuits for 5 qubits   (b) 2-qubit amplitude estimation

Fig. 4. Performance comparison between compiled textbook circuits and circuits created with our QCG approach for the IBM Lima and Manila quantum computers

hardware. Using our quantum circuit generation method we learned a quantum circuit to mimic the thin circuit operation for 5 qubits and the amplitude amplification step of Grover's search for 2 qubits. We note that for the Quantum Inspire results we exclusively made use of the non-gradient based PSO approach.

Upon running and comparing the thin circuit results, using both our QCG circuit and a textbook circuit that we turned into an executable circuit by hand using theoretical decompositions and manual qubit placement, we found that the probability of finding one of the correct basis states upon measurement remained equal. However, our generated circuit results in a much more even spread of the possible basis states to be found upon measurement, as is desired. This shows that our method can lead to more reliable quantum circuits; see Fig. 5a.

In Fig. 5b we compare the outcomes of running the textbook circuit of the amplitude amplification step of Grover's search on the Starmon 5 with that of the QCG circuit. Here the QCG circuit performs overall significantly better.

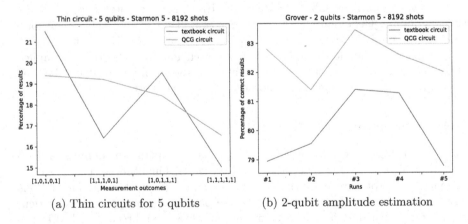

(a) Thin circuits for 5 qubits   (b) 2-qubit amplitude estimation

Fig. 5. Performance comparison between compiled textbook circuits and circuits created with our QCG approach for the Quantum Inspire Starmon 5 quantum computer

8   Discussion

In this paper we have presented a method to make use of NISQ devices, by implementing machine learning methods to learn circuits for mimicking probabilistic and search operations. To this end, we introduced a cost function that only distinguishes between finding the correct basis states upon measurement.

We have shown that our method can be successfully implemented with both gradient-based and non-gradient based machine learning to create thin quantum circuits, which behave as desired. The created quantum circuits are thinner then their compiled textbook counterparts and can lead to more stable results when executed on physical quantum computers. In doing so we have shown the potential of our cost function for generating quantum circuits.

At the current stage, our method is restricted to work on quantum circuits for relatively small numbers of qubits and circuit depth. This is due to the barren plateau issue known in quantum machine learning approaches. In further research we will extend our approach by implementing a discrete optimization method to circumvent the barren plateau issue.

Acknowledgment. This research used resources of the Oak Ridge Leadership Computing Facility, which is a DOE Office of Science User Facility supported under Contract DE-AC05-00OR22725. We also wish to express our gratitude to IBM and Quantum Inspire for making their quantum computers available online for public use. Furthermore the authors thank David de Laat for his useful ideas, fruitful discussions and valuable feedback on the manuscript.

References

1. IBM Quantum (2021). https://quantum-computing.ibm.com/
2. Smith, R.S., Curtis, M.J., Zeng, W.J.: A practical quantum instruction set architecture (2016)
3. QuTech: Quantum Inspire Home. Retrieved from Quantum Inspire (2018). https://www.quantum-inspire.com/
4. Paszke, A., et al.: PyTorch: an imperative style, high-performance deep learning library (2019)
5. Bergholm, V., et al.: PennyLane: automatic differentiation of hybrid quantum-classical computations (2020)
6. Miranda, L.J.V.: PySwarms: a research toolkit for Particle Swarm Optimization in Python. J. Open Sour. Softw. **3**, 433 (2018)
7. Adarsh, S., Möller, M.: Resource optimal executable quantum circuit generation using approximate computing (2021)
8. Khatri, S., LaRose, R., Poremba, A., Cincio, L., Sornborger, A.T., Coles, P.J.: Quantum-assisted quantum compiling. Quantum **3**, 140 (2019)
9. Cincio, L., Rudinger, K., Sarovar, M., Coles, P.J.: Machine learning of noise-resilient quantum circuits (2020)
10. Davis, M.G., Smith, E., Tudor, A., Sen, K., Siddiqi, I., Iancu, C.: Heuristics for quantum compiling with a continuous gate set (2019)
11. Benedetti, M., et al.: A generative modeling approach for benchmarking and training shallow quantum circuits (2019)

322   M. A. Schalkers and M. Möller

12. Zhu, D., et al.: Training of quantum circuits on a hybrid quantum computer (2019)
13. Liu, J.-G., Wang, L.: Differentiable learning of quantum circuit born machine (2018)
14. Martinez, E.A., Monz, T., Nigg, D., Schindler, P., Blatt, R., et al.: Compiling quantum algorithms for architectures with multi-qubit gates. New J. Phys. **18**, 063029 (2016)
15. Nielsen, M., Chuang, I.: Quantum computation and quantum information (2000)
16. Preskill, J.: Quantum computing in the NISQ era and beyond. Quantum J. **2**, 79 (2018)
17. Abrams, D.M., Didier, N., Johnson, B.R., da Silva, M.P., Ryan, C.A.: Implementation of the XY interaction family with calibration of single pulse (2019)
18. Murali, P., Linke, N.M., Martonosi, M., Abhari, A.J., Nguyen, N.H., Alderete, C.H.: Full-stack, real-system quantum computer studies: architectural comparisons and design insights (2019)
19. Schuld, M., Bergholm, V., Gogolin, C., Izaac, J., Killoran, N.: Evaluating analytic gradients on quantum hardware (2018)
20. Banchi, L., Crooks, G.E.: Measuring analytic gradients of general quantum evolution with the stochastic parameter shift rule (2021)
21. Goodfellow, I., Bengio, Y., Courville, A.: Deep learning (2016)
22. McClean, J.R., Boixo, S., Smelyanskiy, V.N., Babbush, R., Neven, H.: Barren plateaus in quantum neural network training landscapes (2018)
23. Grover, L.K.: A fast quantum mechanical algorithm for database search (1996)

A Quantum Approach for Tactical Capacity Management of Distributed Electricity Generation

Frank Phillipson[1,2]([✉]) [iD] and Irina Chiscop[1]

[1] TNO, The Hague, The Netherlands
frank.phillipson@tno.nl
[2] Maastricht University, Maastricht, The Netherlands

Abstract. Matching electricity demand and supply by decentralised generators will be very important in the near future, where more and more electricity has to be produced sustainably. Optimisation problems that address this problem often have quadratic objective functions or constraints, due to the quadratic nature of energy loss. Where classical solvers struggle with quadratic, often integer or binary, optimisation problems, quantum computing (inspired) solvers are well equipped for this kind of problems. In this paper, we present such an optimisation problem and the performance of the quantum annealer in solving this problem, in comparison with classical methods and commercial solvers. We show that the hybrid, quantum-classical, solvers provided by D-Wave can outperform classical solvers despite the small-scale of the available quantum hardware.

Keywords: Hybrid quantum computing · Smart energy and home control · Tactical planning · Distributed electricity generation

1 Introduction

The demand for energy and provisioning of electricity networks will change dramatically in the coming years due to the rise of distributed generation (DG) of electricity, such as wind turbine, photovoltaic cells, micro (gas) turbines, small hydro-power stations and due to the use of heat pumps and electric vehicles. Since most DGs rely on exploitation of natural sources of energy, they exhibit high fluctuations in production over time. For example, a wind turbine produces more energy when there is more wind. However, when a storm produces too much wind, the turbines are shut off for safety reasons. Hence, the maximum power supply goes from the maximum to zero in a non-continuous fashion. Of course this does not just happen for one turbine, but for all the turbines on the 'wind-farm' at the same time, giving enormous local fluctuation. See for example Fig. 4 in [31]. This means that electricity generated by DGs will probably not match demand and can cause over- or underproduction of electricity at certain points in time. Both the peaks in production and in demand will demand a lot from the network infrastructure. The current technological solution to solve possible transport problems is to reinforce the existing grid [4,11] or add, the right amount of, storage capacity [14,19]. This is very expensive and has to be avoided as much as possible. Another solution, still in development, is to make the grid smarter by controlling fluctuations in production and consumption, using smart grids and production planning [7,16,17]. Next to this, many trials have been done on managing the behaviour of customers, as in [8,22,33]. However, before we do grid reinforcements and create smart grids that can perform sophisticated load balancing, we should perform tactical capacity management. One should have some idea about the global demand and supply characteristics and perform tactical planning: try to find the optimal mix of DGs while keeping network capacities in mind. Also in an operational environment, one could be interested in the optimal configuration of the network to fulfil the electricity demand, network balance and preventing overload, by switching on or off specific DG equipment.

The authors of [6] provide an approach for tactical capacity management. A Mixed Integer Quadratic Programming (MIQP) problem is proposed, having binary variables and a quadratic objective function due to the loss function. There the observation is made that MIQP problems are in general hard to solve and often [5,10,21] the choice is made to reduce the problem size, to relax the binary variables or to linearise the quadratic objective function. Also, researchers have proposed different methodologies for optimal DG placement, which can be classified as Artificial Intelligence (AI) Meta-heuristics, Analytical methods, and Hybrid approaches [29]. Each of these techniques has its own merits and demerits [1].

In recent years, a new computation paradigm has emerged: quantum computing. Already in the current, early stage, quantum computers seem to be useful for optimisation problems using Quantum Approximate Optimisation Algorithm (QAOA)[30] or quantum annealing (or adiabatic quantum computing) [20]. Both QAOA and quantum annealing are especially useful for quadratic binary optimisation and would soon be able to compete with traditional quadratic optimisation solvers, using the QUBO (Quadratic Unconstrained Binary Optimisation) or Ising formulation, which are equivalent [18]. We are now in the stage where real life problems are starting to be solved by these solutions, for example in traffic and logistic problems, as shown in [9,13,23,28]. Some examples from the energy domain can be found in [2,24,27,32].

In this paper we present a QUBO problem formulation for the 'Quadratic Tactical Capacity Management' (QTCM) problem. For this, we introduce quantum annealing and the QUBO problem formulation in Sect. 2. Next, in Sect. 3, the mathematical formulation of this QTCM problem is given and translated into the QUBO problem formulation. We show the performance of this formulation using an example. Both the example and the performance analysis are presented in Sect. 4. In Sect. 5 some discussion and ideas for further research complete this work.

2   Quantum Annealing

Quantum Annealing [15] or Adiabatic Quantum Computation [3] is based on the idea that is quite distinct from the gate-based quantum computing model. Whereas in the latter a computation is encoded into a series of quantum gates, in quantum annealing the computation proceeds from an initial Hamiltonian whose ground state is easy to prepare, to a final Hamiltonian whose ground state encodes the solution to the computational problem. The challenge is to formulate the computational problem in such a way that this minimum energy ground state corresponds to the solution of your original problem. The most advanced implementation of this paradigm is the D-Wave quantum annealer[1].

The main input of the D-Wave quantum annealer is an Ising Hamiltonian or its binary equivalent, the QUBO formulation. The QUBO problem [12] is expressed by the optimisation problem:

$$\text{QUBO:} \quad \min_{x \in \{0,1\}^n} x^t Q x, \tag{1}$$

where $x \in \{0,1\}^n$ are the decision variables and Q is a $n \times n$ coefficient matrix. QUBO problems belong to the class of NP-hard problems [18]. For a large number of combinatorial optimisation problems, an equivalent QUBO representation is known [12,18]. Many constrained integer programming problems can easily be transformed into a QUBO representation. This QUBO can then be embedded on the hardware of the quantum annealer to then get solved by searching for the minimum energy state.

D-Wave also offers hybrid, meaning a combination of quantum and classical techniques, solvers, where both classical and quantum resources are used to solve problems, exploiting the complementary strengths that each provides. These solvers, which implement state-of-the-art classical algorithms together with intelligent allocation of the quantum processing unit to parts of the problem where it benefits most, are designed to accommodate even very large problems, up to 1 million variables, where the sole Quantum Processing Unit (QPU) can solve problems in the 600- to 800-variable range [25].

3   Problem Formulation

The problem under consideration in this paper is a tactical planning problem, assigning types of distributed generators to houses, such that the energy loss is minimised. Note that import and export of energy to a housing district means the electricity has to travel a longer distance, thus generates a higher loss. Minimising the energy loss thus indirectly minimises the mismatch between demand and supply.

We propose using the following model, of which the used notation is shown in Table 1. Assume we have M types of generators, N houses in a specific neighbourhood and T time intervals. We can assign generators to houses using the

---

[1] www.dwavesys.com.

Table 1. List of variables, sets and parameters

Variable	Description
x_{ij}^u	$\begin{cases} 1 & \text{if house } i \text{ is equipped generator of type } j, \\ 0 & \text{otherwise, } i \in \{1,\ldots,N\}, j \in \{1,\ldots,M\} \end{cases}$
Parameter	**Description**
M	Number of types of generators
N	Number of houses in a specific neighbourhood
T	Number of time intervals in the analysis
s_{ijt}	Amount of electricity that house i produces using generator of type j in time interval t
d_{it}	Demand of house i in time interval t
I_{it}	Amount of electricity that has to be imported from the grid for house i in in time interval t
O_{it}	Amount of electricity that can be released to the grid for house i in time interval t
S_t	Resulting amount of electricity of neighbourhood in time interval t

variable $x_{ij} = 1$, if house i gets a distributed generator of type j, and $x_{ij} = 0$ otherwise. Important in electricity networks is that demand and supply are equal all the time. This leads to the following constraints. If house i has a generator of type j, it will generate s_{ijt} units of electricity in time interval t. If this amount of generated electricity is less than the demand d_{it} of house i in time interval t, an amount I_{it} has to be imported from the grid. Otherwise, an amount O_{it} is released to the grid. For each house and each time interval this must hold:

$$\sum_{j=1}^{M} s_{ijt} x_{ij} + I_{it} = d_{it} + O_{it} \quad \forall i, t. \tag{2}$$

Next, for the total neighbourhood also an equilibrium in supply and demand must hold. Because we are only interested in the energy loss due to transportation, it is enough to know how much electricity has to be transported from and to the neighbourhood each time interval S_t. For this we define the constraints:

$$S_t = |\sum_{i=1}^{N} O_{it} - \sum_{i=1}^{N} I_{it}|, \tag{3}$$

which can be translated to

$$S_t \geq \sum_{i=1}^{N} O_{it} - \sum_{i=1}^{N} I_{it}, \tag{4}$$

$$S_t \geq \sum_{i=1}^{N} I_{it} - \sum_{i=1}^{N} O_{it}. \tag{5}$$

There could also be restrictions to the capacity of the streams within the neighbourhood, which we will neglect here, assuming that minimising the (quadratic) loss will avoid large deviations from demand. If we assume transportation loss fraction within the neighbourhood of $p_n = 0.00035$ and outside the neighbourhood of $p_s = 0.00231$ (from [5]), we define the following objective function

$$\min \sum_{i=1}^{N} \sum_{t=1}^{T} p_n O_{it}^2 + p_n I_{it}^2 + \sum_{t=1}^{T} p_s S_t^2. \tag{6}$$

This will minimise the transportation losses within the neighbourhood plus the transportation losses outside the neighbourhood due to import. Variables x_{ij} are binary and O_{it}, I_{it} and S_t are non-negative. This leads to the following optimisation problem.

$$\min \left(\sum_{i=1}^{N} \sum_{t=1}^{T} p_n O_{it}^2 + p_n I_{it}^2 \right) + \sum_{t=1}^{T} p_s S_t^2, \tag{7}$$

$$\text{s.t.} \sum_{j=1}^{M} s_{ijt} x_{ij} + I_{it} = d_{it} + O_{it} \qquad \forall i, t, \tag{8}$$

$$S_t \geq \sum_{i=1}^{N} O_{it} - \sum_{i=1}^{N} I_{it} \qquad \forall t, \tag{9}$$

$$S_t \geq \sum_{i=1}^{N} I_{it} - \sum_{i=1}^{N} O_{it} \qquad \forall t, \tag{10}$$

$$x_{ij} \in \{0, 1\} \qquad \forall i, j, \tag{11}$$

$$O_{it}, I_{it}, S_t \geq 0 \qquad \forall i, t. \tag{12}$$

If we look closely to this formulation, we can assume (by taking the length of interval t small enough) that for a specific (i, t) only one of (O_{it}, I_{it}) will be positive when minimising the objective function. This means we can derive:

$$\sum_{i=1}^{N} \sum_{t=1}^{T} p_n O_{it}^2 + p_n I_{it}^2 = p_n \sum_{i=1}^{N} \sum_{t=1}^{T} O_{it}^2 + I_{it}^2 \tag{13}$$

$$= p_n \sum_{i=1}^{N} \sum_{t=1}^{T} (O_{it} + I_{it})^2 \tag{14}$$

$$= p_n \sum_{i=1}^{N} \sum_{t=1}^{T} (O_{it} - I_{it})^2 \tag{15}$$

$$= p_n \sum_{i=1}^{N} \sum_{t=1}^{T} \left(\sum_{j=1}^{M} s_{ijt} x_{ij} - d_{it} \right)^2, \tag{16}$$

where (14) and (15) follow from the assumption that O_{it} and I_{it} are not both non-zero and (16) follow from substituting (8). For the term $\sum_{t=1}^{T} p_s S_t^2$ we can derive

$$\sum_{t=1}^{T} p_s S_t^2 = p_s \sum_{t=1}^{T} \left| \sum_{i=1}^{N} O_{it} - \sum_{i=1}^{N} I_{it} \right|^2 \tag{17}$$

$$= p_s \sum_{t=1}^{T} \left| \sum_{i=1}^{N} \left(O_{it} - I_{it} \right) \right|^2 \tag{18}$$

$$= p_s \sum_{t=1}^{T} \left(\sum_{i=1}^{N} (O_{it} - I_{it}) \right)^2 \tag{19}$$

$$= p_s \sum_{t=1}^{T} \left(\sum_{i=1}^{N} (\sum_{j=1}^{M} s_{ijt} x_{ij} - d_{it}) \right)^2, \tag{20}$$

where (17) follows from substituting (3) and (20) follows from substituting (8). When we combine this all together, we get

$$\min \left(p_n \sum_{i=1}^{N} \sum_{t=1}^{T} \left(\sum_{j=1}^{M} s_{ijt} x_{ij} - d_{it} \right)^2 \right) + p_s \sum_{t=1}^{T} \left(\sum_{i=1}^{N} (\sum_{j=1}^{M} s_{ijt} x_{ij} - d_{it}) \right)^2, \tag{21}$$

$$x_{ij} \in \{0,1\} \quad \forall i,j, \tag{22}$$

which is a quadratic model that can be directly translated to a QUBO formulation using standard qubo manipulating software [34].

4 Example

We now take a example with $M = 1$, using only solar cells, and look at the performance of the quantum annealer for this problem. The quadratic model, as defined in (21) and (22) then translates to:

$$\min \left(p_n \sum_{i=1}^{N} \sum_{t=1}^{T} \left(s_{it} x_i - d_{it} \right)^2 \right) + p_s \sum_{t=1}^{T} \left(\sum_{i=1}^{N} (s_{it} x_i - d_{it}) \right)^2, \tag{23}$$

$$x_i \in \{0,1\} \quad \forall i. \tag{24}$$

We generated the following data, to be used for s_{it} and d_{it}. The yield of the solar panels (s_{it}) has a certain (fictitious) day profile for south-oriented panels on a non-cloudy summer day. For east and west orientation panels, we use shifted patterns, which are less efficient, see Fig. 1. Profiles for the users, $N = 25$ to $N = 1500$ for various instances, are generated with an orientation between 0 (east) and 1 (west) (meaning 0.5 is south). Based on their orientation, they each receive a pattern somewhere between the extreme values. In this way we get users with

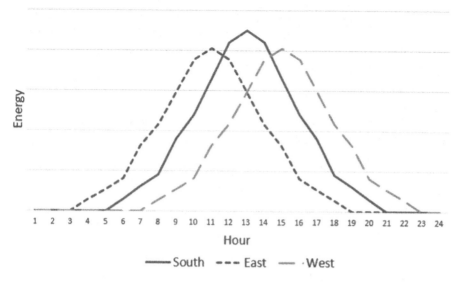

Fig. 1. The three main day profiles for solar panels

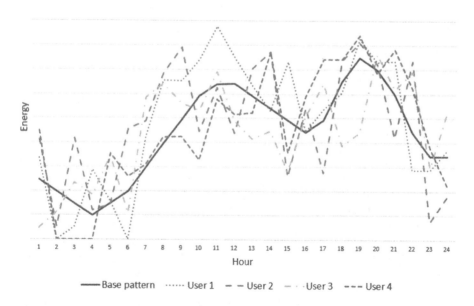

Fig. 2. The base demand pattern together with four examples, sampled from the base pattern

different day-patterns. Same holds for the demand d_{it} for $t = 1, ..., 24$. Here, an energy demand profile is also generated for all users, as deviation from a (ficti-tious) base pattern. In Fig. 2 the base pattern and four user patterns are shown.

We solved the quadratic problem with 3 solvers: Simulated Annealing (SA), the Quantum Annealer (QA) using a hybrid solver and the conventional solvers Gurobi[2] and Local Solver[3]. For SA, we used the D-Wave Neal Sampler[4]. As hybrid solver we used Leap's quantum-classical hybrid BQM solver.[5].

Table 2. Calculation times in seconds for the solvers Gurobi (GU), Local Solver (LS), Simulated Annealing (SA), Quantum Annealing (QA) and the Hybrid Solver. Between brackets is shown the communicated optimality gap at t = 1200 s.

N	GU	LS	SA	QA		Hybrid solver		
				e2e	QPU	e2e	QPU	Run time
25	5 (0%)	2 (6%)	1	6	1.00	9	0.11	3.0
50	4 (0%)	2 (29%)	3	31	1.15	15	0.06	3.0
100	26 (0%)	2 (48%)	6	249	1.42	11	0	3.0
250	–	16 (55%)	37	–	–	12	0.06	3.1
500	–	114 (78%)	207	–	–	13	0.03	3.0
750	–	19 (78%)	405	–	–	25	0.03	3.0
1000	–	407 (79%)	688	–	–	32	0.03	3.0
1500	–	1200 (70%)	2455	–	–	34	0.06	4.1

All solvers find for each case ($N = 25$ to $N = 1500$) the same solution. This means we only have to compare performance, which is shown in Table 2. For Gurobi and LocalSolver we used a maximum computation time of 1200 s and show the timestamp at which the best solution is found. Also we show, in parentheses, the realised optimality gap at 1200 s. Gurobi is able to close the optimality gap. However, solving a this quadratic problem quickly causes memory problems for Gurobi, as was also seen in [26] where the maximum QUBO size was also around 150. Local Solver has difficulties closing the optimality gap and the calculation times goes up quite quickly when the problem grows. For simulated annealing also the calculation grows quickly. For the direct embedding on the QPU we see that sampling 1000 times from the chip is rather fast (around 1 s), however, finding the embedding gets more difficult and time consuming when the problem reaches the limit of the current hardware. This state of the hardware limits the problem size here to around 100 variables. The hybrid solver seems to achieve the best performance. Whilst the hybrid approach does not give any optimality guarantees, the computation time end-to-end (e2e), which includes sending the problem to the machine, composing and decomposing it,

---

[2] www.gurobi.com.

[3] www.localsolver.com.

[4] docs.ocean.dwavesys.com/projects/neal/en/latest/reference/sampler.html.

[5] Using hybrid_binary_quadratic_model_version2, see
docs.ocean.dwavesys.com/projects/system/en/stable/reference/samplers.html.

and returning the solutions, only grows linearly with the size of the problem. Time used by the QPU is limited and the time the solver actually uses is almost constant. The run time comprises the time the hybrid solver uses on the D-Wave machines, thus, the e2e time includes the run time and the run time includes the QPU time.

5   Discussion and Further Research

The current state of quantum computing is very suitable for solving quadratic problems. Especially unconstrained binary optimisation problems fit very well to QUBO models that can be used in quantum annealing and the QAOA algorithm. We showed that for our specific problem such a QUBO formulation exists and that the hybrid solver as provided by D-Wave performs well on this problem, having a better performance than, e.g., the commercial solvers Gurobi and Local Solver. It is possible to solve real world size problems in this way.

However, this solver is, to some extent, a black box, due to the lack of official documentation. It is not always clear how a solution is found and whether the QPU is really used to get this solution. For applications, this is of course not that important, but from a scientific perspective not totally desirable. D-Wave offers more flexibility here, making it possible to create and control your own (hybrid) solver. Further research could go in this direction, making more clear statements whether the use of quantum QPU gives this performance or that a smart heuristic is the real driver of this performance. Also, it would be of interest whether (more) realistic and varied demand and production profiles influence the performance in any way.

References

1. Ahmed, A., Nadeem, M.F., Kiani, A.T., Khan, I.: An overview on optimal planning of distributed generation in distribution system and key issues. In: 2021 IEEE Texas Power and Energy Conference (TPEC), pp. 1–6. IEEE (2021)
2. Ajagekar, A., You, F.: Quantum computing for energy systems optimization: challenges and opportunities. Energy **179**, 76–89 (2019). Elsevier
3. Albash, T., Lidar, D.A.: Adiabatic quantum computation. Rev. Mod. Phys. **90**(1), 015002 (2018)
4. Brinkel, N., Schram, W., AlSkaif, T., Lampropoulos, I., Van Sark, W.: Should we reinforce the grid? Cost and emission optimization of electric vehicle charging under different transformer limits. Appl. Energy **276**, 115285 (2020)
5. Croes, N.: Impact of distributed generation on energy loss: finding the optimal mix. Master's thesis, University of Groningen. Faculty of Economics and Business (2011)
6. Croes, N., Phillipson, F., Schreuder, M.: Tactical congestion management: the optimal mix of decentralised generators in a district. In: CIRED 2012 Workshop: Integration of Renewables into the Distribution Grid, pp. 1–4. IET (2012)

7. Diekerhof, M., et al.: Production and demand management. In: Hadjidimitriou, N.S., Frangioni, A., Koch, T., Lodi, A. (eds.) Mathematical Optimization for Efficient and Robust Energy Networks. ASS, vol. 4, pp. 3–25. Springer, Cham (2021). https://doi.org/10.1007/978-3-030-57442-0_1

8. Faruqui, A., Sergici, S., Akaba, L.: Dynamic pricing of electricity for residential customers: the evidence from Michigan. Energy Efficiency **6**, 1–14 (2012)

9. Feld, S., et al.: A hybrid solution method for the capacitated vehicle routing problem using a quantum annealer. Front. ICT **6**, 13 (2019)

10. Franco, J.F., Ochoa, L.F., Romero, R.: AC OPF for smart distribution networks: an efficient and robust quadratic approach. IEEE Trans. Smart Grid **9**(5), 4613–4623 (2017)

11. Gitizadeh, M., Vahed, A.A., Aghaei, J.: Multistage distribution system expansion planning considering distributed generation using hybrid evolutionary algorithms. Appl. Energy **101**, 655–666 (2012)

12. Glover, F., Kochenberger, G., Du, Y.: Quantum bridge analytics I: a tutorial on formulating and using QUBO models. 4OR **17**(4), 335–371 (2019)

13. Hussain, H., Javaid, M.B., Khan, F.S., Dalal, A., Khalique, A.: Optimal control of traffic signals using quantum annealing. Quantum Inf. Process. **19**(9), 1–18 (2020). https://doi.org/10.1007/s11128-020-02815-1

14. IET: Energy Storage System: A Potential, "Flexibility Resources" to Accelerate the Decarbonisation of Smart Grid Network (2021)

15. Kadowaki, T., Nishimori, H.: Quantum annealing in the transverse Ising model. Phys. Rev. E **58**(5), 5355 (1998)

16. Kopanos, G.M., Georgiadis, M.C., Pistikopoulos, E.N.: Energy production planning of a network of micro combined heat and power generators. Appl. Energy **102**, 1522–1534 (2012)

17. Korkas, C.D., Baldi, S., Kosmatopoulos, E.B.: Grid-connected microgrids: demand management via distributed control and human-in-the-loop optimization. In: Advances in Renewable Energies and Power Technologies, pp. 315–344. Elsevier (2018)

18. Lucas, A.: Ising formulations of many NP problems. Front. Phys. **2**, 5 (2014)

19. Matthiss, B., Momenifarahani, A., Binder, J.: Storage placement and sizing in a distribution grid with high PV generation. Energies **14**(2), 303 (2021)

20. McGeoch, C.C.: Adiabatic quantum computation and quantum annealing: theory and practice. Synthesis Lect. Quantum Comput. **5**(2), 1–93 (2014)

21. Memon, S.A., Patel, R.N.: An overview of optimization techniques used for sizing of hybrid renewable energy systems. Renew. Energy Focus **39**, 1–26 (2021)

22. Mutule, A., et al.: Implementing smart city technologies to inspire change in consumer energy behaviour. Energies **14**(14), 4310 (2021)

23. Neukart, F., Compostella, G., Seidel, C., Von Dollen, D., Yarkoni, S., Parney, B.: Traffic flow optimization using a quantum annealer. Front. ICT **4**, 29 (2017)

24. Nikmehr, N., Zhang, P., Bragin, M.: Quantum distributed unit commitment. IEEE Trans. Power Syst. (2022). https://doi.org/10.1109/TPWRS.2022.3141794

25. Oshiyama, H., Ohzeki, M.: Benchmark of quantum-inspired heuristic solvers for quadratic unconstrained binary optimization. arXiv preprint arXiv:2104.14096 (2021)

26. Phillipson, F., Bhatia, H.S.: Portfolio optimisation using the D-wave quantum annealer. In: Paszynski, M., Kranzlmüller, D., Krzhizhanovskaya, V.V., Dongarra, J.J., Sloot, P.M.A. (eds.) ICCS 2021. LNCS, vol. 12747, pp. 45–59. Springer, Cham (2021). https://doi.org/10.1007/978-3-030-77980-1_4

27. Phillipson, F., Bontekoe, T., Chiscop, I.: Energy storage scheduling: a QUBO formulation for quantum computing. In: Krieger, U.R., Eichler, G., Erfurth, C., Fahrnberger, G. (eds.) I4CS 2021. CCIS, vol. 1404, pp. 251–261. Springer, Cham (2021). https://doi.org/10.1007/978-3-030-75004-6_17

28. Phillipson, F., Chiscop, I.: Multimodal container planning: a QUBO formulation and implementation on a quantum annealer. In: Paszynski, M., Kranzlmüller, D., Krzhizhanovskaya, V.V., Dongarra, J.J., Sloot, P.M.A. (eds.) ICCS 2021. LNCS, vol. 12747, pp. 30–44. Springer, Cham (2021). https://doi.org/10.1007/978-3-030-77980-1_3

29. Prakash, P., Khatod, D.K.: Optimal sizing and siting techniques for distributed generation in distribution systems: a review. Renew. Sustain. Energy Rev. **57**, 111–130 (2016)

30. Preskill, J.: Quantum computing in the NISQ era and beyond. Quantum **2**, 79 (2018)

31. Rehman, S., Alam, M., Alhems, L.M., Rafique, M.M., et al.: Horizontal axis wind turbine blade design methodologies for efficiency enhancement-a review. Energies **11**(3), 506 (2018)

32. Saito, T., Yoshida, A., Kashikawa, T., Kimura, K., Amano, Y.: Combinatorial optimization-based hierarchical management of residential energy systems as virtual power plant. In: 2020 59th Annual Conference of the Society of Instrument and Control Engineers of Japan (SICE), pp. 1833–1839. IEEE (2020)

33. Wolske, K.S., Gillingham, K.T., Schultz, P.W.: Peer influence on household energy behaviours. Nat. Energy **5**(3), 202–212 (2020)

34. Zaman, M., Tanahashi, K., Tanaka, S.: PyQUBO: Python library for QUBO creation. IEEE Trans. Comput. **01**, 1 (2021)

Author Index

Printed in the United States
by Baker & Taylor Publisher Services